THE MEANING OF BLUE
Recovering a Contemplative Spirit

Sub Praesidium Sanctae Mariae

Luke Bell, OSB

THE MEANING OF BLUE

Recovering a Contemplative Spirit

Foreword by
THE EARL OF OXFORD

Sub Praesidium Sanctae Mariae

First published
by Second Spring, 2014
www.secondspring.co.uk
an imprint of Angelico Press
© Luke Bell 2014
Foreword © Raymond Oxford,
The Earl of Oxford, 2014

For information, address:
Angelico Press
4709 Briar Knoll Dr.
Kettering, OH 45429
angelicopress.com

978-1-62138-082-5

Cover image: *The Wilton Diptych*
(Richard II presented to the Virgin and Child
by his Patron Saint John the Baptist
and Saints Edward and Edmund),
circa 1395–1399

Cover design: Michael Schrauzer

CONTENTS

PART THREE: *Contemplating God*

Chapter Seven: The Father of Mercies • 201

Chapter Eight: Christ the Word Incarnate • 229

Chapter Nine: The Spirit • 252

Notes [277]

Acknowledgments

I am most grateful to the following for help with writing this book: Clare Asquith, Countess of Oxford; Mark Asquith; Deborah Bell; Jonathan Bell; Spike Bucklow; Stratford Caldecott; Sam Davidson; Blake Everitt; Nick Gooch; David Hayes; Alice Kitcatt; Raymond, Earl of Oxford; Duncan Smith, OSB; Julia Trahair; Andrew Tulloch; Katherine Tulloch; Laurie Venters; James Wetmore; Andrew Wye.

And I am most grateful to you, for reading the book.

LUKE BELL, OSB
meaningofblue@gmail.com

Foreword
by the Earl of Oxford

his book is a meditation on what speaks most clearly and deeply to the very "eye of the heart," man's intellective apprehension and intuition of reality. It is quite simply a guide to "seeing" on all the many levels of human sensibility, thought, and delight; and it demonstrates how human nature and knowledge, through the love of natural beauty, literature, art, and philosophy (the inclination toward *sophia*), are happiest—and healthiest—mixing the corporeal with the metaphysical. Father Luke Bell draws the reader from the start into an examination of the symbols that surround us in nature and existence. Since all symbols point beyond themselves to a source or presence that transcends them, it is they that give reality its meaning, not the other way round. Just as the essence of "information" lies in its capacity to signify, so the power of words, the mystery of language, the willingness to *look*, to grasp significance, to be captured rather than to capture, lead thought beyond closed systems and toward the point of understanding that "all our awareness is a sort of sharing of God's thought."

The exposition of the book is designed to illustrate how depth and clarity of knowledge is in a literal sense a choice, an "election," one that leads naturally from wonder toward faith and prayer. Indeed faith itself is essentially a decision of the "heart" (the intellect, that is) because "being is being known by God"—and that decision of faith is like the self-yielding of a plant's seed to root and flower in its home soil. The author uses literary texts with precise effect, and through his familiarity with and love of poetry, in particular, the reader is supplied with keys to unlocking meaning or, more accurately, pointers on the journey toward "celestial living." "For a Tear is an Intellectual Thing," a line in Blake's poem on the futility of violence, better illustrates God's immediate and direct response to a suffering heart than a paragraph of exegesis can. "Ah, but a man's reach should exceed his grasp, / Or what's a heaven for?" (from Browning's *Andrea del Sarto*) encompasses in its tiny scope all that unassuaged desire and longing for the infinite that is written indelibly into man's constitution and which we dimly know as strong evidence of God's gravitational pull.

Apart from the literary interpolations that serve to stud the text like the jewels of a necklace, there are some unusual quotations from saints and theologians that help to focus the argument. Reflecting upon her dependence on God for all that she had, Saint Thérèse likened herself to trees lit up by the sun: without that light, the view of the trees would not be especially remarkable. And when she says, rather daringly given what we now know about the nano-world, that God is "bad at arithmetic," the author as it were unpacks her thought to show her insight into God's generosity and superfluity of richness, without measure or calculation of what any of us deserves. *The Cloud of Unknowing*, probably the greatest text on love in the English language (certainly the wittiest on the false loves), is used to cast illumination, as are commentaries of theologians, from Saint Augustine of Hippo to Father Augustine Baker and Abbot John Chapman (whose gem-like definition of God as "nothing in particular" I like to cling to as a life raft).

The book does not have "a philosophy," but it is highly philosophical in the deep tradition of thinkers, from the ancients (Parmenides) to the moderns (Jean Borella, for instance), whose pattern of thought is to resist or move beyond reductive systems of theory—those systems and methods, at least, that by definition exclude the transcendent and the divine—in order to position knowledge as *l'ouverture à l'être*, the ability to open doors, not to bolt them. As one modern physicist has said, "The Real is not what we catch in our nets but precisely what we do not catch," and it is in this spirit that the author absorbs the insights of a Gödel, say, whose Incompleteness Theorem proposes that it is impossible to prove the integrity of a formal system without going *out* of that system (in other words, even mathematics points beyond itself). Heidegger's brilliant demonstrations of the fallacies of reductionism belong to the same tradition—as well as his phrase that language is the "House of Being," by which he sees language not as a closed system but as increasingly open, indeed vanishingly imprecise the closer it approaches transcendent reality. Meister Eckhart's deliberately shocking "I am good, God is not good" belongs precisely here: you can't with any meaning at all pin an attribute on the Divine without diminishing Him, ridiculously, to the status of a being, albeit supreme, among others. Similarly, the author's strictures on science are directed not, as I understand, at "hard science" itself but at what is sometimes referred to as "scientism," the notion that the axioms, or what Thomas Kuhn called the "paradigms," of science are unalterable and closed. By way of context here, it is a fact that within two generations the universally accepted norms of Newtonian mechanics have been subverted by quantum physics, and, in the last twenty-five years only, the Cartesian model of human perception has been almost completely overthrown. The author's contention is that science cut off from theology, divorced from metaphysics or the realm of transcendence, degenerates into utilitarian knowledge and even purposelessness.

The scope of the book is broad, yet what is its purpose? What do you carry away with you as you close it? Perhaps it's best to look at the lines the author takes from Yeats: "I must lie down where all the ladders start / In the foul rag and bone shop of the heart." I know of no true experience or account of despair and nihilism that doesn't reveal this sense of hitting the bottom, where there is nothing but contingency and powerlessness, that nightmare sense of complete unrelatedness and nowhere else for the subject to go. The practical point of the author is to show that while you don't necessarily have to reach this point of rock-bottom nothingness, there is a marvelously fruitful rebirth of the human personality once it learns to apprehend its *relationship* with—the wholeness of its dependency on—God. In the so-called modern age, there has been for too long an emptying of the content of thought, a kind of hollowing out of the transcendental ways of "seeing," a positivist lock upon the scope of educated or inquiring minds. But, as this timely book reminds us, man is not designed to play those sorts of games; rather, he is made to know truth, and it is impossible for him to ignore or renounce the being of things while there is breath in his body.

In a philosophical way we can talk of God as "being" itself, but that, the author says, is really just another useful symbol, because God is "beyond" being, since He must be unconfined by the opposition of non-being. He is the supreme non-contradiction that we could allude to as infinite Possibility (insofar as the possible is that which necessarily can never contain a contradiction).

Through such a condensation, I have perhaps made *The Meaning of Blue* sound all too rarefied. In fact, this book is not concerned with being learned. Its key notes are that God wants our permission to enter our lives with His light, and that we give that permission by becoming poor in spirit, recognizing that we receive everything from God and have no "righteousness" of ourselves. Christ's promise is that for the poor in spirit "theirs *is* the kingdom of heaven"— not *will be*, but *is* now. "The receptivity is all." The action throughout this book is to release the reader into the light of God which shows us things as they truly are, into that colored light which Mary, the Mother of God, bears in herself, into prayer, into the radiant freedom of encountering, in the silent intimacy of true dependency, infinite Possibility.

RAYMOND OXFORD
January 2014

"God's appearance through the sky consists in a disclosing that lets us see what conceals itself, but lets us see it not by seeking to wrest what is concealed out of its concealedness, but only by guarding the concealed in its self-concealment. Thus the unknown god appears as the unknown by way of the sky's manifestness. This appearance is the measure against which man measures himself.

"A strange measure, perplexing it would seem to the common notions of mortals, inconvenient to the cheap omniscience of everyday opinion, which likes to claim that it is the standard for all thinking and reflection.

"A strange measure for ordinary and in particular also for all merely scientific ideas, certainly not a palpable stick or rod but in truth simpler to handle than they, provided our hands do not abruptly grasp but are guided by gestures befitting the measure here to be taken. This is done by a taking which at no time clutches at the standard but rather takes it in a concentrated perception, a gathered taking-in, that remains a listening."

MARTIN HEIDEGGER, ". . . Poetically Man Dwells . . ."

Introduction:
Restoring the Wonder of a Child

"Verily I say unto you, Except ye be converted and become as little children, ye shall not enter into the kingdom of heaven."

Some Poetry

"We need to recover a contemplative spirit," wrote Pope Francis in his first apostolic exhortation. Such is my conviction also. I agree with him that "true love is always contemplative" and that to receive the love that God offers us, to reciprocate it, and to show it to others, we need to be able to contemplate that love. Recovering this contemplative spirit involves getting back a way of knowing that has been increasingly eclipsed in recent centuries. This book is about that rediscovery. It is concerned with how we look, how we listen, how we know. It is about our relationship with the world, with words, and with God. It is about the meaning of what we see, what we hear, and what we know in our hearts. It looks at how what we can perceive speaks (if we can but listen) of what is beyond itself. A color, itself often linked to the beyond, stands for this speaking and what is spoken of: the color blue. In writing of it, I am dependent on the ponderings, the prayer, and the poetry of others.

Let's start with poetry. William Wordsworth wrote, in celebrated verses, of the loss that afflicted him as he left childhood behind:

> There was a time when meadow, grove, and stream,
> The earth, and every common sight,
> > To me did seem
> Apparelled in celestial light,
> The glory and the freshness of a dream.
> It is not now as it hath been of yore—
> > Turn whereso'er I may,
> > > By night or day
> The things which I have seen I now can see no more.

7

To him as a child things wore a "celestial light." They spoke to him of heaven. They had a wonderful meaning. They intimated a life beyond death. The look of wonder on a child's face remains for us a sign of the possibility of this meaning and life. It may remind you of a loss, like Wordsworth's, of glory and freshness, or it may remind you of being weathered by the passing years as "shades of the prison-house begin to close / Upon the growing boy."

To me, the things which the poet can see no more speak of something more than that. They speak of a loss endured by the whole of our culture. It has grown old. It now sees things in an earthly rather than a heavenly light.

This book argues that this can be changed. The "visionary gleam" can be restored. Our common culture can see things with the wonder of a child. It can be reborn.

The Bible speaks of this possibility for an individual person. It says, "Except a man be born again, he cannot see the kingdom of heaven." To see God's sovereignty in everything, to see celestial light shine through all things, it is necessary to become once more a little child. To such belong the kingdom of heaven. Being born again is being born from above. In fact, the Greek word translated "again" (ἄνωθεν) also means "from above." This human capacity for spiritual transformation is known, if often forgotten. I am saying it can happen to a culture, taking that word in the broad sense of how people in a given society live and think.

The Doors of Perception

Another William, Blake, got to the heart of the matter. He wrote, "If the doors of perception were cleansed, every thing would appear to man as it is, infinite." That is to say, if we change the way we look at things so that it is not a distorting way, we will be able to see the celestial light that clothes everything. An undistorting way of looking at things is a contemplative one. Contemplation is attentive viewing. The words "contemplation" and "contemplative" are commonly used as shorthand to mean "contemplation of God" and "one who contemplates God." These are meanings I recognize and use, but I argue in this book that in order for it to be natural and normal for people to contemplate God in our culture, we need to learn to contemplate *every* thing. Man is irreducibly religious, and however hostile the culture, there will always be people who are "contemplatives" in the religious sense. But if the way they look at God is different from the way people in general look at every thing, then they live in a kind of ghetto, and those among the latter who would like in some measure to join in what they do can only participate through (to use a phrase of Wordsworth's friend, Coleridge) a kind of "willing suspension of disbelief." They disbelieve because their idea of what is true is formed by what they can see using their habitual way of looking at things, being unaware that the doors of perception need cleansing. There comes about a kind of schizophrenia: there is the religious part of their mind (fundamental to their nature) that tells them there is a God and they can contemplate Him, and there is another part of their mind (formed by their culture) that tells them that there is only what they can see in their customary mode of perception.

Another way of saying this is that there is in them a childlike way of looking at things and a way that has been formed by the habits of their education and their cultural milieu. Often this results in the former being dismissed (wrongly) as childish. Sometimes people rediscover it through their children. Yet there hovers over their lives the sense that it is not intellectually serious. They can lose it again when the children grow up and leave home, and the children themselves can also lose it when they become adults.

My contention in this book is therefore perhaps counterintuitive. It is that through serious intellectual work we can remove the barriers to becoming childlike again. This spiritual rebirth is of course a gift of heaven. People do not give it to themselves—rather, they receive it from God—but we can clear out of the way the obstacles that make people divided and hesitant about opening themselves to it. In doing that we can get back to seeing steadily and seeing whole what life shows us. We can cleanse the doors of perception.

Wonder or Wander

By considering where we have wandered from the way of an attentive gaze and how we get back to it, we can restore the wonder of a child. We can link thought with contemplation. It has been observed that nowadays there are not many intellectual saints, after the manner of, for example, Saint Augustine. There is not the culture that nurtures them. Yet this need not be so. We can develop a contemplative way of thinking. We can think about how a contemplative spirit has been thwarted and how we recover it.

To do this, it will be helpful to divide our looking into three, although it is in reality only one looking, one gaze. Hence the nine chapters in this book are divided into three parts, relating respectively to contemplating nature, contemplating the word, and contemplating God. Getting right the first two means that undertaking the third is not swimming against the tide. It is as though the telescope through which we are looking out to sea is focused first on the waves and then on the name of the ship, so that when we move it to bring into view the monarch standing on the bridge we see him in all his glory. Perhaps when we first look through that telescope, before it is adjusted, the focus has wandered so far from what is needed that we are looking at an empty soft drink can in a puddle on the beach and imagining that this is the horizon. No wonder there is no wonder.

Each and Every Thing

There are books about how our relationship with nature lacks a mutually nurturing respect, and there are books about how we understand what is spoken, written, or shown, and there are books about contemplating God. This book is about how we look at each and every thing, how we understand each and every thing, and how we look toward and understand the source and sustainer of each and every thing, God. In considering how we relate to nature, it takes in light, life, and humankind; in reflecting on our relation to the word, it includes language and symbols, Holy Writ, and sacred rites; and in pondering our contemplation of God, it asks what is involved in adoring Him as Father, Son, and Holy Spirit: three chapters for each of three aspects—nine chapters for one gaze. The one gaze is, in essence, toward God, but it sees Him evidenced in nature and explained in word.

Just a Monk

It may seem that all this means that the book is written by a philosopher, a scholar, and a theologian, or each part by the respective specialist. It is not. I am simply a monk. However, this does give me the privilege of leading a form of life that in a particular way enables contemplation: the Benedictine life. The Rule of Saint Benedict begins with the word "listen." It is all about receiving with attention the things of faith. "Faith cometh by hearing," says the Bible, and the monk is one who tries to listen to the still small voice that is speaking to his heart about the things of faith. The monk daily reads and hears sacred texts and takes into his heart their meaning. The monk looks with the awareness that all beauty is from God. Monks are eyes in the Body of Christ, looking toward the Godhead. That perspective does not mean, however, that this book requires the reader to know anything about monastic life. It is enough that you want to open your heart. If you don't want to do that, I hope that you will let me give you some reasons for considering doing it. The blindness of rapacity that infuses our spiritual ecosystem may make you afraid to do so. I wish and pray that in that case you may get beyond this blindness, and that seeing yourself everywhere gifted by a bountiful Providence you may respond with the gentle laughter of your heart. I hope that you will see that, if things are deeply considered, God is not, after all, implausible.

Blessings are given to be shared. Here at my abbey, I am privileged to live in an area of outstanding natural beauty. I have the benefit of serious intellectual work done by others, and I am a member of a congregation of monks devoted directly to contemplation. I want to share how I see and understand these blessings, and—more than that—I want to convey my sense of how all three of them (nature, word, and God) are deeply linked. They are of course simply one in God, but they can also be united in the human soul by being received in a whole heart in one single act of contemplation. Nature is filled with a meaning disclosed by language, and together they point beyond themselves to the Lord of all goodness.

Others Have Helped

In telling of these things, I am not in the main expounding ideas that I have worked out for myself. I am deeply grateful for their thinking to those who have worked them out, and to God for the thinkers. A lot of other people's books have helped with this one. To enable you to contemplate it without distraction, they are not normally referred to directly in the main text, but my debts are obvious and huge. There are notes to each chapter at the end of the book, not only to acknowledge these debts but also to assist anyone who wants to join fully in the conversation of which this book is a part. If you are of a scholarly inclination, or want to pursue some of my themes in greater depth in authors of greater authority, these notes are for you. If all you want is the possibility of opening your mind to some things you may not have considered before, you do not have to look at them at all. It is enough that I am a channel through which these thinkers can speak to you.

In being this, I want to help restore a mentality, an attitude of heart instinct with the love and trust of a child, that has been eroded during recent centuries and to which the culture of the moment is not friendly. This, I hope, will lead you to a place where contemplative prayer is not an arcane, ghetto-based practice, but a natural outflowing of a healthy and happy life. If in achieving this the book enables anyone who thought it not within the compass of her or his doing to enter into the supreme good of such prayer, it will have superabundantly fulfilled its purpose. If all it does is persuade one reader to be open to the true beauty of things efficaciously enough for that person to feel a little less lost and lonely, it will have been more than worth writing. In fact, I wouldn't even be bothered if you read no further than here, if at least you were to look at the notes and find one book among them that helped you as much as it has helped me.

Some More Poetry

By way of introduction, it simply remains to give a clearer indication of what is impeding a contemplative spirit and a more precise characterization of what it will be like when it is recovered. The latter will not be fully apparent until the final chapter of the book, but some idea of where the argument is heading will aid understanding. Wordsworth again articulates the trouble. In his *Prelude* he addresses his friend, Coleridge, saying:

>   to thee
> Science appears but, what in truth she is,
> Not as our glory, and our absolute boast,
> But as a succedaneum, and a prop
> To our infirmity. Thou art no slave
> Of that false secondary power, by which,
> In weakness, we create distinctions, then
> Deem that our puny boundaries are things
> Which we perceive, and not which we have made.
> To thee, unblended by these outward shows,
> The Unity of all has been reveal'd.

Wordsworth is saying that science is a help to us because it enables us to do things that we need done because of our weakness. It is not the culmination of our wisdom. The problem with considering it as such is that we end up mistaking our *way of seeing* for *what we see*. If we impose a template (such as mathematical science) on nature for the sake of gaining data that give certain advantages for particular purposes and then we think of that data as the complete truth, we can imagine that this template (with "our puny boundaries") is all that there is in nature. The math becomes the message. The truth is that the revelation given to us in nature is incomparably greater. The visionary poet, such as Coleridge, can see it. There is a unity. That unity is a reflection and a revelation of the unity of God. It is also an indication of life, God-given and God-reflecting life. Wordsworth calls people who don't see this wholeness or holiness (he calls it "sanctity") in nature:

> ye who are fed
> By the dead letter, miss the spirit of things,
> Whose truth is not a motion or a shape
> Instinct with vital functions, but a Block
> Or waxen Image which you yourselves have made,
> And ye adore.

Seeing the waxen image as though it were what is really there, rather than as a model representing selected aspects of what is there, misses the spirit and unity of things. Missing the spirit and unity of things is missing God, because this spirit and unity show us God—not directly but at the level of being that belongs to the things that have them. That is a narrowing of vision.

The Atoms of Democritus

The other William also saw this narrowness and can help us see where it comes from. Immediately after his reference to the doors of perception, Blake wrote, "For man has closed himself up, till he sees all things thro' the narrow chinks of his cavern." The narrow chinks are the extent of his vista, in other words. He has closed himself up so that he is not really looking. This self-closing comes from a particular philosophy and a method of science based on it. These are indicated, and also put into perspective, in the final stanza of a poem by Blake:

> The Atoms of Democritus
> And Newton's Particles of Light
> Are sands upon the Red sea shore
> Where Israel's tents do shine so bright.

Democritus was an ancient Greek philosopher who thought that reality is essentially an unbounded space filled with indivisible atoms—that is, multiple unchanging and indestructible material principles that persist and merely rearrange themselves to form the changing world of appearances. All changes in the visible objects of the world of appearance are brought about by relocations of these atoms. Our world and the species within it arise from the collision of atoms moving about. It follows that this perspective envisages the source of the cosmos as being within the material rather than transcending it, and as divided rather than unified. This view of reality is presented as something we can perceive by thought rather than by our senses. Democritus denies that perceptible qualities other than shape and size (and, perhaps, weight) really exist in the atoms themselves.

In line with this tradition of thought, Galileo explicitly argued in his book *Il Saggiatore* that only what can be measured is real—the sense of quality (such as color), rather than quantity, being in human consciousness. *Saggiatore* means "tester." Galileo is arguing that what can be extracted from nature is real in a way that what is given by or received from nature is not. He accounts as real only what a mathematical physics shows him. It follows from this that qualities such as color and smell that can convey meaning or value ("beautiful" or "putrid") are systematically ignored. Meaning or value conveys the sense of God; therefore, this partial way of seeing becomes in time a blindness to God. It is by its very nature a partial and thus anti-contemplative way of looking. This is not to say in any way that people holding to it are atheists—far from it, especially in the case of its pioneers—but rather that they confine God. In this way of thinking, He is a brilliant mathematician whose presence is divined by the abstracting mind rather than the whole seeing, feeling, hearing, tasting, smelling person. When the mathematical physics becomes a means to an end—manipulating nature so as to produce certain outcomes—the true end (God, as reflected in the mathematical order) becomes the means, and the particular end (for which nature is manipulated) becomes what the human person wants. Human desire or will becomes God. This is now more or less the official teaching of our Western democratic societies, although there are difficulties getting these desires and wills to coalesce—difficulties that are only partially solved by the ballot box.

Newton's Particles of Light

The atomism that Galileo took from Democritus flowered in Newton's *The Mathematical Principles of Natural Philosophy*. The title says it all: thinking wisely about nature means reducing it to mathematical formulas. This thinking is presented as though it came into being through being proved by experiments. In fact, it came about because historically a selection was made of a particular way of seeing—one that in effect reduces the cosmos to physically measurable characteristics. Newton's "particles of light" belong to a theory that tries to reduce what (as we shall see in the first chapter) is the most spiritually revealing aspect of nature to what is material and quantifiable. Blake's description of them and the atoms of Democritus as sands upon the "Red sea shore" suggests that they are trampled underfoot by Israel's people, whose tents shine "so bright" because they are the people of God. In other words, the spiritual, not the physical, is the primary reality. This is the opposite of Democritus's contention that in reality there are only atoms and void, qualities (such as color) being "by convention." In Blake's poem, each "sand" (meaning each grain of sand), far from being colorless, "becomes a Gem / Reflected in the beams divine." Those who mock the revelation of the divine in nature "throw the sand against the wind, / And the wind blows it back again." These grains of sand do not affect the ability of God's people to be guided by His light mediated in creation, but they stop the mockers from seeing:

> Blown back they blind the mocking Eye,
> But still in Israel's paths they shine.

In other words, the mockers' mistaken way of thinking about the grain of sands substitutes for seeing a *way* of seeing based on their ideas. Sight therefore eludes them, whereas the godly simply look (or contemplate) and see. The grains of sand blown in the wind are an apt image for the reductionism of atomism and its scientific descendants. Because Democritus's void is unbounded, there can be no direction in the world as he sees it, no focus, no meaning. There are only quantities, there is mere measurement. There are fragments without any wholes, and the very void in which they are supposed to exist expresses how devoid these are of color and savor. The manipulative meaning-draining way of looking that this philosophy spawned has perhaps an apt nemesis in a world dominated by currency no longer linked to gold—a currency which goes on being "quantitatively eased" until it is on the brink of being eased out of any value.

Galileo, Violence, and Rape

The limited kind of seeing that registers as real only what can be measured mathematically and according to preconceived ideas is not content simply to specialize in what can be analyzed in this way: it seeks (by placing them off-limits) to force out other kinds of knowledge—that is, the sort that a contemplative spirit will receive. This is clear from the language of its post-medieval pioneers. Galileo, for example, wrote, "I cannot sufficiently admire the eminence of those men's wits, that have received and held it to be true, and with the sprightliness of their judgements offered such violence to their senses, as to prefer that which their reason dictated to them, to that which sensible experiments represented to the contrary." This is not reason offering violence to nonsense: it is a particular philosophy refusing to admit the thought that looking (and otherwise engaging with the world naturally) evokes. Galileo goes on to say that he cannot find any bounds for his admiration for people whose reason is able "to commit such a rape on their senses." Kant, commenting on Galileo's work, says reason "after a plan of its own" must approach nature as "an appointed judge who compels the witnesses to answer questions which he himself has formulated." It has been observed that Francis Bacon, another pioneer of the mathematical way of extracting data from nature, often used court imagery, as though nature were a woman being tortured during a witchcraft trial. The spirit of aggression conveyed by the language of these pioneers suggests an insecurity. Their way of thinking has aptly been called "a fragile mythology of the moment." Anyone who really looks, as Wordsworth did, can see through it. Only in the absence of contemplation can it be plausible.

Solid Body Thinking

This aggressive way of looking, this eschewing of contemplation, has consequences. A tendency to destroy the planet is perhaps the most immediately obvious. This is the material expression of the violence that it attempts to offer to what is spiritual. Because it can only recognize solid bodies (which can be measured), it tends to miss spiritual goods. Economists speak helpfully of "rival goods" and "non-rival goods." The former are those which can be fought over. The latter are those which are good for everybody who is not an enemy of the common good. On the one hand, there are material goods, such as land and minerals; on the other hand, there are civic or spiritual goods, such as justice, peace, and the rule of law, which benefit all who are positively engaged in society. A way of looking that sees the former as the primary reality is going to undervalue what makes for the common good. It also values the feeblest goods. As Plotinus pointed out, solid bodies are weaker than spiritual bodies. They can be moved, damaged, or even disintegrated by other solid bodies. Spiritual bodies are not dependent on exclusion (keeping other bodies out of their space) for survival, because they do not live a life extended in space. That is why the Bible says, "Fear not them which kill the body, but are not able to kill the soul."

A philosophy (like atomism and its descendants) that recognizes only what is weak (solid bodies) and ignores what is strong (spiritual bodies) is going to be a weak way of thinking. Because it applies only to what has an extended and replaceable existence, it is going to miss the stronger and more primary reality. Its "calculative thinking" (to use Heidegger's phrase) as it measures and quantifies will be unable to perceive what is not chopped up into mutually exclusive pieces. Integrity and life are beyond it. It cannot see what is organically cohesive as a living whole, only as a quantity of lifeless parts. The characteristic process of this philosophy's reasoning is exclusion: it is solid body thinking. It excludes the recognition of a reality that includes in a whole at the same time as distinguishing. It can only separate. Its artistic expression is in painting that shows distance and separation by means of perspective. This is in contrast with the older way (characteristic of holy icons), which shows everything as equally near (with nothing blocking anything else) and so is ultimately more realistic, since everything is equally near to God, who alone knows everything in its true reality. Its sociological expression tends to think of society as separated individuals rather than as an organic unity of distinct persons. This is because it uses a mathematical logic as its way of looking. Its logical structure is to say that a thing is the same as itself; it cannot therefore be both itself and not itself, and it follows that either it has to be what this thing is or it is not this thing: there is no middle alternative. This is totally efficacious for working out mathematical proofs, but its logic is that of materialism. It applies when things occupy a particular space that cannot therefore be occupied by other things, but it is inapplicable to more spiritual considerations, such as that of the communion of persons. This is true in life as we know it here. Someone can totally belong to a family—in a sense *be* that family, representing it as if an ambassador—without losing a personal identity. This does not mean that there is not a solid body and mutually excluding aspect to that person's life in the family—there can still be quarrels about someone spending too long in the shower; it means simply that this aspect is not the whole of it. In life in heaven, eternal life, life that is totally real, the consideration of who is to occupy a particular place does not arise. In other words, this way of thinking is directed toward the relatively unreal.

As with thought, so it is with language. If language is reduced to statements that exclude all but one completely unambiguous meaning, any sense of the richness of life, its connectedness and mutual interpenetration, is lost. It is simply atoms in Democritus's void. It has no spiritual dimension. This sort of language is useful and even necessary for particular purposes, such as air traffic control, but it is useless for poetry. Its exclusive adoption leaves people without a notion of everything that poetry conveys: what is beyond the material, the visionary, that which gives meaning and purpose to life. Society becomes atomized, people become lonely, and insofar as they do associate, it is—as Matthew Arnold wrote in his poem about the tide of faith going out—as "ignorant armies" that "clash by night." The end, life's birthright and purpose, is sold to pay for the means, the mess of pottage, the capability to get things done.

Getting Things Done

Looking only with a view to getting things done, knowing only what is needed for manipulation, collecting information only to control is in the end self-defeating. An intelligent book about Britain's pris ons argued that merely trying to control prisoners, excluding any freedom on their part, is to fail. Of course input from them needs to be limited, in some cases severely limited, but if they have no input at all then no cooperation is possible, and even the goal of control is missed. So it is with nature, so it is with all with which we interact. Unless we recognize its own quality, we will, like the fallen angels in Milton's *Paradise Lost*, end up eating not fruit but ashes. Everything has a meaning, everything in its way communicates wisdom, everything speaks of something beyond itself. Regarding as real only that knowledge which allows us to manipulate closes us off from this meaning, this wisdom, from what is beyond what we see. God is blocked off. He cannot be manipulated. People looked at in this way can no longer share with us the light and love that they radiate. The servant, a way of knowing that enables us to get things done, has instead become the master, a bad master. The emptiness that only God can fill echoes with the noise of the distracting activity of getting things done. We forget why: as the ability to impose our will increases, any value that might guide our will in the way of truth, beauty, or goodness diminishes. There is only emptiness. There is nothing in us that might be worth carving on the tree of being.

The Receptive Heart

It has been necessary to clear the ground, to show the blindness of identifying knowledge with calculative thinking, but that is only so that we may begin to dig for the buried treasure. This pearl of great price is the receptive heart. Solomon asks for a listening heart and is given everything else. The priestly prayer of Jesus identifies how the heart is transformed to receive the fullness of life: "And this is life eternal, that they might know thee, the only true God, and Jesus Christ, whom thou hast sent." It is in knowing that we live: in knowing God, source of all being, and in knowing Jesus Christ, God made manifest, for "without Him was not any thing made that was made." It is not with the miser's squint, or the narrowed eyes of the schemer, or the cautious glance of one preparing to attack, that we know: it is with the full, trusting gaze of a child. That trust contains a belief: a conviction that the world is meaningful, a confidence that words have value and power, a confession that God is the Creator of all. That gaze takes in everything unflinchingly, unafraid to claim that "There is some soul of goodness in things evil, / Would men observingly distill it out." And the wonder is that it is reciprocated.

The receptive heart is happy to not know in advance what it is to find, happy to take in rather than give out, happy to receive meaning rather than impose it. It prefers knowing to utilization and consumption, meaning to logic, beauty to power. It is happier being changed by what is true than twisting what is true to avoid changing. It seeks its destiny in a knowing without *arrière-pensées*. It does not take pleasure in a knowing that enables it to put others in their place; it is joyful even in a knowing that reduces it to helpless ignorance. It understands that sometimes grasping something clenches a fist that could be open to receive a greater gift. It simply contemplates what is there. All of this does not mean that one with a contemplative spirit never applies the mind to practical work—indeed, one with such a spirit will tend to be more practical on account of being able to see what is really there—but it does mean that he or she will see this application not (as Wordsworth wrote) an "absolute boast" rather as an aspect of the Fall that leads to Adam being told, "In the sweat of thy face shalt thou eat bread."

A Fresh Look

Nonetheless, recovering a contemplative spirit is walking in the direction of the "garden eastward in Eden." To walk in that direction is to learn to change the mind and heart from the narrowness of utilitarianism to the openness of enjoyment. This book is intended as company for that walk. Even if it won't get you back to where Adam and Eve first were, it offers keys to unlock you from imprisonment in the errors of recent centuries. It is a guide to contemplating afresh nature, word, and God. It shows the cosmos as a symbol rather than a machine, nature as meaningful rather than ripe for exploitation and as a presence to be approached with love rather than fear. It makes its own the prophetic sentiments of Lord Northbourne:

Nature is only squalid to those who do not understand her, and when misunderstanding has upset her balance. She is imbued above all with the power of love; by love she can be conquered, but in no other way. That has not been our way. We have attempted a less excellent way, and have upset the "balance of nature" so that she no longer appears to us in pleasant guise but in a guise in which the appearance of an opposition of forces—a "struggle for existence"—predominates over the appearance of a balance of forces.

Reading Nature, Word, and God

This is echoed by a young man who spent a couple of months in my monastery learning something of the contemplative life: he reported a consequent growing awareness of the benign nature of creation. This book trusts that benignity and sees the world, in the words of a notable Benedictine teacher, as "the great book of God." It seeks to read there so as to understand something of what is spoken about that which is higher than nature. It aims to read with a fresh and whole gaze whatever is written, but especially Sacred Scripture and the words of worship. It aspires to read not by imposing the self on what is read but by the interpretation of the Holy Spirit. It realizes that a way of reading that murders to dissect cannot reach the heart of meaning, which is the unlimited wholeness of God. His oneness cannot be analyzed, only contemplated, and only by one who is willing to be changed by it. It requires the risk of not being in charge of knowing and where it leads: being, to speak grammatically, not subject but dative—the one to whom meaning is disclosed.

It is, in the end, a matter of considering how we know—what in philosophical discourse is called epistemology. This matters because how we think about knowing affects how we know. Upon how we know depends whether we have a healthy relationship with nature, meaning, and God; upon that depends whether we live or die. I have a memory of a philosopher-monk in his last two days of life in a hospital bed, with another monk in quest of truth trying to get an epistemological question sorted out with him before his last breath. It is that important. Treating this sort of question as settled before it really is risks being unable to see any meaning. Meaninglessness is the climate of self-destruction.

Tradition

Our time has not been friendly to receiving meaning as a gift. It would make its own, but since one's own meaning is by definition different from those of others, this leads to a fissiparous and fragmented society where community is replaced by loneliness and—ultimately—persuasion by violence. It is no way to live. Only by reaching back into the wisdom of the ages, or by attentiveness to those who have done so, can life be found again: only a recovery of tradition can ground rebirth. By the mercy of God, I was blessed to read an author of the last century who helped me with this recovery, who cleared the ground for a life of faith by rescuing me from relativism and concomitant strayings. Of course, it is all there in the old books, and yet humanly speaking we need someone of our own age who will show it to us as living now. This book is addressed to you who seek seriously, especially if you are young and working out your way in and to life in this century. May you be helped as I was helped, and may you have life and have it abundantly.

The final chapter will say more about what it is to have arrived at the place we started from and to know it for the first time, about what it is to know everything as a child of God, about what it is to have recovered a contemplative spirit. I invite you to allow me to lead you there through the intervening chapters. We will start our consideration of how we see and receive meaning with the *sine qua non* of looking: light.

PART ONE
Contemplating Nature

"For the invisible things of Him from the creation of the world are clearly seen, being understood by the things that are made, even His eternal power and Godhead."

Chapter One:
Light and Color

God Is Light

he Scripture verse from Saint Paul's letter to the Romans that is at the head of this section of this book (consisting of the first three chapters) points to the fact that each thing in creation speaks to us of God. Each thing has its particular word to say about God. In this chapter, we will consider what light, color, and darkness—the very palette of the painting of the picture that is God's creation—have to say about Him and our relationship with Him, and how we can be attentive to what they are saying.

In the introduction, we saw that how we know is important: if we are not looking properly we will, to put it mildly, miss stuff. The Bible says this very directly: "The light of the body is the eye: therefore when thy eye is single, thy whole body also is full of light; but when thine eye is evil, thy body also is full of darkness. Take heed therefore that the light which is in thee be not darkness. If thy whole body therefore be full of light, having no part dark, the whole shall be full of light as when the bright shining of a candle doth give thee light." The eye is how we see. Therefore it is in effect light, since we can receive no light except through the eye. By its agency it is what it transmits. Everything that can possibly be seen is seen by light transmitted through the eye. It therefore needs to be "single" or sound and healthy, taking everything in as whole, not complicating or dividing it. The Greek word translated by "single" (ἁπλοῦς) means, literally, simple or unmixed, and hence a "single" eye is one that sees clearly. The *Oxford English Dictionary* defines "single" in this biblical context as meaning "simple, honest, sincere, single-minded; free from duplicity or deceit." The word can therefore carry the implication of a sort of seeing that is free of the will to manipulate and impose desire that characterizes the "false secondary power" of seeing that has dominated modern epistemology. It also points to a seeing that is not physical, to the intuitive awareness of uncreated (divine) light that is sometimes said to be the function of the "eye of the heart" or "third eye." This eye looks neither to the future (traditionally symbolized by the right eye) nor to the past (symbolized by the left eye), but simply to eternity. It does not look at what is spatially present—as do the left and right eye, working together to establish perspective—but at what transcends space: the divine.

If the eye is single, it will receive light and everything with it. What does it *mean* to receive light? The Bible is again direct: "God is light." God is the meaning of the light. If our eye—our way of looking at things—is healthy, we will be able to know God and in that knowledge have a right and healthy awareness of everything else. Light speaks God for us on the level of what is created. This sense of the divine meaning of light has endorsements ancient and new, quite apart from the biblical witness. Plato saw the sun as a symbol of the ultimate reality, the Idea of Good. In Hermetic literature, the *Poimandres* says, "God the Father is light and life." The Hellenistic Jewish philosopher Philo of Alexandria, who lived around the time of Christ, writes, "God is light, for in the Psalms it is said, 'the Lord is my light and my saviour'; and not only light, but the archetype of every other light, or rather more primitive and higher than every archetype." He makes the point that light is self-revealing: light is seen by light, so "God, being His own ray, is beheld through Himself alone." This indicates the inherent aptness of light as a symbol of God: just as we see other things only by virtue of light, so what exists does so only through the work of God. Other traditions testify to an analogous symbolic interpretation of light. In Buddhism, it symbolizes truth and transcendence of the world and of conditioned being; in the Greco-Roman tradition, Zeus; in Islam, the manifestation of divine knowledge. The Koran says, "God is the light of the heavens and the earth." Appropriately, light is sacred to the Magi, among whom were those led to Bethlehem by a star. There is a universal sense of light as manifestation of divinity, a widespread conviction that it points to ultimate reality, that it is at the beginning and the end of all things, that it denotes that which is immaterial and spiritual.

Contemporary physics accords with this. It teaches that the closer anything gets to the speed of light, the more slowly time passes relative to what is not traveling at that speed. So, in a science fiction scenario of people going off in a spaceship traveling at nearly the speed of light, they can come back after a few adventures to find that many years have passed on earth whereas they have hardly aged. The implication of this teaching, developed from the theory of special relativity, is that light stands apart from time. It partakes somewhat of the life that belongs to eternity, the life that belongs to God.

Light in a sense transcends space as well as time. It consists, modern physics tells us, entirely of energy rather than mass. Of everything that is in creation, it is among the least material. In this too it speaks of God. "God is a Spirit," says the gospel; there is nothing of matter in Him. "God is light, and in Him is no darkness at all," says the first letter of Saint John. The "darkness" corresponds to what is unlike light: that which is wearied by time and weighed down by matter.

A Glory Passed Away

There is a proverbial Russian phrase—"clear as God's daylight"— that expresses what an obvious sign of God's presence light is, and yet the heart in our age seems insensitive to it. Light shows it everything except that which it most directly expresses. Wordsworth articulated this loss of sensitivity. In the stanza immediately following that quoted at the beginning of this book, he wrote:

> The Rainbow comes and goes,
> And lovely is the Rose,
> The Moon doth with delight
> Look round her when the heavens are bare,
> Waters on a starry night
> Are beautiful and fair;
> The sunshine is a glorious birth
> But yet I know, where'er I go,
> That there hath passed away a glory from the earth.

Wordsworth gives multiple sources of light, direct (the sun, the stars) and reflected (the rainbow, the moon, the rose, waters), but he observes that a glory has passed away from the earth. He implies that there is some trace of it in the sunshine, calling it "a glorious birth." This is apt, since the sun, among the various sources of light, is the most direct symbol of the divine, with which in some cultures it has indeed been identified. Yet glory has passed away. What is this glory but the *meaning* of light, the glory that clothes the Most High? That is what has been lost. Nature with its natural light shines in all *its* glory, but the glory of God that it signifies has passed away from the earth because it is no longer in the hearts of those who behold it. That it expresses what is beyond itself has been forgotten. There was a time when each of the sources of light in this stanza meant something beyond itself. We will come to all of these meanings in due course, but for the moment let us just consider the meaning of the rose.

The other poet William again helps us. He writes,

> O Rose, thou art sick.
> The invisible worm
> That flies in the night
> In the howling storm
>
> Has found out thy bed
> Of crimson joy,
> And his dark secret love
> Does thy life destroy.

The rose is a very rich symbol. It is perfection, the heart-center of life, the point of unity in the center of the heart. In Christian tradition, it is the flower of paradise in its beauty, perfection, and fragrance, and the red rose is charity and martyrdom, growing from the drops of Christ's blood on Calvary. Yet it is also earthly passion, denoting the love that belongs to time as well as that of eternity, and this meaning seems to be touched on in the "love" of the second stanza. Yet it is not a healthy human love that is here in question. It is the love of "the invisible worm that flies in the night." In other words, it is a love *without light*. It is a way of relating that ignores what the senses perceive: ignores light, color, and fragrance. The atoms of Democritus and his unbounded void are determining the mind-set with which the rose is embraced. In this way of grasping the rose, it can only be measured. Its qualities of light (reflection of the divine), color (red, the color of love—supremely, Christ's love), and fragrance (sanctity) are blanked out, and so its life, which is in and from these things, is destroyed. The worm, symbol of death, kills the life of the rose by turning the human heart away from the image of its integrity and happiness.

Let There Be Light

Yet we still have a way of getting back to the glory that has passed away. God has given us two books. If we can no longer read the book of nature, there is also the Bible. Let us look together at what it says about that most primordial symbol, light, and let us think about what it teaches us about the book of nature. This thinking can bring us back into the light, God's glorious light. We will look first at the biblical teaching about light, and then consider what nature shows us through color.

The first mention of light in the Bible is in the third verse: "And God said, Let there be light: and there was light." The childish (not childlike!) objection that this is contradicted by the sun and moon not being thought of until verse fourteen is answered by the text of the first verse: "In the beginning God created the heaven and the earth." Heaven comes first. Light on earth is a weak rendering of the glory of celestial light, God's own clothing. The latter is brighter far yet gentler too: unlike the light of the sun, it cannot hurt. As the last book of the Bible declares, it renders otiose light of candle or sun. The childish objection forgets that this light comes first and that the lights that illumine the earth are a constricted and relatively insubstantial reiteration of it, given to remind us to set our affection "on things above, not on things on the earth." They speak of heaven, where God's glory remains in all its brightness. They are His gifts, but they are not God Himself, for "every good gift and every perfect gift is from above, and cometh down from the Father of lights, with whom there is no variableness, neither shadow of turning." The Father of lights gives us these symbols of His presence—which, like light, is known by itself alone—but unlike them, He does not change. This dis-identification of God and His gifts (in the letter of Saint James) is significant. As well as showing that God transcends even the most central aspect of His creation, it implies the promise given through the prophet Isaiah: "The sun shall be no more thy light by day; neither for brightness shall the moon give light unto thee: but the LORD shall be unto thee an everlasting light, and thy God thy glory. Thy sun shall no more go down; neither shall the moon withdraw itself: for the LORD shall be thine everlasting light, and the days of thy mourning shall be ended." This is entry into the realm where "there is no variableness, neither shadow of turning." The separation of time and place does not extend to the life of eternity, and so there is no cause for mourning there. There it is as if the sun does not go down, as if the moon never retreats behind a cloud.

God in the Dark

And yet this primal symbol of God—the light of the sun and the moon—does not give us the whole. It cannot, for it is part of creation, and the whole is greater than the part. God, supreme Unity, is not exhaustively symbolized by any part. Darkness too is a symbol of God. According to Nicholas of Cusa, opposites coincide in God. God is light and darkness. In this world, where light and darkness war as players on a chessboard, God is identified with light. (The white pieces move first.) The division between light and dark, like the parallel division between up and down, characterizes this world of struggle and becoming. Beyond this world, in Himself and not shown to this world, God is darkness. He is utter mystery. Hence in the beginning "the earth was without form, and void: and darkness was upon the face of the deep." It is only in creation, when He showed forth something of Himself, that "God divided the light from the darkness." In His unity they are one. So darkness too speaks God. It is not essentially evil, since it is the ground of light, which emerges from it, and in this sense it is unmanifest light. "An horror of great darkness" fell upon Abraham, and "when the sun went down and it was dark," God ratified His covenant with him. "A smoking furnace, and a burning lamp"—light out of darkness—manifested His presence.

Darkness is in a sense the symbolism of the absence of symbols. Saint John of the Cross taught that the divine is darkness to us because our normal modes of perception, adapted to sensing what is in this world, are not able to reach it. Any symbol veils as well as reveals; any thinking is not that which is greater than what can be thought. It follows that the experience of the quest for God is an experience of darkness. First, according to Saint John, there is the dark night of sense. This is the mortification of the appetites, in which a denial of what comes through the senses creates a feeling of loss and deprivation. It is the beginning of a life that is spiritual rather than sensual. The dark night of the spirit that follows is much more terrible; it comes when the customary symbols and thoughts no longer convey the meaning of the divine because they are transcended by the divine reality that is beyond them. It is terrible because subjectively it seems like a total loss of God. In reality, it is a loss of a partially adequate way of relating to Him and is thus the finding of Him as He is in Himself. Yet Saint John of the Cross does not leave us with darkness as the ultimate symbol of God: he writes, "The endurance of darkness leads to great light." His account of the spiritual journey into the depth of God corresponds to the Bible's account of God's first manifestation, which tells us that first "darkness was upon the face of the deep" and then that "God said, Let there be light, and there was light." So everything shows us God, our seeing and our not seeing: "In Him we live, and move, and have our being." It is also the case that the *interaction* between light and darkness (from which color emerges) teaches us about God, but before we look at that let us pursue the way the Bible explains for us the celestial light hidden within the earthly light.

The Sun and the Moon

Let us ask what it tells us about the glory that Wordsworth records as having passed away from the "glorious birth" of the sunshine and the "delight" of the moon. It relates, "And God said, Let there be lights in the firmament of the heaven to divide the day from the night; and let them be for signs, and for seasons, and for days and years." God introduces division and time. That is, He creates duality (light and dark) and separation. This is in the cosmos, but it reflects the primal darkness in God and then (because He shows Himself) the light in God and the concomitant light and darkness in Man, reflected the other way around in His image because light has to precede darkness for God to show Himself. God says of these lights, "Let them be for lights in the firmament of the heaven to give light upon the earth." They show what is heavenly to the earth. They remind us on the earth (to quote Wordsworth's poem again) that "trailing clouds of glory do we come / From God who is our home." To give light upon the earth, "God made two great lights, the greater light to rule the day, and the lesser light to rule the night: He made the stars also." We will come to the stars in a moment; first, we will consider the sun (the greater light) and the moon (the lesser light). The sun represents God's light as it is in itself: its own source. The moon is God's light reflected. Although night indicates a degree of separation from God, it is not total. Just as God makes for Adam and Eve coats of skins to clothe them when they are expelled from the Garden of Eden, so He allows the comfort and guidance of His light to reach Man in his relative darkness through the obscure light of the moon.

Traditionally, the sun and the moon correspond to the two inner channels of light for Man: the heart and the brain, respectively. This teaching needs explanation to be properly understood. In this context, the heart is the seat of the *intellect* rather than mere feeling, which is subordinate to intellect. The intellect here does not mean that sort of intelligence that is good at chess and math problems; it means the capacity to look intuitively at God, the capacity for spiritual vision or divine inspiration. It is thus Man's ability to grasp directly self-evidencing truths that can inform his life as the sun lights up the world and makes it possible for one to see one's way around it. The brain, corresponding to the moon, is the seat of rational discursive thought. Starting from the premises that the direct light of the heart gives, it is able to work out implications and consequences of these directly received illuminations. It is a different way of perception, just as seeing by moonlight is different from seeing by sunlight. The difference may be clearer if we look at Saint Thomas Aquinas's definitions of reason (corresponding to the moon: indirect, discursive discovery of truth) and intellect (corresponding to the sun: direct, intuitive perception of the spiritual).

"Reason," he says, "designates a certain discursiveness by which the human soul from knowing one thing comes to know another; intellect, however, seems to designate a simple and absolute knowledge (without any motion or discursiveness, immediately in the first and sudden apprehension)."

The Mother of All Journeys

The absence of "simple and absolute knowledge" in the discourse of our culture indicates that we are, generally speaking, nowadays not governed in our steps by light received directly from God. We are, as it were, walking by the light of the moon. Yet moonlight is real light. Man's capacity to think is still a way to the truth, although it is not as direct and by no means as reliable a way as the direct contemplation of God's truth. Yet one needs to face the reality that moonlight may not be the predominant light guiding people in choosing where to place their steps in our epoch. How often do you notice the moon among the bright night lights of the city? Artificial light is more often what guides steps: a light that does not come from heaven; that is not a reflection of God's light; that is arbitrary and contrived; that reflects no more than the wilful whim of the individual. It follows that to recover a contemplative spirit, we need to fast from this sort of light: to learn to prefer truth to what we would like to be true, to go where disinterested inquiry takes us rather than where we would prefer to go—or where a machine tells us to go.

Perhaps a whole book can be written on this, but without claiming that I have myself learned to live entirely by natural light, so to speak, I will assume that you have done so. (Perhaps significantly, Saint Benedict says in his Rule that the evening prayer and supper are always to be completed by natural light. Maybe he felt its importance intuitively.) With this assumption, our task in recovering a contemplative spirit is to make the journey from the head to the heart. This is the mother of all journeys and the quest hidden within all quests. It is the peregrination from the pallid and cold glimmer of the ratiocinative to the warm glow of spiritual certainty. Our spiritual destiny is to transition from moonlight to sunlight. Even if in this life that is only accomplished "in part," in the next life we shall see the divine radiance "face to face" and know even as we are known. In the meantime, we can move toward that spiritual destiny, and our natural reason, a reflection of the divine, can help us.

The Stars Also

It is not simply a question of the sun and moon, however. God "made the stars also." Wordsworth, in the stanza with which we began this chapter, recalls the beauty of waters on a starry night. Water is the liquid counterpart of light, with something of the same symbolic importance: it indicates the eternity of God and the total possibility that is in Him. If the poet sees stars reflected in the waters, then he is seeing in their light the light of God's eternal power shining in His saints. He is seeing those whose inner glory is spoken of by the prophet Daniel when he says, "And they that be wise shall shine as the brightness of the firmament; and they that turn many to righteousness as the stars for ever and ever." Wordsworth seems to allude to this identification in his description, later in the same poem, of "the Soul that rises with us, our life's Star." We are made for this: to shine like a star in the vault of heaven. Nature, speaking for its Artificer, teaches us this through the light of the stars. Saint Thérèse had a sense of this as a child. She noticed stars in the sky in the shape of the letter "T" in a prophetic intuition that her place was in heaven. After her death, one who loved her was walking in Lisieux utterly desolate, wishing to herself that at least the miserably overcast sky might clear. With miraculous rapidity this happened: the star-studded firmament, the symbol of the blessed in bliss was revealed.

Children of Light

The Bible points us to this destiny. It calls us to "walk as children of light." This involves having a childlike openness to what we can see, letting the light in its many colors and shades teach us about the uncreated Light. It means having the curiosity that children are born with about the meaning of the natural symbols that light brings into vision for us. Yet "to walk in the light" also means to battle the powers of darkness, to "put on the armour of light." The sublunary world is one of struggle. To engage in this as "the light of the world" we need to "believe in the light" that we "may be the children of light." The darkness of doubt and mistrust is dispelled by belief and confidence. This belief and confidence are enacted in "good works" that enable the light to "shine before men." Iconographically, those who thus reflect "the light of the LORD" are traditionally represented as having a halo or aureole: the halo showing light around the head, the aureole around the whole body. Walking "as children of light," they "shine as lights in the world." Their light, however, is not *of* the world, so it is not to be extinguished. As the Bengali poet Rabindranath Tagore observed, "Death is not extinguishing the light; it is only putting out the lamp because the dawn has come." They shine "as the stars for ever and ever."

The Dayspring from on High

This is possible because the light of "the one Morning Star who never sets" has come into the world, because "the dayspring from on high hath visited us," because "the light shineth in darkness; and the darkness comprehended it not." This last account (from the Gospel of Saint John) of the uncreated Light coming into the world consciously echoes the Genesis account of the first light. Both begin "in the beginning," and both tell of the articulation of celestial light. In Genesis, God speaks and there is light; in Saint John's Gospel, God's Word is the light. Saint Matthew's Gospel cites the prophet Isaiah to the same effect: "The people which sat in darkness saw great light; and to them which sat in the region and shadow of death light is sprung up." The "region and shadow of death" is that realm where change and mortality rule; the light that springs up is the unchanging and immortal divinity from which it has been separated. He is given "for a light" so that there may be "salvation unto the end of the earth"—that is, a healing from separation and fragmentation, a making whole and living. The one who follows Him "shall have the light of life." He is "the light of the world." He is "the true Light, which lighteth every man that cometh into the world." He makes the claim, "I am come a light into the world that whosoever believeth on me should not abide in darkness."

These claims of and about Christ, identifying Him as divine, are an extension of the identification of God with light in the psalms, the basic words of worship of His people. The psalmist tells God, "Thou wilt light my candle; the LORD my God will enlighten my darkness." He calls his Lord "my light and my salvation," and prays, "O send out thy light and thy truth: let them lead me." The psalm that praises God with the words, "O LORD my God, thou art very great; thou art clothed with honour and majesty. Who coverest thyself with light as with a garment," anticipates the evangelist's account of the transfiguration of Christ, in which "his face did shine as the sun, and his raiment was white as the light."

The transfiguration itself anticipates the victory of Christ's light over death in the resurrection, when "the darkness is past, and the true light now shineth." Here, "the darkness comprehended it not" in the sense of swallowing the light up. The primordial pattern of darkness "upon the face of the deep" and of God speaking light is replicated. Saint Luke records, "And it was about the sixth hour, and there was darkness over all the earth until the ninth hour. And the sun was darkened." The three hours of darkness correspond to the three days before the dawn of dawns, when, "In the end of the Sabbath, as it began to dawn toward the first day of the week, came Mary Magdalene and the other Mary to see the sepulchre. And behold, there was a great earthquake: for the angel of the Lord descended from heaven, and came and rolled back the stone from the door, and sat upon it. His countenance was like lightning and his raiment white as snow." The messenger with the face like lightning announces the lightning-like breaking of God's revelatory light into the world: "Fear not ye: for I know that ye seek Jesus, which was crucified. He is not here: for he is risen, as he said." With light comes life, and light in the sense of understanding too: "Then opened he their understanding, that they might understand the scriptures, And said unto them, Thus it is written, and thus it behoved Christ to suffer, and to rise from the dead the third day."

Every dawn that happens is an announcement both of this great dawn and of the first genesis of celestial light that the Bible begins by proclaiming. The dawn speaks; it means something. It is an invitation to open one's heart to "the dayspring from on high." I am reminded of a breakfast dialogue between a philosopher-monk and a conversationally challenged monk: "Did you see the dawn this morning?"—"Where was it?"—"The usual place I suppose." (Breakfast conversation was discontinued after the brief experiment during which these words were uttered.) The true place of the dawn is the human heart (in the sense explained above of being the seat of the intellect rather than mere feeling). The dawn is primordial and eternal. What *happens* at the beginning of each day is merely a reminder of the dawn of the absolute in the beginning of God's self-manifestation and in His Word triumphing over the darkness of the human heart and over death on the morning of the third day. This happening articulates the deep drama of the heart; the cosmos embodies the odyssey of the soul—it is all significant.

Color

With the help of the Bible, we have seen something of the meaning of light as such, but this is not the only meaning we find in light: its colors too speak to us. They speak first of the diversity of the world as created in the train of the genesis of celestial light. They symbolize the manifestation of God "by the things that are made," but they have also their particular meanings. Colors occur when light negates darkness, as creation comes into being when God (symbolized by light) negates nonbeing. Creation, as Meister Eckhart taught, is God's no to nothing; color is light's no to darkness—what appears when light encounters darkness and the light, as it were, refuses to be occluded. Exactly which color occurs depends upon the particular relationship of light and darkness, and that relationship is connected with its meaning. The connection between color and the relationship between light and darkness can be seen by looking at the sky. If you look at the sky overhead on a clear day, it is bright blue. This is because you are looking at darkness (the darkness of outer space) through the atmosphere illuminated by the sun. You are in effect looking at darkness through light, or (we could say) from the viewpoint of light. When you look at the setting sun, it is red. This is because you are looking at light (the light of the sun) through the darkness caused by the thickness of the atmosphere.

Red occurs when light is seen from the viewpoint of darkness. Now let us consider the meanings of these colors, starting with their relation to how they arise.

The Meaning of Blue

Blue is dark seen from light. It is therefore the color of the light-filled, the spiritually realized. It is first of all the color of heaven. (In Italian, the same word—*celeste*—is used to indicate a shade of blue and to mean "heavenly.") From a heavenly viewpoint, no darkness enters in: darkness (meaning the absence of light or God) is completely exterior. It follows that darkness does not trouble heaven. It is seen only in a completely serene and peaceful mode, which the color blue conveys. It is no accident that if we look up to the sky we see blue. That says to us: reach heaven (which the sky symbolizes—the word for sky and for heaven are identical in some languages) and you will be completely at peace. One who is light-filled contemplates darkness in peace. The light-bearer herself, Mary the Mother of God, is traditionally associated with blue. It is her color because she bears the light of the world in her, and in her there is no darkness. She is immaculately conceived. I will have more to say about her in the last chapter of this book, since she ("our tainted nature's solitary boast," to quote William Wordsworth again) is the exemplary realization of where we are aiming to arrive in recovering a contemplative spirit. But here let us simply reflect further on the meaning of her color, blue.

Blue is the color of mystery. It belongs to the heavenly rather than the earthly: the naturally blue object is a rarity on earth. This is reflected in the language of yore. As the nineteenth-century British prime minister, Gladstone, discovered, there is no explicit mention of this color in the writings of Homer. Indeed, a word for blue tends to be absent from very ancient languages. It is as though it is too sacred to mention, like the Name of God. The blue light of the sky is everywhere, like the presence of God. It makes possible the seeing of all things, as God makes possible their existence, yet like God Himself it is in a sense too obvious to see. And when we name it, as we now do, it is as though we have made a thing of what is beyond the things of this world. If we could see it as no thing, we could see beyond it to the mystery it symbolizes: the mystery of heaven, the mystery of God. To name and claim it as a color among others, to make a thing of it, is to block that mystery by limiting ourselves to an earthly knowing, refusing to contemplate what is beyond.

For blue is the color of contemplation, of one who ponders in the heart what is heard and seen. It is the color of one who sees deeply, who looks into the water (as into the sky) and, from light, sees the darkness of its depth. It is the color of one who contemplates eternity. The sea, in its vast depth and breadth, is a symbol of eternity; according to an Arab proverb, looking at the sea is as good as praying. Its blue color reflects the gaze of one who looks toward God. The earth is largely blue when viewed from space. The color is indicative of one who is receptive to the mystery of creation and sees it (and its God-gifted meaning) whole. Blue is the color of one who is in no way benighted, who is light-filled, who sees everything in its totality.

If we consider blue now from the point of view of the color itself, rather than the one who sees it, we can see its aptness for symbolizing contemplation. It takes in rather than gives out, as a contemplative person will take in what is being said to him or her rather than giving out opinions. Blue is a cool color, not just because water can be cool (it doesn't need to be) but because in taking in rather than giving out light it concomitantly takes in rather than gives out heat. The coolness is apt for contemplation: if you look at something coolly, you are looking at it in a way that is not distorted by the heat of passion. You are looking at it objectively, as it really is; you are contemplating it. Blue is associated with purity undistorted by passion. "Unto the pure all things are pure." Blue stands for truth and the intellect (in the traditional sense explained above of the capacity for spiritual vision and intuitive knowledge of God), as well as chastity, piety, and peace. Because the color of the sky is blue, it symbolizes the void: primal simplicity and infinite space, which, being empty, can contain everything. The one who contemplates is similarly empty of preconception and prejudice and, having no partiality, can see everything and take in the whole. Note that the contemplated, the contemplator, and contemplation are, each of them, symbolized by the one color, blue, just as Father, Son, and Holy Spirit, the Holy Trinity, is one God. I will have more to say in Chapter Three about how a contemplative outlook, rather than one that is analytic and tends toward manipulation, alters the way what is seen, the one who sees, and the seeing (or what is known, the knower, and the knowing) are conceived. But for now let the color blue stand for that peace and rapture that can characterize the sense of wholeness in which perception transcends the fragmentation of individuality. This peace is an obscure glimpse of our ultimate home, paradise. Blue speaks of that home. As the color of the sky and of water, it is associated with what is far away, deep, transparent, and immaterial; it is therefore the color of God, who is Spirit, and of those who worship Him "in spirit and in truth." It is the color of fidelity, since heaven, symbolized by the blue firmament, does not change.

The Red Horse

The symbolic import of red is opposite to that of blue. In medieval Christian art, the two colors are used to indicate the struggle between heaven and earth. Red is the color of the infernal, the lower depth opposed to the starry height. This corresponds to the fact that red is light seen from the point of view of darkness. The devils in hell are aware of God's light—they could not exist without it— but as something totally exterior to themselves. To them therefore it is red, as is the sun on the edge of the horizon seen through the darkness of the thickness of the atmosphere. Red is their color, as it is the color of the molten lava that comes up from the depths of the earth and, thus, the color of unbridled passion. It is the color of violence, discord, and the shedding of blood. The bloody violence of the end times is indicated thus in the Bible: "And there went out another horse that was red: and power was given to him that sat thereon to take peace from the earth, and that they should kill one another: and there was given unto him a great sword." As blue is the color of peace, so red is the color of the taking away of peace. It is a sign of danger, hence its use in traffic lights to indicate the need to stop. Chairman Mao wanted traffic lights to use red for "go," but this, like his idea of abolishing flowers, was unnatural. We know viscerally that red is associated with the danger to life of blood being shed.

Red heralds the imminent end of the world, when the moon, symbolizing Man's thinking, becomes "as blood" and the third of "the seven angels" pours out one of "the vials of the wrath of God . . . upon the rivers and fountains of waters," turning them to blood, turning the blue of the light-filled to the red that starts from darkness. It is the color that points toward the final absence of light, when "shall the sun be darkened, and the moon shall not give her light, and the stars shall fall from heaven"—the severing of the world from God, whose light keeps it in existence. It is the color of fire as well as of blood: after the red horse of the apocalypse there is the destruction of the world by fire, when "the elements shall melt with fervent heat, and the earth also and the works that are therein shall be burned up."

Yet red is not pure evil. In fact there cannot be pure evil. Evil is not good enough to be pure: of itself it does not have the good of existence and depends on a good outside itself for its being. Red is good as well as evil, and never more so than when it is the good of God Himself entering into our darkness to redeem us. Christ takes on our position, of looking toward light from within darkness, in order to set us free from darkness. He is cut off from the light of the sun when at the sixth hour there is "darkness over the whole land until the ninth hour," and at the ninth hour He is cut off from the light of His heavenly Father that the sun symbolizes, crying "with a loud voice saying, Eloi, Eloi, lama sabachthani? Which is, being interpreted, My God, my God, why hast thou forsaken me?" He is made sin for our sake; He is baptized by fire. Red in its beneficent aspect is the blood of Christ shed for us. It is the color of love: His sacrificial self-giving for us, which loves "unto the end." It is the color of the love for Christ shown by martyrs in the shedding of their blood for Him, as memorialized in the red robes worn by the leaders of the Church. It is the color of the love proclaimed by the Scottish poet to be "like a red, red rose." It is the color of the heart's blood, its love and life.

Green Grows the Grass

Associated with red are the other colors that we see as the sun sets behind the relative obscurity of the atmosphere: orange and yellow. These too are colors seen from darkness rather than from light, colors associated with heat. Red, orange, and yellow are the colors of fire. (It is true that there is also a blue flame, but significantly this is to be observed when a gas burns without admixture of solid impurities.) Between blue with its light and coolness and the hot colors there is an intermediary that partakes of the characteristics of both and, as it were, mediates between them. It is the color with which God's Providence clothes the earth. Hildegard of Bingen, the visionary medieval nun, wrote a song entitled, "O the greenness of the finger of God." Greenness is evidence of the work of the creating Spirit. Seeing green, in the grass and leaves of the trees and so on, soothes and promotes good health. Green is God's gift to our weary spirit. Areas of natural green are the lungs of the earth: through photosynthesis they produce oxygen so that we can breathe, as well as the food that we eat. They are the meeting place of light and life. Green speaks of the mystery of God's communication of Himself to creation: compounded of yellow and blue, heaven and earth, it is the mystic color. It also combines the cool blue light of the intellect with the emotional warmth of the yellow sun to produce the wisdom of equanimity. As the color of annual renewal in nature, it represents hope, renewal of life, and resurrection. However, it is an ambivalent color: it speaks of the life communicated from heaven (blue) but also of the changeability of the earth (yellow), and thus it denotes transitoriness and change. It is not only the green of new life but also the green of the livid dead. Not perduring, it knows lack and is traditionally associated with jealousy. The ambiguity of green enables it to stand for the fundamental choice we make in this life by our actions, as well as for this life itself. This is the choice between the infernal fire or the empyreal blue, the fire that burns or the pure fire of light. Green is our life here on earth. The first thing God says after gathering the waters together so as to let the earth appear is, "Let the earth bring forth grass." Green is the ordinary color for our earthly life, hence its liturgical use for ordinary time.

They Clothed Him with Purple

If green is the color that denotes the downward movement from heaven to earth, purple, or violet, is the color that denotes the upward movement from earth to heaven. It contains the red of the lower depth and the blue of the celestial height. It is the liturgical color of the seasons of penance: Advent and Lent, the seasons when the heart is purified and the mind tends toward the things of heaven. It denotes penitence (especially as exemplified by Saint Mary Magdalene), humility, temperance, fasting, and sanctity. Purple is the color of redemption. Saint Mark's Gospel recounts that the soldiers led Christ "away into the hall, called Praetorium," and they called together "the whole band. And they clothed him with purple, and platted a crown of thorns, and put it about his head." Purple—a costly cloth—is the color of kingship, here intended in mockery, albeit a mockery that speaks more truly than it knows in thus arraying the King of kings. Furthermore, the ancient dye used for this cloth would not fade when exposed to the sun, making it a symbol of Christ's immortality, although its ingredient acquired its color from exposure to the sun, a symbol of His divinity. Most profoundly in this context, the color purple signifies the journey of one who has come down into the place of those in darkness (associated with red, the color seen from darkness) in order to bring them up into the place of light (associated with blue, the color seen from light). Purple, midway between red and blue, is the color of the suffering borne for us through which we are brought out of darkness into light.

How Colors Relate

Let us summarize our reflections on how the colors we have discussed relate to one another. Both purple and green come between blue (the color of light) and red, orange, and yellow (the colors of heat and fire). Blue is the light of heaven, and red, orange, and yellow the fire of hell. Green is the light of heaven coming down to clothe the earth; purple is the devotion of Man seeking to ascend to heaven in the power of the sacrifice of the Son of Man. These colors can be arranged in the form of a triangle. At its base are the earth and the fire beneath: red, yellow, and orange. At its apex is blue, the point of aspiration for us on earth. In the middle of the right side of the triangle is green, the descent of light and life. In the middle of the left side of the triangle is purple, the ascent of Man's spirit. Green and purple therefore are alongside each other on the second level of ascent, above the earthly and thus more spiritual, as the narrowing of the space occupied by the triangle suggests, but not as completely spiritual as blue, which transcends the earthly, as being at the topmost point suggests.

There is another way of representing the relations of these colors. Instead of forming a single triangle, they can form two triangles: one with blue, yellow, and red at the points, as in the triangle already described, and another with green, orange, and purple at the points. If the second triangle (of the same size as the first) is inverted and superimposed on the first to form a six-pointed star, we have the coordinates of a circle. This circle can include all the shades of color at the indefinite number of points intervening between the points of the main colors. If blue remains at the top (as it is naturally in the sky), then its position symbolizes how light and life come from heaven and how it is possible for Man to return to the source of his being.

Blue is the summit as manifest in creation through color: it is not the Creator Himself. The true beginning and end of all things is symbolized by white, which is not itself a color. This is, as it were, the center of the circle around which colors and shades are arrayed: it is the source of them all. It denotes the absolute: purity and perfection. Those who "put on Christ" in baptism wear white robes. The color belongs to Him by whom "all things were made." It is the color of light, and "God is light." It represents the seventh day on which God rested, a rest which He as unmoved mover never left and from which issues all His creation. It is equivalent to the point from which issue the six directions of space, corresponding to the six colors.

The Rainbow

These colors are God's reaching out, not only in creation but also in mercy. They are the colors of the rainbow, which (as Wordsworth's poem says) "comes and goes," that sign of God's mercy, of which He proclaims, "This is the token of the covenant, which I have established between me and all flesh that is upon the earth." In the prophecy of Ezekiel, "The appearance of the bow that is in the cloud in the day of rain" is "the appearance of the likeness of the glory of the LORD." In medieval paintings of Christ as ruler of the world, He reigns on a rainbow, a sign of mercy. The six colors plus white give the number seven, sign of the uniting of heaven (denoted by the number three, indicating the spiritual) and earth (denoted by the number four, indicating the earthly, as in the four directions or the sides of a square). The rainbow occurs naturally when rain falls and the light of the sun shines. God's mercy, which "droppeth as the gentle rain from heaven / Upon the place beneath," is symbolized by this vivifying rain, and His presence is symbolized by this light. Tears of repentance, expressing sorrow for turning away from God's light, are the human equivalent of the rain; as they fall, God's merciful presence is beautifully shown. The rainbow bridges and unites heaven and earth, giving hope to sinful humanity. It is also a reminder of creation, when colors first broke into being. According to Talmudic thought, the rainbow was created on the evening of the sixth day of creation. Traditionally (as in the *Iliad*), the rainbow is symbolically assimilated to the serpent, which, moving without arms or legs, is associated with the all-pervading spirit. In this context, the serpent is linked to creation. It has a good as well as an evil spiritual significance, as evidenced by the Bible presenting it as a symbol of Christ as well as of the devil.

Unweaving the Rainbow

It is in this positive creative sense that the poet John Keats imagined, in his poem *Lamia*, a rainbow/serpent/spirit who became a beautiful woman. This eponymous heroine of the poem bonds in love with a beautiful youth called Lycius. They are happy together, but he wants her to marry him. She is reluctant, but agrees on the condition that his mentor, the philosopher Apollonius, not come to the marriage feast. Apollonius is a sophist, standing for skeptical philosophy. He belongs with Newton and his "particles of light." Keats spoke of Newton at a dinner party attended by, among others,

William Wordsworth, lamenting that he had "destroyed all the poetry of the rainbow, by reducing it to a prism," and proposing a toast to "Newton's health, and confusion to mathematics." In the poem, Apollonius has a similarly reductive role with his "juggling" and "demon eyes": his "impious proud-heart sophistries" undo the fashioning of Lamia's mortal frame accomplished by the god Hermes. "The bald-head philosopher" fixes "his eye, without a twinkle or stir, / Full on the alarmed beauty of the bride / Brow-beating her fair form." This eye is not "single" in the biblical sense of being healthy, as discussed at the beginning of this chapter. Lamia breathes her last and, denounced by Apollonius as a serpent, fades away; Lycius dies of grief. They are in effect killed by a defective epistemology. "Do not all charms fly / At the mere touch of cold philosophy?" the poet has asked, reflecting thus on the destructive new way of knowing:

> There was an awful rainbow once in heaven:
> We know her woof, her texture; she is given
> In the dull catalogue of common things.
> Philosophy will clip an Angel's wings,
> Conquer all mysteries by rule and line,
> Empty the haunted air, and gnomed mine—
> Unweave a rainbow, as it erewhile made
> The tender-person'd Lamia melt into a shade.

The way of knowing that would argue that color is simply an arbitrary construct of human subjectivity, that it is not the work of a creating Spirit, that it does not convey meaning, murders to dissect. Unable to see or receive the spiritual that gives wholeness and life to creation, it focuses only on the secondary, which in the case of colors is the wavelengths of the light that transmits them. The direct quality that color expresses is ignored because it cannot be measured, because it defeats the epistemological limitations of the beholder. This defective epistemology does not see, as Wittgenstein did, that color cannot be grasped by organizing concepts, by the measuring mind. This philosopher observed in his last work (*Remarks on Color*), "There is merely an inability to bring the concepts into some kind of order. We stand there like the ox in front of the newly-painted stall."

My argument is that color, like light, is intrinsically meaningful. It really does convey truth, though I do not claim that I have disclosed that truth in fullness and with total accuracy. Others also have received and will receive something of that truth, and theirs may well be the better rendering. The issue is not a perfect accounting of it, but whether there is such a thing as that truth. I say that if we look aright, there is, and that if we do not look aright then our epistemology, like that of the old Apollonius, is deadly. Life belongs with wholeness that is seen and received in contemplation, not with the "peering eyes" (to quote another poet) that divide and separate to grasp and manipulate. This living wholeness is the subject of the next chapter.

Chapter Two:
Life and Wholeness

Life and Light

tarting with the link between life and light, this chapter considers the former as reflecting God, particularly His unity. As the word "wholesome" suggests, life is bound up with integrity, and for Man this is true for body, soul, and spirit. A holistic rather than a fragmented epistemology is a living one and points us toward the spiritual and transcendent. God's unity, I argue, is in fact evidenced throughout creation, and to see rightly is to see the whole. This contemplative seeing takes us beyond solid body thinking, discussed in the introduction, to the living spiritual reality underlying creation. It leads to a peace that is very different from the agitation that characterizes much of contemporary activity.

Scripture links life and light. The psalmist sings, "With thee is the fountain of life: in thy light shall we see light." The prologue to Saint John's Gospel echoes this, saying of the Savior, "In him was life; and the life was the light of men." He who announces Himself as "the resurrection, and the life" also claims to be "the light of the world." He is the union of life and light. The themes of life and light dominate Saint John's presentation of the signs that he narrates. Jesus comes into the world that His followers "might have life, and have it more abundantly," and He is "the true Light, which lighteth every man that cometh into the world." He is the "green tree" where light becomes life.

Beyond Time and Space

Both light and life reflect God's transcendence: light, as we saw in the last chapter, because it is the thing in creation that comes closest to being beyond time and matter, and life because it has a unity that is above and beyond its moments and its materiality and that partakes of God's unity. When we speak of a life, we speak of a whole, stretching from conception to death. Indeed it is proverbially experienced as a whole when people see their life flashing before them at the moment of death. That experience is an experience of the whole that constitutes the life. It cannot be a moment from the life; still less can it be part of the matter that it animates. To speak of a life as less than this—as in "his life as a diplomat"—is to speak metaphorically, the metaphor indicating, precisely, wholeness. Life is the miracle of oneness.

The most obvious sense in which life is correlated with being whole is that the body needs to be whole for there to be life: a chopped up person is a dead person. Even when parts of it are removed through surgery, accident, or war, the body adapts and makes of what remains a new whole. When it is no longer able to do this, it becomes a dead body. Wholeness is life. This life is more than the sum of its bodily parts, just as it is more than the sum of the moments during which it exists. It transcends these. It is spiritual, belonging beyond space and time, while operating within them. In this it reflects its source and Creator.

The correlation between life and wholeness is more subtle when it comes to the psychic realm, the life of the soul rather than the body. To put it simply: people are more fully alive when they accept the reality of everything they experience, without trying to block out parts of it. Saint Thérèse of Lisieux, when as a child she was offered a choice of little gifts from a basket, famously said, "I choose them all." She lived this out by accepting everything that God sent her: the sufferings and pains as well as the joys and graces of her life. This was in effect an acceptance of God. It is not just that she was accepting His will as expressed by Him allowing everything in her life to happen; in accepting the whole of what her life brought her, she was in effect accepting the whole *as such* and in doing that welcoming her life, the essence of which was its wholeness. In welcoming that living wholeness, she was welcoming the One whose image and token of love it was; she was welcoming God. She triumphed over the temptation to refuse life because parts of it were painful. Each part of life is in a fashion the whole of it, and to refuse that part is to refuse life in the person of its ambassador, the present moment. And the ambassador represents not just life as we know it below the moon but also the celestial life of eternity in all its beauty and wonder.

The Pattern He Has Planned

Something of this is expressed in these popular verses:

> My Life is but a weaving
> Between my Lord and me;
> I cannot choose the colours
> He worketh steadily.
>
> Oft time He weaveth sorrow
> And I, in foolish pride,
> Forget He sees the upper,
> And I the under side.
>
> Not till the loom is silent
> And the shuttles cease to fly,
> Shall God unroll the canvas
> And explain the reason why.
>
> The dark threads are as needful
> In the Weaver's skilful hand,
> As the threads of gold and silver
> In the pattern He has planned.

The "pattern He has planned" is the whole picture. That picture is beautiful. To look at one thread of it separate from the others is to miss the whole and the beauty; it is missing the life of it. Contemplation is seeing the whole and the beauty; it is life-giving. Ultimately, it is an intuitive grasp of God Himself, perfect and absolute wholeness and beauty, and the very source of life. Contemplative acceptance of one's life as deep as this, reaching to the ground of its being and the source of its oneness, so avoids being snared by dark threads of sorrow that these are subsumed in the beauty of the whole, even if that is only seen through a glass darkly. When we see the whole in the part and the whole as a whole, we don't get thrown off balance by parts that separated from the whole are painful or even intolerable. We receive the joy of God Himself. "The sufferings of this present time" are jewels whose darkness serves only to make sparkle in glorious color the bright radiance of eternity. When the Lord Jesus says, "Your sorrow shall be turned into joy," He is indicating that sorrow can be contemplated as joy in seed form, or in His own metaphor, as a giving birth to life. That life has the beauty of wholeness.

Adam, Eve, and Us

Focusing the attention of one's soul on a dead fragment instead of a living whole is shrinking from life, refusing the whole as it presently manifests itself. It is a turning from beauty. Adam and Eve ate from "the tree of the knowledge of good and evil," thus dividing their awareness of life so that it was no longer received as a whole. Consequently, they "hid themselves from the presence of the LORD God amongst the trees of the garden." No longer knowing the wholeness of life, they cannot face the absolute wholeness of God. In the upshot of their falling from wholeness, it is easy for us to refuse the whole, refuse God, by being resentful about something or unforgiving toward someone. This is equivalent to saying, "I will not accept the whole: I will take only part of my life." Yet only the whole is life: the part is dead. The refusal is a refusal of life and its beauty. He who taught us to pray "Thy will be done" and to forgive did so that we might have life and "have it more abundantly." If we welcome the pain—and the person who is "a pain"—then we have only a pain, not a loss of wholeness and life. Relaxing into what we might feel inclined to tense against opens us to life. Abandoning the non-sense of refusing permission to reality because we are resentful about a part of it that we have chosen to focus on instead of the whole, we give permission to God to manifest His wholeness in the fullness of our life. No longer chopping up time and space with our preferences ("knowledge of good and evil"), we see everything— even the darkness within ourselves—with an equanimity that draws us back toward Eden. To be open to seeing everything with the eye of an all-welcoming heart is to have the gaze of God, to be as Man when he walked with his Maker in paradise.

Looking at Darkness Within

Contemplating the whole includes facing "the dark threads" within our own hearts as well as those visible to our outward gaze. To exclude or attempt to exclude our dark feelings and motives from our attention because we don't like them is also equivalent to saying, "I will not accept the whole: I will take only part of my life." Contemplating our dark feelings is not at all the same as identifying with them. It is in fact an act of dis-identification. Precisely because we are looking at them we know that we are not those feelings. Our true self is rather located at the eminence from which they are surveyed, as one on a mountain might see clouds in the valley far below. We are not obliged to descend; we do not have to act on our feelings and desires unless that can be rightly judged proper. Open to seeing all, we can simply be at peace with ourselves and the world.

This outlook, and this inward looking, of course means being at peace with others. As both modern psychology and traditional ascetic writers (such as the author of *The Imitation of Christ*) point out, it is especially those failings that we have in ourselves that we will tend to home in on and excoriate in others, even if the ratio of faultiness from ours to theirs is that of the beam to the mote. If we see everything as it is, we do not feel the need to hide away the part of the inward picture that we do not want to see by projecting it onto another person. That is not to say that we are precluded from taking appropriate restraining action with regard to evils perpetrated by others, but simply that we will not on account of inner darkness imagine it is appropriate when it is not. Indeed, we are in general more able to take right action when we are willing to see everything. It is those who do not see the big picture who do wrong. Great contemplatives, such as Saint Teresa of Avila, are great at getting things done.

Loving Welcome

If we do not project our sins and failings onto others, we will not shrink from other people; we will welcome them. To be contemplative is to love; eschewing the post-lapsarian "knowledge of good and evil," contemplation does not harbor prejudices against people either by singling out individual people as embodying evil or by singling out particular characteristics of them as objectionable. It welcomes the whole, and therefore all persons and the whole of each person. It makes for peace. That does not mean that it says, "Peace, peace; when there is no peace." Precisely because it sees clearly, it is able to show to others (as well as itself) the true love that is willing to say (as Hamlet does to his mother), "Repent what's past, avoid what is to come." It brings peace to others and seeks it itself, by reflecting on and speaking of the will of God, in which, as Dante observed, is our peace. Only when we want what God wants is there an absence of inner strife.

Contemplation diminishes not only strife but also sorrow. Sorrow is a resistance to a state of affairs that we do not want. If we accept the state of affairs as it is, give it permission to exist, *contemplate* it seeing the whole, then we are conformed to it without resistance to its existence. This does not mean failing to take appropriate action (measures to cure illness, for example)—it simply means sparing ourselves the grief of complaint (or "murmuring," as Saint Benedict calls it in his Rule). We do not do the harm to ourselves of tensing against being. We say yes to absolutely everything we see or hear or say. In Christ, as Saint Paul says, there is "not yea and nay"—there is only yes. In Him is the perfect affirmation of all being of the perfect contemplative, the One in whom the very ground of being is perfectly contemplated.

Contemplation—wanting all, wanting the whole—not only enables peace with others and in the heart but also positively enhances and enables the life of others. It is only on the lower, material level that life depends on rival goods. On this level, sharing one's bread with the hungry can possibly diminish at least somatic life, but the life of the soul positively facilitates the life of other souls. It does this not simply by example. If one is accepting all with the gaze of one's heart, then other people sense that they are accepted. Accepted, they can accept their own darkness—not projecting it onto others—and knowing themselves as loved, they can love other selves. Love is undivided. To know oneself as loved is to know love; to know love is to be able to radiate love to others—a sort of benevolent reversal of projecting failings onto others. As light and life are connected, so are life and love. Life is wholeness, and love is the outcome of a whole heart wholly open to all. In the presence of this openheartedness, others flourish. Indeed, an entire therapy has been established on the healing efficacy of attentive listening to others. The one who contemplates heals. As we shall see in the next chapter, this healing in fact extends to the whole cosmos. Here let it simply be reiterated, in the spirit of the poem about the weaver, that the contemplative in receiving the whole into her heart receives concomitantly its bright and sparkling beauty. That of course is why people happily watch plays and operas about sad things and go away not dejected and depressed but rather uplifted by the beauty of the interplay between "the dark threads" and "the threads of gold and silver." They are contemplating.

Wholeness of Spirit

As for the soul, so for the spirit: wholeness is life. Personal integrity is the way to eternal life, a life that is the fruit of the wholeness of spiritual being and thus is capable of gazing on the absolute oneness of God. Inner division is the root of spiritual suffering, a suffering that can become what the book of Revelation calls "the second death," a death far more serious than that of the body. This spiritual wholeness of life is implicitly acknowledged in law: one can be tried for a crime committed many years ago—it is no defense to say that because it was a different time it was a different person who did the deed. Traditionally, one function of punishment for crime is to restore spiritual wholeness. If it is broken, it can be repaired by repentance, which, as it were, gives a new and positive direction to the past. Spiritual wholeness is also assumed in the making of promises and vows. Perhaps one reason why commitment to marriage or religious vows is considered difficult in our own time is the prevalence of an epistemology of fragmentation, where the analyzed part is awarded superiority over the uncontemplated whole. Simply telling the truth, with lips speaking what is in the heart, is another example of spiritual integrity. Moses presents it in the Decalogue as the way to life.

Chapter Twenty-Five of Saint Matthew's Gospel presents a further connection between wholeness and eternal life. If, like Blessed Mother Teresa of Calcutta, one welcomes the stranger, feeds the hungry, and gives drink to the thirsty, or if, like Saint Martin, one clothes the naked, then one hears the Lord Christ say, "Come ye blessed of my Father, inherit the kingdom prepared for you from the foundation of the world." The kingdom, a sharing in the unbounded life of God, comes as a result of acknowledging by the generosity of one's deeds the wholeness of humanity. When Christ goes on to say, "For I was an hungred, and ye gave me meat: I was thirsty, and ye gave me drink: I was a stranger, and ye took me in: Naked, and ye clothed me," He is proclaiming that in Him all humanity is one—He is the summing up and wholeness of human-kind. To know the oneness of humanity and act on it is to know Him, and to know Him is eternal life. Having an unfragmented epistemology is more than a matter of life or death—it is a matter of eternal life or the second death. Selfish individualism and the con-comitant spiritual torment follow from seeing the part (whether one's bank balance, one's pleasure, one's power, one's reputation) rather than the whole—the common good. Unselfish generosity and bliss follow from seeing the big picture: the good of all and the oneness of humanity in Christ.

Seeing the Whole

To make this link between selfish individualism and an epistemol-ogy that eschews wholeness is not to make a moral judgment on the epistemologically challenged—many fine and generous people tac-itly accept an epistemology that fragments to analyze simply because it is the one that prevails. It is merely to say that unless we have a way of seeing that is open to the whole, it will be difficult for us to con-ceive the presence of God, who is love and the source of life. I would spare people that difficulty. That openness to the whole is exempli-fied for us by poet, physicist, and philosopher. Wordsworth, whose thinking on the question we have already touched on, writes appo-sitely (in the context of his experience of the grandeur of nature) of "the imagination of the whole." David Bohm, particle physicist, writes, "My main concern has been with understanding the nature of reality in general and of consciousness in particular as a coherent whole." Robert Sokolowski, philosopher, explains the phenomenological concept of "eidetic intuition," the grasping of an *eidos*, or a form of a thing. To have insight into the form of a thing is to see what makes it whole.

That intuition, that insight, is necessary for perception. It is not simply a question of data streaming through the eye, so to speak, and things thereby being perceived. There needs to be an active grasp of the whole by the person perceiving. Essentially, this is beyond time. When you understand a sentence, or a paragraph, or a chapter that I have written, you have not simply piled up bits of information acquired moment after moment. You have also gained a sense of the whole: the overall meaning that the sentence, paragraph, or chapter conveys. In a similar way, nature is read; the expression on someone's face is read; the performance of a piece of music is read. Each, in its fashion, is a whole. Each whole is an echo of God's wholeness, "for the invisible things of him from the creation of the world are clearly seen." If we are willing to subordinate the question "How can I manipulate and use this?" to the question "What is this?" then we can see that everything points to God. We can contemplate. Really great poets, such as Shakespeare, see life in its wholeness. Minor writers will see their little corner of it or their angle on it and mistake it for the whole. Yet this isn't a question of breadth of experience, as though one who has traveled a lot necessarily sees the whole; it is rather a question of seeing the whole in the part instead of seeing the part in the whole. Jane Austen, with her "little bit (two inches) of ivory," saw the whole; a man who is caught up in a private preoccupation can travel the high seas and never see the whole, being unable to detach himself from this preoccupation in order to receive contemplatively.

Meaning and Means

I am not saying that analysis and working out how things can be used are wrong, only that they do not give us a paradigm of reality. Intuitive perception of the whole, ultimately of God, gives us the *meaning* of life. Analysis and working out how things can be used give us the *means* to sustain that life. It is when the means becomes the meaning that we are epistemologically stranded. We get the fork without the food, the sound without the music, the words without the meaning. We miss the living and see only what is dead. The wholeness that is contemplated is the messenger of life; the part that is analyzed is inert. To see the kingdom of God, we need to be born from above: we need to *see* from above—not the fragments, but the whole that is a reflection of God's unity. This whole is everywhere in God's creation, if we have the eyes to see it. Each life is a whole, each thing is a whole. To know truly (to be wise), we need to let go of the partial knowledge that says, "If you do this to something, then that will happen." We need to let the whole of reality take from us the cleverness of the particularities of inspection and the thought schemes that coordinate them. We need to receive all that is with simplicity, aware that we are children being given a gift, not lords and masters taking our due. Then we will be people whose whole-seeing makes them fit to behold the Whole of wholes who is above all: the one, true, and living God.

The Music of Eternity

This Whole is above time and space and is the source of the wholeness that gives life to what moves in time and space. One thing after another is not a life: a life is the whole that finds expression in its events. It is therefore a spiritual reality. Each thing in creation is not just a bundle of particles in space: it has a wholeness that comes from above. It has a spiritual source. To see truly any life or any thing, we need first to know the whole—to receive all that is as a single gift. Only then can we see the life or the thing as what it is: an echo of the One. Then, to quote William Wordsworth again,

> with an eye made quiet by the power
> Of harmony, and the deep power of joy,
> We see into the life of things.

Then we will understand what the particle physicist, Heisenberg, meant when he told his students that the world was made not of matter but of music. The creation will sing to us of its Creator and

His "eternal power." The song is a song of eternity because its harmony is from beyond time, its wholeness impossible in one moment after another. True attention of the soul to any of "the things that are made" is timeless because the whole cannot be dribbled out one drop at a time in a series of moments on pain of not being a whole. Similarly, it is beyond space because the whole cannot be one part and then another and so on without losing its identity. It is spiritual.

All Is Everywhere

The Scholastics linked being and oneness; Saint Thomas Aquinas taught that all of God is in each and every thing. God is the source of being, God is one. The oneness that a thing has is from God. That is why, to the one who has ears to hear, it sings of its Creator. As in a well-written text (such as Saint John's Gospel) each episode can contain the theme of the whole, as in a well-written symphony each movement can be a musical variation on the theme of the whole, so each individual whole in creation can speak or sing of the oneness of God. In announcing that wholeness it *a fortiori* announces the whole of creation, all of which is contained in God. All is everywhere. Hence Blake, a true seer, was able "to see a World in a Grain of Sand." Each particular speaks the whole, and that whole symbolizes God.

This pattern of relation also applies to people. Saint Paul makes the point in his description of the body of Christ, by which he means the totality of His people. Although the members of this body are different—"there are diversities of gifts"—they are all animated by "the same spirit." If one member suffers, "all the members suffer with it," and if one member is honored, "all the members rejoice with it." The common suffering and the common joy show that all are involved in what happens to each. Conversely, each represents all, just as in each celebration of the Mass, the Body of Christ is present both in the sacrament and in the gathering of His Church. It is not just in religious association that these patterns show themselves. If one child is lost, everyone looks for her: all are concerned. Wisdom or inspiration in one person benefits all; a single perpetrator of murderous outrage can shock and involve all, from the lowest to the highest. Each policeman is the law. Acting in the name of the law, he can arrest someone even though due process only happens afterwards. The actual way that society works belies the concept that it is a collection of atomized individuals. Oneness is everywhere.

Wholeness and Existence

To know any particular thing truly, we must first know the whole. Trying to understand it without an intuition of wholeness is like a person with poor visual imagination looking at pieces of a jigsaw puzzle in random order and expecting to see a picture. Nothing particular can exist without wholeness. This is strikingly illustrated by the work of quantum physicists. Looking at the raw material from which things are formed, they find particles with no determined place. These "non-localized" particles acquire a position in space only when they become a particular thing: in other words, oneness—the oneness of the thing they become—gives them existence within the coordinates of space. Some such physicists (like David Bohm, quoted above) see the importance of this oneness; others (like Stephen Hawking) are so wedded to the assumption that the whole of reality is within time and space that they cannot admit that there is a Creator who gives wholeness and form to matter. These votaries of Democritus and his atoms are nonetheless constrained to account somehow for the fact that their particles are, so to speak, all over the place, and so they come up with weird and wild hypotheses about there being quantities of parallel universes in each of which a particle can enjoy an existence in one of its many possible positions!

The Spiritual Life of a Potato

If each thing that exists is an expression of oneness, then each living thing is a fuller expression of it. Take the potato, for example. If you keep a potato until it is a bit past the time before which it is best to eat, you will notice growths coming out of it. If instead of eating it you plant it in the ground, from these growths new potatoes will come. This is how you got the potato that you forgot to eat in good time: it was grown from another potato. This in turn was grown from yet another potato. In fact, given the way potatoes are actually grown for sale in the shops, all the potatoes of a particular variety after the original one are grown in this way. It follows that all of them—and all the chips and mashed potato and so on made from them—are in fact actually one potato! Yet a potato from this week's shopping does not occupy the same space-time coordinates as one from last week's shopping. The oneness is not a material oneness that joins all the particular potatoes together in one place: it is a spiritual oneness, above time. It is nothing less than a reflection of the oneness of God.

The God-given oneness that is exemplified in each individual potato is not at all the same as the oneness in man-made products of industrial factories, since each individual potato is different. This difference does not contradict the potato's oneness: it is a difference within its oneness. The difference is characteristic of God's creating, a reflection of His uniqueness, and is to be found even in blades of grass. It is a sign of life. By contrast, mass-produced items have no life. Replication is not wholeness. These items are the expression of a death-dealing epistemology that wants to divide and conquer nature rather than love and nurture her. It is not their human origin that makes them lifeless. (It can be argued that the process is inhuman.) Rather, their lifelessness comes from the fact that the "dark Satanic Mills" (to quote Blake again) of the industrial process are not a reflection of the life and life-giving of God. Human activity *can* be a reflection of God's life and wholeness. Traditionally, before the advent of the new epistemology of domination, it was.

Indeed, tradition itself is a very apt exemplification of the divine life and wholeness. It echoes nature. Take the tradition of Morris dancing: however many Morris dances there are, it is the same dance, yet each individual dance and indeed each dancer is different. As with traditional arts, so with the traditional crafts: a traditionally made pot can be the same as one made of yore and yet have its own individuality. Tradition is alive. Its wholeness follows from that. This is true of spiritual tradition also. Take the Benedictine tradition, to which I belong. No two Benedictine monasteries (even in the same congregation of monasteries) are the same, and yet all Benedictine monasteries have a spirit each monk will readily recognize as his own. The Benedictine tradition is alive, and so it is one. Yet it would be death to a series of communities to force them all to be the same.

Creatures Great and Small

We can see a reflection of God's oneness in all living things. Each animal is one over time. It will be different when it is old from when it was little, but it will be one and the same animal. The differences show the creativity of its Maker. This creativity of difference within oneness is also visible across a species of animals. You can have a whole flock of sheep and (so the Bible tells us) the shepherd will know each individual, and yet it will be quite clear that it is one species of animal that you have here. There is difference and oneness, manifesting God's creative unity. That diversity in wholeness, the sign of life, is visible in larger groups of animals. It is there, for example, in mammals. This group itself could be seen either as one in a greater group (all animals) or as comprising smaller groups (for example, carnivores). The point I want to make is that there is a wonderful interplay of oneness in God's creation. It is not just one thing tacked onto another. There is a living wholeness, which can be seen across time and space. There are wholes within wholes that are themselves within wholes. Life is not linear. It has an inner dimension: like so many Russian dolls, there is life within life—whether that be a cell in a body containing a DNA code for the whole body or one goose flying in a flock.

Other People's Wholeness

This means something. It speaks of a higher reality. To see what it says, let us reflect a little more on what was said about the life of the human person consisting of wholeness of body, soul, and spirit and about how that life finds its fulfillment in a disinterested wholeness of gaze. This gaze does not, as it were, pick a quarrel with anything it sees but rather takes it all in lovingly. Although the person so looking will have occasion to see things from the point of view of their usefulness, this will not be mistaken for full knowing, which, on pain of being vitiated by partiality, is directed toward the whole and is in principle all-encompassing. This whole person, gazing wholly, will know other persons who are also whole. They too will (potentially, at least) have an all-encompassing gaze. Here the image of Russian dolls breaks down: if one person seeing other persons is like a doll containing other dolls—one whole encompassing other wholes—the other persons are not just like dolls within the particular doll but also like dolls containing that doll, for they too are wholes encompassing other wholes. Of course in our fallen world we do not always realize the awe-inspiring integrity of the other people with whom we are dealing. We may even see them simply as a source of profit.

Heaven

However, the destiny we are called to realize is a celestial one: the full awareness of heaven. Here will be fulfilled the gospel saying: "nothing is secret, that shall not be made manifest"—that is, what is hidden on earth will be known in heaven. The full inner dimension of other people will be known in its wholeness. Each person will know the whole of what each other person's heart (in the fullest sense of the word) knows. That means that the whole joy (for joy characterizes heaven) of each person will be known by each other person. It will be, to compare great things to small, like a party where everybody gets happier when anybody has a drink. Yet it is more than that, since it will not just be other people's experience of joy that we know; it will also be other people's experience of other people's joy. Then there is their experience of this latter to be known, and so on without limit. That is why it is called infinite bliss. And we haven't even begun to consider the promised experience of knowing God's joy.

Seeing with a whole gaze, then, is seeing into the life of things: things on earth and in heaven. It is seeing the wonder of creation in all its variegated wholeness; the wonder of the other person in that person's awe-inspiring wholeness; the multifaceted wonder of all that the other person gazes upon. Ultimately it is gazing upon a majestic wholeness that evokes such awe that any fragmented partiality or selfish interest is melted away: the wholeness of God Himself.

Holiness

This is (as the root meaning of the word suggests) holiness. Precisely because holiness is disinterested, because it does not look for a usefulness favorable to the beholder, it tends in our epoch to be considered ignorant, naive, or even childish. It is in fact providentially concealed from those who would use it for selfish purposes. Indeed, Christ thanked His heavenly Father for concealing such things from the wise and learned and revealing them to mere children. To such belongs the kingdom of heaven; to their innocent gaze are revealed things hidden from the foundation of the world; to their wonder is unfolded life in its poised dance at the heart of all that is. Yet it is always there for those who seriously seek it, at whatever hour of the day they begin their toil in the vineyard. Although we cannot make anyone want it, at least by sorting out our epistemology, and otherwise clearing the ground of the error that has accumulated in recent centuries, we can offer its possibility to those of goodwill who do not want to turn away from the truth.

Family and Community

The way the whole is multiplied in heavenly bliss points to what Jesus meant when He said, "I am come that they might have life, and that they might have it more abundantly." With God, there is always more abundance. Each whole, with the life of which it is an icon, illustrates this, for a whole is always more than the sum of its parts. This is abundantly clear in marriage, where two become one flesh and a third (or more!) results. The love between two people blossoms in conception and is fruitful in offspring. New life comes from the living whole of the union. It is also true that new love comes from it. The beloved is not only a particular person—she or he is also the whole of humanity. Marriage is a training in loving each and every person. So is religious life. The latter is wonderfully exemplified in Blessed Mother Teresa of Calcutta. She loved Jesus; every person she spoke with was Jesus to her, and therefore she loved all people greatly.

Marriage is one actuation of the urge to wholeness, the instinct to return to pre-lapsarian wholeness. Life in community is another. Communities express the connection between life and wholeness: their life is always different from the sum of the lives of their individual members. Relations within the community as a whole will be different from relations between two individual members. And in religious communities, such as monasteries, there will characteristically be a wholeness that extends over time, even over centuries: a living tradition. The instinct of the human spirit for life and wholeness is also seen in the urge to join clubs, societies, unions, guilds, and so on. Although they may not be explicitly religious, these associations are fed by the longing for life and wholeness that is at bottom a longing for God.

The Catholic Church

This longing does find an explicitly religious expression in membership of the Catholic Church. "Catholic" means "universal" or "including everyone," and it is in the Church (this word in its original Greek form—ἐκκλησία—means "gathering") that the life that Jesus came to give us is found most abundantly, precisely because of the wholeness of the Church. This wholeness is not an imposed uniformity after the manner of a production line; rather, it is a living diversity in which wholeness is expressed locally. Each bishop is the center of the Church where he has his diocese. When bishops gather in a particular country, there is not one who is in charge of the others; rather, they come together in a bishops' conference when they wish to establish a common policy on something. Yet, for there to be life there has to be wholeness, and so to ensure that the Church is not fissiparous there is one bishop, that of Rome, who provides unity for the worldwide body by making judgments when necessary. Within the Church there are communities of very different character, just as there are individuals of very different character. It is this diversity within unity that characterizes living community. It steers a passage between the Scylla of fragmentation and the Charybdis of uniformity. It is the mark of both God's first creation and the new creation in Christ that is his body, the Church.

This unity of the Church is spiritual and encompasses the living and the dead, who help one another. It is rooted in God. As Saint Paul says to the Ephesians, "There is one body, and one Spirit, even as ye are called in one hope of your calling; One Lord, one faith, one baptism, One God and Father of all, who is above all, and through all, and in you all." It is a reflection of the unity of the Holy Trinity and the answer to the high priestly prayer of Jesus: "That they all may be one; as thou, Father, art in me, and I in thee, that they also may be one in us." It is the unity of love, the Love that is the person of the Holy Spirit who makes one Father and Son and who performs what Jesus asked in His prayer to the Father: "That they may be one, even as we are one; I in them, and thou in me, that they may be made perfect in one."

God

To see with a single gaze oneness in all the ways I have adumbrated—in things that exist, in living things, in people, in social and religious groupings—is to see the reflection of the oneness of God. The distinction without separation that this oneness allows is at its most fundamental in the Holy Trinity. Father, Son, and Holy Spirit are distinct, yet They are one. To see oneness in creation is to sense the source of creation, the Creator. To see only fragments in creation is to see creation in its material aspect, missing its source and its life. It is to miss the One through whom all things were made, without whom "was not any thing made that was made." He is the One in whom are united human and divine nature, and thus the One who is able to give eternal life. He is the One who gives the Holy Spirit. The Spirit vivifies and makes whole, as at the first Pentecost, in which the Church was born. That divine gift of life and wholeness is offered afresh in every moment to any who will receive it.

Life and Death

Moses says to the people of Israel, "See, I have set before thee this day life and good, and death and evil." The former is loving God and keeping His commandments, the latter turning away from Him. To love God, we need to know Him. To know Him, even indirectly through His creation, we need to see the whole in its many manifestations with a gaze that is whole. In that is life and integrity. The other way—the one that sees material fragments rather than spiritual wholes—is death and disintegration. The thinking that separates out, that divides into parts, becomes—if it is an end rather than a means—a separation from life and a falling apart of the thinker. Let us consider more fully what sort of life wholeness brings. After that we can cast a glance at the indicators in our contemporary world of the pressing need for this contemplative spirit, before opening a new chapter regarding Man and the cosmos.

Life in all its wholeness includes all of time. An unthinking epistemology may regard our experience as a lot of little moments one after another, but we have already concluded that we do not in fact see things like that. It would be impossible to understand a sentence if we could not see or hear all the words as a whole; it would be impossible to see what a thing is if we could not put together our looking at it from various angles to see the whole. Still less could we know a person without a sense of a whole that goes beyond fractions of time and space. All of this, however, is only an illustration in miniature, as it were, of the truth that we do not really see unless we see all that is as one. For God, this seeing is absolutely everything at every moment. This divine viewpoint gives the truest picture. For us, the truest picture is to see all that we experience as a single whole. Separating off parts for purposes of calculation and manipulation is a secondary sort of looking; it has its uses, but if mistaken for looking at the whole it loses touch with reality. This reality is in the whole rather than the part, because life and spirit are in the whole—the part on its own is dead. God in His eternity is real and living: time and space are the canvas on which His picture is drawn—of themselves they are dead.

Stillness

This seeing the whole rather than the fragment is perhaps more characteristic of the child, who can be lost in the wonder of it all, than it is of the person immersed in the changing business of the world. Yet the old too can have some natural awareness of it. Nearer the end of life, it is easier to see it as a whole, even without waiting for that last moment when the whole of it is said to rush past one's eyes. An intuitive glance can take in all that has been together with all that the senses now present. Such intuition can be supposed to extend on some level to what is to be: it is not uncommon to have dreams that say something about what is to happen. These necessarily touch a level of awareness that is not fragmented by time. One can in any case accept the future, as it were, on trust.

What is it like, then, this seeing all of time at once? There is a hint in our perceiving meaning. I commonly have the experience of hearing sounds and a little time later registering meaning. I know that this is not my experience only, because frequently people ask me to repeat what I have said and I find that by being silent long enough for them to take in the meaning of what I have said, I can avoid doing so. The meaning is in the whole, found when that is paid attention to. So if we assume, as I do, that creation means something, a total experience of the world is going to be an experience of meaning. To the objection that no one has a God-like experience of the whole world, we can oppose the spiritual wisdom of the Jewish Talmudic saying, "Whoever saves a life, it is considered as if he saved an entire world." Each life is in a sense *the* world. That will be explored more fully in the next chapter; here the point is that the world is a gift of meaning to each person, that is understood when it is perceived as a whole.

It is an experience of meaning, but it is also an experience of peace. The reason for this is that to see the whole is to not be identified with any particular part and therefore to not be disturbed by the fate of that part. For example, if one accepts the whole in one's gaze, one is not staking one's happiness on particular outcomes in the future or reacting to particular events in the past. In fact, to see the whole is to see that in reality there is no movement or change in the world. Of course this sounds counterintuitive, since much of the time we are not seeing whole. We are identified with some particular part, and relative to that particular part other parts are moving or changing. The whole is something else. If we imagine time as though it were a dimension of space—that is, imagine that it is present to us as a whole in the same way that it is present to God— then a ball being thrown up into the air and away from one person to land at the feet of another person will look like the structure supporting a suspension bridge from underneath: it will form a parabola curving up and then down. And it is always just that. It never changes. No part of it ever changes. This divine viewpoint is the view from eternity. Yet translating time into space does not fully represent this viewpoint, since the separation of space as well as of time is overcome in the divine seeing: the aim of such a translation is to evoke the possibility of contemplating all moments as one. To the extent that we can see time whole we are entering into eternity. That is a journey into eternal reality: the living meaning that is behind and beyond—and expressed by—all that is.

Peace comes from seeing this way. There is no movement or change. Everything just is, met with a serene gaze. Of course people interact with what is around them and there are outcomes in this world of space and time, yet—properly seen—all of that is secondary to the whole and its meaning (as in the weaver poem). Grasping the meaning contemplatively relativizes these outcomes, even if they involve acute personal suffering. A comment by Saint Thérèse of Lisieux on the suffering of Jesus suggests how this happens. She said, "Our Lord in the Garden of Olives enjoyed all the delights of the Trinity, and nevertheless His agony was not the less cruel on account of it. It is a mystery, but I assure you that I understand something of it through what I experience myself." Enjoying "all the delights of the Trinity" is of course seeing the whole in the most fundamental way: the oneness at the root of everything, the oneness of God in which Jesus (and therefore Saint Thérèse) participated.

Saint Thérèse was knowing in her own experience the truth of the promise of Jesus: "Peace I leave with you, my peace I give unto you: not as the world giveth, give I unto you. Let not your heart be troubled, neither let it be afraid." In another context Saint Thérèse wrote, "All was sadness and bitterness. . . . However *peace*, always *peace* was found at the bottom of the chalice." She longed to communicate this peace, writing to a sister, "Ah! . . . if I could communicate to you the peace that Jesus has put in my soul in the thick of my tears." This is the peace that Jesus gives, the peace of the meaning of the whole that He, the Word of God, of course is. Regarding the objection that looking at the whole world including its undoubted horrors cannot be expected to give peace "not as the world giveth," it can be replied that the world *as such* does not give peace: rather, what it *means* gives peace. And it cannot but express Him of whom it is written, "All things were made by Him; and without Him was not any thing made that was made." One does not find a book of consolation comforting just by putting it under one's pillow: one *reads* it. The meaning comforts.

So how do we read the book of the world and find its comforting meaning? How do we see all time as a whole so as to grasp what it adds up to? Where is this much-to-be-desired life to be found? The answer, in a word, is in *stillness*. "Be still, and know that I am God," sings the psalmist. If there is no agitation, if there is no change or movement of turbulence in the soul, we are still and can look into the deep meaning of things. Knowledge, say the Scholastics, is according to the knower, and if we are still we can gaze on the utter stillness that is in everything when all time is perceived as a whole. This is of course a detachment from the way we are normally involved in the world. It is as though we are considering a great play in which much suffering is depicted—such as *King Lear*—but we have so absorbed it that there is nothing of the "what is going to happen next?" in our response. We know the script and the words are always the same. They exist in utter stillness. This detachment is a detachment from commitment to the particular fragment. It is not at all the same as detachment from the senses. One does not achieve spiritual enlightenment by sensory deprivation. On the contrary, in this detachment every tale that the senses tell us is accepted as belonging to the whole. We do not refuse to let in reality as it is signaled to us. We do not fight its existence. We read the signals as showing us something beyond what our senses show us: a reality ever still, ever crystalline in its beauty. This is the light-filled way of looking in the sense that, as we saw earlier, light is the nearest thing in creation to the timeless and eternal.

This is more than a matter of looking at things calmly, helpful as that may be. It is a spiritual practice in a long tradition. The custom of going on retreat is part of it. This is spending time in quietness and stillness, apart from any particular concern with doing things. Monastic life involves this. Indeed the congregation to which my monastery belongs stipulates that no particular work (apart from worship of God, who is in Abbot John Chapman's phrase "nothing in particular") is to be allowed to become the main purpose of a monastery, on pain of expulsion from the congregation. A Benedictine monk takes a vow of stability. He is rooted in one place, a physical prelude to a spiritual stillness. Going further back, there is the whole Greek hesychastic tradition. A particular form of prayer in the context of stillness and quietness, established by the pattern of breath, is characteristic of this tradition. Further back still, before the advent of Christ, there is the ancient Greek religious practice of incubation, in which a person would be utterly still in a cave or suchlike so as to be able to pass beyond this world into the realm of those who from its perspective have died. From there they would be able to bring back the wisdom of eternity and become lawgivers. They would, to quote an outstanding commentator on the writing of Parmenides (a pre-Socratic philosopher belonging to this tradition), be able to pass on a teaching about "how to find stillness in the middle of movement, the proof of oneness in apparent separation, the evidence of something beyond our senses through the use of reading and hearing." In other words, they could through their guidance help people to find life and wholeness by learning to see all time and space as one. To put it in terms that belong to the later Christian tradition, they could help people to hear the Word through which the world was made and in knowing that Word to find eternal life. Such is the comfort of meaning. The illusion of distance and movement disappears. The human heart in utter stillness sings to the heart of all that is and finds its song reciprocated, for the harmony sung between them is one.

Chapter Two: Life and Wholeness

The Present Moment

If we see all of time as one, then the present moment contains both past and future. It is all. The whole of our being is in the present: there is not part of it regretfully wrapped up in the past, nor is there part of it anxiously constrained by thought of the future. The spiritual practice of living like this has been called the sacrament of the present moment. A sacrament is a means by which God makes Himself present to us. It is fitting to call the present moment a sacrament because it is in this moment that God is present to us. The present moment is the image in time of eternity; it is the point of contact with eternity. "Behold, now is the accepted time; behold now is the day of salvation," says Saint Paul, alluding to the prophet Isaiah, meaning not just that it is unwise to put off turning to God but that it is only *now*—ever—that we can know God. We cannot reach Him in the past or the future because these times are not present to us, though they are to Him. Wholehearted acceptance of His will for us now—as expressed in all that is, including our own inner disposition—is contact with His life-giving presence; to look at all that there is with unfragmented attention is already to know obscurely the fullness of life. All fragments are gathered into living wholeness in this, "the seal's wide spindrift gaze towards paradise," to borrow the words of a poet.

It looks, this gaze of wholeness, back to paradise as humanity first knew it as well as forward to the life of heaven. In God who is One they are of course one: the beginning is the end. Yet we in time see them separately. Looking back we see a time nearer to eternity. As the world gets older and its freshness from the hands of God fades ever further, so time speeds up. It is enough even to reflect on the last ten or twenty years to see that this is so. Whereas a decade or two ago it was the accepted thing to respond to a written communication within a week or so, now people apologize if they do not respond the same day! Urgency has overcome us. The process is analogous to the way time has a more unmoving quality to it when one is young. Polixenes, in Shakespeare's *The Winter's Tale*, reflects that he and his friend as boys were "Two lads who thought there was no more behind / But such a day to-morrow as today, / And to be boy eternal." They thought there was nothing in the future ("no more behind") except what was in the present: they lived as boys in eternity. To live in the present moment is to "become as little children" like these boys. In living again our own youth and the youth of our race, we prepare ourselves to enter the kingdom of heaven. The remembrance of a time nearer eternity is a foretaste of eternity, as in Wordsworth's *Intimations of Immortality from Recollections of Early Childhood*, the poem with which I began this book.

The higher life from which we have descended and to which we aspire to ascend is less fragmented by time, less one thing after another and more a single whole. We approach it when we take "no thought for the morrow," when we do not calculate by focusing on a fraction of the whole and overlooking everything else. We approach it in a contemplative gaze that is not concerned with a mere fragment of time but rather shares in the life of Christ, of whom it is said in the Easter liturgy, "All time belongs to Him and all the ages." Facing everything in the moment, we are not ambushed by what we have neglected in our preoccupation with a part. Looking with the "third eye" neither to the past nor to the future (represented by the left and right eyes) but to the indivisible instant between them that is the reflection of eternity in time, we see all as a whole. In this contemplative gaze the sense of direction of time is relativized. After all, it is only in our own scheming that one thing prepares for another in the future: in God's Providence a future good can, more efficaciously than any human planning in the opposite direction, determine a present necessity. For example, His awareness of the destiny of two people to share their lives can cause Him to bring them together. As the Author of all, He is quite free to write the last chapter first. He calls us to this freedom, the freedom of life in its wholeness.

Intensive Living

This life in its fullness transcends the fragmentation of space as well as of time. In our consideration of solid body thinking in the introduction, we saw that it considered only what is separated by space, ignoring the stronger spiritual reality where one does not exclude another. The two aspects of life can be called extensive living and intensive living. "Intensive" does not mean "intense" but rather life within an inward dimension that includes others rather than excluding them as an extensive—or material—existence does. Intensive life is all that there is in heaven: there people do not trip over one another. Rather, they dwell in one another, without losing their identity, in the manner implied in Christ's saying, "Abide in me, and I in you." That is why they do not need to get married, of course. In heaven, all goods, including intimate relationships, are spiritual, or "nonrival" in the sense explained in the introduction in the discussion of the different kinds of goods that we know in this life. Life in its fullness allows nothing to be unshared.

It is possible to cultivate this life in its fullness even here. Avoiding the sin of envy is obviously a help since it looks away from partial—because extended and exclusive—goods to those that are spiritual and shared. For the same reason, it also helps to be generous. The contemplative life, however, goes further than that. It deliberately cultivates the inward or the intensive. In doing so it looks to the whole in which all is included (within) rather than the fragments that exclude one another (without). Life in a Benedictine monastery is organized for this. Saint Benedict says in his Rule that as far as possible everything needed should be within the monastery rather than outside it. This is spiritually better for the monks because the arrangement of the monastery expresses an inward movement rather than an outward one. Their lives are centripetal rather than centrifugal. Traditionally (as in the writing of Saint Bernard, for example) a monastery is an image of heaven or the New Jerusalem. That is because it is a place where the heavenly life is cultivated. This is the life that is found in the wholeness that does not exclude. It is therefore an inward, spiritual life whose depth can include the other, rather than an outward, material life whose dissipation fragments and isolates. It is a life that has a way of looking that appreciates the whole rather than one that would manipulate the part for advantage. It is contemplative and leads to gratitude, rather than analytic and (because there are never enough rival goods to go around) leading to resentment.

To avoid extensive living and cultivate intensive living, Saint Benedict stipulates that monks should have goods in common as the first Christians did. They are not to have private property, and the abbot is to look under their mattresses to make sure that they don't. The sixteenth-century abbot, Louis of Blois, summed up how to move from the extensive (outward, material) life to the intensive (inward, spiritual) life by saying that one should cast out all sense of proprietorship. Giving up the ownership of space is part of this. Courteous making way for others prepares the way for life beyond "our bourne of Time and Place." Of course there are sacrifices—at least of temporary, rival goods—involved in this, but contemplating the beauty of the whole and the spiritual joy of facilitating one's participation in it relativize the sacrifices. Seen in perspective (contemplatively), they are not the main issue.

Celestial Living

The main issue is life and wholeness, and that is something that cannot unwillingly be lost. It is "hid with Christ in God." In heaven it is realized in all its fullness. There "God shall wipe away all tears . . . and there shall be no more death, neither sorrow, nor crying, neither shall there be any more pain: for the former things are passed away." That is to say, the separation of time and space is no more; there can therefore be no more grief because there can be no more parting. Space and time involve parts that are outside one another and our earthly bodies exist in space and time, but "there are also celestial bodies" of which earthly bodies are simply the seed. These have inward rather than outward dimension; they include others rather than exclude them, so love is perfect in heaven: no one is cold-shouldered there.

Of course it is difficult to conceive of this if our primary organizing principle is that of Democritus, but he was wrong: space is not the absolute template of creation. Rather, life is the organizing principle of creation, and so it is the whole that is the basic form of creation. Each whole speaks of other wholes in a way that directs the intuition to the undying celestial reality of wholes within wholes, wholly contained in the thrice holy God. There are other helps to intuition. Every love, every sort of sociability even, points to this wholeness. Then there are those exceptional people who already live a celestial life of sorts while on earth and enjoy some of its privileges. Such was Padre Pio, a saint who could bilocate, that is, he could be present in more than one place at the same time. In this he had something of the risen Christ, who could, "the doors being shut," come into the midst of His disciples. This of course contradicts Democritus even more decisively than quantum theory does! Space is not king, love is.

There is a further help to the intuition of the whole of heaven that will be explored more fully in Chapter Six—namely, the Eucharist. This is the sacrament of unity. In it, Christ's people are one and receive Him, undivided though given to many. They receive His celestial Body, a pledge of celestial life, where there is no division of heart, of place, or of time. It is the life of mutual indwelling, peace, and harmony, where many are together in love, distinguished but not separated by space or time. There nobody wants or needs to be queen or king of the sidewalk. The nourishment of the Eucharist, "which endureth unto everlasting life," points to this. The one who takes it already knows mutual indwelling, for he has heard the great promise, "He that eateth my flesh, and drinketh my blood, dwelleth in me and I in him." To sacrifice material wealth or dominance for the sake of this is like giving up Monopoly money, of use only in the context of a game, for hard currency. It is done in the knowledge that our physical presence, like our participation in a game, is not our entire being. Our true life is spiritual and indestructible.

Difference and Hierarchy

This celestial life is reflected in life on earth, which partakes of its character while also having a material aspect. If the latter were all that it is (as the votaries of Democritus would have it), then it would simply be one thing alongside another in space. It would be merely mechanical and in effect therefore not life at all. Atomism—seeing creation simply as atoms in space—looks at creation without seeing life, since it does not see the indicator of life: the whole, whether that is the absolute whole or the showing forth of it in a particular whole. In reality, because there is life there is wholeness, and because there is wholeness there is an organizing principle. This principle means that everything does not fall apart into atomic existence: instead, there is an intrinsic relation in every distinction. This relation is not that of uniformity or one imposed from outside: it is a relation within wholeness that allows difference.

In order for the little wholes to be contained within a greater whole, there needs to be a hierarchy. This is the guarantor of life, since it is what makes wholeness possible. We can see this if we take the human body as an example. The body as a whole is higher in the hierarchy than the individual cell, which is subordinate to it. If a single cell claims dominance for its particular whole over the whole of the body by multiplying without reference to its subordinate position, then it becomes cancerous, and the life of the body is threatened. Life is when a multiplicity of lower wholes is contained in a higher whole. This is possible because of levels or degrees of hierarchy. This principle applies in its way to the body politic— social organization—as well as to the human body. What happens without it is eloquently told by Shakespeare:

> O, when degree is shak'd,
> Which is the ladder of all high design,
> The enterprise is sick. How could communities,
> Degrees in schools, and brotherhoods in cities,
> Peaceful commerce from dividable shores,
> The primogenity and due of birth,
> Prerogative of age, crowns, sceptres, laurels,
> But by degree stand in authentic place?
> Take but degree away, untune that string,
> And hark what discord follows.

In this speech it is being argued that degree, the principle of proper subordination, is needed to fulfill one's purpose in a healthy way. Social harmony, the music of society, depends upon it. You can argue that the particular social forms described here could or should be replaced with other ones, but unless these also contain ordering at different levels then what you have is social atomism, which is to say, anarchy. With no higher level at which social life is coordinated, there is rivalry. This is especially so if the coordinating function of the life of the whole is replaced by the deathly imposition of uniformity, as in totalitarianism, whether cultural or political. In this case, because they are the same, the individuals are rivals for the same role and are not held together by a living organic unity. They are indeed like atoms clashing with one another at random. On the other hand, a living unity, which is embodied in a person of higher rank, is the guarantor of difference. Here, individuals each have their role to play in a way that helps rather than rivals others, like parts of a body working together. Because there is a higher authority, none need oppose another.

Shakespeare describes the opposition that arises in its absence in the continuation of the speech quoted:

> Each thing meets
> In mere oppugnancy: the bounded waters
> Should lift their bosoms higher than the shores,
> And make a sop of all this solid globe;
> Strength should be lord of imbecility,
> And the rude son should strike his father dead;
> Force should be right, or rather, right and wrong
> (Between whose endless jar justice resides)
> Should lose their names, and so should justice too!
> Then every thing include itself in power,
> Power in will, will into appetite,
> And appetite, an universal wolf
> (So doubly seconded with will and power),
> Must make perforce an universal prey,
> And last eat up himself.

In other words, without different levels there is self-destructive chaos. "Mere oppugnancy" rather than cooperation is the relation between individuals; the identity of righteousness and justice is lost. Power becomes the only arbiter, waiting on the will of the individual and thus serving appetite. The body politic then becomes self-devouring. The "universal wolf" of appetite recalls the opponent of the One who came that His followers "might have life, and that they might have it more abundantly" (since when they are not in His care, "the wolf catcheth them, and scattereth") and hints at the Antichrist. Without degree there is scattering; there is no wholeness and so no life.

Fragmentation in Our Time

We have considered at length how life is linked to wholeness. If we are to recover a life-giving contemplative spirit—one that knows the whole—we need to consider also the effects of the dominant epistemology of our time: one that fragments to analyze. The way of looking that predominates in our days is one that looks at reality "in tiny shreds and shards." To us can be addressed the prophetic words of Isaiah: "Seeing many things . . . thou observest not." We do not see the whole. Our attention itself is fragmented. Let us consider briefly the history of this fragmentation.

In primordial times, communication was always in the present moment, from the whole person, and, assuming that there were not great throngs of people speeding around the globe, from a fairly limited number of people: the arrival of a new person would be exceptional. With the advent of writing there was already a fragmentation: the person who communicated was no longer there and so it was no longer a living and whole communication made in the present moment. We can say that a book contains the lifeblood of a master spirit, but that is a metaphor. A living presence is no longer there: the living presence is to the book as freshly made vegetable soup is to the sort that is made by adding water. Printing meant that written communication was no longer personally prepared, and by its replication it offered that parody of unity which is known as uniformity; furthermore, its relative ease encouraged writing that did not come from the depth of the soul. These considerations apply to an even greater extent to radio, television, and the internet. Telephone communication by definition involves the absence of the one speaking, and furthermore it interrupts and fragments what the person called is doing. Smartphones with their ability to receive messages from anywhere at any time are a masterwork of the fragmentation of attention. Of course several of these media can claim attention simultaneously! Often a present living person may lose out to their claim.

This is an account of the integrity and life of communications as they are given, but a corresponding fragmentation of the ability to receive whole can be assumed: skipping from one thing to another precludes the giving of whole attention to one thing, however necessary. Long before the use of the internet and smartphones, T. S. Eliot wrote that we are "distracted from distraction by distraction." It is a common experience now for people at work to forget what it is that they have been distracted from. The fragmentation takes place over space: no longer is the natural human range of sight and hearing respected. It also takes place over time, mostly now with a forward direction. Much of the news, not to say the anxiety, is about what is expected to happen! We hurtle toward the apocalypse, forgetful of the gospel injunction to take "no thought for the morrow." It is in this latter being present to the moment that the defragmentation of time is found—that eternity is touched.

Fragmented Thought

This fragmentation of time is paralleled by the fragmentation of learning. It is assumed that a wide-ranging learning is going to be a superficial one, since nothing will receive the depth of inquiry that is supposed to be necessary for the acquisition of worthwhile knowledge. This assumption is possible because of an ignorance of hierarchy. If there is only (as Democritus thought) one thing alongside another thing, then one can only hope to acquire bits of learning. If there is a higher whole that contains other wholes, then wisdom is possible even with only representative pieces of information. Before fragmentation became widespread, theology was acknowledged as the queen of the sciences. Such an enthroning does not mean that theologians have any right to interfere where they are ignorant: each branch of learning is rightly accorded its own suzerainty of judgment. It simply means that the tree has a trunk and is not yet dead. Nowadays, however, even living things tend to be studied as though they are dead. Their separate parts are considered in terms of mechanical interaction. Significantly, Descartes, the father of much modern thought, considered animals to be in effect machines. By looking at parts only one loses a sense of unity and thus of spirit and life. Even the human person is not invulnerable to being treated this way, especially with regard to the spiritual dimension of being. An epistemology that works for what is dead is brought to bear on what is living, and so much that makes for life is occluded thereby that dreariness and desperation are the natural outcome. Seeing whole, looking contemplatively, is the cure. An integrated learning fostering the ability to make intuitive decisions that can take in the full picture is the outcome of such an epistemology.

Integrating thinking is not simply about individual people seeing the life and wholeness of creation. It is also about thinking together with other people: about having a common mind. That allows a depth and richness of thought not otherwise possible, but it also means that thought, because not private, is alive with the life of a greater whole. It depends on an idea of truth, grounded finally in God. It is the loss of this (the loss of the life and wholeness that comes from welcoming God's presence) that has led to the glum postmodernist notion that individuals each have their own thought and one cannot hope for much more than a negotiated truce among them. This is where chopped up thinking has led us. A contemplative spirit offers a better intellectual polity (in the sense of the relations thinkers have with each other) and a better life to those willing to pursue it.

Entropic Collapse

This spirit sees beyond what is dead and fragmented. Looking by way of life and wholeness, as seen in creation, toward the very Giver of life and wholeness, it escapes "the shadow of death." It transcends what necessarily belongs to the physical world as such: the gradual loss of distinct being. The second law of thermodynamics indicates that every physical process involves an irreversible net increase of disorder or entropy. This entropic collapse leads to homogenization—the erosion of distinctions (including those of life-enabling hierarchy) and the fading of identity from the world. As contact with the life and spirit found in the oneness of God is attenuated, what is material tends to its original state when "the earth was without form, and void: and darkness was upon the face of the deep." In its sociological aspect, this entropic collapse (concomitant with a society increasingly divorced from God) is manifest in high streets in many towns having just the same shops, in women and men having increasingly identical lifestyles, and in the sheer difficulty of any person simply being himself or herself. Only in contemplation, in looking to the living God in and from whom is all life and wholeness, is there escape from this. Left to ourselves, we tend to lose the oneness—the singular identity—that reflects the One. Without His spirit, we go the way of matter as it, by immutable physical law, loses its own distinctness.

A Binary World

It is perhaps significant that we live in a binary world: one that is increasingly so structured ("organized" would be a word too associated with life to be apt here) digitally by computers. This is an indication of distance from God in whom opposites coincide, an indication of multiplicity without the life-giving unity that comes ultimately from Him. Interestingly, Plato thought that two was a number without meaning since it implies relationship, which introduces the third factor. We have an increasing amount of information through our technology together with a diminishing amount of meaning. That third factor, the Spirit through whom we can recognize the Son who reconciles and atones (makes one), is absent, so we are left with the opposition and conflict of the binary, far from the peace and unity of oneness. Life in this digital world is relatively unreal, as though the dwellers in Plato's cave were to people hidden in a more subterranean cave as those walking outside were to them and this life of a digital world were in that more hidden cave. In it there is awareness lacking meaning, the meaning of the Logos: the Word of God whose oneness with Him is attested by the one Spirit. An exemplar of this meaningless consciousness is money that is entirely a digital creation, such as the bitcoin: accepted as having value, but having no referent of either goods or authority outside of itself.

In a sense this binary world, where everything is reduced to one or the other and there is no wholeness, is a working out of the consequences of the first falling away from God, from divine unity.

When Adam and Eve eat of "the tree of the knowledge of good and evil," they begin to look at things no longer as one (an outlook indicated by "the tree of life") but as divided. They discriminate and analyze: they no longer look with a simple and all-including gaze. As suggested above, recovering a contemplative spirit is walking in the direction of Eden. It is recovering a wholeness that began to be lost at the Fall.

Recovery

Such is our task. It is a matter of receiving: receiving God in His wholeness. Being who He is, He always gives—and wants to give—Himself totally and wholly. Our undertaking is to meet Him in that: to give ourselves totally and wholly to Him—to give all for all, or "all for You and nothing for me," in the words of Saint John of the Cross. That comes from knowing God, knowing that from our point of view He is—in the same saint's words—"all for me and nothing for You." The wholeness is all. We are in quest of "A condition of complete simplicity / (Costing not less than everything)," a simple gaze, a single eye, a heart whole, that looks toward that which it images and "selleth all." To find this simple, single whole outlook is to be ineluctably rewarded with the Whole toward which it looks. To "love the Lord thy God with all thy heart, and with all thy soul and with all thy mind" is to live eternally because to give all is to receive all. Giving whole attention to Him, whom to know is to love, is to live. This is why recovering a contemplative spirit matters.

I shall look more fully at this direct gaze toward God in the last three chapters of this book. Now, there is one further consideration to be made regarding how we look at what He has created: the relationship between Man and the cosmos. In this there can be a wholeness no longer generally dreamed of: if we can see this, then union with *Him* need not seem remote. It points us toward the ultimate goal of contemplation. The next chapter is about this relationship.

Chapter Three:
Man and Cosmos

The Great Book of God

he prophet Isaiah says to those who have lost wholeness of vision, "And the vision of all is become unto you as the words of a book that is sealed, which men deliver to one that is learned, saying, Read this, I pray thee: and he saith, I cannot; for it is sealed: And the book is delivered to him that is not learned, saying Read this, I pray thee: and he saith, I am not learned." In our epistemologically challenged age, the cosmos is as a closed book that we cannot read. Our learning closes it to us, for we have learned to see in a limited and limiting way, and our lack of learning stops us from reading it, for we have forgotten what it truly is.

It was not always so. Abbot Louis of Blois saw the world as "the great book of God." He remembered the tradition that had celebrated expression in the Latin verse *Omnis mundi creatura / quasi liber et pictura* ("Every creature of the world is as a book or picture for us, and a mirror"). Shakespeare remembered it too, in presenting a rural life, "exempt from public haunt," which

> Finds tongues in trees, books in the running brooks,
> Sermons in stones, and good in every thing.

Of what do these books and tongues speak? What do these pictures and mirrors show? The answer is twofold. First of all, they speak of their Maker, God. Then, analogously, they show Man, whom He made, male and female, in His own image.

They speak and show God and Man—and the great love God has for Man—to those who contemplate (seeing "good in every thing") rather than to those for whom nature is an adversary from whom something is to be extracted. The poets are receptive to this. Wordsworth reflected:

To me the meanest flower that blows can give
Thoughts that do often lie too deep for tears.

These thoughts are hidden in the heart in the traditional sense in which, as was said in Chapter One, it is the seat of the *intellect* rather than mere feeling. The intellect perceives directly what God has to say in His creation, without the intervention of human reason or feeling. The one who knows the world through it can read flowers. Blake had this ability. As one who contemplates, he saw both wisdom and happiness in flowers growing in the wilderness. He wrote in his poetical sketch entitled *Contemplation*:

> Who is this, that with unerring step dares tempt the wilds, where only Nature's foot hath trod? 'Tis Contemplation, daughter of the grey Morning! Majestical she steppeth, and with her pure quill on every flower writeth Wisdom's name. . . . Those who want Happiness must stoop to find it; it is a flower that grows in every vale.

Nature can speak of God and Man at the same time. The emergence of a butterfly from a chrysalis tells of the resurrection in a glorious body of Christ and of the promised resurrection of Man. The chrysalis is a reminder of when Saint Thérèse of Lisieux wrote to a sister distressed about not having known of her poor physical condition that her body was an envelope, with the implication that the message within would be revealed when it was put aside.

It is not just beautiful flowers and butterflies that have something to say to us: it is *everything* in creation. We have already considered the import of light, color, life, and wholeness. By way of further illustration, I shall look at three important strands in nature in greater depth: water, trees, and birds. Then I shall consider Man's relation to the cosmos as a whole and the implications of this for how we think of ourselves and our knowing.

Water

Water, like light, is a symbol of the divine. Of the four traditional elements, it has the most universal presence. It can even be present in the other elements: frozen, in earth; as steam, in fire; as mist, in air. It echoes God on the material plane by being the source of life.

Saint Cyril of Jerusalem takes it to be a symbol of the Holy Spirit in particular. As water can vivify very different kinds of growth, such as that of a palm tree or a vine, so the Holy Spirit gives life in all its diversity. Meister Eckhart says that God is distinguished by His indistinction. As God is present in all without distinction, so water is present in all plants and animals. As God gives life to the soul of Man, so water gives life to his body—making up a very large proportion of it. All things are possible to God; water, in its very fluidity, has the greatest possibility in where it can be and what it can become. God is infinite; water, in the sea, appears unbounded.

Water is associated with the color blue, and all that it means. It is redolent of heaven and its peace. It is also associated with the color green, with its ambivalent representation of life and death. To cross through the waters of the River Jordan is, according to Christian tradition, to die. One can drown in water, as well as be revivified by it. These two aspects of death and life are both present in the sacrament of baptism, by which people die to sin and are reborn to new life in Christ. Baptism cleanses from sin as water cleanses from dirt. The symbolism of baptism will be explored more fully in Chapter Six, but here it will be appropriate to look more fully at water as a universal symbol of God's redeeming as well as His creative power.

Water falling as rain is a symbol of His mercy; water falling as dew is a sign of His benediction. Water evaporating and being reincorporated in the atmosphere is a sign that as we come from God, so we return to God. The prophet Isaiah explains miracles of healing—from blindness, deafness, lameness, and dumbness-—by referring to the divine presence as evidenced by water, saying, "For in the wilderness shall waters break out, and streams in the desert. And the parched ground shall become a pool, and the thirsty land springs of water." Elsewhere in announcing the Lord's lament, "O that thou hadst hearkened to my commandments! then had thy peace been as a river, and thy righteousness as the waves of the sea," he uses the symbols of a river and the sea to indicate (respectively) the peace and justice of being guided by God. The prophet Ezekiel sees a river pouring from the Temple that gets deeper and deeper till it cannot be passed through. He is told, "Every thing shall live whither the river cometh." On its banks will be trees whose fruit is for food and whose leaves are for healing. This anticipates the celestial vision in the book of Revelation of "a pure river of water of life, clear as crystal, proceeding out of the throne of God and of the lamb."

Water is the symbol that Jesus Himself uses to indicate the life given through His Spirit, saying to the woman of Samaria, "Whosoever drinketh of the water that I shall give him shall never thirst; but the water that I shall give him shall be in him a well of water springing up into everlasting life." He even offers the possibility of becoming through faith a fount of this water, announcing, "He that believeth on me, as the scripture hath said, out of his belly shall flow rivers of living water." Lest there should be any misunderstanding, the evangelist adds, "This spake he of the Spirit, which they that believe on him should receive."

Trees

If water is a symbol of God's immanence—His presence within everything—then the tree by contrast points to His transcendence. Reaching up to the sky (or heaven), it expresses Man's destiny. "A man's reach should exceed his grasp, / Or what's a heaven for?" wrote the poet Robert Browning, and the tree's reach toward the sky, touching but not containing it, gives form to the unsatiated longing for the celestial that is written in Man's spirit. Its verticality contains its meaning. It represents what is traditionally called the *axis mundi*: the pole of the earth, which connects it with higher states of being. This is echoed in columns in sacred architecture, and in the implicit vertical pole connecting the sanctuary of a church to the top of the spire or tower above it. Robert Frost gives expression to the tree's meaning in a poem using the image of a tent with "its supporting central cedar pole / That is its pinnacle to heavenward /And signifies the sureness of the soul." Since what is in the world speaks not only of God but also of Man, the tree has a correspondence within him too. The spinal column (or vertebrae) represents the same reach that the tree has. It moves upward from the passional (the loins) to the spiritual, that is, from wanting what belongs to this world to wanting God. There is a somatic correspondence to the spiritual journey so symbolized in the therapy that makes subtle adjustments to the spine to improve the flow of fluid in it, which can bring healing to feelings as well as posture.

Trees are symbols of reaching toward the blue beyond, but they are also symbols of God's manifestation. His arboreal presence announces His power to conquer the enemies of David, who is told, "And let it be, when thou hearest a sound of a going in the tops of the mulberry trees, that thou shalt bestir thyself: for then shall the LORD go out before thee, to smite the host of the Philistines." More directly, God speaks to Moses from the burning bush, saying, "I AM THAT I AM." The very ground of being is apparent in a tree. This is an echo of "the tree of life . . . in the midst of the garden" in the first book of the Bible and in the last, where it yields "fruit every month" and leaves "for the healing of the nations." Between these two books (in the arrangement of the Bible) is the cross of Christ. According to traditional symbolism, it is made from the wood of "the tree of the knowledge of good and evil." This represents the power of the cross to regain for Man the domain of the tree of life, from which he was exiled by eating of the fruit of "the tree of the knowledge of good and evil." It is in a special sense the *axis mundi*, the vertical axis of communication between heaven and earth.

Movement along this vertical axis is not simply upward: life from heaven can come down to earth. This is symbolized by an inverted tree, with its roots in heaven. The analogy within Man is the nervous system. The brain (indicating the spiritual) is the root of the inverted tree: in form it is like a bulb or other concentrated root mass in the plant world. From it the nerves spread; those in the spinal column are like the trunk of a tree, and those radiating from it like the branches. The openness to God in Man's highest nature is thus transmitted throughout his body. Man's role as a pontifex, a bridge between heaven and earth, is replayed in miniature in his body. "Look unto the rock whence ye are hewn," urges the prophet, and Man, made through Christ and in the image of God, carries into this world something of his origin. The summons to becoming aware of this origin and his role in connecting the world to it is as evident in the form of his body as in the Scriptures. Heaven would reach to earth through him even as earth reaches to heaven in him. Downward and upward he is as a tree.

Birds

Like water, like a tree, a bird can be a symbol of the divine. When Jesus was baptized in the River Jordan, "the Holy Ghost descended in a bodily shape like a dove upon him." This recalls the dove that Noah sent out of the ark, which "came in to him in the evening; and lo, in her mouth was an olive leaf pluckt off: so Noah knew that the waters were abated from off the earth." The dove heralds reconciliation between God and Man and is the Spirit of peace, the Holy Spirit, who is able to give the assurance of forgiveness in the human heart. The dove is also the human soul, as when Saint Benedict had a vision of the soul of his sister, Saint Scholastica, flying up to heaven. Freedom from being constrained by earth makes of a bird a natural symbol of the spiritual. Being able to fly in the blue beyond speaks of the life of heaven, whether that which comes down to us in the Spirit or that which goes up to heaven in the souls of those destined for beatitude. A bird, like the whole of the cosmos, speaks of both God and Man.

Like the dove, the eagle does this in a special way. In its unwavering gaze on the sun, it is Christ beholding the glory of God; carrying its young to the sun, it is Christ bearing souls to God; plunging to take fish out of the sea, it is Christ rescuing souls from sin. It is also the Apostle beloved of Christ, John the Evangelist. He, like the eagle, stands for all those who contemplate God. The one who contemplates God, ever ancient and ever new, finds newness of life in Him, and so his or her "youth is renewed like an eagle's," as the psalmist sings. The gospels of John and the other evangelists are inspired by the contemplation of God, and so the lectern for the gospel is sometimes made in the form of an eagle.

Birds are set before us in the gospel as exemplars of carefree trust in God's Providence for us when Jesus says, "Behold the fowls of the air: for they sow not, neither do they reap, nor gather into barns; yet your heavenly father feedeth them." In the stillness of their absorption in flight, they teach us what He teaches us: "Take . . . no thought for the morrow." They show us how to live in the moment that opens to eternity, how to be present to God who is present to us in that moment. In their soaring into the sky they proclaim the injunction of the Apostle to "seek those things which are above, where Christ sitteth on the right hand of God" and to "set your affection on things above, not things on the earth." Even the most undignified duck waddling along can direct us to where to seek our peace when, disturbed, it takes flight to the blue beyond.

Contemplating the Cosmos

I have offered a few examples of the meaning of nature. As with the colors, it is not my claim that I have given an interpretation of unquestionable authority. I simply affirm that nature is intelligible, that it does have an objective meaning open to one who, like an eagle, is willing to contemplate it. It is a question of being receptive rather than domineering, of being one to whom something is revealed or given rather than one who imposes meaning or takes something. What is created speaks of the Creator. It does not do so in a way that demands that one strain to look beyond it, but by its very earthiness. Indeed, the highest is reflected in the lowest: the beauty of the earth—the lowest aspect of creation—speaks of the beauty of God Most High. Inversely, but in the same reflection of a reality in its opposite, the highest heavens with all their starry multitude speak of the most profound depth: the soul of Man. It is as though the oneness of God, in whom all opposites are reconciled, will not let these very different aspects be separated; rather, He links them with a common meaning and says thereby that He in His oneness is the Source of all and a universal Presence.

The cosmos is instinct with meaning; it is a holy icon. "The heavens declare the glory of God; and the firmament sheweth His handywork," as the psalmist puts it. The meaning of creation is to be read in the same spirit as Holy Scripture. The monastic practice of *lectio divina* or spiritual reading (which will be considered at more length in Chapter Five) with its prayerful waiting on what God wishes to say through the sacred text is aptly transposed to contemplative consideration of nature. Indeed, one might venture to say that God would not have needed to give us Sacred Scripture if we had not forgotten how to read the expression of "the invisible things of him from the creation of the world." The natural world is charged with the glory of God; it is in effect a sacrament—the visible expression of things holy but unseen. It matters that we see it this way, because we are utterly involved with it. On the material level, we are part of it; on the spiritual level, it is part of us. That is why we can be aware of its beauty, and why when we forget to reverence that beauty and treat the natural world as a meaningless thing to be manipulated we are falling into the most damaging self-contempt. Its beauty is our beauty.

When we do reverence that beauty we are acknowledging a presence rather than something—such as a traffic sign—that represents something else by convention. We see what is higher than the natural world present in a form that belongs to that world. So water is the expression in this world of the universal possibility that belongs to God. Contemplating water we see, through a glass darkly, God's immanence in His creation. Contemplating the blue beyond of the sky, we have an obscure realization of His transcendence. These expressions never reduce to something that can be exhausted by a verbal formula, as we can say of a traffic sign, "That means that you mustn't go more than thirty miles an hour here." We can, and indeed this is what I have been doing in this book, express in words what is being communicated to us in nature, but these words are no more than notes to help the contemplator of nature. Poetry (and this is a reason why it has been helpful to cite it) can say more than a mere guide to deciphering meaning, yet it only helps us to enter into the presence of the mystery: it cannot pluck out its heart. The reason is that what is expressed in nature is higher (or deeper) than that in which it is expressed: the latter necessarily belongs to the material plane. We can only look or listen and let our spirit be brought into the presence of what belongs to the spiritual plane. Of course, the Baconian empiriometric enterprise by definition cannot reveal this presence to us. It can only measure what belongs to space and time; it can never show what transcends space and time. You cannot cut up a dead bird and grasp the spiritual height to which the majesty of its flight points.

Yet the contemplative spirit can sense something of what is beyond space and time in everything in nature. I remember hearing the roar of a wild Bengal tiger in its natural habitat: freedom and power were incarnate in it. What Wordsworth saw in the loveliness of "the innocent brightness of a newborn Day" was a glimpse of the beauty of the absolute, which—as Einstein demonstrated—we look for in vain in space and time. That absolute beauty makes itself present for us in light so that we may in some sense know it, just as the human soul communicates something of itself to another in a living body. It can no more tell us all about itself through any aspect of nature than a body can tell us all about a soul, but it can recall us from our blindness to it, for in reality it is never itself absent.

To contemplate the cosmos is to see in this mediated fashion the One without whom "was not any thing made that was made." It is to behold the beauty of Christ, traced upon that which was made through Him. It is to see Him who said, "He that hath seen me hath seen the Father." It is to see "the invisible things" of the Father, "even His eternal power and Godhead." It is to see with Christ, as belonging both to Him and His creation, what He sees eternally. It is to share in the love that unites Him to the One He sees, the Spirit of God who "moved upon the face of the waters" to bring into being what began at the divine utterance: "Let there be light."

And we have a sense that we are more than beholders. C. S. Lewis articulated this thus:

> We do not want merely to *see* beauty, though, God knows, even that is bounty enough. We want something else which can hardly be put into words—to be united with the beauty we see, to pass into it, to receive it into ourselves, to bathe in it, to become part of it.

We want to be at the heart of creation.

The Centrality of Man

Even if we don't have this vision, the contemplative openness to what God has inscribed for us on the fabric of His creation, we have in our very nature an indication that we belong at the heart of creation. We are after all made in the image of God, and He, source of beauty, holds all things in being. He is the true and absolute center of all that is, and in geometric terms He is symbolized by a point from which all extension and design emerge. We are, each of us, a center that reflects this absolute center. Each of us perceives a whole world of which we are the center.

Of course, taking this centrality too literally leads to a clashing of egos and can be identified with the number one sin of pride. Yet it is an echo of God in us and has much to teach us if we but understand it according to the things of the spirit. "The letter killeth, but the spirit giveth life," wrote Saint Paul. If we take our centrality to be according to the letter—to the outward form—then we try to exert domination in the material plane. This is doomed to failure since on the material level we are part of the natural world. Our fate is like that of Nebuchadnezzar, who dreamed of a tree cut down and was told by Daniel, "It is thou, O king, that art grown and become strong: for thy greatness is grown and reacheth unto heaven, and thy dominion to the end of the earth." As a consequence, "he was driven from men, and did eat grass as oxen, and his body was wet with the dew of heaven, till his hairs were grown like eagles' feathers, and his nails like birds' claws." In this he was given the knowledge that he belonged to the natural world in the same way as the beasts and the birds.

Nebuchadnezzar had life of the sort of which Jesus says, "Whosoever will save his life shall lose it." To assert oneself by material power is to stake out in one's suzerainty a false simulacrum of the wholeness that is life. God alone is the source of oneness: a man's rule cannot replace it. Yet, and this is his true destiny, Man can be one with God and so share His oneness. In this real wholeness he finds that "the spirit giveth life." The natural fact that in perceiving the cosmos we find ourselves at the center (since each individual is at the center of all that his senses tell him) points to this destiny. It is possible to *think* of other ways in which the cosmos is organized—for example, that the planets, including our own, circle the sun or (as Democritus would have it) that there is just space with no center or direction—but our senses tell us that we are at the center, and this is providentially meaningful. Scientifically speaking, anything can be relative to anything, so the question of a center cannot be settled in this way, which is in any case indirect compared to sense perception. Galileo, as indicated in my citation of him in the introduction, wanted to offer violence to the senses for the sake of thinking of the cosmos in a way different from how they show it to us. In doing this, he attacked the *spiritual* meaning of direct sense perception. There is a spiritual meaning also to seeing the sun as the center of the cosmos, as is clear from what has been said about light as a symbol of the divine, but it is not so immediately (that is, sensually) available. To say that the cosmos has *no* center or direction is to ignore the spiritual meaning of space, as well as to ignore the evidence of our senses as in fact they operate.

All This Is Mine

Not only are we at the center of the cosmos: it all belongs to us. The real error of Nebuchadnezzar was to want dominion on the wrong plane, material rather than spiritual. He mistook a partial and unstable good for a full and final good. Mystical authors bear witness to this latter, spiritual way of coming into possession of the cosmos. Take Thomas Traherne, for instance, an English spiritual writer of the seventeenth century. He writes,

> You never enjoy the world aright, till the Sea itself floweth in your veins, till you are clothed with the heavens, and crowned with the stars: and perceive yourself to be the sole heir of the whole world, and more than so because men are in it who are every one sole heirs as well as you.

This last point about rejoicing in other people's enjoyment of the world makes it clear that this is not a material-based "get out of my space" enjoyment of dominion. What follows makes its own basis clear:

> Till you can sing and rejoice and delight in God, as misers do in gold, and Kings in sceptres, you never enjoy the world.

The finding delight in God, Creator and Source of all that is, means that this is an enjoyment of the whole world *with* God. Saint Paul makes a similar point about possessing all things, writing to the Corinthians, "All things are yours; . . . all are yours; And ye are Christ's; and Christ is God's." It is in belonging to Christ and to God that we become heirs to all.

Given that we are fallen—that is, that we tend to opt for the temporal and material instead of the spiritual, for the partial instead of the whole—entering into that inheritance is something of a labor. Saint John of the Cross expresses this by writing on his diagram showing how to ascend Mount Carmel, "To come to possess all desire the possession of nothing." If we desire nothing in particular, then we are desiring God who is (as Abbot John Chapman pointed out) nothing in particular. The saint expressed the same idea in the counsel, "Whoever knows how to die in all will have life in all." It is a matter of forgoing private empire; of being willing to receive rather than to take; of letting God choose. It is taking seriously Christ's saying, "Whoever will lose his life for my sake, the same shall save it."

This work of spiritual discipline, of working toward the spiritual and eternal rather than the material and temporal, is in a sense a reclaiming of childhood. Being converted and becoming "as little children," we "enter into the kingdom of heaven." Traherne remembered his own childhood when he wrote, "The skies were mine, and so were the sun and moon and stars, and all the World was mine; and I the only spectator and enjoyer of it." He enjoyed everything because (by his witness) he knew neither "bounds nor divisions." In other words, his mode of perception was not fragmenting. He did not murder to dissect, he did not analyze: he simply received everything with wonder as a gift.

This way of looking has been lost by the educated public at large now. As I argued in the introduction to this book, recovering it can be seen not only as a reclaiming of our own childhood but also as a return to the childhood of the race. It is going back to the way things were at the beginning, when "God said, Let us make man in our image, after our likeness: and let them have dominion over the fish of the sea, and over the fowl of the air, and over the cattle, and over all the earth, and over every creeping thing that creepeth upon the earth." This dominion does not sound good in our day when the planet has been treated so rapaciously, but it is not that kind of lordship; rather, it is that of the innocent child celebrated by Traherne, the child like whom the gospel tells us to become.

It is the same lordship that the psalmist celebrates, putting it into the context of wonder and awe at the greatness of God and His creation:

> When I consider thy heavens, the work of thy fingers, the moon and the stars, which thou hast ordained; What is man that thou art mindful of him? and the son of man, that thou visitest him? For thou hast made him a little lower than the angels, and hast crowned him with glory and honour. Thou madest him to have dominion over the works of thy hands; thou hast put all things under his feet: All sheep and oxen, yea, and the beasts of the field; The fowl of the air, and the fish of the sea, and whatsoever passeth through the paths of the seas. O LORD our Lord, how excellent is thy name in all the earth!

This is not Man making himself God; it is Man amazed that God shares His life and work with him. It is the original state of Man: crowned with the stars, crowned with glory and honor. It is a state that can be recovered if we can but see the world aright. That involves subordinating the epistemology that considers our knowledge of the world to be the same thing as our ability to manipulate it to the epistemology that understands that our knowledge of the world is given to us directly as a gift from God to His children. It involves being aware that the true is greater than the useful, that the whole is more than all of its parts. It is a regaining of our spiritual centrality, a realization of who we really are.

My World, My Body

If we only acknowledge the reality of the material, it will seem that we are just our bodies: very small, very vulnerable in the context of material reality as a whole. This is only one aspect of who we really are, however. The human soul is not material and—in contrast to the body, which is contained in the cosmos—contains the cosmos. Our perception tells us this. We see the trees, the sea, and the sky. They are within our soul. The greater contains the lesser, so the spiritual contains the material. The soul contains the body, as part of the world of which it is aware, and with it all other material reality within its ken. If at first blush this seems counterintuitive, that is because the prevailing epistemology is one that measures the material in order to manipulate it. It therefore has to stand apart from what is measured and to concentrate on the part rather than the whole. This of course is necessary for all sorts of operations: the weakness of the epistemology is that it mistakes what is practically useful for truth in its fullness. The weakness may be clearer if we consider an extreme example of separating oneself in order to carry out a useful operation. A man was climbing when a boulder fell on his arm. He had no way of summoning help and no hope of surviving if he stayed where he was. He therefore distanced himself from his characteristic sense of being one with his arm and cut it off so that he could reach help and safety.

My argument is that operations we perform on the world are of this nature. Of course they may be as harmless and painless as a haircut, but nonetheless they involve an effort of separation and a concentration on the part instead of the whole. That is now an effort that is so habitual and frenzied that it has become what is regarded as normal, and it is the sense of oneness that is regarded as exceptional. People report knowing everything as one as a peak experience. I remember my father telling me that he had such an experience walking along Park Street in Bristol. It stood out in his memory, and his account of it stands out in my memory. Poets and mystics bear witness to such things. I contend that in Man's childhood it was normal. I won't say he experienced it all the time, because time itself would also have been experienced as one, in the manner described in the last chapter, rather than as chopped up. He simply knew that all that he could perceive was part of who he was. When you think about it, that is a very helpful realization to have. It makes sins such as envy and avarice completely pointless. Aggrandizement, ego trips, and power plays have nothing to offer: one already has in whole that of which they offer a false simulacrum in part. Only the simple necessities of life are needed, and even this need is not absolute since it is clear to one who knows that he contains the whole of the material within his soul that his true life cannot be ended by bodily death. Furthermore, there is no sense of isolation and insignificance in being such a small part of such a large thing: that is only the material perspective—in the spiritual perspective, even the most distant galaxy is included in who one is.

I realize that this may still sound unconvincing to the reader used to thinking differently about it, so I shall adduce some hints from poets that this is something that is basic to human identity and has been forgotten rather than invented, and then I shall consider some possible objections. The following poem is subtitled "The fantasia of a fallen gentleman on a cold, bitter night," and it can be read as simply the reflections of one who has fallen in the street, or who must sleep there because of falling fortunes; it also, however, speaks of Man fallen from the integrity in which even the night sky was part of him:

> Once, in finesse of fiddles found I ecstasy,
> In the flash of gold heels on the hard pavement.
> Now see I
> That warmth's the very stuff of poesy.
> Oh, God, make small
> The old star-eaten blanket of the sky,
> That I may fold it round me and in comfort lie.

This speaks first of all of the coldness of lying in the street, but there is also a sense of the coldness of *distance*. A certain distance is necessary for the cleverness ("finesse") of Man's art, a certain coldness for metallurgy and macadam. Yet his deeper need is for the closeness and warmth of familiarity with even the outer reaches of what he perceives—to regain that obscurely remembered first innocence when all belonged to him, all was him.

There is a more direct poetic witness to a sense of being one with nature in these lines, which anticipate the sense of pain now more commonly felt at ecological violation:

> O if we but knew what we do
>   When we delve or hew—
> Hack and rack the growing green!
>   Since country is so tender
> To touch, her being so slender,
> That, like this sleek and seeing ball
> But a prick will make no eye at all,
> Where we, even where we mean
>   To mend her we end her,
>   When we hew or delve:
> After-comers cannot guess the beauty been.

99

The comparison of removing trees from the landscape with destroying sight is telling: the perceived and the perceiver are one reality—an attack on the first is an attack on the second. Pain and loss in the landscape are pain and loss in the one who sees it. Pope Francis writes in a similar vein, "Thanks to our bodies, God has joined us so closely to the world around us that we can feel the desertification of the soil almost as a physical ailment, and the extinction of a species as a painful disfigurement."

This points to the answer to one possible objection to the idea that the cosmos is the self spiritually: the objection that we know what is our self because that is where we are vulnerable to pain. It can be further argued that there are much more obvious examples of feeling pain in what happens outside of our bodies than the reaction of poetically sensitive types to trees being chopped down. People feel huge pain when they lose members of their families. They suffer hugely when the environment is damaged to the point where food can no longer be grown. On the other hand, nails and hair can be cut from our bodies without us feeling any pain at all. In any case, the absence of pain is not an indication of no harm being done. Smoking can cause fatal illness; depredation of the environment to which people are insensitive can nevertheless cause crop failure or another catastrophe, with fatal results.

Theurgy

The idea that the soul of Man contains the cosmos is connected with the idea explained above that Man, being made in the image of God, is at the center of the cosmos. It may be objected that Man does not in fact show much sign of being like the Creator in terms of creating or directing the cosmos. To this I would answer that the idea of space and time as a sort of box in which things can be put, discredited since Einstein's work, still has a hold on the imagination that makes it insensitive to indications of perception and reality being much more united than is commonly supposed. In truth, space and time are abstractions for the purpose of analysis; they are not, as Democritus and Newton thought, an absolute by which all else can be judged. They are relative. God is the absolute, and in the physical world it is light, not time or space, that is the clearest reflection of that absolute. It is work done for the purpose of manipulating nature that has made us imagine that the absolute is out there in a space-time matrix constituting the defining reality, separate from us. In fact, the human soul is nearer to the absolute than the physical universe is: it is not subject to decay or separation like the latter in that it perceives each whole in a way that transcends time (the twin of decay) and space (the enabler of separation).

As for directing the cosmos, Jesus Christ could do it—even "the winds and the sea" obeyed Him—and He promised that His followers would do still "greater works" than He did. And indeed saints have been able to change the course of nature. Saint James writes, "The effectual fervent prayer of a righteous man availeth much. Elias was a man subject to like passions as we are, and he prayed earnestly that it might not rain: and it rained not on the earth by the space of three years and six months. And he prayed again, and the heaven gave rain, and the earth brought forth her fruit." The world is in a sense Man's body that has become paralyzed by alienation from God. Man needs physiotherapy to be able to get back control of the world by the spiritual means most proper to him. That healing comes from the divine Physician. It enables theurgy—the spiritual power to change what happens in the world with the help of God. It is in our present world miraculous since God is allowed so little space for maneuver by Man now, and He always courteously respects Man's will, but it would have been ordinary before Man's Fall. After the Fall, it is a real effort to get the earth to do what one wants. Adam is told, "Cursed is the ground for thy sake; in sorrow shalt thou eat of it all the days of thy life; Thorns also and thistles shall it bring forth to thee; and thou shalt eat the herb of the field; In the sweat of thy face shalt thou eat bread."

The Earth Mourneth

The Bible makes clear that this lack of fecundity can become more acute as people lapse further from God and His ways. Isaiah announces, "The earth mourneth and fadeth away, the world languisheth and fadeth away, the haughty people of the earth do languish. The earth also is defiled under the inhabitants thereof; because they have transgressed the laws, changed the ordinance, broken the everlasting covenant." Rain and harvest, says Jeremiah, are withheld from those rebelling against God, to whom He says, "Your iniquities have turned away these things, and your sins have witholden good things from you." He laments, "How long shall the land mourn, and the herbs of every field wither, for the wickedness of them that dwell therein? the beasts are consumed, and the birds; because they said, He shall not see our last end." When people forget that their destiny is to go to God, not only the harvest but also the beasts and the birds suffer. Furthermore, Man's relationship with other creatures suffers. Before the Fall, Adam gives them their identity by naming them; he has a benign lordship over them. After the Fall, there is enmity between Man and them.

In the wake of the Fall, there is also the more or less degenerate use of spiritual power in magic, which at its worst is simply the devil's parody of theurgy, wielded not for the common good but for partial and malign advantage. And then there is the modern imitation of magic, technology. I do not wish to belittle the real benefits of this—I am personally very grateful for the work of medical science—but I do wish to take issue with the argument that goes something like this: we are now very clever at doing things, so our way of looking at things (our epistemology) and our outlook (tending to the godless) are better than those of the past. A lot of technological interventions (including some medical ones) are attempts to fix problems caused by an overly aggressive relationship with nature: one that would compel it to give up its secrets and make available its goodness, rather than one of loving receptivity. That ungentle relationship is of course bound up with the whole technological mindset, so the approach takes away as well as gives. Harmony with God and nature brought more happiness to Man, I believe. What we are seeing now is by way of compensation for what has been lost. Because the spiritual is neglected, there is a corresponding increase in accomplishment on the material level. That has its value and can even be seen as part of the unfolding of the goodness of creation, but it is not the culmination of Man's wisdom. The second law of thermodynamics has its parallel on the sapiential level.

Healing and Harmony

All the same, God's arm is not shortened when He is called out to. Anyone who has been involved in healing ministry, as I have, will know of cases in which people have had bodily or other wholeness restored without the side effects of conventional treatment. In fact, bodily ailments, being on a lower level than maladies of the heart or the spirit, are those most readily put to rights in this way. Man, fallen as he is, can still work with God to exercise beneficent spiritual power in the cosmos. Theurgy remains an indicator that spiritually the cosmos is within Man, and that he is not without rights to direct it. Specific requests in prayer that are granted are one indication of this right; another is things working out for people who are close to God. This is expressed thus by Saint Paul: "We know that all things work together for good to them that love God." This is God blessing through nature folk who love Him. This makes sense if one understands that the world is kept in being by God and that Man being made in the image of God shares thereby in that work, at least by being friends with God.

Working but in Alliance

Wordsworth saw "the first / Poetic spirit of our human life" in the young child sharing naturally in God's work of creation before being "abated or suppress'd" in most, though not all, people in "after years." (We might suppose a young child is a friend of God since the Savior said that the angels of little children always behold His face. The young in any case in some sense reflect the youth of the race.) The child's mind, Wordsworth wrote,

> Even as an agent of the one great mind,
> Creates, creator and receiver both,
> Working but in alliance with the works
> Which it beholds.

In other words, the mind, unspoiled in the child by a measuring and manipulating epistemology, is in partnership with nature to put in place what it perceives. We tend to think that this cannot be so and even that thinking it is so is an indication of madness, as in

Samuel Johnson's story *Rasselas*, in which a poor soul thinks that only his efforts are stopping the moon from falling to the earth. However, that is because we have a way of understanding how we know things that abstracts from the actual experience. After we have seen something, we analyze what has happened and divide it up into the one seeing and what is seen. In truth, if we consider perception *as it happens*, there is no division, as Wordsworth understood. Both the knower and the known are involved in the appearance of things. "Appearance" is a good word to use, because it indicates both coming into being and the way things look when perceived directly without analysis and thought fragmenting the perceiving after the event. To exist, it is said, is to be perceived by God. For Him, creating and knowing are the same thing. Man, made in His image, shares in this by right. Wordsworth gives an indication of how this power awakes in the growing child:

> His mind
> Even in the first trial of its powers
> Is prompt and watchful, eager to combine
> In one appearance, all the elements
> And parts of the same object, else detach'd
> And loth to coalesce.

Something being an object, that is a whole, is both a gift from God and an assemblage formed by the human mind, "creator and receiver." The whole of the individual object is formed in relation to the human person, the whole reflecting the divine unity. In the depths of the person are the same ideas that are in the mind of God and are expressed in His creation: that is why we are able to know things. Modern physics echoes this in the idea of "the anthropic principle"—the recognition of correspondence between the human person and the cosmos.

When Wordsworth writes that the child's mind "spreads, / Tenacious of the forms which it receives," he is writing both of the child receiving forms directly from God the Creator and of the receiving of forms in nature that is concomitant with the creating of forms in nature. In the latter, creating and receiving are one undivided act. As Parmenides put it, "What exists for thinking is the same as the cause of thought. For you won't find thinking without the being in which it has been uttered." We could translate this pre-Christian and pre-Socratic philosopher into Christian theological terms thus: "What God creates for us to grasp with our minds is the same as what He gives us in our minds that enables us to think about it. There is no division between our thought and what we think about." Such division is in fact the artificial construct of analysis, not reality. They are one in God and therefore in reality one. A fragmenting epistemology cannot know this, but it is true nonetheless. The twentieth-century philosopher Heidegger understood this, saying, "Self and world are not two entities, like 'subject' and 'object.'"

In this, mind is primary: God's knowing creates and Man's knowing participates in this creation. Plotinus (a philosopher in the Platonic tradition and the Christian era, though not a Christian) observed that consciousness gives rise to matter, not the other way around. This makes sense when we reflect that "God is a Spirit" and that the human soul shares this quality, since its apprehension is super-temporal and not confined to a single space. The latter is demonstrated by the soul's ability to grasp as one that which extends over time and its ability to contain within it what is materially far distant. It also outlives the material, having (in God) the power of indestructible life.

Man as Microcosm

The reader may be wondering why, if Man is so wonderful as to share not only in the course but in the creation of the cosmos, he is at all frustrated by any ailment or impediment. It cannot come down to sheer wickedness: holy people have faced obstacles like everyone else. Part of the answer is that Man is not soul alone. He is also body and spirit. All levels of being are contained in Man: the material, of which the world is made; life—the life of the soul, which corresponds to the life of the world; and spirit—which is to say that there is in Man something that corresponds to the timeless and divine, seen variously as the apex of the soul or its virgin point. Traditionally all this is expressed by saying that Man is a microcosm: that is, he contains in miniature everything in the cosmos. He contains material reality, life, and spirit. In his material aspect, Man contains all four traditional elements—air, water, earth, and fire, this last in the heat in his blood. The material reality is subject to decay and separation and is (relatively) unbiddable; the spiritual shares in God's freedom. How far the latter predominates is up to the soul: it depends on where Man invests his life. If he invests in the grossly material, he loses freedom; if he invests in the spiritual, he becomes progressively free. He becomes either a child of necessity or a child of Providence. This is true of the individual and the collectivity. In our own time, the world and its people have become more subject to necessity, hence the trouble involved in getting what is needed or even keeping the planet from disaster.

Ironically, this result of the abandonment of God's Providence is sometimes adduced as evidence of God's nonexistence rather than evidence of abandonment of God's ways! On the other side of the balance, there are those who give themselves to prayer and the contemplation of God in a way that stands apart from the direction of the collectivity. In doing this they win back a measure of freedom and harmony for the world. Part of the hope behind the writing of this book is that it will help people to see their way to being of this number.

Offering It Up

The human soul is where the destiny of the world is determined. What happens in the world is symptomatic of humanity's spiritual state. There is at work on the spiritual level a process analogous to that described in Newton's third law of motion: to every action there is an equal and opposite reaction. Good attracts good; living according to God's ways attracts God's blessing. It might be objected (coming back to ailment and impediment) that saints are martyred and the Savior Himself was crucified. Yet—as calling the day on which the latter happened Good Friday indicates—good comes of this. In fact, deliberately undertaken sacrifices for the sake of the good attract a reaction that is realized on a higher level if it is not realized on the material level. So the material and temporary is, as it were, traded in for the spiritual and eternal—for an everlasting blessing. That is why Jesus says, "Love ye your enemies, and do good, and lend, hoping for nothing again; and your reward shall be great, and ye shall be children of the Highest." The general principle is, "With the same measure that ye mete withal it shall be measured to you again." If that measure should be measured out in eternity, it is in effect without measure: hence the soundness of the advice, "When thou makest a feast, call the poor, the maimed, the lame, the blind: And thou shalt be blessed; for they cannot recompense thee: for thou shalt be recompensed at the resurrection of the just." The pious response to trouble of "offering it up" is based on this principle. The reaction to the bearing of the evil is good on a higher level that can be offered for any good intention.

In a Sense Everything

Aristotle, and Pope Saint Gregory the Great after him, recognized the importance of the human soul, saying, "The soul is in a sense everything." This idea might be a little clearer if we remember that the Latin word for soul, *anima*, also means "life." Human life in a sense contains everything. All that we are aware of is part of our life. We contain it all. Wordsworth expresses this by referring to "The Soul, the Imagination of the whole." Everything appears in the soul, becomes an image in the soul. That is its being. Of course it is possible to underestimate the importance of the soul. Indeed, it can be argued that this is the source of much of the evil in the world. Characteristically this underestimation takes the form of identifying the soul with particular desires and fears, born of predilections and aversions. It then relates to the world as primarily an enforcer, seeking outcomes that accord with this identification. The primary reality of the soul, however, is contemplative, relating to "the whole." Neglect of this leads to conflict, because the more narrowly defined identity can easily be felt to be under threat. Wordsworth writes of how nature finds herself in those who are not narrow. She exerts a power upon the senses that

is the express
Resemblance, in the fullness of its strength
Made visible, a genuine Counterpart
And Brother of the glorious faculty
Which higher minds bear with them as their own.

The "higher minds" are contemplative, in relationship with the cosmos as "creator and receiver both," not as adversaries. They have the faculty of recognizing all as who they are.

Wordsworth's friend, Coleridge, is to be numbered among these "higher minds." He writes, "In our life alone does Nature live." He sees the human soul as animating nature:

Ah! from the soul itself must issue forth
A light, a glory, a fair luminous cloud
  Enveloping the Earth—
And from the soul itself must there be sent
A sweet and potent voice, of its own birth,
Of all sweet sounds the life and element.

The contemplative recognition of "higher minds" of all as who they are includes other people in their greatest fullness. If each person is a world, then that world contains many other worlds that themselves contain the person's world. The full knowing of this is reserved for heaven. In our life here below, however, we can reverence others as other worlds that are part of who we are. This gives us a motive to treat them well for our own sake, just as the realization that we are part of their world gives us a motive to be responsible toward them for their sake. The contemplative way of knowing enables this; obviously, if our way of knowing is reduced to manipulation for the sake of advantage, we won't treat people well. How we know reflects the state of our souls, whether open to God and others or not.

Heart of Man, Heart of the World

If the soul relates to the cosmos by containing it, the body relates to the cosmos by being contained by it. Although the body as such is vulnerable, it is not insignificant. We have already considered aspects of its meaning corresponding to the symbol of the tree. One part of the human body, however, corresponds to the cosmos as a whole: the heart, which lies in it at the same angle as the tilt of the earth in relation to the solar axis. It represents on the bodily level the capacity of the soul to contain the cosmos. It is in anatomy what the point is in geometry: both symbols of the divine center from which all things come. It is significant that the heart is not actually at the center of the body, being somewhat to the left. The fact that the divine does not belong to the order of the world is symbolized by this asymmetry. It makes it clear that the divine cannot be within a system that is merely spatial. The same reason accounts for an altar traditionally not being in the center of the sanctuary of a church. The human heart thus represents both God's immanence and His transcendence.

Since Man, the image of God, is a microcosm of the cosmos (or macrocosm), the heart of Man is the heart of the world. It is the temple at its center, the holy place where worship is offered, the point at which the world connects with God. As explained in the first chapter, it is the locus of much more than feeling. It is where God and what creation tells of Him are pondered and contemplated. It is as it were a sacred cave where God is to be found, as Saint Benedict found Him in such. It is the "closet" where the Sermon on the Mount tells us to "pray to thy Father which is in secret." It is the place where we have to come if we are to meet God.

And one human heart above all is the meeting place of Man and God: the Sacred Heart of Jesus. It is not only the heart of the cosmos but also the heart of all humanity. It is the sacred point from which all creation comes and to which all things converge. The One through whom all things were made is super-eminently the microcosm of the world, and His heart the source of all meaning in the cosmos. In His heart before ever it is spoken is the word that gives meaning to all that is, the word from which every human utterance and every symbol takes its significance. A recovery of that significance in its true depth is a necessary preparation to getting back a contemplative spirit, to being open to God. The next chapter looks at this.

PART TWO
Contemplating the Word

"In the beginning was the Word,
and the Word was with God, and the Word was God."

Chapter Four:
Symbol and Language

Half a Sixpence and the Creed

n the first part of this book, we looked at the symbols in nature. To understand more fully how they convey something of what is beyond nature, it will be helpful to consider what precisely a symbol is. This will then be illustrated by the working of the most fundamental of symbols: being itself. This points us to the depth in all and every being. The meaning of symbols in general follows. Language is in a sense simply a kind of symbolism and works in a similar way. My reflection on it starts with a consideration of the power of words and then looks at how they give us meaning. Language is not its own end: it comes from and leads to thought that transcends it. I give examples of this and conclude the chapter by looking at the symbolism of other kinds of language: numbers and architecture.

The word "symbol" is derived from the Greek word for token (σύμβολον), which is cognate with the verb meaning "to put together." One part of such a token can be produced to demonstrate that it belongs with the other part, vindicating the bearer's claim to something. There is a modern example of this in the musical *Half a Sixpence*. The hero gives his love (Ann) half a sixpence as a token of his love. Later in life, when his status is very much above hers, Ann produces her half of the sixpence (from her bloomers) and returns it to him, since he is abandoning his first love to marry another woman. He is affected by this gesture (especially since she suffers for it) and ends up marrying Ann.

The symbols in nature are such tokens from God of His love for us. They are signs that despite our very much lower status we belong with Him. The blue sky, for example, is a symbol of heaven. The natural phenomenon, caused by light shining into darkness, is our part of the token. The celestial reality of heaven, where God is

113

all in all, is God's part of the token. The two belong together: they fit. What we have expresses our claim to what God has. Of course we rather than God are the ones who really need reminding. The natural symbol is an appeal to us to remember. It is the expression on the level on which we can apprehend it of the higher reality for which we are made but which we cannot sense. It presents, makes present, this reality to us. It is not something whose import we have decided upon: it is something given to us so that by contemplating it we may go beyond it to what it expresses.

Something being a natural symbol does not mean that it cannot also have a practical use. Take trees, for example. Those in the Garden of Eden were "pleasant to the sight, and good for food," the former, as Philo of Alexandria observed, linked to contemplation and the latter to practical use. Seeing a tree reach for the sky reminds us of our longing for the life of heaven; eating the fruit it provides nourishes us for our life on earth. If the people around us don't very often see things in their symbolic aspect, that does not mean that they do not hunger for the significance that symbols convey or that they are content with the practical use of things only. This is seen from the fact that far greater sums of money will be paid for branded goods than for those that simply do the job. Of course buying in significance like this is quite unnecessary since all of creation is meaningful, but recovering a contemplative spirit is necessary if we are to believe in and accept a significance given rather than manufactured.

As mentioned in the last chapter, nature can be pondered in the same spirit as Sacred Scripture. According to Eriugena (an Irish philosopher-monk of the ninth century), both of them are not given to us or to be desired for their own sake but rather as images of invisible beauty by which divine Providence brings the souls of men back to pure and invisible Beauty itself, toward which everyone who loves tends, whether they know it or not. Scripture, like nature, is a symbol. I will look at what it means in more detail in the next chapter, but here it is relevant to mention the digest of the truth that Scripture conveys, the creed, because the Greek word for "symbol" also means "creed." They are indeed both tokens one part of which we can grasp, the other part of which is the invisible reality that they present. Updating the relation between them a bit, we could say that nature is as it were a physical ticket entitling us (for example) to board a flight and that the creed is as it were an electronic ticket giving the data that can be produced to indicate our entitlement to board. The presence of the former tells us that we can soar aloft toward heaven; the information in the latter says the same thing. Contemplating the truth in the depth of nature and of the creed lifts us toward heaven.

Beyond Being

At the beginning of Chapter One, I drew attention to the scriptural identification of God with the natural symbol of light and discussed its aptness. Obviously we cannot take this identification so literally as to claim that it exhausts what can be said about God, since God is also identified with other things, such as, in the same book of the Bible in fact, love. We should rather say that these things point beyond themselves to God. Such is also the case for a primary identification made in the Old Testament. Moses encounters God in the burning bush in the desert and asks Him, "Behold, when I come unto the children of Israel, and shall say unto them, The God of your fathers hath sent me unto you; and they shall say to me, What is his name? what shall I say unto them?" He gets the reply, "I AM THAT I AM." This identifies God with being, and yet if we take it absolutely literally we are left with a pantheism in which everything that is embodies God and that is all that there is. Taking being as a symbol, however, means that the sense of God's transcendence as well as His immanence is not lost. Being points beyond itself to the One who is greater than all. It is, like other symbols, one part of a token, the other part of which we cannot directly apprehend.

And it is an extraordinarily powerful symbol. Since all that we know has being, it says that God is the source of all that we know: He is Creator and Sustainer of the universe. It is consonant with the teaching of Aquinas that all of God is in each and every thing. Or, to put it the other way around (in Saint Paul's words to the Athenians), "In him we live, and move, and have our being." As light, which makes it possible for everything to be seen, speaks of God, so being, which makes it possible for everything to exist, symbolizes God. Light and being (or, to limit ourselves to a higher kind of being, light and life) are almost too obvious to be noticed. They tend to be taken for granted. If instead we accept them as gift and mystery, their voices sing to us of that which is still greater. A fundamental and universal presence is communicated to us by that which points not *to* but *beyond* itself. Being, like light, presents but does not contain God. Meister Eckhart articulated the way in which being relates to God in the lapidary Latin phrase, *Deo esse est dare esse*, which can be translated as "for God, being is giving being."

God is, but is also beyond, being. He is the source of being, unconfined by the being/nonbeing opposition. He needs nothing to make everything. He contradicts nothingness so that there is something. He Himself has not this nothingness in His origin and so unlike that which begins as nothing He knows not the concomitant limitation of death. Yet even this does not limit Him, for He becomes incarnate to know also the specificity of mortal life. Being is *only* the symbol of His absolute and infinite Reality beyond being, beyond all affirmation or contradiction—supreme noncontradiction that can be called infinite Possibility insofar as the possible is that which contains no contradiction.

God Knows Best

Being exists because God knows it. Being is being known by God. Creation is the bodying forth of God's knowing. We are because God knows us. Knowing creation and knowing ourselves, we have a sense of God's knowing, which is His creative presence. Now we know "in part," but our knowledge is a token of when we will no longer "see through a glass darkly" but know even as we are known. Our knowledge is nothing like God's knowing, and yet it is a sign of that knowing that we are called ultimately to share. It is a sign of the knowing that is the source of what is known. What is known is a symbol of the One who knows it best. Seeing anything is like sharing God's knowledge that brings it into being. All our awareness is a sort of sharing of God's thoughts. Sharing His thoughts is an obscure awareness of His presence. The knowing we have in common with Him puts us as it were alongside Him. Seeing, in some measure, what He sees, we are with Him. We are participating so far as we can in His gathering of all into the unity of His single glance. This is so of the seeing that sees whole, that receives rather than measures—the seeing that is contemplative.

This seeing goes beyond what is seen to its source, which transcends it. And in that transcendent presence, imaged in what that presence knows, it finds also the immanent presence in its own knowing. They are one and the same. The transcendent is the immanent. The one who sees in this way is as it were a lover alongside his or her beloved, looking out on the same seascape, seeing the same sunset and the same evening star rise. It is a moment of loving communion. Yet it is possible for what is seen to become a barrier to communion, a distraction from the one alongside. Indeed, it is only possible for them to kiss if they turn their faces away from what they are looking at and toward each other. The moment for this kiss necessarily comes when "the covering cast over all people, and the vail that is spread over all nations" is put aside and there is no need of any symbol, of any mediated communion. Saint Paul spoke of this as seeing "face to face." It is what we are made for; it is what every thing that is points us toward.

Remembering what is beyond and what is within (for they are the same) prepares us for this, prepares us for a blessed death that opens out to this. And that is a question of how we look at what we can see now. Seeing it with a contemplative gaze does not stop at its out-there-ness, does not see creation in a crassly materialist way. Seeing everything as a symbol pointing beyond itself, and intuitively sensing that in the deepest intimacy of our knowing of everything we already have that which is beyond, imaged in the symbol, we relate to everything with great lightness of touch. All creation speaks what is beyond and within: that, not any solidity of its materiality, is the joy of it. William Blake spoke of this kind of joy in this poem:

> He who binds to himself a joy
> Does the winged life destroy;
> But he who kisses the joy as it flies
> Lives in eternity's sun rise.

The poem is called *Eternity*, and it expresses how the eternal dawns for one who lets the evanescent go in favor of the invisible beauty that it images. The joy that the creation brings is properly the joy of what its message is about. To pin it to the lepidopterist's display board is to kill it. It cannot be hoarded, only welcomed and allowed to lead.

Depth of Being

Our joy in what we see leads us to the transcendent reality of which the visible is but a symbol. To put it another way, that joy leads into the depth of being, to where the roots of being draw the sap that gives it reality. My reflections in the previous chapter on contemplating the cosmos touched on this depth. I want to develop them a little further here by way of seeing what needs to be done if we are fully to recover a contemplative spirit. The difficulty we face is the teaching that our culture has given about how to look at things. According to this, symbols have been decided upon by people in order to denote aspects of what is experienced in our lives. This, it is assumed, gives the symbols their meaning. The truth is the contrary: symbols give what is experienced its meaning. This includes the symbols of language, as I shall argue later in this chapter, but here let us reflect on how we have come to lose the sense that nature is the awesome articulation of God's meaning and have substituted for it the illusion that what unfolds in the material realm can somehow make sense of experience.

There is a clue in the book by Galileo referred to in the introduction: *Il Saggiatore*. In it he says that he believes that forms themselves are not noble, or perfect, or vile, or imperfect, except to the extent that he considers that square bodies are better for building than spherical bodies, and circular bodies are better than triangular bodies for making a wagon go. This amounts to saying that usefulness is the only criterion we have for looking. As I have already pointed out, that misses what is conveyed to us by the quality of things. It also means that we are condemned to the attempt to understand things *in terms of themselves*. To undertake this is never to get to the end of it. The end of material things is on a higher (or we could say, deeper) level than they are. It is a spiritual end or purpose. That is why there is no end to scientific investigations, hypotheses, and papers, why "of making many books there is no end." There can be no final theory of everything, because everything can only be contemplated ("theory" comes from the Greek word for contemplation—θεωρία) from above. God sees it all and His saints have sometimes had a glimpse of all creation, but the material does not of itself offer the means to grasp it all any more than (according to Gödel's theorems) a mathematical system can totally demonstrate its own truth and consistency.

Anything that is real has a transcendent aspect to it. Its reality comes from what transcends it. It therefore speaks of that reality as a symbol, which, as Coleridge said, "always partakes of the Reality which it renders intelligible; and while it enunciates the whole, abides itself as a living part of that Unity of which it is the representative." When we contemplate the symbol of nature, what we see is meaning: we are looking at what it adds up to, looking at the reflection in it of the One who is the Source of all. Its very incompleteness on its own level points us beyond it to the invisible reality that completes and unifies it. It frees us from being trapped in the merely contingent, from being entirely enslaved to material necessity. It offers us "the glorious liberty of the children of God."

All About God

Nature when contemplated rather than analyzed with a view to manipulation is indeed all about God. We know from it (to paraphrase the reflection of a French philosopher of our time) that God has the beauty of a rose, the strength of a lion, the purity of water, the splendor of light, the majesty of a mountain, the immensity of the ocean, the smoothness of milk, the nobility of an eagle, the memory of an elephant, the royalty of the sun, the depth of the night, the perfection of the sky, the rigor of death, the joy of life, the centrality of Man—and so on. Yet all of this is in Him in a supereminent way that is beyond all telling. The principle behind this is explained by a French metaphysician of the last century:

Everything that exists, in whatever mode, having its principle in the Divine Intellect, translates or represents that principle in its own manner and according to its own order of existence; and thus, from one order to another, all things are linked and correspond with each other so that they join together in a universal and total harmony which is like a reflection of the divine unity itself. This correspondence is the true foundation of symbolism, which is why the laws of a lower domain may always be taken as symbolizing realities of a higher order, where they have their profound reason which is both their principle and their end.

An example of the "laws of a lower domain" is Newton's third law of motion, which symbolizes good attracting good. Every movement, every current of nature reflects something of the divine nature. This was once generally understood. Indeed, there are traces of it in the very language of texts that have come down to us. In Chapter Three of Saint John's Gospel, for example, the Greek word πνεύμα is rendered in English as both "spirit" and "wind." The later language has to make a point of establishing the symbolism, but the earlier one does not need to do this: the single reality that is Spirit and that is manifest in nature as wind is denoted by a single word. The divine unity is reflected both in the "universal and total harmony" of all things and in the language itself.

Recovering a contemplative spirit involves relearning the symbolism of nature. Many are the old masters who can teach it. For example, Saint Bonaventure, successor and interpreter of Saint Francis, writes in the thirteenth century of the "contemplation by which we are led to contemplate God in all creatures which enter our minds through our bodily senses" that "we can see God not only through them as through His vestiges, but also in them as He is in them by His essence, power and presence." The theologian Hugh of Saint Victor writes in the twelfth century, "The whole of this perceptible universe is like a book written with the finger of God, that is, created by divine power, and every single creature is like a figure, not invented according to human pleasure, but instituted by divine decision to show and as it were in a certain way signify the invisible wisdom of God." The Cistercian Isaac of Stella writes in the same century in a similar vein of the "corporeal...and visible creature...written within and without so that by the understanding of those things which are made . . . the Wisdom which made them is seen."

Missing the Point

If what is created is "written within and without," it follows that it can be read. For that reading to take place, it is necessary to grasp the whole both in the particular symbols of nature and in the way they coalesce, just as we need to grasp words, sentences, and paragraphs to read a book. Analysis of creation according to the methods of science will not yield meaning any more than measuring and counting words will tell us what a book means. Furthermore, to read nature we need to grasp through its symbols what is beyond it: indeed, it is only to the extent that it does not entirely belong to this world that a symbol can be such. This works in the same way that a book functions as such only if it is *about* something. There has to be a connection with something outside the chain of connections within the book for it to function as such. This book, for example, depends on the sky being blue. The cross-references within it cannot of themselves convey meaning. There is a sense in which (I hope) you are seeing more than just words as you read this book.

Analogously, to read nature we need to be able to look at something other than just the things in nature. Saint Paul claimed this ability in writing to the Corinthians, "We look not at the things which are seen, but at the things which are not seen: for the things which are seen are temporal; but the things which are not seen are eternal." There is an apparent paradox here, since the question is raised, "How can you look at something you cannot see?" Yet in fact we do this all the time. For example, we see an unmade bed with no one in it and our looking tells us that the person who was in it has got up. Our seeing on its own is not enough even to look at an object. We see some brown and some green, but it is by looking that we grasp that this is a tree. Our looking is interpretive. Our interpretation can be more or less deep. We may or may not see the implication of the evidence before us. It can be mistaken: we can think we are looking at a tree but really be looking at a cell phone tower disguised as a tree.

In the same way, our looking at or interpretation of the symbol of nature can be more or less deep. For it to have any depth at all, it needs to avoid the sort of seeing that grasps only what is temporal: that is, the seeing that limits its interpretation to information that can be used to predict and control what happens in time. This limitation has its obvious practical uses, but if the limited seeing claims for itself a suzerainty of looking, it is simply mistaken. To look at nature, to contemplate her rather than just see what use she can be, is to see a depth of being that, because it belongs to what is eternal, is unlimited. Of that depth of being, "the things which are seen" cannot speak in their material aspect only. It is of time and limited.

Seeing only that, only the temporal, misses the point. The point of nature is to speak to us of God. The point, of course, is a symbol of God, perfect Unity and Source of all. If we see nature as one large pointillist painting, then every point in it is a symbol of God. So is every larger unity in nature. Each and every thing says something about Him. That is the implication of the Scripture verse I put at the head of the first section of this book: "For the invisible things of Him from the creation of the world are clearly seen, being understood by the things that are made, even His eternal power and Godhead." Yet I left part of it out. It finishes, "so that they are without excuse." Nowadays I think it would be fair to argue for diminished responsibility on the grounds that depth of being is so rigorously ignored in conventional education. It is only by limiting what we choose to know about nature that we can manipulate things. That, practical knowledge, is the only sort allowed by a science that measures and predicts. This cannot simply behold being. It is antithetical to theoretical knowledge in the etymological sense of "theory"—contemplation—because simply to behold or contemplate is to allow reality to unfold without any limitation, in all its depth, wildness, beauty, and glory. It is to behold everything as one in a way that mirrors God's beholding of it and seeing that it is "very good." This beholding allows the eternal, or unlimited; it is useless for practical purposes yet essential for knowing the meaning of it all. It forswears the capture and bondage of nature for the joy of seeing her dance.

Chapter Four: Symbol and Language

Eyes to Look; Ears to Hear

Although we may want to interpret Saint Paul's phrase "without excuse" according to the new circumstances of our age, he still has something to say to us by it: namely, looking is not morally neutral. One can see but not look. Such a failure is rebuked by the prophet Isaiah: "Seeing many things . . . thou observest not." One can turn the mind and heart away from the significance of the whole, seeing only many things; one can ignore the symbol and acknowledge only the disparate particularity. A *willingness* to grasp significance is involved. To read a symbol, we need a conversion of our spiritual outlook, a turning from the outward appearance of corporeal things and their exteriority, which separates one thing from another, to their inner meaning, which binds them to the celestial realm of which they speak. It is, in a particular sense, a question of intelligence: not a question of being clever but of looking to understand, to enter into relation with, the *intelligibility* of things. Will and intelligence work together to open the heart deliberately to the offered meaning and message. They *read* what is truly real.

There is a sense in which it is a matter of faith: faith that the world has this meaning to which we can entrust ourselves. To this apply the words of Jesus (uttered in a different context): "If thou wouldest believe, thou shouldest see the glory of God." The world shows forth the glory of God to those who look at it with a believing heart. The conversion to this faith goes hand in hand with conversion to faith in the One through whom the world was made: "Christ, who is the image of God." He above all expresses in creation the glory of God: to have seen Him is to have seen the Father. We see "the light of the knowledge of the glory of God in the face of Jesus Christ." He is the ultimate symbol.

However, it is not just a matter of looking. "Faith cometh by hearing," and the faith that perceives the glory of God in the instant of a single glance needs to be educated over time by the hearing of words. The verse from Isaiah quoted above about seeing and not observing continues with a reproach to the one "opening the ears" who nonetheless "heareth not." Hearing is also, like looking, a matter of conversion. This is not only true of hearing the words of

Scripture (that is the subject of the next chapter) but also true in general of that special form of the symbol: language. It is to this form that I now turn.

The Power of Words

Like symbols in general, language does not receive its meaning from our sense impressions (as is now generally supposed): it gives our sense impressions their meaning. It does not tag along behind some preexistent matrix of atom-containing space after the imagining of Democritus: it establishes what exists. I shall discuss how this happens on a human level later in this chapter; here I want to look at the primordial instance of it—God's creating word. The third verse of the Bible first tells of it: "And God said, Let there be light: and there was light." The phrase "and God said" echoes repeatedly through the Bible's first chapter: for example, "And God said, Let the earth bring forth grass, the herb yielding seed, and the fruit tree yielding fruit after his kind, whose seed is in itself, upon the earth: and it was so." As with flora, so it is with fauna: "And God said, Let the earth bring forth the living creature after his kind, cattle, and creeping thing, and beast of the earth after his kind: and it was so." These two examples show the pattern of what happens: God speaks, and it is so. His word makes. In a sense, the created world is His speech, awaiting our attention, if we can hear as well as open our ears. In any case, His word is efficacious: indeed, everything we experience results from it. The prophet Isaiah records the assertion that this is so:

> For as the rain cometh down, and the snow from heaven, and returneth not thither, but watereth the earth, and maketh it bring forth and bud, that it may give seed to the sower, and bread to the eater: So shall my word be that goeth forth out of my mouth: it shall not return unto me void, but it shall accomplish that which I please, and it shall prosper in the thing whereto I sent it.

The word has power. In its own right it works and establishes. There is an ancient understanding of human speech having something of the autonomous power of God's word. It explains this reaction of Isaac when he discovers that Jacob has tricked him into giving the blessing due to Esau:

> And Isaac his father said unto him, Who art thou? And he said, I am thy son, thy firstborn, Esau. And Isaac trembled very exceedingly, and said, Who? Where is he that hath taken venison, and brought it me, and I have eaten of all before thou camest, and have blessed him? yea, and he shall be blessed. And when Esau heard the words of his father, he cried with a great and exceeding bitter cry, and said unto his father, Bless me, even me also, O my father. And he said, Thy brother came with subtilty, and hath taken away thy blessing.

Once the words of blessing have been spoken, it is done "and he shall be blessed." The blessing is taken away from the one to whom it is due because it is an accomplished fact. The natural contemporary reaction—that Isaac could just give another blessing and that could count as the more important one—witnesses to a weakening of the sense of the power of words. In this story, words spoken by a man still have something of the irrevocable power of the words of God, in whose image he is made. In it, a firstborn's blessing is unique and unchangeable.

Adam was the first human wielder of words, as the book of Genesis tells us: "And out of the ground the LORD God formed every beast of the field, and every fowl of the air; and brought them unto Adam to see what he would call them: and whatsoever Adam called every living creature, that was the name thereof." Adam does not here describe the creatures: he gives a new expression to that which they express. It can be seen that it is new because the creatures are brought to him "to see what he would call them"—which implies something unforeseen about the names. The names express anew the essence of the creatures: ancient traditions agree in teaching that the true name of a being is one with its very essence. The cultural world that is constituted by the language of Adam is the microcosm identified with Man that corresponds to the macrocosm of the cosmos. It is not an image of the created world as a photograph is an image of what exists in nature: it is rather another expression of what is symbolically expressed by what exists in nature. Both primordial language and nature express divine realities, and these two expressions correspond to each other.

A Confusion of Languages

Now there are many languages, each to an extent expressing those realities in another new way, an echo of fullness and diversity of being. The transition from one language to many is described in the Bible:

> And the whole earth was of one language, and of one speech. And it came to pass, as they journeyed from the east, that they found a plain in the land of Shinar; and they dwelt there. And they said one to another, Go to, let us make brick, and burn them thoroughly. And they had brick for stone, and slime they had for morter. And they said, Go to, let us build us a city, and a tower, whose top may reach unto heaven; and let us make us a name, lest we be scattered abroad upon the face of the whole earth.

People journey from the east: that is to say, from the light that rises over the world, from Eden, from the primordial wisdom that is encapsulated in the Adamic language. "Let us make *a name*," they say: that is, let our language—our cultural world—become itself for us that which it symbolizes. In doing this they render it no longer transparent to the divine realities; they are no longer paying attention to these (contemplating them) but rather to the cultural system they themselves have constructed. This rendering opaque of the cultural system (of language, of *naming* such as that undertaken by Adam, and of a *city* in which they share a culture) parallels that other consequence of the Fall: the natural world no longer being observed as a refulgent expression of the glory of God but merely seen as "many things." Both expressions of divine realities become opaque.

The Lord's response to the effective idolization of language—the allowing of it to replace the divine—is this: "Go to, let us go down, and there confound their language, that they may not understand one another's speech."

This act of divine judgment is simply the allowing of the consequences of people's acts to unfold. In cutting themselves off from the divine unity by making for themselves a name—a language or cultural system that replaces rather than reveals the divine—they no longer have the possibility of true unity. Only in God can all diversity be one. What they are left with is that parody of unity: uniformity, the making of all alike. This cannot contain diversity, unlike the divine unity that was seen *through* language, and thus it fractures, and the inevitable disparateness that characterizes that which is created leads to a multiplication of languages. Only in God (in His oneness) is there total mutual understanding.

Now, with communion with the divine realities through nature and word cut off by people, God can only respond by coming into the particularity of the human situation to make Himself known. Hence there follows in the subsequent chapter of the Bible the calling of Abraham. God is no longer known as it were naturally through all things seen and spoken, since these things have been allowed to obscure observing and hearing rather than being means to them; He therefore reveals Himself. Hence God, no longer known universally in the same way by all, is made known in a particular tradition. This prevents the loss of contact with the divine but comes at the price of the sacred having the potential to divide: to maintain the sacredness of their tradition, people have to separate themselves from others. Such is the price of the loss of the primordial contemplative spirit. It is also an indicator of the scope of the benefit of going even some way toward recovering a contemplative spirit. Contemplation tends to overcome separation.

The Name of the Lord

Man turns away from God; God never turns away from Man. His intervention to make Himself known seeks to restore communion with that unity forsaken as Man chose the outward aspect of nature and word in preference to what they signify. Already in the reaching out to a particular people there is a prophetic sense that it is not for them only. Zechariah conveys the joyful announcement: "Sing and rejoice, O daughter of Zion: for, lo, I come, and I will dwell in the midst of thee, saith the LORD. And many nations shall be joined to the LORD in that day, and shall be my people." Isaiah goes further and speaks of "all nations" whose unity is expressed in a wonderful peace: "They shall beat their swords into plowshares, and their spears into pruning hooks: nation shall not lift up sword against nation, neither shall they learn war any more." The more people turn away from it, the more God speaks His unity. The meaning that words were given to convey keeps breaking through.

It did most wonderfully on the day of Pentecost, God's undoing of what Man did at Babel. Through the Apostles He spoke so that "every man heard them speak in his own language. And they were all amazed and marvelled, saying to one another, Behold are not all these which speak Galileans? And how hear we every man in our own tongue, wherein we were born?" The primordial power of words is restored: Peter announces that "whosoever shall call on the name of the Lord shall be saved." *The* name, given by God, replaces *a* name made by people for themselves. The divine Self-utterance is given to those lost in the byways of a language system closed in upon itself, where people are "ever learning, and never able to come to the knowledge of the truth." This utterance is there for those who want to open the ears of their heart to hear truly and ponder therein the first and the last, the everlasting Man, for God "hath in these last days spoken to us by his Son, . . . the express image of his person."

The Word Was Made Flesh

He is meaning in person, "the way, the truth, and the life." He is the Word made flesh. He is the Word who is God, through whom "all things were made." He is the new Adam, naming creation anew. His words have great power. "They are spirit and they are life"; they are "the words of eternal life." Heaven and earth may pass away but His words will not pass away. Through His word, people are made clean; are healed; come to faith. What happens through His word echoes what happened when God spoke and the world came to be; through Him there is a new creation. His word is the meaning of the sorrows of the world, it is the sense in what seems senseless, it suffuses sadness with the light of heaven. Such is the implication of this poetry:

> The imaged Word, it is, that holds
> Hushed willows anchored in its glow.
> It is the unbetrayable reply
> Whose accent no farewell can know.

It matters critically whether we are able to hear this Word; contemplation is being open to sounds as well as sights, and it is as sound that the Word echoes in the heart, even though it can be received through what is written being seen. Yet in our age words as such have lost their power. As sexual love loses through ongoing random promiscuity its power to bind people together, so the gabbled, chattered word not measured out by silence no longer binds to meaning. Never has it been easier to transmit words to others—it takes only a few seconds to post them on the internet where they can be read from anywhere in the world—and never have they carried less weight. Not only have the all-powerful word of God and His Christ been largely forgotten: the human echo of that word in naming and blessing has faded too. How can we hear when we do not truly know how to speak? How can we listen when we do not know the full purpose and power of words?

Words Give Us Meaning

The beginning of the answer to these questions is reflection on how words work. We can recover a contemplative receptivity to words (and therefore to the Word) if we understand how they function at their most vital. The first step in this is seeing what has happened to our relationship with them. This parallels closely what has happened to our relationship with nature. As I have explained, this has become limited through a tendency to regard as real only what can be measured for the purposes of manipulation. What is useless for prediction and control is discarded. So it is with words: they are regarded as being of use only for accomplishing our purposes. Of course we are still alert to people trying to trick us with words, and we recognize the value of being straightforward in what we say to others, but we have forgotten that words are a revelation of the metaphysical or supernatural essence of things. We imagine that we give them meaning: the truth is that words give us meaning. Fundamentally, they speak of divine realities. That does not mean that it is impious to say, "Pass the salt." It is all right to use words to get things that we want, just as it is all right to eat the fruit of trees that speak to us of aspiring to heaven. It is just that if we limit words to their subservience to our purposes then we miss the glory and wonder of being that they can give us, the heartening hints of our heavenly homeland that every unfolding by language of the meaning hidden in things conveys. We act as though we established language by meeting together and deciding on a code for the purposes of our interaction with one another, forgetting that there would have been no language in which to conduct that meeting. Language is first of all a gift, a revelation of the wonder of being, to be received rather than wrested to our aims: a channel of meaning toward us rather than from us.

We receive language from those who went before us. Our speech is learned from our parents; our writing is learned from those who wrote books before us. It is fairly obvious that language does not gain in subtlety and expressive power as the centuries unfold: Latin is more inflected than Italian, Shakespeare and the King James Bible fuller in the richness of their resonance than more modern texts. Of course individuals can make a positive contribution, but in general we are living off the linguistic capital that we have inherited. That inheritance has the utmost importance: it is our way of understanding the world. Words disclose to us what is in it; representing what is in it is a secondary function. As children, we understand the world through language, even if as adults we sometimes use words simply to represent things. Words are primarily symbols for us with the associated richness of meaning, even though we can and do use them in a more limited way merely to represent something. The former is apparent in the use of words in poetry, the latter in the transaction of business. Recovering contemplative receptivity is linked to rediscovery of the *revelatory* quality that characterizes the use of words in poetry at its best. Receiving them with childlike wonder, we catch an obscure glimpse of the celestial or divine realities of which both they and nature speak.

Generally, we forget how language first disclosed the world to us as children, but there is a much-quoted example of this process being remembered well because it happened later than normal. Helen Keller lost through illness the ability to see and hear before she learned language. She described the moment at which language began to reveal the world to her in this extraordinarily valuable testimony:

We walked down the path to the well-house, attracted by the fragrance of the honeysuckle with which it was covered. Someone was drawing water and my teacher placed my hand under the spout. As the cool stream gushed over one hand she spelled into the other the word "water," first slowly, then rapidly. I stood still, my whole attention fixed upon the motion of her fingers. Suddenly I felt a misty consciousness as of something forgotten—a thrill of returning thought; and somehow the mystery of language was revealed to me. I knew then that "w-a-t-e-r" meant the wonderful cool something that was flowing over my hand. That living word awakened my soul, gave it light, joy, set it free! . . . I left the well-house eager to learn. Everything had a name, and each name gave birth to a new thought. As we returned to the house each object that I touched seemed to quiver with life. That was because I saw everything with the strange new light that had come to me.

The world comes to life for her through "the mystery of language," which gives her the ability to grasp the world with her thought: "each name" enables another thing to be in her mind. The process recalls Heidegger's saying: "Language is the house of being." With this understanding of the way words work, we can see a parallel between limiting language to merely denoting things and limiting knowledge to measurement for the purposes of manipulation, after the fashion of Galileo. Both of them insist that it is only within the confines of the material world that anything can be thought about or known. This method of using the tools of thought, whether words or mathematics, excludes from the start the possibility of knowing the transcendent or divine. Note that this is so independent of whether what is thought about is natural or supernatural: the natural world cannot do its symbolic work of speaking about what is beyond it, nor can religious language—such as New Testament discourse about "the Word"—disclose something of the divine. Recovering a contemplative spirit is a matter of changing the method of looking at the evidence of the divine, which is itself already there.

Poetry, Puns, and Paradoxes

In fact, the way language works shows that it cannot be a closed system wholly containing what it denotes. It breaks up in a way that makes evident that there is a greater reality that it cannot pin down. Its most fundamental function is to open up this reality for people rather than shuffle it around, and it necessarily sheds itself in doing this, as a chrysalis its skin in releasing a butterfly or a doctor his work in making people better. Ambiguity is an indicator that language is not closed, that the irrepressible depth of being fissures it like volcanic lava breaking the surface of the earth. Sometimes this happens in the innocent misunderstanding of a child, as when the Irish boy, asked "How do you get to Ballymena?" by a traveler seeking directions, answered, "My cousin takes me." Sometimes it happens when a poet uses it with skilled deliberation to open up reality for the listener, as when Shakespeare writes,

> Like as the waves make towards the pebbled shore,
> So do our minutes hasten to their end,
> Each changing place with that which goes before,
> In sequent toil all forwards do contend.

The syntactic ambiguity of this brilliantly conveys both the movement of the waves and our experience of time, which the waves symbolize. To the listener it seems at first as though the first two lines are a completed sentence (indeed some editors replace the comma at the end of them with a full stop) with "hasten" as its main verb. Yet tide and time wait for no man, and the third line qualifies and develops the meaning. Hearing this, the listener mentally attaches it to the first couplet, feeling perhaps that it is somehow unsatisfactory since waves do not in fact completely replace each other. However, its meaning is then reassigned so that it qualifies the fourth line, imitating the way that water first belongs to one wave and then to the next, and the way that time seems first to contain one thing and then the next. Finally, the first candidate for the main verb, "hasten," finds a rival in "contend," suggesting (together with the implication of "toil") the pugnacious contest between one wave and the next, and the experience of one moment battling attention away from the preoccupation of the previous moment. The fact that which of them is the main verb is never finally settled points to the fugacity of our experience of time: we cannot rest in anything in it—it moves on. The openness and ambiguity of the language reflects our inability ever to pitch our epistemological tent in this world alone without the prospect of having to fold it up again.

The metaphysical reason for this is that God alone is absolute. The things of time have only a contingent and dependent reality with which the human intellect (in the sense explained in Chapter One) cannot be satisfied. If it tries to wrap up reality in an exact and complete system, whether it is of words, mathematics, or scientific theory, it is like a bird battering its wings against a window that is blocking it from doing what it is made to do: soar into the blue beyond. The very frustration that the attempt causes has a providential purpose, beautifully expressed by George Herbert, an Anglican divine of the early seventeenth century, in this poem:

> When God at first made man,
> Having a glass of blessings standing by;
> Let us (said he) pour on him all we can:
> Let the world's riches, which dispersed lie,
>   Contract into a span.
>
> So strength first made a way;
> Then beauty flow'd, then wisdom, honour, pleasure:
> When almost all was out, God made a stay,
> Perceiving that alone, of all his treasure,
>   Rest in the bottom lay.
>
> For if I should (said he)
> Bestow this jewel also on my creature,
> He would adore my gifts instead of me,
> And rest in Nature, not the God of Nature;
>   So both should losers be.
>
> Yet let him keep the rest,
> But keep them with repining restlessness:
> Let him be rich and weary, that at least,
> If goodness lead him not, yet weariness
>   May toss him to my breast.

The pun on "rest" in the last stanza (like the ambiguously relating third line in the Shakespearian quatrain) brilliantly mimics the way we think we have somewhere to lay our intellectual head in this world but in reality do not. "Rest" means first of all the repose we think we have found in the goods of this world. These (the meaning and the repose) are then taken away when that meaning is contradicted by the line that follows and a new and banal meaning is given: "the other things." This change of meaning mimics the way in which what seems to be absolutely and definitely *it* turns out to be—because of belonging to this world—not at all capable of giving us that satisfaction. The poem is called *The Pulley* because it describes what pulls us up to God.

The lack of rest that draws us to God is also evident in paradoxes, where the logic of language, which is expected to provide a system fully able to contain truth within it, contradicts itself. The paradox points to this world not being the final reality. Meister Eckhart uses paradox for this purpose, saying, "I am good, God is not good." This appears to be very shocking arrogance: it flatly contradicts Jesus's saying that no one is good but God alone. However, the shock is intended to draw attention to the fact that the language of our discourse is transcended by God. We can say that someone or something in this world is good, and in this case the implicit assumption is that the contrary might be the case: other examples could be adduced by contrast. After the eating of the fruit of the tree of the knowledge of good and evil, there is this range of possibility. Such language does not work like this for God. He is the source of all and above any particular characterization. He can be good only in the sense that He is a lion: He includes its qualities and is their source. Eckhart argues that the language of human qualities applies to Him only by the sort of analogy we make when we say, "This man's urine is healthy," meaning that its state indicates health in the man. The indirect knowledge we have from the state of the urine corresponds to the way the word "good" works when applied to God. Yet we cannot truly describe a man in terms of his urine and no more can we describe God in terms of goodness! The paradox is saying by implication, "All our righteousnesses are as filthy rags." "Good" describes an effect that God has, rather than God Himself.

Philosophy as well as theology can use paradox for this sort of purpose. Such is the case in the celebrated paradox of Epimenides the Cretan stating that all Cretans are always liars. The formal system of language seems to guarantee that this could be a true state-ment, yet we can see that if it were true it would be contradicted by the fact that Epimenides—being a Cretan and therefore one who always lies—nonetheless is telling the truth. This points (as may well have been the intention of its first formulation) to the fact that language cannot of itself guarantee its own sense. Only a person thinking not words but ideas can do that. Therefore reality cannot be closed up in words: language points of necessity (as mathematics does, according to Gödel's theorems) beyond itself. It shows that there is a reality greater than what it can contain. It witnesses to the transcendent. The human person is made for the transcendent and is properly lord of language rather than its servant, in a way similar to being lord of creation: a lordship that comes from being able to recognize through the intellect what language and nature express, and not simply the forms of that expression.

These forms are always in some sense provisional. They cannot replace what they express; they cannot be in themselves the still point of the turning world, the absolute from which all forms come. T. S. Eliot gave this fact poetic expression:

> Words strain,
> Crack and sometimes break, under the burden,
> Under the tension, slip, slide, perish,
> Decay with imprecision, will not stay in place,
> Will not stay still.

Language stretches toward where it cannot be: "Words, after speech, reach / Into the silence." Articulated over time, speech yet moves us toward the timeless, the "always now."

Numbers

Language is a special form of symbolism, but it is not the only such. Numbers too are symbols. Indeed, in some ancient languages such as Hebrew, letters have numerical values, and thereby script can be charged with meaning beyond what the words say. In our age, num-bers, and mathematics in general, are seen chiefly as means of mea-surement and calculation, but it was not always so. In the epistemological youth of our race, they had sacred meaning. This is why (famously) those ignorant of geometry were excluded from Plato's academy. Although in the conventional education of our day Pythagoras is chiefly memorialized for working out how to calculate the hypotenuse of a triangle, his real concern was with the sacred teaching that numbers expressed. This change in the way in which numbers are regarded is concomitant with the other turning from a contemplative spirit that I have described: the sort that Galileo espoused with his insistence on measurement and practical use at the expense of discernment of quality. Numbers and mathematics are of course ideal for measuring and for practical applications, and using them for such is not wrong. But if that is the whole of what we allow them to tell us, then we are turning away from meaning written in the very fabric of creation. They speak to us of the Absolute, of God.

Above all, the number one speaks of God. Chapter Two discussed at length how the oneness, or wholeness, of God is reflected in every instance of life and existence. It also touched on the quality of two, expressive of extension and line—as distinct from the point expressing divine unity—and thus of creation fallen from God, as when Adam and Eve prefer the duality of the tree of the knowledge of good and evil to the unity of the tree of life. The number two, however, also expresses God's entering that creation in order to redeem it, since Christ has two natures, the divine and the human. It speaks therefore of creation returning to God, as well as falling from Him.

The number three is another expression of God, above all as denoting the Holy Trinity. Like one, it is a number of wholeness, having, as Aristotle observed, a beginning, middle, and end. It denotes the wholeness of Man: body, soul, and spirit; and the wholeness of the human family: mother, father, and child. Three is the spiritual; four is the material. There are four dimensions, three in space and one in time, and they make possible the material creation. Four seasons mark the passage of time; four directions our journeys on earth. Four elements constitute our material world, and four gospels point us from this world to the next.

Five is the number of Man: with limbs outstretched he forms a pentagon, and he has five senses. Man is the fullness of creation just as a blossom with, most characteristically, five petals is the fullness of growth. Six is the number of perfection, the number of days in which creation was completed and the number of directions in space if we count up and down as well as the points of the compass. The perfection of the cosmos symbolically comes to earth when crystals of snow, little six-pointed stars, fall from the sky. *Cosmos* in Greek means "order," and six is perfect order, being the only number constituted both from the sum of its factors (one plus two plus three) and their product (one times two times three). It stands for the circle: at the sixth hour on the sixth day, Christ brought the creation back to its Creator.

Seven is the uniting of the spiritual (three) with the material (four). There are seven petitions in the Our Father, three about God and four about our life on earth; there are seven sacraments that link our earthly life to heaven; there are seven virtues, three theological to guide our relations with God (faith, hope, and charity) and four cardinal to guide our earthly actions (prudence, justice, fortitude, and temperance). Seven, the number of days in the week, is the number of time, where spirit and matter intersect. Eight is the number of new life. Jesus rose on the eighth day; He gave us eight beatitudes by which to find new life. The font in which the new life of Christ is given in baptism is characteristically octagonal. Eight is the first number that is a cube (two times two times two): it is the entry into a new dimension. With the eight corners of the cube go six surfaces, indicating the perfection of a higher world.

This brief account of the meaning of some numbers is of course by no means exhaustive. There is more both about these and about subsequent numbers in my sources (indicated in the endnotes) and elsewhere. What I have written is simply intended to indicate that numbers are for more than measurement and analysis. Although these latter functions are emphasized in schools, it is the capacity of numbers for spiritual meaning, their telling of the Creator and His creation, that is their primary wonder. With the humility of the truly spiritual, they allow themselves to be used for purposes pertaining to this world, but the depth of their being is elsewhere.

Architecture

Language and number are symbols that people use to allow nature to become real, that is to say, to have meaning. Nature itself, however, can be fashioned so as to become its own language and expression of the harmony of numbers. Nowhere is this more vital for us than in architecture, determining as it does the very pattern of our lives. As with nature, the symbolic importance can be forgotten in the interests of efficiency of manipulation: Le Corbusier notoriously spoke of a house as "a machine for living in." Yet architecture properly practiced forms our hearts and minds for the celestial. This is most obviously the case with sacred architecture. I am privileged and blessed to live in a monastery and worship in a church designed by a monk-architect.

Our abbey church guides the minds and hearts of those who worship in it. It is a symbol through which we contemplate God. Its very structure teaches us about prayer. The first, lowest, and narrowest section is the place for individual, private prayer. The prayer of the Church is recited by the community of monks in the wider, higher, and taller middle section. The highest part of the church is the great tower over the sanctuary, which is raised above the rest of the building and has chapels on either side of it. This architecture emphasizes the great power of the highest possible prayer, the sacrifice of Jesus Christ, made present in the Holy Mass. The way the light works in the building also shows us the power of prayer. The architect said he wanted to make the sun sing before it came into the church, and its song is of God, whom it most aptly symbolizes. Light from the tall windows in the tower floods the sanctuary where the great prayer of Jesus is offered; it is more mediated, by a clerestory wall, as it comes into the choir where monks recite the psalmody in His name, and it comes more from the side than above in the lowest section of the church where private prayer is offered. Everywhere, though, the light shows us how God meets us in prayer.

The bricks too are expressive. Their richer and darker color in the sanctuary, where the hanging tabernacle containing the Blessed Sacrament, presence of the Lord, is seen, draws the mind and heart to worship. In the sanctuary tower they form arches, which make it seem as though they were tossed up by one hand to be caught with the other. The architect spoke of juggling with bricks and of fireworks. That he has got this heavy material to behave in this way teaches us how we, formed of clay and weighed down by its heaviness, can nonetheless aspire to heaven, as the tower reaches toward the sky.

This church is just over a century old, but I am blessed also to live in a country where there remain great cathedrals that memorialize an age when contemplation took precedence over technological prowess and remind us of the possibility of regaining something of that spirit. In Salisbury Cathedral, for example, it is still possible to see some of the original oak beams, hewn well over eight centuries ago, supporting the roof. They lack the straightness of the ones put in when people got better at manipulating the material world and are held together with nothing more sophisticated than dowelling, but they are part of a whole: a building that witnesses to a faith that saw the trees from which they were taken, and creation as a whole, as an expression of God.

A cathedral indeed was the consciousness of a city: the articulation of its faith-filled understanding of creation. It also expressed, and expresses, the theological virtue of hope, with its heaven-pointing great tower or spire demonstrating the triumph of height over heaviness. Its very making was a demonstration of love, since people from all strata of society would have been involved in its creation, and they would all have gathered together in it. Indeed, according to medieval tradition, a church building represents the heavenly Jerusalem: that city made of living stones where all live together in harmony, peace, and joy. A cathedral is still what it was when it was built: a book in which the things of God can be read. It was built as such to allow those who could not read that access to divine truth that the learned could find in the Bible. It is to learning how to contemplate God in the Bible's pages that I now turn.

Chapter Five:
Scripture and Hermeneutics

O Book! Infinite Sweetness!

his is the central chapter of this book. It would be entirely reasonable to start a book about contemplation with a consideration of Holy Scripture: after all, through its pages we learn about God and so begin to turn our minds and hearts toward Him in prayer. It is the beginning of meditation, which leads to prayer and contemplation. Yet our cultural circumstances are different from those of the ancient writers on contemplation. As I have argued, there has been a falling off from a natural and wholesome way of knowing: we have to a large extent forgotten how to see and hear things as they are, in our quest to get a grip on them to make them what we want them to be. It has therefore seemed right to reconsider how we contemplate nature and how we use words before considering the specifically sacred. That reconsideration will inform what follows.

There are people who can live with the mind-set of our age, with its substitution of control for receptivity, and who can just drop it to pick up a Bible and open themselves to what God is saying through it. I admire and honor them, but seek for myself and my readers an outlook that is less demanding of spiritual strength: one that can come to the Bible with a mind already open to depth of meaning because that is how it habitually reads nature and literature. I have been blessed to study and teach poetry, which can open the heart to that depth in natural symbols and in word, and I hope I have been able to share a little of that blessing with you in what you have read so far.

In this spirit, I want to start our consideration of Scripture with some more poetry. Here, then, is the first part of George Herbert's poem *The Holy Scriptures*:

> O Book! infinite sweetness! Let my heart
> Suck every letter, and a honey gain,

Precious for any grief in any part;
To clear the breast, to mollify all pain.

Thou art all health, health thriving, till it make
  A full eternity: thou art a mass
  Of strange delights, where we may wish and take.
Ladies, look here; this is the thankful glass,

That mends the looker's eyes: this is the well
  That washes what it shows. Who can endear
  Thy praise too much? thou art heaven's Lieger here,
Working against the states of death and hell.

  Thou art joy's handsel: heaven lies flat in thee,
  Subject to every mounter's bended knee.

The three quatrains present, in order, the ability of Scripture to assuage grief, to bring health, and to renew how we see things. I have argued in the previous chapter that revelation as such is God's response to Man's allowing nature and word to become opaque so that the eternal is no longer seen through them. Scripture is then the cure for the sadness and the spiritual illness and blindness of being cut off from the eternal. In earlier times, people were not so ill that they could not swallow this medicine. There are still some, as I indicated above, who are strong enough to take it directly. I write this book, however, with special concern for our culture's need to be rescued from the epistemological unhealthiness of our age so that we might all, with the doors of perception cleansed, have an appetite for the medicine of Scripture and receive life from it.

That is the reason why I have looked at the natural before the sacred. Yet, of course, I have been using Scripture also from the very beginning. Scripture helps us to see nature and philosophical discourse aright, just as seeing this discourse aright helps us to be ready to receive from Scripture. The readiness is all. *How* we receive Scripture determines what Scripture is for us. In calling this chapter "Scripture and Hermeneutics," it is not my intention to consider first Scripture then hermeneutics, as in Chapter One I considered first light and then color. "Hermeneutics" is a word similar in meaning to "interpretation," but it is not exactly the same, since the idea of interpretation includes the possibility of translating: putting the same message into another language. Hermeneutics is a little different: it is the art of understanding what is expressed so that the form of expression changes from being opaque to being transparent. It is about seeing meaning. So by "Scripture and Hermeneutics" I mean Scripture *as transparent to the light of the celestial and eternal*—that light which has been closed to us by the opacity of nature and word. Properly understood, Scripture is a text transparent to supernatural light, but just as you can (to an extent) amuse yourself by turning a bicycle upside down and making the wheels go round by turning the pedals by hand, so it is possible to take a different approach to Scripture, for example, one that is interested in scholarship alone or satisfying mere curiosity. As a bicycle realizes its true being as a means of getting somewhere quicker than is possible by going on foot, so Holy Scripture realizes its true being by allowing us to contemplate God through it. Its words establish God in our hearts just as ordinary words build up the natural world for the very young child or someone who, like Helen Keller, first learns them later in life.

That is why it is "infinite sweetness." God is delight without bounds. Scripture is "precious for any grief in any part" because "God shall wipe away all tears." It is "all health, health thriving, till it make / A full eternity" because it heals the fissure between us and God, making it possible for us to be open to what is eternal and thus totally unbounded. It "mends the looker's eyes" because by acquiring the ability to contemplate what is divine through it we can say, with the blind man healed by Jesus, "Whereas I was blind, now I see." It "washes what it shows" because through it we see what is wrong with our lives and through it we can put it right. It is "heaven's Lieger" (meaning "ambassador") because through it we enter into relation with the celestial. It is "joy's handsel" (meaning a "first installment of a payment" and also a "gift") because it gives us the joy of heaven, now in part and ultimately in its fullness.

Hermeneutist and Hermeneutics

Holy Scripture is not all this for us through our own skill in hermeneutics. I wrote in the previous chapter of how, when seeing goes beyond what is seen to its source that transcends it, it finds also the

142

immanent presence of the source in its own knowing. In other words, this seeing is seeing *with God*. So it is with reading Holy Scripture aright. The Holy Spirit is our Hermeneutist. He is "the Spirit of truth" who guides us "into all truth." He reveals the deep meaning of Scripture. Saint Paul tells us what His central revelation is: "No man," he says, "can say that Jesus is Lord, but by the Holy Ghost." Jesus is the Word, in Greek the *Logos*, and the Holy Spirit teaches us that He is the central meaning of all that is: the logic of it all, we might say, for "all things were made by him." Saint Jerome said that he who is ignorant of Scripture is ignorant of Christ, and we might add that we cannot understand the true import of Scripture without the Holy Spirit, for He brings us to know Jesus as Lord.

This does not take away the natural work of hermeneutics. Grace builds on nature: the Holy Spirit leads us to the Lord Christ who is "the way, the truth, and the life," but we can prepare ourselves for being open to a spiritual path, for recognizing truth and receiving life, by learning to know in a healthy way, by developing a sound epistemology. That has been the purpose of the first four chapters of this book. It is therefore appropriate to apply the reflections of the earlier chapters directly to Holy Scripture. What applies to God's revelation in nature will apply to His revelation in Scripture; what applies to the human word will apply to the holy word of the Bible. I shall look first at how the reflections on wholeness (mostly in Chapter Two) apply; then at the application of the reflections on symbolism; and thirdly at the application of the reflections on language. After this I shall consider the way in which Scripture is best read so as to lead us to contemplate God, with special reference to the monastic tradition of *lectio divina* or spiritual reading.

The Whole Thing

I said in the introduction that a way of reading that murders to dissect cannot reach the heart of meaning. Nowhere is this more true than in Sacred Scripture. Analysis can be useful, of course. A detailed examination of fragments can give a clearer understanding of particular implications, yet "the word of God is quick." That is, it lives and a characteristic of life is that the part belongs to the whole and the whole is reflected in the part. We cannot separate parts to read them unconnected without violating life. Sometimes parts will yield their meaning by speaking on behalf of huge expanses, or even the totality, of Scripture. Such is the announcement that "the Word was made flesh, and dwelt among us." Another example is this saying of Jesus: "Thou shalt love the Lord thy God with all thy heart, and with all thy soul, and with all thy mind. This is the first and great commandment. And the second is like unto it, Thou shalt love thy neighbor as thyself. On these two commandments hang all the law and the prophets." Indeed, it would be enough simply to live according to this saying: it fully conveys the teaching of the Bible. Like the first cell of an embryo or a fragment of a hologram, it contains the whole. Other portions of Scripture will yield their meaning if read alongside different texts: these different parts will vary according to the particular message that is apt for a particular person at a particular time. The dynamic of this is beautifully expressed in the second part of George Herbert's poem quoted above:

> Oh that I knew how all thy lights combine,
>   And the configurations of their glory!
>   Seeing not only how each verse doth shine,
> But all the constellations of the story.
>
> This verse marks that, and both do make a motion
>   Unto a third, that ten leaves off doth lie:
>   Then as dispersed herbs do watch a potion,
> These three make up some Christian's destiny.
>
> Such are thy secrets, which my life makes good,
>   And comments on thee: for in every thing
>   Thy words do find me out, and parallels bring,
> And in another make me understood.
>
> Stars are poor books, and oftentimes do miss:
> This book of stars lights to eternal bliss.

This part of the poem also conveys how Scripture is medicine that cures the illness of not being able to read the cosmos. To us now "stars are poor books": the sky cannot be read as it used to be; we do not see heaven in it anymore. We are healed from blindness to heaven by a prescription—"a potion"—made up from disparate elements of Scripture in a combination that is unique for the person for whom it is intended. This prescription "makes good" the life and destiny of this particular Christian. Knowing "how each verse doth shine" is not enough, but we do have enough light, from "the configurations" that we can perceive, to see our true state and say with the poet, "Thy words do find me out." In this way, drawing our attention to the coherence of multiple texts, the Bible gives us enough light to reach "eternal bliss," even if we do not know "all the constellations of the story."

The coherence comes from the oneness of the Holy Spirit, as George Herbert explained in *A Priest to the Temple*: "For all Truth being consonant to it self, and all being penn'd by one and the self-same Spirit, it cannot be, but that an industrious and judicious comparing of place with place must be a singular help for the right understanding of the Scriptures." The Spirit-given oneness goes further than this: it is also in the unity of Christ's followers in the Church, now and through the ages. In the whole of Scripture and the whole of Tradition received in the present and from the past, we find the light and meaning that elude us if we look only in fragments. What is cut up into pieces is dead and cannot animate: what has living coherence gives life.

Eyesalve

The Bible, like nature, has an Author and so a coherent meaning. It therefore makes sense to seek that meaning in the whole text, not just in little sections of it. In order to exemplify this, I shall look at a couple of connections between the first book of the Bible, Genesis, and the last, the book of Revelation. The first is connected with a major theme of this book: how we see things. The devil is recommending eating from the forbidden "tree of the knowledge of good and evil" and makes his epistemological pitch to Eve thus: "In the day ye eat thereof, then your eyes shall be opened, and ye shall be as gods, knowing good and evil." He is saying that they will *see* things differently when they have eaten of the fruit: their way of knowing will be different. His claim that they will "be as gods" implies a divine perspective. Of course (as we know from elsewhere in the

Bible), "he is a liar." In reality the perspective is less than divine. God's knowledge is an undivided unity; He knows only good. "The knowledge of good and evil" is a divided knowledge, belonging to what is extended; it lacks the perception of everything as a single whole because for it the created is opaque, and so it does not see the divine unity through it. Independence of the divine unity (which is also pride of judgment) entails division, conflict, and evil. The immediate effect of this new way of looking is that Adam and Eve know that they are naked. Knowing themselves this way is no longer knowing themselves according to the divine plan and purpose of their creation when "God created man in his own image, in the image of God created he him; male and female created He them." They do not see God *through* their bodies, which image Him: they only see their own nakedness—their vision stops at what is created, no longer seeing what it expresses. It is no longer the case that "they were both naked, the man and his wife, and were not ashamed."

Here, from the book of Revelation, is God's truthful promise corresponding to (and undoing) the devil's mendacious one:

> Because thou sayest, I am rich, and increased with goods, and have need of nothing; and knowest not that thou art wretched, and miserable, and poor, and blind, and naked: I counsel thee to buy of me gold tried in the fire, that thou mayest be rich; and white raiment, that thou mayest be clothed, and that the shame of thy nakedness do not appear; and anoint thine eyes with eyesalve, that thou mayest see.

The "eyesalve," divine medicine, restores the vision lost through the devil's temptation: the ability to see the divine unity in and through all things. The nakedness, which was what Adam and Eve were left with when they no longer saw God through His image, is clothed with "white raiment": the divine refulgence. The white is a symbol of the undifferentiated and transcendent perfection of divine simplicity, innocent of any evil. The "gold tried in the fire" is a symbol of the sacred luminosity, the pure light won by the suffering of Christ. These are offered to Man who thinks he is well-off but looks only at the goods of this world, not at what they signify. The new vision the devil persuaded him to seek is in reality blindness, and he is so far fallen from paradise that he has forgotten what he knew before his exile: that he is naked.

The offer of "eyesalve" is another presentation of the sign given by Jesus in Chapter Nine of John's Gospel. Here is the corresponding narrative:

> As long as I am in the world, I am the light of the world. When he had thus spoken, he spat on the ground, and made clay of the spittle, and he anointed the eyes of the blind man with the clay. And he said unto him, Go, wash in the pool of Siloam, (which is by interpretation, Sent.) He went his way therefore, and washed, and came seeing.

Jesus, the light of the world—God (who is light) with us—redoes the making of Adam from the dust of the earth, restoring his primordial vision. Jesus is "sent" (the meaning of the pool's name, Siloam) by His Father to cleanse Man's blindness. He makes his eye "single" in the sense (given at the beginning of Chapter One where its use in Luke's Gospel is discussed) of making it healthy, but also in the sense of curing the double vision—"of good and evil"—that came through the devil's temptation and deprived Adam of the ability to see "the one thing" that is God in His unity, apparent in all things.

More About Trees

The loss and healing of vision is not the only connection between the first and last books of the Bible. The tree of life also connects them. In the book of Genesis we read, "And out of the ground made the LORD God to grow ... the tree of life ... in the midst of the garden." It is central: Eve and Adam eating of the other, forbidden tree is off-center, and leads to exile. In the middle of the Bible there is a prophecy of restoration in Ezekiel's prophetic vision of a life-giving river with "very many trees on the one side and on the other." This is fulfilled in the apocalyptic vision of the New Jerusalem in the last chapter of the Bible:

> And he showed me a pure river of water of life, clear as crystal, proceeding out of the throne of God and of the Lamb. In the midst of the street of it, and on either side of the river, was there the tree

of life, which bare twelve manner of fruits, and yielded her fruit every month: and the leaves of the tree were for the healing of the nations.

The trees have the symbolic associations outlined in Chapter Three, but the symbolism of the tree of life also parallels that of the eyesalve restoring wholeness and singleness of sight, since life is bound up with wholeness. To eat from the tree of life is to know the oneness of God and in that knowledge to have wholeness. The story of the Bible is the story of losing and finding again that wholeness, the story of the fall from gazing upon the oneness of God and the recovery of that contemplation. It is the primary inspiration for this book.

Not a Closed System

The Bible has a wonderful coherence, but it is not a closed system in which everything is explained by reference to everything else. Like human language, it breaks open under the pressure of the reality it conveys. As we saw in the previous chapter, human language contains paradoxes, such as that of Epimenides, because no system can wrap up reality so that there is no depth or significance beyond that system. This is most especially true where divine reality is concerned. The words of the Bible, human as they are, cannot contain it: they can only open out onto it. It follows that on the level of language, there will be paradoxes. Take, for example, this teaching of the Lord Jesus:

> If any man come to me, and hate not his father, and mother, and wife, and children, and brethren, and sisters, yea, and his own life also, he cannot be my disciple.

This contradicts, among other texts, the commandment given through Moses, "Honour thy father and thy mother"; the saying of Saint Paul, "Let every one of you so love his wife even as himself"; and that of Saint John, "He that hateth his brother is in darkness." This prompts us to look more deeply at it. It begins to make sense in the context of this comment on His teaching here that the Lord makes: "Whoever he be of you that forsaketh not all that he hath, he cannot be my disciple." Forsaking what one has carries the implication of forswearing ownership or private property. It suggests that the love that is being contradicted is a love that relates to the self in that it cherishes what belongs to the self. There is another sort of love that loves the other wholly for his or her sake. This is the love that comes when one can truthfully say, "I live; yet not I, but Christ liveth in me." It is the love that comes when one forsakes self to follow Christ, losing one's life to find it. This is the love that God is, a love of a completely different order from that which comes from our natural inclinations. It follows that what Jesus is saying in the apparently contradicted passage is, in effect, "Clear out the old love, to replace it with a universal love that will much more truly benefit its objects." It is as though He is recommending knocking down a poky little building for the sake of building a much finer edifice.

We can draw meaning from these apparent contradictions in this sort of way, yet on the level of straightforward use of language the contradictions remain. It would never do to codify law by using words like this. A system of legal significance could never tolerate such usage. The breaking in of divine light works differently. It has to reduce words to impotence before it, making them mean the opposite of what they say, to establish its Lordship over the conventions of human word and thought. This is characteristic of the way the divine breaks into the human: there is always more depth (or more weight) than the system can contain. It is at its most dramatic in the crucifixion of Christ: in human terms, health is wholeness of body, and yet it is through the breaking of a human body that health and wholeness (salvation) come to all humanity. Saint Paul was pointing to this breaking of human meaning systems when he wrote, "When I am weak, then am I strong." I will look further at how this sort of use of paradox breaks through language, which since Babel has tended to be the terminus rather than the portal of our perception, when I look at the teaching of Christ in Chapter Eight. Here I simply want to point out that Scripture is given to us to help us get beyond the worldly reification of words, not to become another exhibit in a museum of language that *once upon a time* shimmered with a glory superabundantly greater than anything it could contain.

On the literal level, Scripture is messy and reflective of the mess of human life: sometimes perhaps even shockingly so. Yet if it were squeakily clean, perfectly polished and totally explicable in terms of itself, it would not speak of God breaking into our world as that world really is. It would simply be lying. The truth it tells is greater than such tidy completeness and not literal alone. Of this truth I shall now speak.

Scripture and Symbolism

In the way we think nowadays, we tend to get used to the lazy assumption that things do not mean anything in particular, other than meanings that we want to bestow upon them. I have argued against this assumption, particularly in Chapters One, Three, and Four. I want now to look at the application of this thinking to Scripture. Sometimes the symbolism in Scripture is obvious, such as when Jesus says, "I am the true vine, and my Father is the husbandman." A literal identification is excluded, and the manifold aptness of the symbol is clear. The vine is alive and in its way a tree of life: it denotes the One who came that His people might have life and "have it more abundantly." Each branch of it has a life of its own and yet is not separate, so Jesus can say, "I am the vine, ye are the branches" and explain how not being separated from Him is the way to life. The work of "the husbandman"—the Father—is to remove those branches that do not bear fruit and to prune those that do so that they may bear more. The vine as cultivated expresses His Providence in judging those whose lives are spiritually unfruitful and in allowing difficulties in fruitful lives that make them yet more fruitful. The fruit of the vine, grapes crushed to produce wine, symbolize the suffering of Christ and point to His Precious Blood in the Eucharist.

To say all this is to say what is patent from the passage even in our day, and there is more that any reasonably careful reading of Chapter Fifteen of John's Gospel will reveal. Yet there is meaning that our culture loses, because of what has happened to the way it reads the book of nature. Jesus says, "I am the *true* vine." The words used for "true" and "truth" in the Greek version of the Bible carry the connotation of divine, or more real. Jesus is saying that He is *more* what the vine is than it is itself. The vine is the expression on its own (less real) level of the divine reality that Jesus Himself *is*. We are used to the notion that a symbol is something that can be used for our purposes, as when a company takes something from nature to establish its brand, for example—to take one associated with the original epistemological dysfunction—an apple. Yet, as I have argued earlier in this book, nature exists to show us what is beyond it and thus has a meaning that is given, not taken. The vine is not co-opted by an ingenious teacher to make his point; the Teacher reveals in Himself what the vine of its nature reveals on its own, lower, level. In one sense, the Incarnation is a response to the forgetting of what nature means; it is a direct showing of that meaning.

If we bear in mind this reading of nature, Scripture has a double power. It speaks with the power of words but also with the symbolic force of nature. A less obvious example than that of the vine is this promise from the book of Revelation:

> He that hath an ear, let him hear what the Spirit saith unto the Churches; to Him that overcometh will I give to eat of the hidden manna, and will give him a white stone, and in the stone a new name written, which no man knoweth saving he that receiveth it.

This begins with a reprise of the admonition of the prophet Isaiah, referred to in Chapter Four, about the distinction between opening the ears and hearing. To hear is to get the meaning as well as the sounds. It goes on to say that the one who resists the allure of evil will get two gifts. The first is defined in terms of the narrative in Chapter Sixteen of the book of Exodus, where God gives His people food in the desert. The word "manna" takes its power from those earlier words, indicative of a Providence that meets need exactly. That it is qualified by the word "hidden" tells us more. This is nourishment for "the inner man." The Lord works in secret in the soul to make it strong. The second gift is the "white stone." The whiteness has the same symbolic implications as in the "white raiment" mentioned above. The stone is an extraordinarily rich and powerful symbol. Characteristically, a stone is not affected by other things in its environment: roots and so on go around it rather than through it. Being in this sense impenetrable, it is a whole in its own right; it cannot be made a part of something else. It therefore symbolizes that in Man which transcends his environment: his immortal being. The stone is Man as microcosm, containing all things within his spirit, rather than Man as part of the external world and subject to its forces. The wholeness and immortality the stone expresses correspond to these qualities in God, whose image Man is. Therefore God, in the person of Christ, is also symbolized by a stone. The gift of a stone is thus a share in the life of Christ, the realization of Man's immortal destiny, an eternal and imperishable being. It is white because this life is that of light, purity, and peace.

I have dwelt on the symbolism of the stone because it illustrates how our recovery of the ability to read nature, to look at it contemplatively, facilitates our reading and receiving of meaning through Scripture. The two are synergetic. It is not just our relationship with nature that is relevant to how Scripture works for us, however: the way in which words work for us is also vitally important for what we receive from it. If words are just tokens that we move around, they will not reveal to us as much as they will if words are keys that unlock being for us. Everything in the last chapter, both about symbol and about language, is relevant to how we read Scripture. The "white stone" illustrates this with regard to both symbol and language, because it has "in the stone a new name written, which no man knoweth saving he that receiveth it." To look at it with the carelessness of a contemporary epistemology is to be able to say to oneself merely, "That stone is mine because it has my name on it." Seeing nature with a deeper knowing, one can say, "This stone is me." It can then be pondered in a way that takes one deeper than where words can go.

The words matter too, though. They have power. The "new name" brings about a depth of being. It echoes God's first creating word, as recorded at the beginning of the Bible. Through it God gives to the human soul an identity, as Adam in paradise gave the animals identity. This is a participation in the identity of God. The last chapter explained how *the* name, given by God, replaces *a* name made by people for themselves. Here is something yet more glorious. It is not simply a matter of something factitious being replaced by something universal. The personal and particular *becomes* the universal. The new name is not divisive like that sought at Babel: it is written by God, who "is one LORD," as once He wrote on stone for Moses. Yet it is gifted to the individual alone. No one else knows it. It has something of the mystery of the tetragrammaton: the sacred Name of God not to be profaned by being uttered in public. It is no way external and therefore cannot be manipulated or subjugated. It is irreducible being, containing everything.

History as Symbol

I will come back to words, and their power. Having looked at how they can work with a natural symbol, I want now to consider how symbolism works more extensively. To be precise, I want to consider how symbolism works when extended in time. If it is true, as I have been insisting, that nature symbolizes what is beyond it, presenting supernatural reality to us, then there is no reason why it should do this only statically. Things change in nature, and this reflects the changes in human life, as in the seasons corresponding to different phases of a person's life. But I have in mind not just correspondences between one natural thing and another but correspondences between what is natural and what is spiritual. Just as a stone or a tree can symbolize something spiritual, so can an event. This is generally understood when it comes to fiction. A quest story can illustrate someone finding his true self. Jesus used such stories, like the one about selling everything to buy the "pearl of great price." Yet there is a prejudice that says such stories can only be "not really true"—that is to say, that only fiction can carry the meaning that they contain. To say this is to divorce natural life from meaning. It is to say that the material, extended in space and time, is the ultimate reality and meaning is a humanly constructed add-on. I have argued from the beginning of this book that this is not true. Reality is deeper and greater than this, and the material is a presentation of it, not the thing itself. This being the case, we do not need to limit ourselves to fiction (wonderfully, even indispensably, illuminating though it can be) when seeking spiritual meaning. Just as something that exists in nature can speak of what is beyond it, so can something that happens in nature, and this can be recorded in human history.

In the age of the fathers of the Church, this was taken for granted when reading Scripture. Nowadays there tends to be a tacit and unexamined assumption that this is a fanciful and unreal way of looking at history. In reality, it is the modern way of thinking that is unreal, because it is materialist. Prescinding, therefore, from the atoms of Democritus, we will look at some examples from Scripture of history conveying spiritual meaning. As with the symbol of the stone, types of events can have a natural spiritual meaning antecedent to their scriptural use. An obvious instance is the journey. There are many examples, from Homer's *Odyssey* to a modern political leader naming his autobiography *A Journey*. Pilgrimages are journeys that embody a spiritual meaning: a movement toward the sacred. The outward act of, for example, walking toward Santiago de Compostela gives expression and—at least by aspiration—effectiveness to an inward desire for holiness. Yet a journey does not need to be undertaken for religious reasons to be a true spiritual symbol. Every life is a journey along the extension of time to God; people may have greatly varying degrees of preparation for their arrival at their destination, with corresponding degrees of felicity (or its absence) there, but they are all going to the same place. The trials and dangers of a journey are the difficulties we face in life, and how we respond determines our spiritual development, our readiness for when we arrive.

Get Thee Out of Thy Country

There are three great journeys in Scripture, all of them carrying the meaning of going to God. The first is that of Abraham. It begins because "the LORD had said to Abram, Get thee out of thy country, and from thy kindred, and from thy father's house, unto a land that I will show thee." The land is an identifiable historical and geographical place, but it symbolizes something yet more real: heaven. The fact that Abram (his name is changed to Abraham later, a symbol of spiritual change) has to leave his own fatherland, folk, and family is a symbol of the spiritual necessity of getting beyond the natural and cultural world in order to contemplate God. As I have explained, both these worlds in principle express the divine pres-

ence but have become, through the devil's epistemological devious-
ness, in some sense barriers to knowing God. We have to leave not
so much nature and culture themselves—doing this with any completeness would be harmful even if it were possible—but rather *our
way of knowing them*. In practice, though, this involves a degree of
real renunciation. It is striking how close the requirements for
renunciation placed on Abraham parallel what Jesus says about hat-
ing father and mother and so on in the teaching discussed above.
Both express the demanding costliness of the dynamic of abandoning our own world so as to be open to God's.

The reward, though, is huge, and the enterprise enjoys divine protection. In a vision Abraham hears the Lord saying, "Fear not,
Abram: I am thy shield and exceeding great reward." His journey not
so much takes him to God as brings God to him. The power of Abraham's story is in the awe inspiring extent of his descendants, of the
body and of the spirit. He is told, "Look now toward heaven, and tell
the stars if thou be able to number them. . . . So shall thy seed be."
His seed is the descendants of his body, the stars of his spirit: the latter are the blessed in heaven. These include among them those "that
turn many to righteousness"—those who follow Abraham's path so
far as to become a spiritual father to many. Such was Saint Benedict,
leaving the familiarity of Rome for seclusion in the holy cave till he
emerged capable of leading generations that followed him to God.
The immensity of the blessing of such progeny indicates the power
of renunciation, or rather what God can do when not blocked. Abraham's journey brought him to much more than he left behind.

The Journey to the Promised Land

The second great journey in the Bible is that of a whole people: the
people of Israel. They have settled in Egypt, but when there is "a
new king over Egypt" they find "their lives bitter with hard bondage." Literally, this is making bricks and other servile tasks, but traditionally this has been interpreted as symbolizing the enslavement
of God's people to sin. The beauty of a symbol is that it implies
more than can be conveyed by a verbal equivalent, and I would like
to suggest a particular aspect of this bondage that corresponds to

the theme of this book. This is being kept prisoner within the natural and cultural worlds: that is, being unable to see what they express, considering nature and language to be the terminus of reality. Instead of knowing God, the prisoner knows only the laws that govern the operation of natural processes and the conventions governing the use of language, considered as arbitrarily assigned. This failure can also be expressed in terms of being cut off from the light, a symbol used throughout John's Gospel. In advancing this reading of the people of Israel's bondage, I need to make an important qualification: I do not for a moment imagine that this is the entirety of sin and evil. Indeed, although I have spoken of the moral aspect of conversion from this outlook, I do not think that it is even necessarily sinful in the sense of being a deliberately willed bad choice. *That* is why I think it matters so much that we understand what is going on: people of goodwill are prisoners, are in the darkness. This is because they are *taught* such things.

If somebody is determined to choose evil, there is not a lot one can do. When I worked as a prison chaplain, a governor once described my job as "turning bad people into good people," and I think that was a little naive. Yet it is a different matter to trust the goodwill of people who through no fault of their own have inherited a dysfunctional epistemology. Even if at first the older, wiser way of knowing seems strange, in the longer perspective truth has a gentle persuasiveness. It can be a long journey, but so was that of the Israelites to the Promised Land. It is highly significant that their leader Moses "was very meek, above all the men which were upon the face of the earth." Humility is the ability to see reality as it is, not distorting it with a manipulative spirit that twists it to the prejudices of the self. Because Moses is humble he is open to God, who calls him to lead His people "unto a land flowing with milk and honey." That land is interpreted by the ancient commentators as symbolizing heaven. This is nothing other than seeing God as He is. It is the ultimate seeing aright, the perfect healing of how we know. It is not allowing anything, great or little, to replace Him and thus obscure the vision that alone gives bliss.

Moses leads the people in the decisive break from their bondage: the crossing of the Red Sea. The Bible tells the story like this:

And Moses stretched out his hand over the sea; and the LORD caused the sea to go back by a strong east wind all that night, and made the sea dry land, and the waters were divided. And the children of Israel went into the midst of the sea upon the dry ground: and the waters were a wall unto them on their right hand, and on their left. . . . Thus the LORD saved Israel that day out of the hand of the Egyptians; and Israel saw the Egyptians dead upon the sea shore.

I do not need to interpret this in terms of the theme of this book since William Blake has done it for me, in the poem quoted in the introduction: "The Atoms of Democritus / And Newton's Particles of Light / Are sands upon the Red sea shore." The people of God leave behind, as I said in my commentary on the poem, the reductionism of atomism and its scientific descendants. They get beyond a defective epistemology, an inadequate way of knowing.

This is only the start of their journey, however. They are troubled by the lure of what they were used to. They say, "We remember the fish, which we did eat in Egypt freely; the cucumbers, and the melons, and the leeks, and the onions, and the garlick." They are tempted by what they have left behind. The tendency to succumb to being locked into the limitation of knowing this world (natural and cultural) only for the false certainty and comfort it gives, in preference to being vulnerable to the living God, is perennial. That is why the psalm urges, "Harden not your heart as in the provocation, and as in the day of temptation in the wilderness." It is a journey through the desert, itself an ambivalent symbol. On the one hand the desert is a place of desolation and abandonment; on the other a place of contemplation, quiet, and divine revelation. It is these two for the same reason: the normal distractions of this world are withdrawn.

The journey ends after the death of Moses. This is significant. The journey to God is ultimately a journey beyond this life. In Christian tradition, this passage beyond our mortal existence is symbolized by the crossing of the people of Israel through the River Jordan. This parallels that through the Red Sea. Crossing the Red Sea is, as it were, a death to the things of this world; crossing the Jordan a literal and actual death. Moses is the one who leads through the Red Sea, Joshua the one who leads through the River Jordan. As

157

Joshua promises, the waters of the Jordan are parted so that the people of God can pass "clean over Jordan." They are later reminded through him of the remarkable fact regarding how they take possession of their new land: "Thus saith the LORD God, . . . I have given you a land for which ye did not labour, and cities which ye built not, and ye dwell in them; of the vineyards and oliveyards which ye planted not do ye eat." The Promised Land, the beatific vision, the knowledge of God is ultimately His work: it is He who sets us free, He who liberates us from our bondage with all that it implies.

The Greatest Journey of Them All

The third journey is the greatest of them all. The final stage of the Israelites' journey is a symbol of it especially, and Joshua a symbol of the One who makes it. It is announced in Luke's Gospel: "And it came to pass, when the time was come that he should be received up, he steadfastly set his face to go to Jerusalem." The being received up is the crossing of the Jordan: the death, resurrection, and ascension of Jesus. He is resolute in His undertaking of the journey that is to both the earthly Jerusalem, over which He lovingly laments, and the new or heavenly Jerusalem, where He reigns in glory. It is a journey toward terrible suffering as well as glory, as He explains to His followers: "We go up to Jerusalem, and all things that are written by the prophets concerning the Son of man shall be accomplished. For he shall be delivered unto the Gentiles, and shall be mocked, and spitefully entreated, and spitted on: And they shall scourge him, and put him to death: and the third day he shall rise again."

The tension of this outcome hangs over all He does; He says, "How am I straitened till it be accomplished!" It is in the context of this destiny that He goes "through the cities and villages, teaching, and journeying toward Jerusalem." The circumstance of His teaching is even clearer in John's Gospel, where it is placed between the departure of His betrayer and His arrest. The teaching is therefore as much in the journey He makes and whither He makes it as in what He says. I shall consider Jesus's teaching in greater depth in Chapter Eight, but a particular element of it is relevant here. He is, like the Israelites, making a journey beyond the confines of the natural and cultural worlds that have kept mankind in bondage through becoming the terminus of what is known instead of the expression of the divine. It is of the essence of His mission therefore that He cannot rest in the here below, in the created. When "a certain man" says to Him, "I will follow thee withersoever thou goest," He responds, "Foxes have holes, and birds of the air have nests; but the Son of man hath not where to lay his head." His followers have here, like Him, "no continuing city." He is the source of confidence that there is meaning, and life, beyond what we have become confined in; He is "the author and finisher of our faith; who, for the joy that was set before him endured the cross, despising the shame, and is set down at the right hand of the throne of God."

Prayer

The previous chapter emphasized the power of words: the words of God and the words of Man who is in His image. They have an authority beyond what is generally credited to them in our utilitarian age. Here I want to look at a special category: the words of Man to God. To be precise, I am considering the words God gives us through Scripture to address to Him. They have the performative power of divine words, but their utterance is given to us. God gifts His *fiat* to us, to make strong the weakened grip of our speech on reality.

There are three particular prayers from the New Testament that hallow our speech. The first, the Hail Mary, centers our attention on the divine presence of Our Savior. It comes from the words of the angel Gabriel and of Elizabeth her cousin to Mary, mother of Jesus. In joining in the angelic salutation and making our own Elizabeth's words, "Blessed art thou among women, and blessed is the fruit of thy womb," we are saying yes to the Incarnation with the consent of our hearts. Invoking at the very heart of the prayer the Name of Jesus, announced by the angel and "the name which is above every name," is reaching out to God who has come to save us, for the name indeed means (in Hebrew), "God saves." The final petition of the prayer, though not in the Bible, draws on its presentation to us of the Mother of God and calls for her intercession at those two moments that contain everything: the present and the time of our passing.

Praying the Hail Mary in the rosary helps to form a contemplative spirit, since the mysteries of the rosary focus the attention on Jesus, to see whom is to see the Father. The central prayer for this formation, however, is the Our Father. As I pointed out when discussing numbers, its very structure links heaven and earth, with three (the number of the divine) petitions relating to God and four (the number of the earth) about our terrestrial life. Its words are from God and directed to God, and thus they have an especial power: indeed, there was a time when the uninitiated were not allowed to participate in its recitation. When, taught by the Lord Jesus, we pray the words recorded in the gospel, "Our Father which art in heaven, Hallowed be thy name," we are not of course adding to God's holiness, but rather reverencing it so that the eye of our heart may be turned to it. When we pray, "Thy kingdom come. Thy will be done in earth as it is in heaven," we are asking that God's kingship and power fulfill His purposes with us being helped to play our part in that, but also we are accepting reality as it is. In this (comparatively neglected) sense, the prayer helps us to be open to life and its beauty, since it is an accepting of the whole of life rather than tensing against a part of it. Similarly, when we pray, "Forgive us our debts, as we forgive our debtors," we are accepting or contemplating the whole of reality, including people who have done things that harm us; this is an opening of ourselves to God's merciful love. Finally, in praying, "Lead us not into temptation, but deliver us from evil," we ask for help in not being diverted from openness to God and for protection from malign powers that would foster that diversion.

The third of the prayers with words directly from the New Testament is the Jesus Prayer, "Lord Jesus Christ, Son of the living God, have mercy on me a sinner!" It conflates the appeal of the blind men for sight with the humble acknowledgment of the publican's prayer, "God be merciful to me a sinner." To acknowledge the darkness within oneself in the words of this prayer is already to begin to be able to see the light that is God. These three prayers, God-given through Scripture, are an efficacious orientation of the mind and heart toward the Most High. Primordially, language itself by the very meaning and truth it disclosed would have had this effect: in these darker times, a particular divine intervention with particular words makes good the falling from the beholding of what is beyond and within. These are not the only prayers from the Bible, of course: for example, the psalms are hugely important, but I will reserve discussion of them to the consideration of liturgy in the next chapter.

A Loving Letter

Addressing words, especially those given by Him to us for that purpose, to God in prayer opens us to Him, but so does attending to His words to us. This is the basis for the monastic practice of *lectio divina* or spiritual reading. Here a very helpful model is the contemplative attitude toward nature of which I wrote in the first section of this book, drawing attention to its loss and the desirability of recovering it. That is why I dealt first with our relation to nature: if we read the book of nature aright, then reading the book of Scripture in a fruitful way will come easily. This is not reading for the purpose of proving or disproving something or for our own satisfaction or for any use at all: it is simply being receptive to what the words say. I argued in Chapter Three that the cosmos is more fundamentally part of who we are than something we inspect: the latter approach, which we can also apply to our own bodies, is useful for practical purposes, but it is less illuminative of the truth of our being than the former. We can take Scripture also to be integral to who we are. It simply makes explicit what is written in the heart. It is like a series of notes that are written as a reminder. It reminds us of who we really are, of what is in the depths of our spirit. Not being separated from it, over and against what we are contemplating, is of the essence of reading it aright.

A way to begin moving to this closeness is to see Scripture as a personal letter written to us out of love by someone who knows us intimately: intimately enough to remind us of our deepest aspirations. Being loved and known like this awakens us to what matters to us at the core of our being. Teresa of Avila wrote, "Contemplative prayer in my opinion is nothing else than a close sharing between friends; it means taking time frequently to be alone with him who we know loves us." We can add that contemplative reading of Scripture is also "a close sharing between friends"—receiving what is shared with us by the all-wise God, who we know loves us. It is taking time to read His loving letter. If that love means something to us, we will be inclined to read it more than once and go back over particular passages. If that wisdom means something to us, we will attend especially to the counsel that is being offered in the letter. We will want to go beyond our own concerns and troubles and enter into the way of thinking of the One who writes to us. There will be no need to write back, since God knows the heart of Man: it is enough that our own heart is changed by what we read.

This reading will be in the spirit of love. Indeed, it will be in the Holy Spirit who is the love between the Father and the Word. This Love will help us to understand: the Lord said, "He shall teach you all things, and bring all things to your remembrance, whatsoever I have said unto you." The Holy Spirit teaches gently, and by attraction. He speaks in our heart. According to Saint Ignatius of Loyola, we can discern what God wants to draw our attention to by a feeling of consolation that certain words give us. It is to these words that it is helpful to return for further meditation. Yet the intimacy of this sharing is not merely cozy, still less a flattering intimacy. It can challenge us as well and draw attention to what needs changing in our life, to what we need to do to find a deeper peace.

For the words come from the One who is transcendent, as well as immanent. That aspect is well captured in these words of Pope Saint Gregory the Great to Theodore:

> What is Scripture if not a letter from Almighty God to His creature? If Your Excellency lived somewhere else and received a letter from an earthly monarch, he would have no peace, he would not rest, he would not shut his eyes until he had learned the contents of that letter. The King of Heaven, the Lord of Men and Angels, has written you a letter that you might live. . . . Strive therefore, I beg you, to meditate each day on the words of your Creator. Thus you will long for the things of heaven with greater desire, and your soul will be more eager for the joys that are celestial.

The Word of God puts us in touch with what is deepest in our hearts and what is highest. The stars in the night sky correspond to what is deep within each human person. They speak of a noble destiny. Scripture speaks of the same: "greater desire" and "joys that are celestial." It is a letter offering life: eternal life. This life is nothing less than the life of God. Saint Jerome, as mentioned earlier, said that ignorance of the Bible is ignorance of Christ. If we read, mark, learn, and inwardly digest its teaching then we have Christ living in us. This is the high sense in which it becomes something no longer exterior: it becomes a way of making our own what Saint Paul had reached when he wrote, "I live; yet not I, but Christ liveth in me." This life is a participation in the love the Son receives from and gives to the Father through the Holy Spirit. It is knowing the Father whom the Son reveals to us. It is the contemplation of God. I shall consider this contemplation at length in the third and final section of this book. Here I want to examine further the actual practice of spiritual reading of the Bible in the context of developing a contemplative spirit.

Spiritual Reading

This reading is personal. It follows that different people will find that different words of a text will speak to them. These are the ones through which God has given consolation to which each individual will return. Also, particular individuals may find that different words from the same text have this quality at different times of their lives. What is most apt at one point on one's journey to God may be superseded by something else. To illustrate this, I will consider three possible responses to this text from Luke's Gospel:

> And I say unto you, Ask, and it shall be given you; seek, and ye shall find; knock, and it shall be opened unto you. For every one that asketh receiveth; and he that seeketh findeth; and to him that knocketh it shall be opened. If a son shall ask bread of any of you that is a father, will he give him a stone? Or if he ask a fish, will he for a fish give him a serpent? Or if he shall ask for an egg, will he offer him a scorpion? If ye then, being evil, know how to give good gifts unto your children: how much more shall your heavenly Father give the Holy Spirit to them that ask him?

This text might speak to a serious seeker at an early stage of her or his quest simply with the words "seek, and ye shall find." They would be an affirmation and an encouragement, an indication that life does indeed have a meaning and that it is worth looking for. The same person could be further along in the journey to God and revisit the same text at a time of trouble and difficulty. At this point the words "every one that asketh receiveth" may take the attention, together with the theme that follows them: that even an unholy human father is a reliable provider, so how much more can God be trusted. This reflection could encourage trust in God's Providence and the conviction that there is a gift hidden within the darkness that is being endured. Finally, yet further on in the journey to God, there could be a thirst for a deeper spiritual life; here it could be the promise of the Holy Spirit that especially claims the attention, and this could lead to prayer for the gift of the Holy Spirit. All this, of course, does not exhaust the "infinite sweetness" of the passage: indeed, it could be argued that all the responses belong to an earlier stage of the journey since they are about what God can do for the reader rather than what the reader can do for God. The final response, however, does lead to incorporation in Christ: knowing Him as Lord, and through Him knowing the Father.

Seven Wonderful Promises

In this spiritual reading, the important thing is the willingness to *hear* what is being spoken. That is the essence of the contemplative spirit. "Opening the ears" is not enough. This point is made most emphatically in the second and third chapters of the last book of the Bible. Here there are seven wonderful promises made to the one who overcomes, who is victorious in the spiritual struggle. They are the following: eating of the tree of life; being unhurt by the second death; eating of the hidden manna and receiving a white stone with a name unknown to others; receiving power over the nations and receiving the morning star; being clothed in white raiment and having one's name in the book of life, with it being confessed by the Son before the Father and the angels; being a pillar in the temple of God forever and being inscribed with the Name of God and His city, the New Jerusalem, and with the new Name of the Lord Jesus; sitting with Him in His throne with the Father in His throne. One of these has already been considered at length; the others are similarly rich with symbolic meaning, but I will leave the details of them for your own pondering in spiritual reading. The point I want to make here is that each of them is accompanied by the same words: "He that hath an ear, let him hear what the Spirit saith to the Churches." Exactly the same words occur seven times: the number linking heaven to earth. The Bible could hardly be clearer about the importance of hearing, of having a contemplative spirit. The promises are awe inspiring. It is hard to imagine greater prizes for victory than these, which include a divine name and divine kingship.

Hearing

The words of Jesus as He goes to His passion and death are indeed true: "Blessed are they that hear the word of God, and keep it." Hearing endures as vital to the Christian tradition. Saint Benedict starts his Rule with the words, "Listen O son to the teaching of the master and incline the ear of your heart." The first encyclical of Pope Francis, owing much to the work of his predecessor named for Saint Benedict, explains the special quality of hearing:

> Knowledge linked to a word is always personal knowledge; it recognizes the voice of the one speaking, opens up to that person in freedom and follows him or her in obedience. Paul could thus speak of the "obedience of faith." Faith is also a knowledge bound to the passage of time, for words take time to be pronounced, and it is a knowledge assimilated only along a journey of discipleship. The experience of hearing can thus help to bring out more clearly the bond between knowledge and love.

This tradition of hearing, personal contact, and a journey of discipleship goes back to the words of Jesus about Himself as shepherd, reported in John's Gospel: "The sheep hear his voice; and he calleth his own sheep by name, and leadeth them out. And when he putteth forth his own sheep, he goeth before them, and the sheep follow him: for they know his voice."

Looking and hearing: these are the father and the mother of the contemplative spirit. Saint Benedict, father of monks, tells us to open our eyes to the divinizing light and with astonished ears to listen to the divine voice calling every day. The next chapter considers an activity that is quintessentially Benedictine and involves both looking and hearing: the celebration of the liturgy and the sacraments.

Chapter Six:
Liturgy and Sacrament

The Beginning and the End

he last chapter drew attention to the way the first and last book of the Bible are connected by the loss and healing of vision and by the tree of life. There is a further connection, implicit in the beginning but explicit at the end: praise and honor of God. In the book of Revelation, this is loud and clear:

> And a voice came out of the throne, saying, Praise our God, all ye his servants, and ye that fear Him, both small and great. And I heard as it were the voice of a great multitude, and as the voice of many waters, and as the voice of mighty thundering, saying, Alleluia: for the Lord God omnipotent reigneth. Let us be glad and rejoice, and give honour to Him.

In the beginning, before Adam and Eve fall from grace, it is there in its essence. Before their knowing of God is subverted, they can but praise and honor Him by all that they are and do. Adam is the first priest. Before the Fall, his every movement is liturgical in the sense that his whole life is a loving contemplation of God. Every gesture, every word is charged with a meaning beyond the mundane, filled with the praise and honor of God.

Liturgy, the formal worship of God, is at one and the same time a movement to recover that first honoring of God in its exuberant innocence and an anticipation of the final praise of heaven. Like Scripture to which it is intimately related, it is a way of healing our failure to see and hear what life really means. It is a return to the tree of life, to an openness to the life-giving wholeness of God. It is eyesalve to enable us to contemplate Him.

Emphasizing Meaning

It is a sort of emphasis. Before the Fall, ordinary language and behavior praised and honored God. Now we have to do it specially. There is a parallel with theater, which (at least in its ancient Greek origins) in the beginning had a liturgical import. Dramatic discourse and interaction highlight aspects of our life so that we can better understand their value and importance. They convey meaning. That is true for tragedy as much as for comedy, as Yeats brilliantly observed in his poem *Lapis Lazuli*:

> All perform their tragic play,
> There struts Hamlet, there is Lear,
> That's Ophelia, that Cordelia;
> Yet they, should the last scene be there,
> The great stage curtain about to drop,
> If worthy their prominent part in the play,
> Do not break up their lines to weep.
> They know that Hamlet and Lear are gay;
> Gaiety transfiguring all that dread.
> All men have aimed at, found and lost;
> Black out; Heaven blazing into the head:
> Tragedy wrought to its uttermost.

The poem goes on to consider a sculpture "carved in lapis lazuli," a most precious stone. Lapis lazuli is blue, the color of heaven. Tragedy, like the sculpture, conveys the celestial import of "all the tragic scene." In the greatest darkness, there is "Gaiety transfiguring all that dread" and "Heaven blazing into the head." It is not fiction alone that conveys meaning. Life as such has it, but on the stage we can through the dramatist's art contemplate it with special clarity. Similarly, life is to the praise and honor of God, but in the liturgy that ultimate meaning of our lives is realized with particular emphasis.

That meaning is the contemplation of the Father with Christ. According to the teaching of Dom Guéranger, the nineteenth-century French priest and monk who founded the congregation of monks to which I belong, Christ is formed in us through our liturgical participation in the mysteries of His life. He is alluding to Saint Paul writing to the Galatians, who compares his formation of Christ in them to giving birth. They are receiving the new life of which

Jesus speaks when He says, "Except a man be born again, he cannot see the kingdom of God." Great saints, such as Saint Gertrude, have been made through a life of contemplation rooted in the liturgy's Christ-centered praise of the Father. In people such as her are realized the blessings of which Saint Paul wrote to the Ephesians: "Blessed be the God and Father of our Lord Jesus Christ, who hath blessed us with all spiritual blessings in heavenly places in Christ: . . . Having predestinated us unto the adoption of children by Jesus Christ to himself, according to the good pleasure of his will, To the praise of the glory of his grace wherein he hath made us accepted in the beloved." A liturgical life is precisely "the praise of the glory of his grace." Such praise is contemplation because it is *seeing* God as He truly is, wonderful beyond all telling. It grows from *hearing* the mysteries of the life of Christ as they are unfolded in the cycle of the liturgical year in spoken and sung words drawn from Scripture.

A Great Ring

A remarkable feature of that year is that as soon as it ends, it begins again. It is not like, for example, the academic year, after which the people involved take holidays before beginning the following year refreshed by them. There is not a break marking the end of the liturgical year. The worship of the morning and of the middle of the day belong to one liturgical year; the worship of the evening belongs to the next. There is nothing whatever by way of an interval. Quite why this should be is suggested by these lines from a poem by the seventeenth-century English writer Henry Vaughan:

> I saw Eternity the other night
> Like a great Ring of pure and endless light,
>   All calm, as it was bright;
> And round beneath it, Time in hours, days, years
>   Driven by the spheres
> Like a vast shadow moved, In which the world
>   And all her train were hurled.

The significance of eternity being "pure and endless light" will be clear from the consideration of the symbolism of light in Chapter

One. The poem also distinguishes it as being like "a great Ring." In other words, it has no beginning or end. So it is with the liturgy: it is like a ring in which there is no break. It is above the linear movement of time in which there is a start and a finish. In this world of time, we are born and we die. In eternity, we simply are. The liturgical cycle takes time and makes of it a symbol of eternity. It is a means by which we contemplate eternity.

The Day, a Life, and Eternity

This is perhaps clearest in the way in which the hours or offices of worship of each day follow the same pattern. This repetition, as it were, stops time, so that there is only one day: symbolically, the great day of eternity. The offices of each day also symbolize a human life. This symbolism builds on the natural symbolism of a life being expressed by the extent of the day. The first office, of readings or vigils, corresponds to the phase of life when one is learning, involving as it does listening to the words of Scripture and its ancient commentators being read. It is, like childhood, a time of stories. It is also the time of awakening, literally and to our eternal destiny. Lauds, the office of praise that characteristically accompanies the dawning of the day, is like the first flush of life. The little offices that are interposed during the work of the day match the phase of life where work is uppermost. The evening office of vespers, when the sun is low, is consonant with the evening of life. The final office of compline culminates with the recitation of the *Nunc Dimittis*, the song of Simeon: "Lord, now lettest thou thy servant depart in peace, according to thy word"; this office is the yielding of one's life into God's hands, made explicit in the responsory, "Into your hands, O Lord, I commend my spirit," echoing and in union with the last words of Jesus on the Cross, as reported by Saint Luke. To engage with this office is, symbolically, to offer the day of one's life to the Father in union with the Son. To do it each day is to make an eternal offering of one's life: the repetition of the day makes it as it were stand still, as though it were eternal.

After the Pattern of Christ

The most fundamental union with Christ is in the Mass. I will consider this later in the chapter, but here let us look at some more links between the offices and the life of Christ. Vigils, which is often prayed while it is still dark, corresponds to His time in the tomb, sleeping in death. Lauds reflects His resurrection since it happens around the time of dawn (symbol of the resurrection) and includes the *Benedictus*, the canticle of Zechariah, with its celebration of "the tender mercy of our God; whereby the dayspring from on high hath visited us, To give light to them that sit in darkness and in the shadow of death, to guide our feet into the way of peace." It praises God for the resurrection and anticipates the eternal praise of heaven. The little office of sext, the sixth hour according to ancient reckoning, recalls His crucifixion, which happened at "about the sixth hour." Perhaps the little offices in general can be seen as recalling the hidden life of the Lord in Nazareth, since they punctuate the working day. Vespers, with its singing of Mary's canticle of praise, the *Magnificat*, recalls the Incarnation of the Lord in her exultation: "He that is mighty hath done to me great things; and holy is his name." It also points to the Cross of Christ because the greatest of the "great things" is the work of redemption accomplished upon it, and because the forthcoming ending of the day is a symbol of death. Compline as the very last office is associated with this symbol and echoes the Lord's death as well. It also recalls the presentation of the child Jesus in the Temple through Simeon's song.

Christ's death and resurrection are more clearly patterned in the liturgical cycle of the week, being marked particularly on Friday and Sunday respectively. The clearest patterning, however, is in the yearly liturgical cycle, which images the entire work of Christ. It is important that this pattern should be in the liturgy. To ignore the life of Christ and simply offer praise to the Father is to forget what Scripture says: "No man hath seen God at any time; the only begotten Son which is in the bosom of the Father, he hath declared Him." To know the Father, to recover the spirit of contemplation, we need to come to the Son who "will reveal Him." In the liturgical year, we are patterned according to Christ so that we may know the Father.

The Meaning of Blue

In it we are made one with the One who said, "Before Abraham was, I am"—we enter into the eternity He shares with the Father in the love of the Holy Spirit.

The liturgical year begins (if, in the light of what has been said above, it can be considered to have a beginning at all) with the season of Advent. This, in itself, is an indication of the liturgy's impetus toward the transcendence of time, since it has a triple reference. It recalls the ancient prophetic longing for the coming of the Messiah; it looks to His Second Coming, when God will be all in all; and it urges Christ's faithful to open their hearts that He may be born in them. This last is a being caught up in the eternal love within the Godhead. Of it Meister Eckhart wrote, "All that could ever be conceived of delight and joy, of happiness and pleasure, is no joy at all when set against the bliss which is in this birth." The season that follows, Christmas, celebrates this birth as it happened in history but also the concomitant possibility of it happening in the soul of the individual Christian.

The birth of Christ in a soul implies the unfolding of His life in that soul, and this is facilitated and celebrated as the liturgical year continues. The ordinary time of the year following Christmastide is reminiscent of the hidden years at Nazareth, and Lent remembers His wrestling with temptation in the desert. I will look more closely at the central three days of the liturgy, in which His death and resurrection are enacted, at the end of this chapter; here let me simply remark that these three days are a sharing with Him in the greatest journey of them all, discussed in the last chapter. It is a journey with Him to the Father. The seven weeks of Eastertide—seven times seven days, with all that this implies for the linking of heaven and earth—are by being a celebration of His resurrection also a celebration of the possibility of our breaking through death into the life of eternity. Humanity's place in this life is celebrated in His ascension. Pentecost celebrates the birth of Christ in His entire Church, the birth of His Body the Church, through the gift of the Holy Spirit. The eternal life in heaven that is won for us through the birth of Christ (in history, in the soul, and in the Church) is already, through a glass darkly, open to us through contemplation. We know it as we look to the Father with Christ in the power of the Holy

172

Spirit. This life that we share, the life of the Holy Trinity, is celebrated a week after Pentecost. The next great feast, of the Body and Blood of Christ, celebrates its ongoing sacramental presence among us. The great feast of the Assumption that follows some weeks later celebrates the full entry into this life of Mary, first among Christians, God's mother and the mother of this life in us.

This has been a very brief outline of an extraordinarily deep and rich subject. If you want to consider it more closely, Dom Guéranger's *The Liturgical Year* will be a guide for you. My point here is that the pattern of the year's celebration patterns us after Christ so that we may share His life of contemplation of the Father. It fosters in us a contemplative spirit. It enables us to live already in a sense out of time, in eternity. The ordinary time that comes after Pentecost until the year begins again (if, once more, it is appropriate to talk of liturgy, that images eternity, beginning) is really neither ordinary nor time. It is a continuation of an extraordinary sharing in the life of Christ, which is eternal. The imaging of the eternal by the cyclical in the liturgical day, week, and year also characterizes the three-year cycle of gospel readings for the Mass, the number three expressing God.

Soaring Above

The liturgy offers the possibility of contemplating the eternal beyond the material creation that we are now all too apt to mistake for the term and boundary of reality, instead of seeing it truly as the messenger of reality. However, it is not the only way. As suggested in the previous chapter, the rosary also offers an entry into the mysteries of Christ's life, and Scripture is a means to a living relationship with Him. Yet this entry into the eternal, this sharing of eternity with Christ, is not something that comes to us whether we seek it or not. This point is made in the lines that follow those quoted above from the poem by Henry Vaughan. They present various characters (such as, for example, the miser) who are as it were beneath eternity, caught up by their preoccupations in the toils and travails of time. The final lines of the poem show us others who do enter eternity, contrasting them with those who remain below:

Yet some, who all this while did weep and sing,
And sing, and weep, soared up into the Ring,
  But most would use no wing.
"O fools", said I, "thus to prefer dark night
   Before true light,
To live in grots, and caves, and hate the day
   Because it shows the way,
The way which from this dead and dark abode
   Leads up to God,
A way where you might tread the sun, and be
   More bright than he."
But as I did their madness so discuss
   One whispered thus,
This Ring the Bridegroom did for none provide
   But for his Bride.

The singing and weeping is praise of God and sorrow for their sins. The soaring up into the Ring corresponds to what Eckhart, further on in the sermon quoted above, says about the soul in which Christ is born:

> The soul in which God is to be born must drop away from time and time from her, she must soar aloft and stand gazing into this richness of God's: there is breadth without breadth, expanseless expanse, and there the soul knows all things, and knows them perfectly.

This is entering eternity where there is no dimension of space and separation; this is recovering the fullness of knowing because it is a sharing in *God's* knowing; this is contemplation in its integrity. The ones who prefer dark to light (with all that this symbolizes) are like Plato's dwellers in the cave who prefer shadows (what belongs to this world) to the daylight (the reality that the things of this world signify). They do not soar up because the Ring of eternity is given by the Bridegroom only to His Bride: by Christ to His Church. Nuns making their profession of consecration to Christ literally receive a ring; all who share Christ's life in the Church, whether through the liturgy, through reciting the rosary, or simply through knowing Him in the Scriptures, receive what the Ring means: eternal life.

Chapter Six: Liturgy and Sacrament

The Value of Uselessness

The liturgy belongs to what I called in Chapter Two intensive living. In that chapter, intensive living was considered with regard to one's relation to space and the goods of this world. There is of course a further dimension to our life in this world: time. Liturgy does for time what generosity and sharing do for space: it takes away its dominion. Not only does its cyclical nature do this: so does the fact that the liturgy has no practical use. It doesn't do anything, or at least it does nothing relating to this world. It is not a project of some kind, preparing for a particular outcome. And although people who are present at it may be deeply affected and may even have their lives changed by the experience, it is not primarily celebrated for their benefit. I remember once a guest in a monastery being surprised that the early office of vigils was celebrated even if no one apart from the monks attended it. He had missed the point that it is directed to God, not an audience. Its celebration is part of celestial living in the sense given in Chapter Two. It joins "the voice of a great multitude" in heaven saying, "Alleluia." It belongs with the treasured things that are useless, that is to say, the most valuable. This statement may seem paradoxical at first glance, but if we think about it then it makes sense. If something has a use then it is undertaken for the sake of something else: its value is subordinate to the value of that other thing. For example, somebody might work very hard for the sake of providing his family with food and lodging. The work is useful: it brings in money. Yet the money's value is subordinate: it is treasured because it can provide the necessaries of life for the members of the worker's family. They are his true treasure, and if the little ones are too young to work and are themselves more than enough work for their mother, they will all be useless. So is the liturgy. It does not manipulate anything to effect a change; it does not lead to anything different in this world; it opens only to heaven.

The spirit of the liturgy is expressed in this prayer:

> O God, who cause the minds of the faithful to unite in a single purpose, grant your people to love what you command and to desire what you promise, that, amid the uncertainties of this world, our hearts may be fixed on that place where true gladness is found.

The liturgy is about fixing our hearts where true gladness is found. That is why it is essentially a joyful thing! It is also about unity, with all that this implies concerning wholeness and life as explained in Chapter Two, and about singleness of purpose. That purpose (the fixing of hearts where true gladness is found) is shared by the whole Church: not only the Church of today but also the Church through the ages. It is a timeless purpose, linking those striving to fix their hearts where true gladness is found to those who no longer strive because their hearts are thus fixed irrevocably, for they are in heaven. This purpose is single in that it is not adulterated by any other purpose: there is no swerving from it as time goes on. The spirit of that singleness is well captured by John Henry Newman in a passage I want to quote. He is writing about how people worshipped in ancient times, but I would want to add that this spirit is alive today in our monasteries. These are his words:

> Unwavering, unflagging, not urged by fits and starts, not heralding forth their feelings, but resolutely, simply, perseveringly, day after day, Sunday and week-day, fast-day and festival, week by week, season by season, year by year, in youth and in age, through a life, thirty years, forty years, fifty years, in prelude of the everlasting chant before the throne,—so they went on, "continuing instant in prayer," after the pattern of psalmists and apostles, in the day with David, in the night with Paul and Silas, in the dark, in the day-break, at sun-rising, in the forenoon, at noon, in the afternoon, at eventide, and on going to rest, still they had Christ before them; His thought in their mind, His emblems in their eye, His name in their mouth, His service in their posture, magnifying Him, and calling on all that lives to magnify Him, joining with Angels in heaven and Saints in paradise to bless and praise Him for ever and ever.

The fact that this is all one long sentence shows how far away we are in the spirit of the liturgy from the culture of the sound bite, the urge to grasp hold of the next new thing that time proffers. The beauty of the liturgy is its timelessness and openness to eternity.

Daily Fare

I have indicated the structure of the liturgy and its spirit. I want now to look at what constitutes its daily fare. A feast is not an inappropriate metaphor for it, yet it is not like Dives in the parable, who "fared sumptuously every day." The daily bread of the liturgy is the psalms. They are Christ's prayer to the Father, not just in the sense that He would have prayed them on earth but also in the sense that in Him all of humanity is summed up, and the psalms contain and offer to God the whole of human experience. For reasons given when wholeness was discussed in Chapter Two, it is important that we not edit our humanity when we bring it before God. It may be appropriate before an earthly sovereign to put on our best clothes and politely not mention our more anguished and less presentable feelings. But God knows everything, and it is only by bringing the whole of who we are, by coming before Him in our integrity, that we can give Him due honor—give Him what He wants, which is our very selves. Hence the psalms contain verses of complaint and cursing; anguish and aggression; dissatisfaction and desperation. Some of these are sometimes edited out for worship, but that is, I think, a mistake. We bring the whole of our humanity before God, or we bring in effect nothing.

That does not mean that, when in a bad mood, monks or nuns pick out psalms that convey their feelings for choral recitation. As Newman observed in the passage quoted above, they are not in the business of "heralding forth their feelings." Rather, they pray with and on behalf of Christ for the whole of humanity. Thus the discipline of the psalmody may oblige them to sing joyful psalms of praise when they are not feeling so inclined. It is a matter of receiving the texts as they are. This belongs to the contemplative spirit. It does not manipulate to impose self but rather beholds and listens. Its way of knowing is directed not by self but by God, as revealed in His word. It allows itself to be drawn into the ecstatic and joyful contemplation of the Father by the Son. Hence it willingly makes its own words such as these:

> O COME, let us sing unto the LORD: let us make a joyful noise to the rock of our salvation. Let us come before his presence with

thanksgiving, and make a joyful noise unto him with psalms. For the LORD is a great God, and a great King above all gods. In his hand are the deep places of the earth: the strength of the hills is his also. The sea is his, and he made it: and his hands formed the dry land. O come, let us worship and bow down: let us kneel before the LORD our maker. For he is our God; and we the people of his pasture, and the sheep of his hand.

To pray like this is to recover a sense of a world instinct with divine meaning; it is to know God's dependability and to trust Him; it is to be happy.

In praying the psalms, we bring not just the whole of our humanity in all its variations of mood but also the whole of the Bible and the whole of sacred Tradition into our prayer. What was said in the previous chapter about an integrated understanding of Scripture applies especially to its use as prayer. Above all, we bring into our prayer Christ as He looks to the Father. To make this entire context clearer, I want to look at some psalmody in more detail.

Poor and Needy

Let us start with Psalm 86. I will look at it little by little. It begins, "Bow down thine ear, O LORD, hear me: for I am poor and needy." Saint Athanasius comments that the psalmist speaks like a weak, sick man who needs the doctor to lean over to hear him. This brings to mind the divine Physician who said, "They that be whole need not a physician, but they that are sick." To pray as one who is "poor and needy" is to open oneself to His mercy; it is to know oneself truly as "wretched, and miserable, and poor, and blind, and naked"; it is to be able to receive the promised blessing, "Blessed be ye poor: for yours is the kingdom of heaven." The healing, the mercy, the blessing are available because, as Saint Paul tells us, "For your sakes he became poor, that ye through his poverty might be rich." The "poor and needy" is not just the one who prays—it is also Christ, to whom she or he is united. Saint Augustine says that it is Christ in the form of a servant, Saint Jerome that it is Christ near His passion. In knowing in prayer our poverty and neediness, we know Our Savior who has entered the heart of our need.

This is evident in the words of the psalm that follow: "Preserve my soul; for I am holy." We offer in our prayer not our own holiness but that of Christ, "the Holy One of God." We do this with trust, saying with the psalmist, "O thou my God, save thy servant that trusteth in thee." Origen comments that the servant of God puts all his hope of salvation in God alone. The psalm continues, "Be merciful unto me, O Lord, for I cry unto thee daily." This is, for the Christian who prays it, an identification with the publican in the parable, who prayed "God be merciful to me a sinner" and was justified. The singer seeks the joy of this justification, continuing, "Rejoice the soul of thy servant; for unto thee, O Lord, do I lift up my soul." In effect, this is asking God to enter the soul of the one who prays, for He is the source of joy. It is imperishable joy, as Saint Augustine's commentary makes clear: "Our hearts will not go mouldy, if raised up to Him. If you had grain down in the basement, you would move it higher up, lest it rot. You find a better place for your grain: will you allow your heart to moulder on earth? If you think it right to take your grain upstairs, lift your heart to heaven. . . . You are in heaven if you choose God as your love." The joy is asked for with confidence: "Thou, Lord, art good, and ready to forgive; and plenteous in mercy unto all them that call upon thee."

The confidence comes from the fact that it is Christ Himself speaking in the following plea: "Give ear, O LORD, unto my prayer; and attend to the voice of my supplications. In the day of my trouble I will call upon thee: for thou wilt answer me." To pray it is to join with Him who "offered up prayers and supplications with strong crying and tears unto him who was able to save him from death, and was heard." The next verse of the psalm, in asserting that God does not divide His sovereignty, focuses the heart on the oneness of God, saying, "Among the gods there is none like unto thee, O Lord; neither are there any works like unto thy works." This universality means that, as the psalm goes on to say, "All nations whom thou hast made shall come and worship before thee, O Lord; and shall glorify thy name." This looks to the final gathering of the elect announced in the book of Revelation: "A great multitude, which no man could number, of all nations, and kindreds and people, and tongues." All are drawn by the greatness and oneness of God, saying to Him in the words of the psalm, "Thou art great and doest wondrous things: thou art God alone."

In the next verse, the psalmist asks to be formed by God: "Teach me thy way, O LORD; I will walk in thy truth: unite my heart to fear thy name." To contemplate God truly, to come before Him with awe, we need a heart made one. Only a heart whole and simple in its innocence can behold Him. He is hidden from the heart divided and dissipated among the things of this world, and thus the psalmist prays, "I will praise thee, O Lord my God, with all my heart: and I will glorify thy name for evermore. For great is thy mercy toward me: and thou hast delivered my soul from the lowest hell." This deliverance is in union with Jesus, who "was not left in hell, neither his flesh did see corruption." The verse that follows in the psalm can be applied to Him when His enemies "consulted that they might take Jesus by subtilty, and kill him." It laments, "O God, the proud are risen against me, and the assemblies of violent men have sought after my soul; and have not thee before them." It can also, as Origen observed, refer to demonic attack.

The psalm ends, as many of the psalms do, with a renewed confidence in God and His qualities of mercy, truth, and patience:

> But thou, O Lord, art a God full of compassion, and gracious, long-suffering, and plenteous in mercy and truth. O turn unto me, and have mercy upon me; give thy strength unto thy servant, and save the son of thine handmaid. Show me a token for good; that they which hate me may see it, and be ashamed: because thou, LORD, hast holpen me, and comforted me.

A Christian praying this psalm knows that the Son of Mary, God's handmaid, has indeed been saved from death and hell, and he or she with Him. The "token for good" has been given: it is (as Saint Bede observed) "the sign of the prophet Jonas." This is help and comfort indeed.

The Mother of Us All

I have commented in detail on this psalm to show something of the richness of meaning that psalmody can have when understood in the context of the whole Bible and the commentary on it by the fathers of the Church. It can form our prayer in Christ, molding us so that we, like Him, can contemplate the Father. It does so with full recognition of the fact that our life here is limited, that "we spend our years as a tale that is told." Yet, together with awareness that this life "is soon cut off," it holds before us the fullness of life "hid with Christ in God."

It was argued in the previous chapter that history can be symbolic as much as anything in nature. This symbolism is not absent from the psalms, which speak not only of the great Exodus from Egypt but also of the Babylonian Exile, when the Jewish people were separated from Jerusalem, their home. The latter is a symbol of the "Jerusalem which is above, . . . which is the mother of us all." This is our homeland, "a better country, that is, an heavenly." The terrestrial Jerusalem symbolizes this because it is a focal point of pilgrimage and worship. People come to this one sacred place to worship in a way that represents their coming at the end of their journey of life to the one all-holy God to adore Him for eternity. As the Jewish people look from their exile with longing to Jerusalem, so do the denizens of time and space long for the unbounded life of eternity.

Psalm 137 tells the tale, orienting our gaze toward our true home:

> By the rivers of Babylon there we sat down, yea, we wept, when we remembered Zion. We hanged our harps upon the willows in the midst thereof. For there they that carried us away captive required of us a song; and they that wasted us required of us mirth, saying, Sing us one of the songs of Zion. How shall we sing the LORD's song in a strange land? If I forget thee, O Jerusalem, let my right hand forget her cunning. If I do not remember thee, let my tongue cleave to the roof of my mouth; if I prefer not Jerusalem above my chief joy.

The rivers of Babylon contrast with the rivers of paradise, where "a river went out of Eden to water the garden; and from thence it was parted and became into four heads." Babylon is identified in the book of Revelation as "the habitation of devils, and the hold of every foul spirit, and a cage of every unclean and hateful bird." Its name is cognate with "Babel," meaning "confusion," for this was the name given to the place where a tower was built to reach heaven, and "the LORD did there confound the language of all the earth."

The multiplication of languages—because people no longer perceive the unity of God through their tongue and culture, so that these become a false and rival absolute (as explained in Chapter Four)—is associated with the sin and division that come of separation from the divine unity that prevails in the heavenly Jerusalem. "Jerusalem" means "vision of peace"—peace flows from unity, the divine unity. The willows are a symbol of weeping: sorrow for sin, and the sorrow of separation from God, of exile from the heavenly Jerusalem. Though we are held captive in "our bourne of Time and Place," the time will come when our captivity will pass and we will be happy in that city where, in Saint Augustine's words, "we delight in God, where free from all anxiety, we live in united fellowship with our brothers and sisters." We are in Babylon not as citizens but as captives: our true citizenship is in heaven, "for here we have no continuing city, but we seek one to come."

The world in which we are for a time prisoners would like to seduce us into finding joy in what passes, requiring "of us mirth, saying, Sing us one of the songs of Zion," yet we are forbidden to "cast pearls before swine." The loss of dexterity and speech, and of the ability to play the harp, is preferable to not subordinating every joy to that of our heavenly homeland. This psalm is a lament for a real historical exile, but it is also universal in singing about exile from the happiness for which we were made and to which all right endeavor tends. To sing it as this is to orient the heart toward that happiness and already to glimpse it "through a glass darkly."

Praying Twice

Singing is the characteristic way in which the psalmody is recited in the monastic tradition. Words from the psalms are also sung in Gregorian chant during the Mass. Music is significant in the liturgy because it accomplishes the same action as the liturgy: taking time and making it into a symbol of eternity. Music as such represents the various changes that come through the passage of time, but the underlying harmony makes a whole of it, and this whole is a symbol of eternity. The oneness that a musical composition has reflects the oneness of God, and the beauty of its ordering, His beauty. Saint

Augustine famously said that to sing is to pray twice. Perhaps this is explained by another remark of his to the effect that singing is the mark of one who loves. Sung prayer reaches out to God with love. Longing and love: these connect us with the Jerusalem above.

Sacraments and Symbolism

There is also a formal connection. That is established through the sacraments of the Church. A sacrament is an efficacious symbol: at one and the same time it does something and signifies what it does. It uses both nature and word, particularly the words of Scripture. There is therefore a sense in which everything written in these first two sections of this book has been a preparation for reflection on the sacraments. Knowing nature and word in a contemplative spirit enables us to receive what is being communicated through the sacraments. They are God's formal means of giving us His grace, through which we have communion with Him. Yet, as Scholastic theology taught, God is not bound by the sacraments. As I have repeatedly insisted, something of His realm is reflected in everything: every flower that blooms, every word that is spoken. They would have no existence otherwise. And God is in no way blocked by lack of formal apparatus from reaching out to any soul who wishes to establish a bond of love with Him. The sacraments do not exclude any other work of grace; rather, they are the work of grace clearly and formally manifest. It is as though "in these last days," when Man has become so insensitive to the presence of the divine, it has been necessary for Providence to give him some means he can unhesitatingly rely upon to open himself to that bonding which alone can save him from the dispersion and division of his soul.

This means uses what has always spoken of the divine. I hope that the earlier chapters have given you some sense of this speaking: the radiance of nature and the power of the word. Sacraments set apart as sacred certain actions and words so that the divine radiance and power can be received by one whose heart is open to them. In doing this they are in relation to the natural and cultural worlds what revelation as such is in relation to the world before Man sought to make "a name" for himself, instead of honoring that of God. To use the words used in Chapter Four of revelation in general, they are God coming into the particularity of the human situation to make Himself known. Through the sacraments, we know God, we can contemplate Him. I have emphasized looking and hearing in what I have said about recovering a contemplative spirit, but the sacraments in fact appeal to all five senses. We see actions and hear words, but we also feel the touch of anointing in the sacraments of confirmation and extreme unction, and taste and smell are at work when Holy Communion is received, to say nothing of the fragrance of incense.

The senses work together to convey one thing: the healing and redeeming presence of God in Christ. We can therefore speak in a way of a sixth sense: the sense of a presence received through the other senses. This sixth sense used to be called the common sense, meaning that which the five senses have in common—the intuition of the reality that the other senses, working together, convey. A notion of how the senses work together is conveyed by the awareness that people sometimes have that the meaning conveyed by one sense can, as it were, be translated into the language of another sense, so that, for example, the soprano's notes are sweet, the bass's savory. This is given poetic expression by Wordsworth's friend, Coleridge:

> O! The one Life within us and abroad,
> Which meets all motion and becomes its soul,
> A light in sound, a sound-like power in light,
> Rhythm in all thought, and joyance everywhere—
> Methinks, it should have been impossible
> Not to love all things in a world so filled;
> Where the breeze warbles, and the mute still air
> Is music slumbering on her instrument.

The third of these lines ("A light in sound, a sound-like power in light") points to different senses conveying the same thing, and in view of what has been said in Chapter One about light and in Chapter Four about the primordial creating speech of God, it can also be said to point to the divine presence in creation. "The one Life within us and abroad" is God sustaining His creation, and the sounds of creation the music whose harmony He is. Since God is love, Coleridge's sense of the lovability of all creation follows. It can also be ascribed to the fact that he was on his honeymoon when he wrote these lines, but this human love is in any case a symbol of the divine love, as will be explained more fully later in the chapter. Coleridge is of course writing about the senses working together to convey the divine presence in nature rather than in the sacraments, but the latter is an intensified instance of the former. The God who is love makes known in a special way in His sacraments the goodness and mercy evident in His creation.

Baptism

First among these sacraments is baptism, because it is the first sacrament of initiation (the others being confirmation and the Eucharist). It is sometimes called "the gateway to the sacraments." It is given by threefold immersion in or sprinkling with water accompanied by the words of the minister: "I baptize you in the Name of the Father, and of the Son, and of the Holy Spirit." The symbolic importance of water has already been discussed in Chapter Three. It represents the One for whom all is possible, the Omnipotent, because of the universality of its presence and the variety of forms it can take. It is a potent symbol of both life and death, apt therefore for the One who is master of both and transcends them both, for to Him "the darkness and the light are both alike." Only contingent being, God's negation of nothingness, knows life and death. In Christ, in His descent into contingency, God triumphs over death. It is this triumphant life that He shares through water in baptism. As water cleanses from dirt, as the great inundation swept away the wickedness of the world, so baptism cleanses from guilt. As the Israelites went through the water of the Red Sea to flee from Egypt and as they went through the water of the Jordan to enter the Promised Land, so through the water of baptism the Christian escapes the consequence of sin and the judgment that comes with death. The threefold immersion or sprinkling corresponds explicitly to the three persons of the Holy Trinity, and the power of God's speech is lent to the minister who invokes their Names, invoking also the name of the person baptized in token of entry into God's life fulfilling, rather than subtracting from, her or his identity.

Baptism is the seed of contemplation because it initiates us into Christ's life, and thus incorporated we can contemplate the Father with Him. It is a sharing in His great journey to the Father, since "so many of us as were baptized into Jesus Christ were baptized into his death." That journey leads ultimately to the direct contemplation of God, the beatific vision, but even to set out on it is to orient what we do to what is consonant with that vision, since "as Christ was raised up from the dead by the glory of the Father, even so we also should walk in newness of life." The new life interrogates each prospective action to see if it is friendly to God, for in that friendship is its whole substance. It is guided in this discernment and strengthened in its resolve to act on it by the gift of the Holy Spirit, which is given to the person baptized as a sibling of Jesus, on whom "the Holy Ghost descended in a bodily shape like a dove upon him." This manifestation during His baptism is for our benefit, namely, so that we may know what we are receiving. So also is the voice "from heaven, which said, Thou art my beloved Son; in thee I am well pleased"—an articulation of the infinite love that is the Holy Spirit, a love that is the dynamo of our contemplation of God.

Oil

There are other symbols used in the baptismal ceremony: the white garment, whose import was discussed in Chapter Five; the candle, the meaning of which will be discussed later in this chapter; and oil. This last is used in several sacraments, and so I will consider its use here. My guide is Gulielmus Durandus, a thirteenth-century French bishop. In his *Rationale Divinorum Officiorum*, he gives a detailed commentary on the symbolic significance of the liturgy. In entering into the liturgy with a view to recovering a contemplative spirit, it can help to go back to a time like his, when there was a lively and widespread sense of how this symbolism worked. Not all points of ceremonial in the celebration of the sacraments are the same now as in his day, but some remain, and about these he can enlighten us.

During the baptismal ceremony as it now is in the Catholic Church, there comes a point when the parents are asked to adjust the garments in which the baby is swaddled so that the priest or deacon can get his thumb on his or her chest for the anointing with the oil of catechumens. This is generally explained as a sign that the child will need to be taught the Christian Faith as he or she grows up, and so it is. Durandus, however, takes us deeper. "First," he writes, "it is to be noted that there are two sorts of anointing: the outward, which is material or corporal and visible, and the interior, which is spiritual and invisible. The body is anointed visibly by outward anointing." The anointing is, as it were, a word of God: the exterior the sound He utters, the interior what it means. This word is what linguists call "performative language." It *does* what it says. It is not like everyday human speech, "For my thoughts are not your thoughts, neither are your ways my ways, saith the LORD. . . . My word . . . that goeth forth out of my mouth . . . shall not return unto me void, but it shall accomplish that which I please, and it shall prosper in the thing whereto I sent it." Durandus explains what is accomplished inwardly by the anointing with the oil of catechumens: "The one to be baptised is anointed with oil on the chest in which is the place of the heart first of all so that through the gift of the Holy Spirit, he or she abjures error and ignorance and receives the faith aright, for the just man lives by faith, and it is through the heart that one believes in justice." It is through the gift of the Holy Spirit that the child will receive faith, not by parents or priest holding forth to him or her, since "no man can say that Jesus is Lord, but by the Holy Ghost."

The oil then is the word of God performing the work of teaching the child faith. It is the presence of the Word of God, whose Spirit teaches. It is the presence of Christ, whose name is derived from "chrism" (consecrated oil)—"or rather," says Durandus, "chrism is named from Christ." His name means "the anointed one": He is anointed by the Holy Spirit, as shown at His baptism, and He shares that anointing with His sisters and brothers. Christ as teacher is also at work in the sacraments of confirmation and ordination, again by the anointing of oil. His presence is tangible in these two sacraments: the hands of the bishop who acts in His person are laid on the head of the one who is receiving the sacrament. Furthermore, it is audible: the bishop says to the person to be confirmed, "Be sealed with the gift of the Holy Spirit," and he prays over the one to be ordained for the outpouring of the Holy Spirit and the gifts of the Spirit needed for his ministry. Although "the invisible things of him from the creation of the world are clearly seen," God condescends to us whose eyes are prone to seeing without beholding; He does so by acting in a way perceptible through several senses. In the sacraments of confirmation and ordination, He gives the Spirit who guides "into all truth" to those who need the strength to "be ready always to give an answer to every man that asketh . . . a reason of the hope" that is in them, and to those who need inspiration to teach through their preaching. The creation declares the glory of God, but He teaches us also in the intimacy of our hearts in the person of the Holy Spirit. That we might apprehend that we are being thus gifted, He gives this best and most personal gift visibly, tangibly, and audibly. Our natural senses are invited to work together so that with a sense common to them we might perceive the holy presence and be drawn into the ways of contemplative love.

Healing

There is a fourth sacrament in which oil is used: the anointing of the sick. The source text for this is in the letter of Saint James:

> Is any sick among you? let him call for the elders of the church; and let them pray over him, anointing him with oil in the name of the Lord: And the prayer of faith shall save the sick, and the Lord shall raise him up; and if he hath committed any sins, they shall be forgiven him.

Durandus cites this as referring to the exterior anointing and comments that this exterior anointing is the sign of the interior anointing, "and the interior anointing is not only a sign, that is the meaning of something, but also a sacrament, because if it is worthily received, it without doubt either does or increases what it designates: health and salvation." The state of a soul is truly known to God alone, but I have seen this sacrament increase the health of the body. Because its intention includes this, it perhaps gives the clearest examples of meaning that God wishes to express having observable results. The mechanistic view of life in the tradition of Democritus would exclude this sort of agency, but it can be aware of its effects.

The accomplishment of the deeper purpose of this sacrament is, however, known only in eternity, for it is essentially about healing a person's relationship with God. This is always what God means—love is His meaning, as Julian of Norwich taught—and the healing of relationship is the sole purpose of the sacrament of reconciliation, or confession. It is highly significant that this healing is received through hearing: the spoken word has a special power to heal, as it has to wound, for "the tongue is a little member, and boasteth great things." The healing that this sacrament gives also has a guarantee in the letter of Saint James, who writes, "Confess your sins one to another, and pray one for another, that ye may be healed." The absolution that the sacrament gives is a manifestation of the healing words of Christ: "Be of good cheer; thy sins be forgiven thee." The supernatural healing builds on the natural, for confession is a contemplation of one's own reality, itself a liberating thing since, as George Herbert wrote in this context,

> Smooth open hearts no fastening have; but fiction
> Doth give a hold and handle to affliction.

This honesty, this escape from the tangled web we weave when we labor to deceive, is a prerequisite for looking with an honest gaze toward God, to whom all hearts are open. The truth of God is known alongside the truth of oneself. That is why—to touch on writing that will be considered more fully in the next chapter—the author of the great medieval treatise on contemplation, *The Cloud of Unknowing*, recommends confession before undertaking the direct contemplation of God. In the forgiveness of sins, God Himself removes the barriers that impede the knowledge of Him.

The Ultimate Bonding

Anointing of the sick and confession are sacraments that heal a person's relationship with God. However, the greatest sacrament of relationship—the greatest sacrament—is the Eucharist, which establishes communion between God and Man. It is about the love between them, beautifully expressed in these lines by George Herbert:

> Love is that liquor sweet and most divine,
> Which my God feels as blood; but I as wine.

Durandus points out that the chasuble, the garment that the priest puts on to celebrate the Mass, symbolizes charity, without which he is "as sounding brass, or a tinkling cymbal." This charity, or love, is ultimately the bonding between God and Man, because God is the perfection and pattern of unity, the source of all peace and concord. It is this that was lost when Man no longer habitually contemplated God but rather saw only what was presenting God (nature and word) instead of beholding what was being presented (the divine presence). This book is about recovering this beholding; as was said above, everything in it so far has been in a sense a preparation for reflection on the sacraments. This is true above all for the Mass. The way we receive nature and the word, which were given to us that we might know and love God, affects deeply how meaningful for us is the Mass, which is our communion and bonding with God. I will therefore now consider in order how each of the chapters so far is relevant to our understanding of the Mass. I do not propose to give an introductory explanation of the Mass, as I suspect that most of my readers will not need it, but if this is unfamiliar territory to you there are many books, including the *Catechism of the Catholic Church*, that will help. My emphasis is on ways of understanding that foster contemplation.

Light, as discussed in the first chapter, is especially relevant to the Easter liturgy; its treatment is therefore reserved for the end of this chapter, where I shall look at the ceremonies of the final days of Holy Week as the culmination, unlocking of the meaning, and summary of the liturgy. Color, which the first chapter also discussed, is immediately relevant. The color of the chasuble worn for Mass is variable. The meaning of its color, as I hope will be clear to you by now, is not given arbitrarily by ecclesiastical authority but is in the very nature of things. Let us begin the explanation of usage with a quotation from Durandus: "White vestments are used on feasts of confessor saints and virgins who are not martyrs on account of their purity and innocence . . . however red vestments are to be used on solemnities of Apostles and Evangelists and Martyrs on account of the blood of their passion, which they shed for Christ." Red is also, concomitantly, the color of love—supremely, Christ's love. Green is the color of life on earth and is therefore appropriate for when no extraordinary manifestation of the celestial is being celebrated. Chapter One explained the appropriateness of purple, or violet, for penitential seasons, it being the color that denotes the upward movement from earth to heaven. Blue vestments (although not used universally) are for feasts of the Blessed Virgin, the light-bearer who ponders deeply. The aptness of this color for her was also explained in Chapter One, and more will be said about it in the last chapter.

Chapter Two explained how life, and indeed existence, is related to the presence of the whole: each and every thing images the unity of God. This understanding of nature helps us to understand the presence of Christ in Holy Communion: this presence is undivided, however many receive Him. The genetic identity contained in a single cell is an image of this. As each new cell retains this identity as it multiplies, so each particle of the consecrated host is the Body of the Lord, whole and entire, however many times it is broken. When discussing wholeness and life, I referred to the teaching of Aquinas that all of God is in each and every thing. In the Mass, this presence is, as it were, raised to a new power: communion with God no longer depends on a primordial sensitivity to His presence everywhere; it is available explicitly in the sacred banquet of the Eucharist. This shares the form of ordinary eating, but the good is the ultimate nonrival good: we cannot deprive another person of the Lord simply because we have received Him. His unity without rival is received with no provoking of rivalry. His presence is wholeness incarnate and is multipliable without limit.

The oneness of the communicant with Christ in the Mass is conveyed in the fourteenth-century English poem *Piers the Plowman*. Its author, William Langland, reports how he fell asleep while men in the offertory procession were taking the bread and wine up to the altar:

> In midst of the Mass, when men went to offering
> I fell eftsoons asleep, and suddenly I dreamed
> That Piers the Plowman was painted all bloody
> And came in with a cross before the common people,
> And right like in all limbs to our Lord Jesu.
> And then called I Conscience to ken me the sooth:

> "Is this Jesus the jouster" quoth I "that unjustly was done to death?
> Or is it Piers the Plowman? Who painted him so red?"
> Quoth Conscience, and kneeled then: "These are Piers' arms,
> His colours and his coat-armour, but he that cometh so bloody
> Is Christ with his cross, conqueror of Christians."

This (somewhat modernized) extract from the long narrative poem shows Piers, who represents human nature, looking like Jesus. The dreamer consults his conscience as to who it really is. The signs of identity of the person he sees (the arms, the colors, and the coat armor) belong to Piers, yet the wounded and victorious person is Christ. They are one: Christ, the winner of healing, has identified Himself with the whole of humanity. That oneness can be seen by a way of knowing that distinguishes without dividing and intuitively grasps life and wholeness rather than focusing analytically in the manner apt for considering what is dead and fragmented. This intuitive knowing can apprehend the vivifying transformation that the bread and wine undergo on the altar as they become the Body and Blood of Christ, effecting the sanctifying change that Christ brings to the people who bring them to the altar as tokens of themselves.

Chapter Three pondered what is written in nature, the great book of God, seeing in each created thing a showing of God and His image, Man. In the Mass, God responds to the failure to notice what is shown of Him, the resting in the created that is allowed to block what it manifests, by Himself *becoming* what belongs to time so that we may not be deprived of His love. Man retreats from eternity; the Eternal One enters time. The Mass is the prolongation of the miracle announced in the gospel: "The Word was made flesh, and dwelt among us." No longer does Man need to see God *through* the world, for God is *in* the world. This is the sublime generosity of God showing itself according to the principle articulated by Saint John of the Cross: "The Lord has always revealed to men the treasures of His wisdom and His spirit, but now that the face of evil more and more bares itself, so does the Lord bare His treasures the more." The more myopic Man becomes, the more visible God makes Himself.

Chapter Four looked at the power of words, instancing God's creating word. The archetypal power of His *fiat* created Man with the words, "Let us make man in our image, after our likeness." Man forgets to listen to the word that gives him being. God's response is humbling in its generosity: He allows Man to say that word that gives *Him* being! First of all, that is Mary's *fiat*, "Be it unto me according to thy word," at which God becomes incarnate in her womb; then it is the word of each priest—however unworthy—who says the words of consecration, "This is my body . . . this is the chalice of my blood," at which God becomes present in the Most Holy Sacrament of the Altar. No longer does Man need to hear God through the word that He speaks in all His creation (including himself): Man can himself speak the words through which God becomes present, so much does God want to give all that He is.

Chapter Four also looked at the creed as a symbol in the original sense of a token, one part of which fits together with another. The creed is proclaimed in the Mass on Sundays and solemn feasts in token of our connection with God. It is a summary of the truth of Scripture, which is itself a means by which God reaches out to us so that we may bond with Him. Chapter Five's exploration of how this works is particularly relevant to the Mass, since the first part of it is the liturgy of the word, in which Scripture is read aloud and may be commented on in a homily. This divine reaching out is a preparation for the even more generous outreach in the liturgy of the Eucharist that was discussed above. The scriptural text can on occasion directly illuminate what is to happen in this latter part of the Mass. For example, the sixth chapter of Saint John's Gospel contains teaching about it. Jesus says, "My Father giveth you the true bread from heaven. For the bread of God is he which cometh down from heaven, and giveth life unto the world." Following the line of argument given in Chapter Five in connection with the true vine, we can say that Christ is more truly the bread that is brought up to the altar than the bread is itself, *even before* it is consecrated, since all of creation is an expression on a lower level of the Word through whom it is made. In this sense, the bread has become Him (by its existence) before He comes in the appearance of the bread (in the consecration). In the great sacrament, the showing forth of Christ the Word becomes more intense and explicit: always, the more Man's eyes are dimmed, the brighter is His presence.

Sex as Symbol

This chapter itself has of course been an introduction to the consideration of the Mass, since everything about the pattern of the year applies particularly to its celebration, and everything about the liturgy and sacraments as a means of bonding with God applies most of all to the communion it offers. The final sacrament to be considered is also about bonding. I have left marriage till last not because it is the only sacrament that I have not received, but because it is a special case of something natural having a supernatural meaning. Weddings are often thought of as getting a minister to bless a couple, and this is all good and proper. Yet something more remarkable takes place. To grasp this, it is helpful to recall that in the Catholic tradition the sacrament is not in fact given by the minister but by the couple to each other, and that it is not regarded as being valid until it is consummated. This was a bit clearer in medieval times when there was less clerical involvement. I touched on the symbolic meaning of marriage in Chapter Two, pointing out that the married couple is an image of the creative oneness of God, but there is more to say. Sexual union, which establishes the married state, is a natural symbol of union with God. In it wholeness and love are found; in a certain way, it heals a sense of incompleteness. From what has been said in this book about how what is in the cosmos gives expression to what is celestial, it follows that union with God is the greater reality that is bodied forth on the lower level in sexual union. The latter and lower is also a means to the former and higher, since being married fosters habits of unselfishness.

Saint Paul writes about marriage being a symbol of the union of Christ with His Church (that is, the union of God with all the faithful) in the letter to the Ephesians:

> Husbands, love your wives, even as Christ also loved the church, and gave himself for it.... So ought men to love their wives as their own bodies. He that loveth his wife loveth himself. For no man ever yet hated his own flesh; but nourisheth and cherisheth it, even as the Lord the church: For we are members of his body, of his flesh, and of his bones. For this cause shall a man leave his father and mother, and shall be joined unto his wife, and they two

shall be one flesh. This is a great mystery: but I speak concerning Christ and his church.

In speaking here of the union of Christ and the Church being reflected in marriage, Saint Paul is not simply picking out something natural to illustrate a point; rather, he is drawing attention to a primordial symbol. The bliss of union is a symbol of the bliss of the soul's eternal union with God. (The devil Screwtape in C.S. Lewis's *The Screwtape Letters* says that pleasure is "His invention, not ours.") That is why sex is sacred. It points also to the union of Father and Son, who bring forth the Holy Spirit, as in the human family father and mother bring forth a child.

More About the Greatest Journey

Everything in the liturgy and the sacraments is oriented to our entry into this supreme union of the Holy Trinity, in order that we might love and praise the Father with the Son in the joy of the Holy Spirit, but nothing more so than the celebration of the final days of Holy Week, from the Mass of the Lord's Supper on Thursday evening to the Easter Vigil on Saturday night. This breaks into the regularity of the offices as the glory of Christ's resurrection breaks into the world, so that where He has gone we might follow. It is the pattern by which everything else is patterned: the very heart and meaning of each Mass, each liturgical day, and each liturgical year. It is the summary and summit of all that the liturgy does.

These three days act out the greatest journey of them all, fore-shadowed by the crossing of the Red Sea and the Jordan, the journey beyond sin and death. Their celebration passes through the agony of the weight of the world's sin to a threefold declaration of peace; through death to life; through three hours of darkness to the light of dawn accompanied by a celestial messenger "whose countenance was like lightning." To be present at these ceremonies is to contemplate the blazing of the trail that leads to our Homeland; to walk on that path in our hearts; to unite ourselves to the One who has gone before. There are three days; three ceremonies; three stages to the journey. They mark humanity's recovery of the vision of peace, of fellowship with God.

The first day is about love, the second about self-effacement, the third about transcendence. It is easy to mistake feeling good around people for love. True love is love "unto the end" that continues despite being "troubled in spirit" by betrayal; it is love that serves others most humbly; it is love that says, "This is my body, which is broken for you." Holy Thursday presents this love; it invites those present to be in communion with it.

Good Friday presents the opposite of the spirit that would impose its own name on what it sees, blinding the eye of the heart. It shows us One who when accused "answered nothing" and gave "never a word" in reply to false testimony; it shows us One who asks for forgiveness for those who wrong Him; it shows us One who finishes the work of love with His own death. The ministers echo this self-effacement by silently prostrating themselves before the bare altar at the start of the liturgy. The universal sweep of intercession gathers the troubled of the whole world into the embrace of the limitless grace that the sacrifice of the Cross brings upon the earth. The thrice held high cross presents this sacrifice, and people humble themselves before it. Finally, communion with this supreme love is offered.

The third day, the great day, "the day the LORD has made" in which we rejoice and are glad, is the day that (through a glass darkly) reveals eternity to us. It shows us that "the light shineth in darkness; and the darkness comprehended it not"—it cannot be swallowed up because "the darkness and the light are both alike" to God. Both symbolize Him, yet on this night light especially. In the great Easter Vigil, this light, showing God victorious, is kindled from sacred fire. The paschal candle, its malleable wax a symbol of the suffering Savior, with five grains of incense thrust in to indicate His wounds, is lit from this fire. Three times it is lifted up with the announcement "the light of Christ," as the cross was lifted up the day before: it is the same One lifted up, and viewed without fragmentation it is the same lifting up—the darkness and the light are both alike—and the words He spoke are fulfilled: "I, if I be lifted up from the earth, will draw all men unto me." The people follow the paschal candle into the church and light their candles from it. The *Exultet* is sung in its praise, proclaiming that it is "a fire into many flames divided, yet never dimmed by sharing of its light." This corresponds to the fact that the life of the risen Christ is not a terrestrial good, diminished by sharing, but a celestial one unlimited by time and place and wholly present wherever it is received.

Then a whole panorama of Scripture is read, starting with seven readings from the Old Testament—the number signifying the union of earth (four) with heaven (three). These include the story of the creation of the earth, the crossing of the Red Sea (anticipating the exodus Jesus was to accomplish in Jerusalem), and the sacred promise, "A new heart . . . also will I give you, and a new spirit will I put within you: and I will take away the stony heart out of your flesh, and I will give you a heart of flesh." They are followed by two readings from the New Testament, taking the number to nine: the number of heaven multiplied by itself. The first proclaims that this great journey is also our journey, "for if we have been planted together in the likeness of his death, we shall be also in the likeness of his resurrection." The final reading is the gospel proclamation of Christ's victory over death, His transcending of the limitations of this life here below, where space and time separate, and decay and loss dissolve. The preacher then propounds the momentous implications of the readings.

In the third section of the ceremonies of the third day, our sacramental incorporation into Christ risen from the dead is celebrated. This is accomplished first by baptism (or simply the renewal of baptismal promises if there is no one to be baptized) and then by the Eucharist, in which the risen Lord becomes present to us, fulfilling once again those words which, like all of God's words, do what they mean: "Peace be unto you." This is the peace of being made whole through our entry into the wholeness of God's eternal life that cannot be taken away. The whole celebration of this wonder, greater than the creation of the world, is ended with the simple declaration of praise: thanks be to God, alleluia, alleluia!

PART THREE
Contemplating God

"And this is life eternal, that they might know thee
the only true God and Jesus Christ, whom thou hast sent."

Chapter Seven:
The Father of Mercies

Beginning Again

t may seem that everything has now been said. We have seen how human perception has become dulled in its beholding of nature and its listening to the word, and how God in His Providence has used these in a special way to lead humanity back to Him. Yet equally it could be argued that nothing has yet been said: I have only been dealing with means of knowing God, whether natural or sacred, and have not touched on the direct contemplation of God as He is in Himself. Indeed, I could repeat what I said at the start of Chapter Five when first broaching the subject of Scripture: it would be entirely reasonable to start a book about contemplation here, bypassing everything that has been said and beginning with the direct gaze toward God as He is in Himself. Indeed, many books about contemplation do start at this point.

The more discerning of these books, however, assume at least a familiarity with Scripture, liturgy, and the sacraments. And the best writers on these subjects would not presume to be able to wrap them up so as to preclude them from opening into the mystery of God in ways beyond the ken of their discourse. The truth is that both what has been discussed already in this book and what has not yet been discussed are needed. In finishing what I have written, I am beginning what I have to write. Let me explain why.

If we trust to our celebration of the liturgy to bring God to us, we are in the position of those mentioned in the psalm that says, "Some trust in chariots, and some in horses." That is to say, we have substituted means for end. The psalm goes on, "But we will remember the name of the LORD our God." Significantly, the Name of the Lord could not ordinarily be spoken: the tetragrammaton was too sacred for utterance. This conveys the truth that God is beyond human speaking. If we say our liturgical celebration has got Him nailed up in a box, there is no truth in us. Nature after the Fall became opaque for Man, who allowed it to replace for him what it was intended to convey, as though mistaking an envelope for the letter inside it. Chapter Four explained how a further such fall is conveyed in the story of the tower of Babel: here a cultural or language system becomes the absolute, the name Man makes for himself, replacing the Name of the Lord. It is entirely possible for this opacity, this replacing of meaning with means, to happen with regard to the explicitly sacred. I have already commented, in Chapter Five, on how the Bible cannot be a closed system. Neither can the liturgy or the sacraments. If they are merely self-referential, they are closed to the divine.

The attempt to make of them a closed and self-sufficient system frustrates their purpose. If the heart rests in the things of nature and the words used by the liturgy and the sacraments, that is just a religiously pretentious version of making an idol of the natural world and human cultural or language systems. It is the Fall again, a fall from a higher level. The same is true of theological systems that pretend to contain all truth. To the constructors of these the Lord's words to the lawyers speak: "Ye have taken away the key of knowledge: ye entered not in yourselves, and them that were entering in ye hindered." Unless there is a sense in which it falls silent before the mystery of God, theology cannot speak of Him. There can be no saying it all.

To put all this in theological terms, we need to supplement the cataphatic with the apophatic. The cataphatic way of doing theology is making positive statements about God. It is not enough on its own. We also need the apophatic way, which is denying that such statements have any final truth. This is because God cannot be entirely defined (with the implications of limitation that definition has) with words and concepts that are appropriate for and oriented toward His creation, those being the sort at our disposal. That would be as if we tried to talk about a cook entirely in terms of the food she produced. We could say, "She is a blancmange sort of person," or, "She is characterized by her signature dish of steak with lightly fried onions," but we would have to add that this doesn't really give the full picture of her life. The cook might not even be a woman! So in our contemplation of God, we need to be able to let go of the limitations that our world- and time-related words and concepts have and to go beyond them to His bare reality. It is with recovering contemplation in this sense that this last section of this book (particularly this chapter) is chiefly concerned.

God in Ordinary Life

Yet it is not good either just to cast oneself straight into the void, trying to act as if one had no body or senses. A total abstraction from creation is very difficult for us, and it is psychologically unhealthy to rush heedlessly into it. God is known in particular circumstances even though He is never tied to any particular circumstances. The whole is known in the part, but the part is never the only way the whole can be known. God is there in ordinary life, but if ordinary life were different, He would still be there. The circumstances or the form of our life can never themselves be God for us. There is a parallel point to be made about language. Just as nature shows God but does not contain or limit Him, so language can speak of God but cannot contain or limit Him. This is true even of sacred formulations like that of the creed. Saint John of the Cross compared the expression of the truths of faith to silver plating on gold: the silver is valuable, but not as valuable as that which it covers. The truths of faith are valuable, but not as valuable as the reality of God that they hide; they are oriented to rational discursive thought, symbolized by the moon rather than the sun. These considerations are germane to my use of poetry to illustrate what I am saying about contemplating the super-terrestrial. Poetry says something that can be understood, but it says nothing that can be tied down in the sense of a legal or technical definition. It is open.

So here is some more poetry, in this case to illustrate the above point that God is known in ordinary life:

> O WORLD invisible, we view thee,
> O world intangible, we touch thee,
> O world unknowable, we know thee,
> Inapprehensible, we clutch thee!

Does the fish soar to find the ocean,
The eagle plunge to find the air—
That we ask of the stars in motion
If they have rumour of thee there?

Not where the wheeling systems darken,
And our benumbed conceiving soars!—
The drift of pinions, would we hearken,
Beats at our own clay-shuttered doors.

The angels keep their ancient places;—
Turn but a stone, and start a wing!
'Tis ye, 'tis your estrangèd faces,
That miss the many-splendoured thing.

But (when so sad thou canst not sadder)
Cry;—and upon thy so sore loss
Shall shine the traffic of Jacob's ladder
Pitched betwixt Heaven and Charing Cross.

Yea, in the night, my Soul, my daughter,
Cry,—clinging Heaven by the hems;
And lo, Christ walking on the water
Not of Gennesareth, but Thames!

The poem is called *The Kingdom of God*, and the first stanza expresses both the fact that the celestial realm is invisible, intangible, unknowable, and inapprehensible, *and* the fact that we nevertheless perceive it. In theological words, it takes both an apophatic and a cataphatic approach. The second stanza hints at how this perception occurs. Just as the fish and the eagle are in their element and do not have to leave it to find it, so in God "we live and move, and have our being." We could say that it is in our knowing that we know God. It is not one thing rather than another particular thing that shows us God; rather, it is the fact that we know a particular thing. At the deepest level, that is a sharing in His creating and sustaining presence, and evidence that He is. "The drift of pinions"— the wings of an angel or even the Holy Ghost—is there, but characteristically we are not open to it. Our doors are "clay-shuttered" because we are focused on the outward, material, and passing rather than the inward, spiritual, and eternal, which in fact never leaves us. It is "estrangèd faces" that stop us from being aware: the angels are there as ever, but we are looking the wrong way. The "many-splendoured thing" is the unlimited possibility and glory of God.

The poem is not telling us to buy a train ticket to Charing Cross station and walk by the River Thames in order to find this glory. It is saying that God was *even there* for the poet, Francis Thompson, who knew times of particular dereliction thereabouts. God is in everything. Yet God transcends everything, so there is also a sense in which He is nowhere. The practice of going apart to pray, of retreating from the business of ordinary life, of leading a solitary and secluded life in quest of God, does therefore have a purpose. God is hidden in mystery. How then do we contemplate Him in His hiddenness and mystery? Let us start by going back to the liturgy for a moment.

The Father

The characteristic prayer of the liturgy is directed to the Father through the Son. The praise of the psalmody is offered to the Father in the Son. Yet compared to the Son, the Father has very little explicit attention in the liturgy. Indeed, one could say that He has only the third part of a feast dedicated to Him: the Feast of the Holy Trinity, which He shares with the Son and the Holy Spirit. There is a sense therefore in which the mystery of God, His hiddenness, belongs especially to the Father. Jesus tells us that no one knows the Father "save the Son, and he to whomsoever the Son will reveal him." He indicates that this revelation is in His own person in the words, "He that hath seen me hath seen the Father." We come to Jesus by the Holy Spirit, so we can say that the Son and the Spirit bring us to the Father. Saint Irenaeus teaches that the Son and the Spirit are the two hands through which God created the world; we can see them also as the two hands by which He redeems the world. They are the hands by which the Father clasps to His breast the prodigal who has wandered to a far country where he has spent all his living. That clasping is possible despite the fact that "no man hath seen God at any time," because "the only begotten Son, which is in the bosom of the Father, he hath declared him." We can be clasped to the Father's breast because of our incorporation into the Son, who is already there. What is in that breast? Love, evidently, since "God is love." That love calls to us, and with our love we call back: "Deep calleth unto deep."

Yet the mystery remains. We know that we reach out to the Father with Christ in the power of the Holy Spirit by our love, yet He remains hidden. It is not an oversight that the Father is so little shown in the liturgy: the liturgy on pain of being ungodly cannot contain and explain the divine mystery, and this paucity of representation acknowledges and places before us this mystery. The Spirit and the Son bring us into the mystery. Even the name "Father" speaks of mystery. By definition, a father is one who was there before us and knows what we do not know. My own father fought in the Second World War and had direct knowledge of what can only be history to me. God the Father is all-knowing and more hidden than a human father: Julian of Norwich said that Man in this life is blind and cannot see God, our Father, as He is. As with the cook and her (his?) blancmange, we know Him rather by His gifts. As an earthly father does, He knows "how to give good gifts." Like the father of young children, He knows what our needs are. He is "the Father of mercies, and the God of all comfort."

Touching the Truth of God

Reaching out to the Father is essentially a mystery of love reaching out to love, or rather of love seeking to return love, since "herein is love, not that we loved God, but that he loved us." Yet love seeks the truth of the beloved. Without it, can it be anything but a sentimental fantasy? On the human level, we would not take seriously one who said he loved another and yet could give no account of seeing or hearing that other or at least of some grasp of the other's reality. Can loving and knowing ultimately be separate? If we love God, then what kind of knowing can be involved? Although the focus of my consideration of the mystery of God is on the Father, the Son and the Spirit are in essence no less mysterious. Love for them too is unseeing: Saint Peter writes of the Son, "Whom having not seen, ye love," and the Lord says to Nicodemus that the Spirit is like the wind— "thou . . . canst not tell whence it cometh and whither it goeth." The questions come down to this one: How can we touch the truth of God? The rest of this chapter pursues this question. I will first of all look in depth at a couple of pertinent Scripture sayings, and then I will consider the teaching of two old English writers on the subject.

One Thing Needful

One portion of Scripture is quoted above all others on the subject of contemplating God. Its importance merits its quotation in full:

> Now it came to pass, as they went, that he entered into a certain village: and a certain woman named Martha received him into her house. And she had a sister called Mary which also sat at Jesus' feet, and heard his word. But Martha was cumbered about much serving, and came to him, and said, Lord, doest thou not care that my sister hath left me to serve alone? Bid her therefore that she help me. And Jesus answered and said unto her, Martha, Martha, thou art careful and troubled about many things: But one thing is needful: and Mary hath chosen that good part, which shall not be taken away from her.

Mary in this passage is traditionally the model of the contemplative. Sitting at Jesus's feet, she hears His word; she hears God. The contemplative is one who hears God. What was said in Chapter Four about the power of words is very relevant to this hearing. God's word creates the cosmos and Man, its summary and His image. His word in Christ re-creates Man, restores His image in him so that he becomes like Christ and fit to behold the Father with Him. Mary hears and is made whole. She enters the wholeness, the oneness of the Holy Trinity. She with her "one thing" is contrasted with Martha with her "many things." The "one thing needful" is the undoing, through this contemplation, of the division that entered the world with the fruit of the tree of the knowledge of good and evil. Duality and separation and the willful choosing of this rather than that, as though Man were God, the arbiter of all, lead to people being "troubled about many things." There is a loss of wholeness and life, as discussed in Chapter Two. The way back to God is

the way that goes beyond distinction and duality to find His wholeness. It is the way of an unfragmented epistemology. Nicholas of
Cusa, cardinal and scholar of the fifteenth century, cries out to God
thus:

> I have discovered that the place where you are found unveiled is
> girded about with the coincidence of contradictories. This is the
> wall of paradise, and it is there that you reside. The wall's gate is
> guarded by the highest spirit of reason, and unless it is overpow-
> ered, the way will not lie open. Thus, it is on the other side of coin-
> cidence of contraries that you will be able to be seen and nowhere
> on this side.

The "spirit of reason" corresponds to what I called "solid body
thinking." In space, one thing being there contradicts another. In
the spiritual realm, it is not like that. For example, as Meister Eckhart observed, God's justice and His mercy are the same thing, and,
as Saint Augustine observed, God can be contained in the smallest
thing but cannot be limited by the largest thing. In Him, all is one.
"Reason," in the sense of the way of thinking that is adapted to our
way of knowing the material, will not reach Him; rather, it keeps us
outside His realm, in which "the wolf . . . shall dwell with the lamb,
and the leopard shall lie down with the kid; and the calf and the
young lion and the fatling together; and a little child shall lead
them." This is a non-adversarial realm; the "little child" is Christ the
Lord, the Word incarnate who gathers all that are contrary into
unity. To enter this realm, we have to go beyond dividing into this
and that, beyond choosing one thing or another: we have to accept
totally everything that is, turning from any partiality or imposition
of self, in loving union with the will of God.

The author of the anonymous English medieval treatise *The
Cloud of Unknowing* (whose teaching will be discussed more fully
later in this chapter) writes—in terms similar to those of Nicholas
of Cusa—about God not being found by rational choice between
contrary pairs, and how to reach Him by going beyond this. The
language of the original is very beautiful, but I will modify it slightly
here (and in subsequent quotations from the same author) for ease
of reading. He explains,

> Silence is not God, nor is speaking God; fasting is not God, nor is eating God; solitude is not God, nor is being in company God; nor even any of all the other such two contraries. He is hid betwixt them, and may not be found by any work of thy soul, but only by love of thine heart. He may not be known by reason. He may not be thought, acquired, or discovered by understanding. But He may be loved and chosen with the true, loving will of thine heart. Choose thee Him; and thou art silently speaking and speakingly silent, fastingly eating and eatingly fasting; and so forth for all the remnant.

The distinction between "soul" and "heart" is in effect the distinction between the human faculty that thinks and acts in this world and the faculty within that simply beholds or hears the immutable things of God—the intellect, as defined in Chapter One. We cannot reach God by distinction and analysis, only by reaching out in love from our immortal and transcendent spiritual center. That is a deeper thing than any spiritual practice such as silence, fasting, or solitude. It is neither any of these nor their opposites.

It may be objected to what I have just said that love is an act of the will and therefore cannot be linked to the work of the intellect. Yet will *is* involved in knowing: this is an act of intentionality, as phenomenological philosophers put it. We can turn our souls to God or not. The distinction between love and knowledge is more an analytic one than a descriptive one: in reality they work together, they are aspects of the same relation. I touched on this knowing involving willingness when I spoke in Chapter Four of reading a symbol. Certainly it can be said of God—as it is said of some people—that to know Him is to love Him. The reverse could also be said, that to love Him is to know Him. Different schools of spirituality have emphasized different aspects, but the difference is more in the mode of exposition than in what is being expounded. If these considerations about knowing and love are now generally lost to view, that is because the epistemology that is tacitly adopted in our epoch is one that gives a false impression of passivity in the knowing self: as though it were a cinema screen onto which projection is made. Yet that neglects the full reality of the human mind, which—as argued in Chapter Three—is in partnership with nature to put in place what it perceives. It follows that, even if its relationship with God must be radically different from that with nature since Man is a creature and God the Creator, it does choose whether or not to be in that relationship, however passive it might be. And that choice is one of love.

Before leaving the subject of transcending contraries, I want to adduce a third text by a twentieth-century writer with an intuition similar to those of the two ecclesiastical authors. Samuel Beckett insisted that this is not a poem but rather a short story, although it is very poetic. It has been hauntingly sung in German translation. It is called *Neither*:

> to and fro in shadow from inner to outer shadow
> from impenetrable self to impenetrable unself
> by way of neither
> as between two lit refuges whose doors once
> neared gently close, once away turned from
> gently part again
> beckoned back and forth and turned away
> heedless of the way, intent on the one gleam
> or the other
> unheard footfalls only sound
> till at last halt for good, absent for good
> from self and other
> then no sound
> then gently light unfading on that unheeded
> neither
> unspeakable home

Here both the self and the world veil the ineffable, and it is always the one not paid attention to that seems to offer hope of finally seeing it. Yet this hope is "heedless of the way" that is by neither. The "unheard footfalls only sound" echoes Francis Thompson's "O WORLD invisible, we view thee"—in both cases there is an apprehension of something beyond what senses can perceive, yet received as though through a sense. The "footfalls" (also the title of a short play by Beckett about a solitary woman) suggest a presence. Finally, there is an end to looking in the wrong places, a "halt for good." The sound ends. It was no more than the effect of the presence, and the "light unfading" (the immutable divine presence) is known where it had hitherto not been looked for, "on that unheeded / neither"—the "coincidence of contraries," as Nicholas of Cusa put it. "He is hid betwixt them," as the medieval text put it. There, where God is, is heaven, is home. It cannot be spoken of.

This quest for what is beyond our thinking is the "good part" spoken of to Martha; it means going beyond or betwixt our self and the world, going beyond or betwixt the duality of our sublunary life, going beyond or betwixt any pair of opposites. Martha is "cumbered" because she has made an absolute (which she expects her sister to obey) of what belongs to this world. The only true absolute is God, in whom all things are one. To see how we behold His "light unfading," let us turn to another Scripture text that is vital to the whole contemplative tradition.

Purity of Heart

"Blessed are the pure in heart: for they shall see God." The other beatitudes from the Sermon on the Mount will be looked at in the next chapter, but this one needs to be considered now. Contemplation of the Father—beholding God, listening to God—*depends* on purity of heart. It is the *sine qua non* of seeing God. The eye of the heart needs to be single, to be whole, because without this wholeness there is insufficient likeness for any perception of God—like recognizes like and God is perfect wholeness. Any adulteration of motive in the quest for God is disabling; any wanting His gifts in preference to Him is a block on the way; any division in how we see frustrates the vision of the One who is God. That division is never in what is, still less in God: it is only in the human heart. It can be divided by a selfish wish, by a failure in the confidence that He is all in all, by seeing in a divided way. That selfishness is a hindrance to openness to the God of love is obvious enough, and that trust and belief in Him are the great enablers of the quest for Him is clearly central to the spiritual teaching of the Christian tradition—but perhaps in this age it is more difficult to grasp the need for undivided seeing. That is because we are so trained to know by what works for getting what we want: seeing is allowed to become the same as dividing and judgment.

How pernicious this is for seeing God is clear from the parable that Jesus spoke "unto certain which trusted in themselves that they were righteous, and despised others." Of two men praying, one "stood and prayed thus with himself, God, I thank thee, that I am not as other men are." The other said, "God be merciful to me a sinner." The latter only is "justified." More than anything else in the gospels, self-righteousness is excoriated. William Blake speaks in the same vein with prophetic trenchancy: "In Hell all is Self Righteousness; there is no such thing as Forgiveness of Sin; he who does Forgive Sin is Crucified as an Abettor of Criminals." Self-righteousness divides; forgiveness unites. Judging others creates a center that cannot include all: only God's mercy can do that. "Judge not that ye be not judged," teaches the Lord, because judgment leaves the soul divided and therefore not capable of the merciful unity that is God. Such is its judgment.

It could be objected that judging people is not at all the same as judging things. This is true, yet to judge either is not to see whole. The danger is that the division and judgment that go with analysis become a dominant epistemological model, so that just as nature is looked at with a view to its usefulness or friendliness to our particular purpose, so are people. This of course happens when people are viewed in terms of their economic function. They are judged. Indeed, the particular boast of the unjustified Pharisee in the parable just cited is, "I give tithes of all that I possess." Judging nature to achieve an outcome that is beneficial to others or oneself can, in context, be meritorious, yet people are not separate from nature, and this outlook, this way of knowing, can all too easily drift to include them. There is a proper judgment of people, but it can only ever be provisional, for a particular purpose, as when we judge whether or not a person should be employed in a specified capacity. There is an improper judgment of nature: rapacious, depredatory, and in violation of the spirit of God that inhabits it. That can spread not only to the malign judgment of people (under, as Blake was acutely aware, the color of moral virtue) but also to the judgment of God Himself. In its common form, this is the despising of God because such and such an ill exists in the world. Of course, it is necessary to be an arbiter of righteousness to be able to make this claim.

You need to block God by taking His place. You need to divide yourself from God.

That is ultimately hell. Heaven and hell is the great divorce, as C. S. Lewis put it. It is not actually a division made by God in the sense that He wants anyone not to receive His mercy. It is rather a division in the soul reflected in its spiritual destiny. It is in reality the same light that illuminates the blessed in heaven that radiates toward those in spiritual torment. God is never other than one. It is simply that in the latter case light is perceived under its aspect of duality. That is to say, it is known in its interaction with the material, the extended rather than unified. And light's interaction with the material is fire. The symbolism of nature makes the point clear: there is a single radiance, and we can receive it either as one, that is, spiritually, or as divided, that is, materially. We can choose unity or division: the light of heaven or the fire of hell. That is the same, as will be clear from Chapter Two, as the choice between life and death: eternal life or "the second death" identified in the book of Revelation with "the lake of fire."

Joy and Woe

In its fundamental outlook on the world, people, and God, singleness of heart does not judge. It accepts all. Everything that is has been given permission to be by God: who are we to countermand that? This is not to say that we do not work to remove evils: that we do, but the *heart* is not caught up in the judgment and analysis needed for this. The heart contemplates all as one. Chapter Two will have made clear that this includes all of one's own experience. It means not tensing against the difficult parts. That is why Blake wrote,

> Man was made for Joy & Woe,
> And when this we rightly know,
> Thro' the World we safely go.

We are safe because we accept God's will in both the good and the bad. Like Saint Thérèse, Blake understood that the difficult aspects have their purpose, and gave this insight an expression similar to that of the weaver poem cited in Chapter Two:

> Joy & Woe are woven fine,
> A Clothing for the Soul divine;
> Under every grief & pine
> Runs a joy with silken twine.

The difference between the joy and the woe is that the joy is forever for those who are pure in heart and can see the whole here below and concomitantly the beatific vision of the supreme Unity in heaven. The woe "is but for a moment."

This means that complaining is not consonant with a contemplative spirit. That is why Saint Benedict, father of Western monasticism, is so insistent that monks should not "murmur." This is not because he wants monks to have a difficult life: he is also insistent that their needs should be properly catered for. It is just that they should not allow bitterness or resentment about anything that seems imperfect to them to eat into their singleness of heart. They seek the perfection of accepting the imperfect. They aspire to follow the gospel injunction, "Be ye perfect, even as your Father which is in heaven is perfect." They want to have that wholeness, oneness, and purity of heart that enables them to contemplate God. How is this to be found?

God's Work

To answer this question, I will now turn to the two old English writers I promised to consider in connection with touching the truth of God. They will be our guide in the quest for purity of heart that enables us to touch it. They are first the medieval author of *The Cloud of Unknowing* (who has already been introduced) and second Augustine Baker, the seventeenth-century English Benedictine monk who did much to preserve the teaching of the *Cloud* author. The latter was also aware of the doctrine of the great Carmelite teachers of contemplative prayer, Saint Teresa of Avila and Saint John of the Cross. He was therefore a channel through which the contemplative spirit was kept alive in England even when the old way of knowing was being lost from the culture in general, just as the earlier English author was himself a transmitter of ancient Christian wisdom. With these two I will look first of all at prayer;

then at what needs to be forgotten for the purposes of contemplative prayer; next at the experience of the total mystery of God; following that at the concomitant sense of our wretchedness in the light of God's glory; and finally at the goal of union with God.

The first thing to be said is that the work of prayer is God's work. Our whole outlook in these days is one fashioned by the notion that we make our world and ourselves as we want them to be. Prayer, especially contemplative prayer, starts from the premise that God is the ground of our being and therefore we are contingent. Unlike God, we do not have absolute being. In prayer, therefore, it is God who fashions us rather than we who present design proposals to Him. Our part is essentially giving Him permission to do this, since in His love He will not violate our freedom. The project management is all His. Hence *The Cloud of Unknowing* teaches, "He will be seen to work as He pleases, where He pleases, and when He pleases." *The Book of Privy Counselling*, a related treatise, says, "It is necessary that Almighty God with His grace always be the chief stirrer and worker, either directly or indirectly; and thou, or any other like unto thee, shall be only the consenter and sufferer: saving that this consent and this suffering shall be, in the time of this work, actively inclined to and made capable of this work." This inclination and capacity are of course also gifts of God.

Specifically, our prayer is the work of the Holy Spirit. As Saint Paul says, "We know not what we should pray for as we ought: but the Spirit itself maketh intercession for us with groanings which cannot be uttered." It is the Holy Spirit who brings us to Christ, incorporates us into Christ, and forms us in Christ through the liturgy and the sacraments. The *Cloud* author takes this for granted: he is concerned with how the prayer goes after this. He tells us how the Holy Spirit inspires us to pray to the Father in the Son. We are to pray with "a sharp dart of longing love." This is directed at the "thick cloud of unknowing" that hides God. The longing is directed toward the mystery of God, hidden in the depths of our intuition rather than in the elaboration of our thoughts. Our guide advises,

> When thou . . . feelest by grace that thou art called of God, Lift up thine heart unto God with a humble stirring of love, and mean

God that made thee, and redeemed, and hath graciously called thee to this work: and receive no other thought of God. And yet not all these but if it pleases; for a naked intention directed unto God sufficeth, without any other cause than Himself. And if it pleases thee have this intent wrapped and folded up in one word, for thou shouldst have better hold thereupon, take thee but a little word of one syllable; for so it is better than of two, for ever the shorter it is, the better it accordeth with the work of the spirit. And such a word is this word GOD or this word LOVE. Choose thou which of the two thou wilt, or another as it pleaseth thee: that which thou likest best of one syllable. And fasten this word to thine heart, so that it never goes thence for anything that befalleth.

The emphasis is on simplicity of thought about God and simplicity of address to God. These reflect the simplicity *of* God: His simple unity. The trend is to integrity. This is in the sense that this prayer leads to honest and right living and also in the concomitant sense of leading to oneness and life. In God, right living and life as such are not divorced. There is no separation in Him.

We live in a world that is given its coordinates of space and time by separation. Augustine Baker teaches the spiritual tradition of how to move the attention in prayer from this to the divine unity:

He that would become spiritual ought to practise the drawing of his external senses inwardly into his internal, there losing and, as it were, annihilating them. Having done this, he must then draw his internal senses into the superior powers of the soul, and there annihilate them likewise; and those powers of the intellectual soul he must draw into that which is called their unity, which is the principle and fountain from whence those powers do flow, and in which they are united. And lastly, that unity (which alone is capable of perfect union with God) must be applied and firmly fixed on God.

The trend is to unity within that enables openness to God's unity. Something of this internal unity is suggested by the reflections in the previous chapter in connection with the sacraments and the verse of Coleridge that was cited about how we can perceive a presence with more than one sense, or, more accurately, with the sense that is common to all the senses. There is an inward self within which God dwells, and His presence is perceived with a similarly common inner sense. Baker's expression of this process is very abstract, and his use of the word "annihilate" may seem negative. However, the apophatic spiritual tradition teaches that we need to deny what is less real for the sake of apprehending that which is more real. What is perceived by senses directed outward belongs to the passing and therefore relatively insubstantial; what is apprehended by the unified heart of our being contains and transcends all of this. This contemplative apprehension is "a pure, simple, and reposeful operation of the mind, in the obscurity of faith" by which a soul "simply regards God as infinite and incomprehensible verity, and with the whole bent of the will rests in Him as (her) infinite, universal, and incomprehensible good." The simplicity is all.

Forgetting

This simplicity is the goal of contemplative prayer, and the closer it approaches this simplicity, the less it can be expressed. It can start with words and thoughts that take their form from this world and gradually become more immaterial in a process that Baker compares—because of its lack of obviousness—to wheat growing. It is a movement from the outward to the inward. Traditionally, this can take the form in an individual's life of deciding to "leave the world" to enter an enclosed religious life. I have put the traditional phrase in quotation marks to indicate that the difficulties of ordinary living in the world are in no way escaped by the movement. Yet the phrase does express what is symbolized by the decision: the aspiration to move from what is outward and dispersed to an inner, immaterial reality where what is grasped by the senses ceases to command the heart. This aspiration is expressed in this poem by Gerard Manley Hopkins:

> ELECTED Silence, sing to me
> And beat upon my whorlèd ear,
> Pipe me to pastures still and be
> The music that I care to hear.

Shape nothing, lips; be lovely-dumb:
It is the shut, the curfew sent
From there where all surrenders come
Which only makes you eloquent.

Be shellèd, eyes, with double dark
And find the uncreated light:
This ruck and reel which you remark
Coils, keeps, and teases simple sight.

Palate, the hutch of tasty lust,
Desire not to be rinsed with wine:
The can must be so sweet, the crust
So fresh that comes in fasts divine!

Nostrils, your careless breath that spend
Upon the stir and keep of pride,
What relish shall the censers send
Along the sanctuary side!

O feel-of-primrose hands, O feet
That want the yield of plushy sward,
But you shall walk the golden street
And you unhouse and house the Lord.

And, Poverty, be thou the bride
And now the marriage feast begun,
And lily-coloured clothes provide
Your spouse not laboured-at nor spun.

The poem is about withdrawing from the things of the senses and how that leads to greater awareness because of openness to the divine. It is called *The Habit of Perfection*. It is about getting into the habit of being perfect even as our "Father which is in heaven is perfect" and about taking the monastic habit. Each sense is drawn inward as Baker advises. Silence is a new kind of music leading to "pastures still"—the phrase evokes the Good Shepherd and the stillness of taking in the whole as discussed in Chapter Two. Silence, which has a "great value" according to Saint Benedict, involves not speaking, a surrender to God who is the source of all speech. The withdrawal of the sense of sight from being caught in this world is in quest of "the uncreated light." This is what "simple sight"—the single, undivided eye of the heart—seeks. The sense of taste is given less scope, with confidence in the promise, "Blessed are ye that hunger now: for ye shall be filled." The sense of smell is directed to what is beyond this world through the incense rising to heaven. The sense of touch has contact with the Lord Jesus in the consecrated host, which it can "unhouse and house"—take out of and return to the tabernacle. It is a wedding to poverty, a marrying into a kingdom as promised by the Lord when He said, "Blessed be ye poor: for yours is the kingdom of heaven." This abandonment of the things of this world is not the same as being abandoned in this world. There is no need to take "thought for raiment"—like "the lilies of the field," the one who seeks "first the kingdom of heaven" will find that clothing and every other material need "shall be added." This is a withdrawal from the outward to be dedicated to its source, God. He can but reciprocate the love this movement toward Him expresses and as Lord of all give all that is needed. It is all about love: as Baker writes, "All our perfection consists in a state of love."

Love forgets all except the Beloved. And so *The Cloud of Unknowing* tells us, "Put a cloud of forgetting beneath thee, betwixt thee and all the creatures that have ever been made." This is the same advice that Baker gives in telling us to draw external senses inward. It may appear that this leaves us with nothing, but the *Cloud* author asks and answers a very pertinent question: "Who is it that calls it nothing? Surely it is our outer man, and not our inner. Our inner man calls it All." The appearance of "nothing" does not matter, therefore, since "though our outward man perish, yet the inward man is renewed day by day." The inward man lives with the immortal life of God Himself. This is truly all, were it but known. It is only the deviant epistemology of recent centuries that is limited to seeing nothing.

Love in quest of the Beloved leaves behind the outward things that can be perceived by the senses. It also needs to leave behind what its thought can grasp, since

> of God Himself can no man think. And therefore I will leave everything that I can think, and choose for my love that thing that I cannot think because He may well be loved, but not thought. By love He may be gotten and held; but by thought neither. And

therefore though it be good sometimes to think of the kindness and the worthiness of God in particular and though it may be illuminating and contribute to contemplation nevertheless in this work it shall be cast down and covered with a cloud of forgetting.

The Book of Privy Counselling (a treatise attributed to the same author) supplements this teaching of *The Cloud of Unknowing* with the advice, "Look that nothing remains in thy working mind but a naked intent stretching into God, not clothed in any special thought of God in Himself, how He is in Himself or in any of His works, but only that He is as He is." The working of the rational mind compared to this operation is, the treatise affirms, as the moon to the sun at "the brightest time of midsummer day." The former's light cannot survive the advent of the latter: "As soon as a soul is touched with true contemplation, as it is in this noble making nothing of itself and making all of God, then surely and truly then dieth all man's reason." This comparison corresponds to what was said in Chapter One about the moon representing the light of Man's reason and the sun God's truth. The journey from one to the other is, as was said there, the journey from the brain to the heart, given that the heart is not understood in any merely sentimental sense but rather as the seat of the intellect, by which we apprehend God without ratiocination. The author of these precious medieval treatises is teaching us how to make that journey.

This teaching corresponds to the more systematized exposition of the sixteenth-century Spanish Carmelite, Saint John of the Cross. He explains the making of the journey in terms of growth in the three theological virtues: faith, hope, and love. Faith is the reaching out to God without the evidencing of the senses and reason that we have just considered. The virtue of hope (in God) is considered by John of the Cross to take over the human memory, and this corresponds to the advice in *The Cloud of Unknowing* about forgetting, since if in the time of contemplation anything other than God occupies the mind, "then is that thing above thee for the time, and betwixt thee and thy God." Turning the attention of the soul to less than God is a thwarting of the soul's longing, a frustration of its hope. Man's thought is worth more than all the world, and God alone is truly worthy of it. The third theological virtue, love, is of course exercised in the "sharp dart of longing love" directed toward God in the cloud of unknowing.

In offering God attention, it is important to withdraw it not only from the senses, reason, and the memory of things but also from any qualities of one's own being. The author of the treatises describes it as an "offering up" of a "naked blind feeling of thine own being," advising, "Look ever . . . that it be naked and not clad with any quality of thy being. For if thou clothe it with any quality, as with the worthiness of thy being or with any other personal condition that falleth to the being of man, . . . then as fast thou givest meat to thy wits, by the which they have occasion and strength to draw thee to many things, and so to be scattered." Just as God is apprehended in His simplicity, so the one praying offers himself or herself in complete simplicity.

Unknowing

The work of contemplation is difficult not only because one has to forget senses, reason, memory, and one's very self, but also because what is contemplated is at the outset very unclear. One is in a "cloud of unknowing." It is a "blind beholding of God." It requires great perseverance, as is implied by this exhortation: "If thou wilt stand and not fall, cease never in thine intent but beat evermore on this cloud of unknowing that is between thee and thy God with a sharp dart of longing love, and be loath to think of anything under God, and go not thence for anything that befalleth." *The Cloud of Unknowing* cites a saying of Dionysius, an early Eastern Christian writer whose thought was foundational for the apophatic tradition: "The best knowing of God is that which is known by unknowing." The apparent paradox points us to the utter inefficacy of any epistemology of this world as a way to reach God. It is only when we know that we have no such knowledge of Him that we can be open to Him. All our pretended knowledge blocks Him.

Augustine Baker explains this more fully in this exposition of the teaching of *The Cloud of Unknowing*:

> The soul loses all remembrance of itself and of all created things, and all that she retains of God is a remembrance that He cannot be

seen nor comprehended. All creatures, therefore, being removed, and no particular distinct image of God admitted, there remains in the soul and mind, as it were, a nothing and mere emptiness, which nothing is more worth than all creatures, for it is all that we can know of God in this life; this nothing is the rich inheritance of perfect souls, who perceive clearly that God is nothing of all that may be comprehended by our senses or understanding. The state, therefore, of such souls, forasmuch as concerns knowledge, is worthily called the "cloud of unknowing" and the "cloud of forgetting" by the author of that sublime treatise so called; and this is the most perfect and most angelical knowing that a soul is capable of in this life.

Being a Stinking Lump

To know God like this requires us to "strive to work at perfect humility." Only emptiness of self can accommodate the all-capacious emptiness of God. This means acknowledging sin, though without going into details that distract. The *Cloud* author advises us, "Feel sin as a lump, thou knowest not at all what, but none other thing than thyself. And cry then spiritually always the one thing: 'Sin, sin, sin; help, help, help!'" Feeling sin as "a lump, . . . none other thing than thyself" is the anguish of being other than God: separated and contingent. Yet to know that one is this lump, this congealing of separation, is the beginning of healing; to recognize one's powerlessness is to be able to invoke help; to know one's nothingness is to be open to what the inner man acknowledges to be God's all. It is a matter of facing reality.

W. B. Yeats gave poetic expression to this resting in the darkness of the heart that is the foundation of all aspiration in his poem *The Circus Animals' Desertion*:

> I sought a theme and sought for it in vain,
> I sought it daily for six weeks or so.
> Maybe at last, being but a broken man,
> I must be satisfied with my heart, although
> Winter and summer till old age began
> My circus animals were all on show,
> Those stilted boys, that burnished chariot,
> Lion and woman and the Lord knows what.

He describes the themes that had engrossed him and reflects,

> Players and painted stage took all my love,
> And not those things that they were emblems of.

This is a recognition that the "circus animals" were forms in which he rested, and not reality itself. This is only found within, so he concludes the poem with this couplet:

> I must lie down where all the ladders start
> In the foul rag and bone shop of the heart.

This is eschewing resting in what is intended to point beyond itself and recognizing the need to know oneself as a sinful "lump." Only from one's own sinful reality can one reach out to God. It is necessary to face that darkness.

This corresponds to the teaching of Saint John of the Cross that was considered in Chapter One in connection with the symbolism of darkness. The dark night of the senses is the withdrawal from resting in what our senses convey to us; the dark night of the spirit is letting go of what our minds can tell us even of spiritual truths. Subjectively it is a terrible thing:

> All other sorrows are compared to this as game to earnest. For he sorrows earnestly who knows and feels not only what he is, but that he is. . . . This sorrow, if it be truly conceived, is full of holy desire; and else might never man in this life abide or bear it. For were it not that a soul were somewhat fed with a manner of comfort of his doing right, he should not be able to bear the pain that he hath of the knowing and feeling of his being. For as oft as he would have a true knowing and a feeling of his God in purity of spirit, as far as is possible here, he feels that he may not—for he finds always his knowing and his feeling as it were occupied and filled with a foul stinking lump of himself.

Augustine Baker simply calls it "the great desolation." He says God permits the soul "to feel her natural infirmity." In this state, "she now sees her own natural misery so perfectly (yea, and can see nothing but it) that she cannot see how God can comfort her if He would." Such is the subjective experience, yet objectively something wonderful is happening:

She practises tranquillity of mind in the midst of a tempest of passions in sensitive nature; she exercises resignation without the least contentment to herself therein; she learns patience in the midst of impatience, and resignation in the midst of irresignation; in a word, she yields herself as a prey unto Almighty God, to be cast into this most sharp purgatory of love, which is an immediate disposition to an established state of perfection.

Being Made One with God

The Cloud of Unknowing says this state of perfection is "to be made one with God in spirit and in love and in accordance of will." *The Book of Privy Counselling* puts it in similar terms: "I say that perfection of man's soul is nothing else but a union made betwixt God and it in perfect charity. This perfection is so high and so pure in itself, above the understanding of man, that it may not be known or perceived in itself." Augustine Baker says that in this union "there is neither time nor place" and that "this happy state" is "the most perfect that the soul is capable of in this life, being almost an entire reparation and restitution of the soul to the state of primitive innocence." It is, in effect, a return of the soul to the childhood of the race. It is "a state of love and an entire conformity with the divine will." It is called "the union of nothing with nothing," because "the soul, being nowhere corporally or sensibly, is everywhere spiritually and immediately united to God, this infinite nothing."

This makes sense in another way if we reflect that "nothing" applied to Man and God can have different meanings. Saint Thomas Aquinas wrote that "whatever naturally pertains to something in itself is prior to what that thing only receives from another. A creature does not have being, however, except from another, for, considered in itself, every creature is nothing, and thus, with respect to the creature, non-being is prior to being by nature." This establishes that Man is basically nothing, since that is what he was before receiving being from God—this being is an added characteristic, as it were. Saints have always recognized this. Saint Thérèse, for example, compared her dependence on God for all that she had to a beautiful view of trees lit up by the sun: it would be nothing if the sun were not there, and so would she without God. God, on the other hand, *appears* to be nothing when viewed by senses oriented to the created. They can see only an "insubstantial pageant"; God is not that, and thus He is invisible to them. In union with God our real nothing becomes one with His apparent nothing. Nothing becomes something: it is a repeat of the process of creation, in which nothing became something. To put it another way, it is a full embracing of being.

Abbot Louis of Blois has this to say about it:

> It is a great thing, an exceeding great thing, in the time of this exile, to be joined to God in the divine light by a mystical and denuded union. This takes place when a pure, humble, and resigned soul, burning with ardent charity, is carried above itself by the grace of God, and through the brilliancy of the divine light shining on the mind, it loses all consideration and distinction of things and lays aside all, even the most excellent images; and all liquefied by love, and, as it were, reduced to nothing, it melts away into God. It is then united with God without any medium, and becomes one spirit with Him, and is transformed and changed into Him, as iron placed in the fire is changed into fire, without ceasing to be iron. . . . For, being raised above the operation of its natural powers, it reaches its silent and tranquil essence; where is simplicity and unity, and where God inhabits; and having found the Eternal Truth, it possesses inexhaustible riches.

The being "reduced to nothing" is severing our ties to the evanescent and "being delivered from the bondage of corruption into the glorious liberty of the children of God." What seems to be our life, played out in time and space, is "such stuff as dreams are made on." Union with God is an awakening to our true, immortal destiny, as the prince in C. S. Lewis's novel *The Silver Chair* escapes the enchantment of the wicked witch, designed to persuade him that there is no such thing as life above ground, with a sun rather than a lamp, a lion rather than a cat. It is the Word of God being spoken in us when—in Meister Eckhart's words—"the powers have been completely withdrawn from all their works and images." These works and images are our engagement with what passes, and the withdrawal corresponds to what Baker wrote about the movement inward. The speaking of the Word of God, the sharing of His life, is the final triumph of intensive over extensive living. It is the triumph of wholeness over fragmentation.

The Connection with Earlier Chapters

I appreciate that the talk in this chapter of clouds, dark night, and nothingness may seem far removed from where we began, contemplating the blue sky and thinking of heaven. The great desolation may seem very different from the happiness that is "a flower that grows in every vale," referred to in Chapter Three. The forgetting of what thought can grasp may seem at variance with what was said in Chapter Four about the significance and power of the word. The cohesion is this: what I wrote about nature and language speaking to us was intended to convey that there was something beyond them. They are not the term and goal of our knowing. They point beyond themselves. This chapter has been about *what* they point to: God in His mystery, God *as* mystery. It has been named for God the Father because, revealing Himself through the Son and Holy Spirit, He remains *as Father* relatively unknown. The first six chapters are intended to show that this mystery exists or at least to encourage confidence and trust (faith) in its existence. Yet you may still ask why, if the things of nature and speech are so many glad messengers of the radiance beyond being, there has been an emphasis in this chapter on withdrawing senses and attention from them.

The answer is implicit in the earlier chapters: they have become in practice a substitute for what they tell of. C.S. Lewis makes the point in his book *The Discarded Image* that in the medieval way of thinking the important thing about writers was that they *gave* fame to others; it was only in later times that they were thought of as being famous *in themselves.* In primordial times, nature and word gave glory to God; latterly, they have been gloried in for themselves. One way of talking about this is to say that people have become addicted to them. It is like an addiction to alcohol or opiates. These have a good use as food and analgesic, but when they become subjectively a necessity that the addicted person is compelled to get in violation of all other values, then the way to tackle this (as in the twelve steps of Alcoholics Anonymous) is for the person to recognize that there is an unmanageable difficulty with the substance concerned, to give it up completely, and ask God for help. This does not mean that it is bad in itself: just that, for this person at this time, not having it is the lesser evil. It is in this spirit that the (remarkably unanimous) teaching about the path to union with God directs the seeker to withdraw from the things of sense and the workings of the mind. That has its difficulties. There are dark nights and the feeling of being a "stinking lump." Yet these are like the withdrawal symptoms of a recovering addict. The dark nights are the cravings of the addict; the feeling of being a "stinking lump" is cold turkey. The outcome is freedom from addiction to what will not truly satisfy, since Man is made for and finds his happiness in God alone.

It will not have escaped your notice that in writing of the way to union with God I have used many quotations from other authors. That is because I have not wanted to pretend to be qualified to speak of this in a way that I am not. All I bring is a deep conviction that the destination is real and that the undertaking of the journey is worth all that we have. This is not to say that it is always accomplished in this life: for some the final withdrawal from what the senses offer happens only with the surrender of death. Yet, "A man's reach should exceed his grasp, / Or what's a heaven for?" It is by reaching for this ultimate prize that we will find ourselves going in the right direction when we die, at which point God will supply the remaining momentum needed. And there is something gained by being on this path, even in this life. Louis of Blois writes of those who "although they do not attain to this height in the time of this exile, yet feel in themselves a certain simplicity of thought, when, excluding tumult from their minds, they dwell in silence, humbly, calmly, and lovingly upon the joyful presence of God." This is no small good.

Furthermore, the spiritual masters whose teaching I have been expounding insist that one should not enter on the path of imageless contemplation without a clear calling to it from God. It is folly for a non-swimmer to leap into the ocean. The wise thing is to learn to swim in the shallow end of a swimming pool. Self-awareness and the guidance of others will indicate when the time comes for the ocean depths. God in His Providence makes provision for us to learn how to move through the waters of eternity in a way consonant with what we can manage. As I have repeatedly said, He has revealed Himself to us through the Son and the Holy Spirit. The remaining two chapters are dedicated to these respectively.

Chapter Eight:
Christeritalicize the Word Incarnate

Recapitulation

here is only one more chapter after this one, so it is appropriate now to begin to gather together the threads of this book with a view to a final weaving. This chapter is about Christ, so this will echo the purpose of the Author of creation: to "gather together in one all things in Christ, both which are in heaven, and which are on earth; even in him." He has of course been present throughout, for He is "Alpha and Omega, the beginning and the end, the first and the last." Yet here I want to reflect more particularly on how the ways of knowing considered in the earlier chapters, particularly the previous one, are connected with Christ's work and teaching. Then, in the final chapter, about the Holy Spirit, we can look at what the Spirit's communication to us of this work and teaching makes of us: what, indeed, it is to have recovered a contemplative spirit and to look with Christ toward the eternal Father.

To contemplate with Christ or to be one who in Him "hath seen the Father" is, first of all, to want the truth. He is "the way, the truth, and the life"—the way to the truth that gives life. He prays for those following this way, saying, "This is life eternal, that they might know thee the only true God and Jesus Christ, whom thou hast sent." It is in knowing the truth of God that life is found. In God's oneness is our life. Yet it is necessary to want the truth for its own sake. Hence the way of knowing that was looked at in the introduction, the interrogation of nature to gain an advantage over it, has to be put aside. If it has become the only way of knowing, it has to be unlearned as such. It is only in coming to Jesus, to God, for His own sake that we can ever know Him. It has to be for truth, not usefulness. Blake bluntly expressed the distance between His way and Bacon's way in this couplet:

> To teach Doubt and Experiment
> Certainly was not what Christ meant.

Indeed, Christ's sternest words are for those who disturb faith. His followers, with their childlike faith, are protected by this malediction: "Whoso shall offend one of these little ones which believe in me, it were better for him that a millstone were hanged about his neck, and that he were drowned in the depth of the sea"! He links faith to wholeness and health, saying exactly the same words to the blind man, the leper, and the woman with a hemorrhage when they are cured: "Thy faith hath made thee whole." Faith is knowing God, knowing wholeness and life. Faith sees beyond the senses, for, again in Blake's words,

> This Life's five Windows of the Soul
> Distorts the Heavens from Pole to Pole
> And leads you to Believe a Lie
> When you see with, not thro' the Eye.

This seeing of faith is *through* the eye: in other words, it sees through the sensation that the eye brings. It does not see *with* it: that is, use data derived from the senses for the purposes of calculation to manipulate nature. It intuitively grasps the whole that is transmitted through the eye by the signs of nature. It is clear from a marginal annotation in his manuscript of this poem that Blake had Bacon in his sights in writing this. The empiriometric enterprise will not bring us to the Savior. Childlike trust does. It does not have its vision blocked by doubt and experiment, and can behold "the Lord from heaven."

To it, "the greater light" and "the lesser light" and "the stars" speak of the One who is "the light of the world." It can say to the setting sun,

> If with exultant tread
>   Thou foot the Eastern sea,
>   Or like a golden bee
> Sting the West to angry red,
> Thou dost image, thou dost follow
>   That Kind-Maker of Creation,
> Who, ere Hellas hailed Apollo,
> Gave thee, angel-god, thy station;

Thou art of Him a type memorial.
> Like Him thou hang'st in dreadful pomp of blood
>> Upon thy Western rood;
> And His stained brow did vail like thine to night,
>> Yet lift once more Its light,
> And, risen, again departed from our ball,
>> But when It set arose in Heaven.

Childlike faith knows that "There lives the dearest freshness deep down things." It looks toward the sun and sees through it the freshness of the uncreated Light, "the true Light, which lighteth every man." Through the red of its setting it sees the love for which Christ shed His blood; through the brightness of its rising it sees the new life He won for us; through the blue that comes from its mid-day shining it sees the empyrean home of His blessed ones.

This faith sees Christ through every living thing because He is "the resurrection, and the life," and life is wholeness. It sees His divine unity through each thing that is. It sees through the wonderful bond of nature, the "golden section"—which divides a length so that the ratio of the whole to the longer segment equals the ratio of the longer to the shorter segment—the One who is able to "gather together in one." It sees Him through the wholeness of the human body, articulated with the proportions of the golden section; it sees Him through the wholeness of each family and each community and in the wholeness of His Church.

Seeing Him through every instance of wholeness, this faith believes His promise to those who follow Him: "I am come that they might have life, and that they may have it more abundantly." It trusts in His wholeness as the gift of this abundance; it trusts that His wholeness contains the whole of humanity and can make each human person whole; it is confident that He is the true self of the human race and that to find Him is to find one's true self. It recognizes Him as that true self in every person, especially the hungry, the thirsty, the indigent, the sick, and the imprisoned. It joyfully loves them as its true self. Such is the contemplation of Christ.

The contemplation of Christ sees Him through all things "made by him." It sees (for example) His dependability through every rock; His innocence in every lamb; His sacrifice in every bull; His glorious life in every butterfly; His warmth through the fire of every hearth; His grace through the bubbling of every stream; His celestial beauty in every flower; His love in every provision of food; His guidance in every event of life; His invitation to share His life in every good to be done; His blessing in every good received; His truth in all that is.

It can do this because it answers the question "Whom say ye that I am?" with the declaration, "Thou art the Christ." It knows He is the One who was in the beginning and by whom all things were made. It knows that He is the Word of God, the meaning of creation, the essential meaning of being.

The Word of God

I want to reflect a little more on this, because it bears on how we come to that life-giving contemplation of "the only true God and Jesus Christ" and how we live with one another in that spirit. Looking up "the word" (ὁ λογος) in a Greek lexicon yields more than two large pages of quotations. They include its first use in John's Gospel, where it is defined as "the word of wisdom of God, personified as his agent in creation and world government." The word also carries the implications of general and earlier meanings. It means at one and the same time the interior and the exterior word: that which is thought and that which is spoken. It means reason, and it means law. In the Septuagint (a Greek version of part of the Bible) "the ten words" (ὁι δεκα λογοι) are the Ten Commandments. It means divine utterance or oracle, or, if one goes far enough back, persuasive speech. Our word "logic" is connected.

All of this meaning illuminates what is written in the letter to the Hebrews: "GOD, who at sundry times and in divers manners spake in time past unto the fathers by the prophets, hath in these last days spoken unto us by his Son whom he hath appointed heir of all things, by whom also he made the worlds." In His Son, God not only shows us the meaning at the heart of creation: He reveals His inner self. That is why Christ teaches, as Saint Matthew says, "as one having authority." He is both the author of creation and God's explanation of everything.

Yet perhaps that oldest meaning, "persuasive speech," is the most important. It means that God respects our freedom. Contemplation, this side of the Second Coming, is not having something thrust upon us will we, nill we. God speaks in "a still small voice," not in wind, earthquake, or fire. God speaks in such a way as to invite our attention and then elicit our agreement, not so as to impose His will on us. And in doing that He also allows us to agree with one another. In a godless, postmodern view of life, there is no agreement: only arbitrary individual views with at best a mutual tolerance, at worst an imposition by violence of a prevailing view. In a godly view of life born of contemplation, the authoritative Word of God wins agreement from people and therefore among them. If we listen to Him, peace and freedom to those of goodwill follow from God speaking to us. God speaking allows us to respond to Him and to other people in freedom. We can see that He does not want to threaten us. He appeals to us first as a little child, and then as a man who can suffer.

He also develops our freedom, so that (as explained in Chapter Three) we become children of Providence, less constrained by the material because linked to God who transcends the material and guides all things. Jesus says, "If ye continue in my word, then are ye my disciples indeed; and ye shall know the truth, and the truth shall make you free." Jesus is the Word, through whom we know the truth of God, who is spirit, and in whom there is no constraint of time and place. In God we are free from these constraints. Hence Isaiah prophesied that Jesus would set prisoners free. Prisoners of time and place are set free by Him, and, as He says, "If the Son . . . shall make you free, ye shall be free indeed." It is as though, instead of dealing with a person sitting at a computer who can only give us what the computer—that is, the system—allows, we are dealing with the top manager who can bypass anything in the system. We no longer are merely subject to the laws of nature—the system—but are in communication with the One who is responsible for the system and can override it.

It may be that we have only glimpses of that in particular acts of Providence and the reports of occasional miracles, but these glimpses prepare us for our greatest freedom, for when we leave the world of constraint of time and place behind. They speak to us of our true home. That is the home which Jesus has left for the constraint of swaddling bands and the Cross, becoming a prisoner so that we might "be free indeed."

It therefore matters greatly that we should hear Him. Saint John of the Cross says, "The Father spoke one Word which was His Son, and this Word He always speaks in eternal silence, it must be heard by the soul." It helps greatly therefore in this if we cultivate an inner silence. For this purpose an outward silence can be helpful, and so can a simplification of life so as not to be "troubled about many things." A contemplative spirit walks quietly without perturbation.

A Most Excellent Book

We can understand this listening as hearing a single word, and it is indeed single in the sense of being one—whole and containing all things. Yet, being adapted to us as we are, it is also given to us in many words. It is in effect a book. Abbot Louis of Blois described the life of Christ as "a most excellent book." Hearing the words of this book enables us to understand life, creation, and indeed the whole caboodle. It is a pattern for us to follow, or, better, contains a Spirit that can guide us, a Spirit who is present to us when we grasp Christ's life intuitively by reflecting on it. It is a book most worth contemplating: not only the book of the life of Christ when He walked this earth in the flesh but also His life through the Spirit in His body the Church, particularly in those members who have been most open to His holiness.

We can also read and reflect on the book of that life through what is literally a text: the Bible. This was dealt with at sufficient length in Chapter Five for it to be unnecessary to say much more here. I want simply to add that this reflection is, if undertaken in a contemplative spirit, one with the contemplation of Christ in everything else: nature, other people, the events of our life, and so on. It is not as though we study the Bible for a bit then take a break and later go out to have a look at Christ in nature. The very unity of our life is something through which we contemplate Him, so that contemplation includes everything, even eating and sleeping, for indeed He ate and slept.

Books can have pictures in them that illustrate what they teach, and the liturgy and sacraments of the Church can be seen as such in this book of the life of Christ. Chapter Six dealt with this at length, so here again I want simply to tie this thread together with the others and to say that it belongs to the unity of the contemplation of Christ. It conveys the meaning in life as a whole and shows what it is concerned with. This little medieval poem, *The Sacrament of the Altar*, conveys the mystery of it all:

> It seems white and is red;
> It is quick and seems dead;
> It is flesh and seems bread;
> It is one and seems two;
> It is God's body and no more.

We could say of the whole creation, "It is one and seems two." The duality of it is finally appearance: it is one in God—eternally, that is. The red of love, as expressed in the sacrificial shedding of blood, is at the heart of it; it all has life, whatever the appearance; it all shows Christ; it all expresses God. The Eucharistic interpretation of the poem is more obvious: the appearance of bread covers the living presence of Christ, which is there whatever fraction takes place.

More About Prayer

One undertaking in the book of Christ's life is solitary prayer— "when he had sent the multitudes away, he went up into a mountain apart to pray: and when the evening was come, he was there alone." The being alone contrasts with the multitudes, reflecting the difference between the oneness of God and the multiplicity of creation. The mountain indicates closeness to heaven and rising above the things of this world, sensually apprehended. Christ is doing here what is described in *The Cloud of Unknowing*: reaching up beyond the many things of this world to divine unity. He is touching the truth of God. When we undertake the seemingly daunting and solitary work of prayer described in this treatise, we are in one sense not alone at all. Christ is praying with us. He is our model and also our human comfort and support. The Spirit—His Spirit—brings us to Him, binds us to Him, and "itself maketh intercession for us." If we feel ourselves to be in the night in the way described by Saint John of the Cross and to be on our own even to the extent of having others against us, we can look into the life of Christ and see how when those around Him were "filled with madness; and communed one with another what they might do to Jesus, . . . He went out into a mountain to pray, and continued all night in prayer to God." It may feel isolated and desolated, but in fact we are not so much praying *to* God as *in* God.

There is a poem by George Herbert, simply called *Prayer*, that conveys something of how it is in fact God's work:

> Prayer, the Church's banquet, Angel's age,
>   God's breath in man returning to his birth,
>   The soul in paraphrase, heart in pilgrimage,
> The Christian plummet sounding heaven and earth;
>
> Engine against th'Almighty, sinner's tower,
>   Reversed thunder, Christ-side-piercing spear,
>   The six days' world-transposing in an hour,
> A kind of tune, which all things hear and fear;
>
> Softness, and peace, and joy, and love, and bliss,
>   Exalted Manna, gladness of the best,
>   Heaven in ordinary, man well drest,
> The Milky Way, the bird of Paradise,
>
>   Church-bells beyond the stars heard, the soul's blood,
>   The land of spices, something understood.

It is "God's breath" that rises. The images in the poem work against each other and are paradoxical, conveying the unknown character of God and His work. The "engine" and the "tower" are instruments of war, and yet prayer is also "softness, and peace." The "plummet" sounds "heaven and earth," suggesting that it completely transcends the operations of space, within which it might be expected to sound only earth, with a downward motion. "Reversed thunder" is also against expectation and implies that something is being directed at God that only comes from God. The idea of fighting the "Almighty" is even more paradoxical. It can only be God at work here: "Christian" means the plummet is Christ's as much as it is His followers'. "The six days' world-transposing in an hour" suggests the wonder of an even greater marvel than the creation of the world, the new creation in Christ proclaimed by Saint Paul: "If any man be in Christ, he is a new creature: old things are passed away; behold all things are become new." It is something far away ("the Milky Way . . . beyond the stars . . . the land of spices") and yet something very intimate ("the soul's blood"). It is the ultimate harmony ("a kind of tune") of the disparate that comes from the oneness of God. There is even a paradox in the final identification of prayer as "something understood," since the contradictoriness of the images suggests something that cannot be known in terms of this world. Prayer is the unknown knowing of the *Cloud*; it is the mysterious work that God Himself accomplishes within us; it is our realization of our life *within* God.

It is a reversal of entropic collapse, with Christ restoring the freshness of the first creation. When "the LORD God formed man of the dust of the ground, and breathed into his nostrils the breath of life; and man became a living soul," the spiritual animated the material, but the gradual falling away from God left Man more and more vulnerable to the blind unfreedom of matter. In the prayer of Christ, freedom is won again, and "though our outward man perish, yet the inward man is renewed day by day." Decay and death ultimately do not matter because the spirit of Man is made new.

This is a good point to clarify, by drawing together its various threads, what I have been saying in this book about Man's gradual falling away from God. My basic thesis is that a contemplative spirit has been lost and that it can be recovered, and at various points in the book I have referred to different steps in this falling away. (Of course these steps do not indicate the whole history of the matter, which is beyond the scope of this book: obviously what comes later is prepared for by what comes earlier.) In chronological order they are the following: the first Fall of Man, when the ability to know all as one was lost by the eating of the fruit of the tree of the knowledge of good and evil; the building of the tower of Babel, when language and culture became opaque to the celestial; and the new way of looking at things that developed around the seventeenth century, when nature began to be interrogated rather than beheld. This last has been a major focus in the sense that I have been concerned with showing the need to undo the epistemological outlook of these recent centuries in favor of a way that allows us to be aware of depth of being rather than that limits us to what helps us to use things. The aim is to recover awareness of meaning and the aptitude for contemplation, including finally the contemplation of God, in whom all is contained. Yet in another sense, the most recent stage of falling is not the most significant, since the whole of the falling away from God is contained in germ in that first Fall. For each and every falling away, the remedy is the same: the prayer of Christ.

That is the manifestation of God's utter generosity: the further we go away from Him, the further He is prepared to go to bring us back. It is wrong to look back to ages of faith with bitterness, because there is a special grace attached to our own age for precisely this reason. God in Christ comes however far we are away from Him. In fact, He becomes precisely what the last chapter quoted the *Cloud* author as saying we become (subjectively, at least) when we set out to reach God in contemplation: a stinking lump. Saint Paul says as much when he teaches that God "hath made him to be sin for us, who knew no sin; that we might be made the righteousness of God in him." This burden fell upon him in the garden of Gethsemane, when "being in an agony he prayed more earnestly: and his sweat was as it were great drops of blood falling down to the ground." His dereliction on the Cross, when He cries out, "My God, my God, why hast thou forsaken me?" is *our* unknowing. He enters the cloud of our unknowing, that we might know God. The cloud overshadows Him on the Cross as a cloud overshadowed Him when He was transfigured. He bears "our griefs" and "our sorrows"—the desolation of not knowing God. Yet, all the while He *did* know His Father, who could say, "By his knowledge shall my righteous servant justify many." The apparent contradiction of not knowing and knowing is implicit in the teaching of *The Cloud of Unknowing*; it also recalls the citation from Nicholas of Cusa in the last chapter, which says that the place where God is found is "girded about with the coincidence of contradictories." Christ really suffers yet really knows the delight of communion with His Father. This is the experience of the one who prays in his great sorrow being "somewhat fed with a manner of comfort of his doing right," also cited in the last chapter, and the experience of Saint Thérèse (cited in Chapter Two) that helped her to understand that Christ in His agony nonetheless "enjoyed all the delights of the Trinity." He brings these delights to where we are, although that is agony for Him. In His body being torn, our vision is made whole: it becomes indeed beatific.

Being Made Conformable

As He comes to where we are, so are we called to be where He is. In order to "know him, and the power of his resurrection," Saint Paul seeks "the fellowship of his sufferings, being made conformable unto his death." This is the teaching of Jesus, who said, "If any man will come after me, let him deny himself, and take up his cross daily, and follow me." There is a sacrificial aspect to the Christian spiritual path. To put the things of sense under oneself in a cloud of forgetting, as described in the previous chapter, is a sacrifice: taking the "habit of perfection" is leaving the world. Yet to one doing this these words of Shakespeare may be addressed: "Thou losest here, a better where to find." The promise of Jesus—"Seek ye first the kingdom of God; and all these things shall be added unto you"—assures us not only of God's Providence for our natural needs if we are on this quest but also of the fact that in Christ, the Word of God, we find the essence of all things, since "without him was not any thing made that was made." In God, nothing is neglected; all things are in Him. Therefore the aspect of sacrifice of this spiritual path appears from the perspective of this world: in following it, we are losing things *as we are used to knowing them*; we get them back in their essence when we have learned to know in depth—which is to say, in God. The subordination of the accustomed outer knowing is the cross; the inner knowing—the knowing as God knows—is being within the blissful life of the Holy Trinity. Seen from *this* perspective, such a subordination is a good deal rather than a sacrifice: like the "one pearl of great price" which more than merited the merchant's sale of all that he had.

Twin Sisters

In one sense, the path that involves giving up life as we know it for the sake of finding life as God knows it is simply about learning to know differently. However, in making how we know my focus in this book, I am not wanting to minimize, still less contradict, other perspectives on the great mystery of salvation. The unambiguous witness of Scripture and Tradition is that Christ's offering of Himself is an act of infinite love and that we enter into the life of God by reciprocating that love. It is love that motivated Christ to offer up the sacrifice of His life in this world so that, according to the spiritual equivalent of Newton's third law of motion, an unbounded blessing should descend on people in this world. Yet love and knowledge—if they can be separated at all—are twin sisters. Their relationship was discussed in the previous chapter, but I want to add here some explanation of why it seems good to me to give the latter sister particular attention in our own time.

There is a prevalent way of looking that divides our life into, on the one hand, what (in its view) can be known and, on the other hand, what is private, arbitrary, or even merely sentimental. This kills saving truth. Wholeness is life, and the separation of knowledge from love is death to the spirit. Having divided the two sisters, this prevalent (but mistaken) way of looking can pick them off individually. To knowledge it says, "You can only verify the material, and that by way of measurement and experimentation: you are not related to the source of meaning or value." To love it says, "Of course we like you because you make people feel good, but your only claim to be here is that individuals have chosen to invite you: you do not have an objective or true claim—that belongs to knowledge."

An integrated way of looking does not divide these sisters. In the wholeness that belongs to the contemplative spirit, they are one. Yet it is knowledge in particular who will lead us out of the darkness of the prevailing epistemology, because of the way we are. It is natural (and in normal circumstances wholesome) to give a priority of respect to what is commonly identified as true and good. If we say "I believe this is true, though everybody else thinks otherwise" and "I choose this because it is good for me, even though it is bad for everyone else," we lay ourselves open to suspicion of being mad and bad. Love, being entirely confined to the private, is in danger of being so dismissed! True knowledge can rescue her sister by traveling to the realm beyond this world, to "the other side of coincidence of contraries," where they are one. This is the way to address the situation prophesied in Saint Matthew's Gospel in these words: "And many false prophets shall rise, and shall deceive many. And because iniquity shall abound, the love of many shall wax cold." Yet the danger does not affect love alone. The isolation of love is modern thinking, but now in postmodern thinking, knowledge—even when allowed only a very restricted scope—is being confined to the private, where she can be accused (by those to whose agenda she is inconvenient) of being mad and bad. The answer to this threat is the integration, the making whole, the healing of knowledge. That is, on the one hand, the building of a consensus (her sister might help here) and, on the other hand, the seeing of things in an undivided way, where they are one and therefore alive. If we do this, we see things from God's perspective and, to quote Shakespeare again, "take upon 's the mystery of things / As if we were God's spies." In a word, the answer is God.

More About Paradox

The return to God is the healing of knowledge and the rescue of love. In this we look "unto Jesus the author and finisher of our faith; who for the joy that was set before him endured the cross, despising the shame, and is set down at the right hand of the throne of God." He teaches us the way beyond "the other side of coincidence of contraries" that is the way to paradise. It follows that, as seen with a way of knowing adapted to this world, it is going to seem paradoxical. It is only where what is divided is united that it escapes paradox. That divine perspective is the goal that is reached by way of paradox. Jesus, "the author and finisher of our faith," presents this to us in two ways, which I will consider in turn. The first, and more important, is by what He did. The second is by His teaching.

The work of Jesus—that He suffered, died, and rose again—was the first aspect to be proclaimed. Already there are paradoxes apparent. What brings the greatest blessing to the world, its greatest work, is in a sense the greatest passivity: the passion, the suffering and being put to death. This implicitly shows us that it is the contemplative spirit—the receiving rather than imposing—that is the way to wholeness and life. Allowing ourselves to be fashioned is a work—the *Cloud* author calls it such—but like the work of Christ it is one in which things are done to us. They are both works of love, which "suffereth long." Another, and great, paradox is in Jesus enduring the Cross and despising the shame "for the joy that was set before him." It makes more straightforward sense to think of Him undergoing what He did out of love, so that although He suffers, others benefit. Yet by this account He underwent it that *He* might have joy. That joy might include the joy of loving others who would benefit and of loving His Father who willed this, but the text implies that joy beckoned directly in what was about to happen. Like the unknowing knowing, the sorrowful joy is hidden within. The veil is torn and the Most Holy made known; the goods of this world—its life and honor—hide the good that is their source, and to know that good is joy supreme.

More Twins

The biggest paradox of the Cross and its biggest challenge to how we know things in the world, however, is that death leads to life. This is brought out in the opening lines of the poem about the setting sun quoted above:

> ALPHA and Omega, sadness and mirth,
>> The springing music, and its wasting breath—
>> The fairest things in life are Death and Birth,
>> And of these two the fairer thing is Death.
> Mystical twins of Time inseparable,
>> The younger hath the holier array,
>>> And hath the awfuller sway:
> It is the falling star that trails the light,
>> It is the breaking wave that hath the might,
>> The passing shower that rainbows maniple.

Death and Birth are twins, and the final words of the well-known so-called "Prayer of Saint Francis" bring out their connection: "It is in dying that we are born to eternal life." They are "alpha and omega," which, in the context of the Scripture text quoted at the beginning of this chapter, identifies them with Christ, who is "Alpha and Omega, the beginning and the end, the first and the last." In Him, because He is God, all contraries are reconciled: the powerless, swaddled baby and the One whom "even the wind and the sea obey"; the One who is judged yet judges all; "the Lamb that was slain . . . that liveth for ever and ever." Death and Birth are "twins of Time" because their dwelling is only in time, on this side "of coincidence of contraries." Time, like all that belongs to creation, comes of God's denial of nonbeing, and thus it has this double aspect of nothingness and being. Death and Birth are "mystical twins" because by their consanguinity they point to "the wall of paradise," which is "the coincidence of contradictories." They take us to heaven.

The final lines of the poem (which immediately follow the passage quoted first about the setting sun) explains more fully their closeness and ultimate identity, on account of the Savior's great work that is like the gloriously beautiful setting sun:

> Thus hath He unto death His beauty given:
> And so of all which form inheriteth
>   The fall doth pass the rise in worth;
> For birth hath in itself the germ of death,
>   But death hath in itself the germ of birth.
> It is the falling acorn buds the tree,
> The falling rain that bears the greenery,
>   The fern-plants moulder when the ferns arise.
>   For there is nothing lives but something dies,
> And nothing dies but something lives.
>   Till skies be fugitives,
> Till Time, the hidden root of change, updries,
> Are Birth and Death inseparable on earth;
> For they are twain yet one, and Death is Birth.

Nature (the oak, the rain, the fern) gives clues, but the final oneness of Death and Birth is found in God: in Christ, who by His death gives us birth into eternal life, and in the Father, into the life of whose house we go through our own death.

This is the primary paradox, but there is a concomitant one: separation is unity. Jesus says, "I tell you the truth; It is expedient for you that I go away: for if I go not away, the Comforter will not come unto you; but if I depart, I will send him unto you." The Spirit of Unity, which unites us to Christ and to one another, comes because Jesus is separated from His followers. There is a parallel to this in people who separate themselves from the society of others in order to seek God: it may seem to be total separation, but in the deeper sense there is a total unity in the presence of the Spirit of Love that their relatively solitary life has enabled them to open themselves to. The seventeenth-century English poet John Donne gave this expression in his poem *A Hymn to Christ*, written on the occasion of his quitting the shores of his native land:

> I sacrifice this Island unto Thee,
> And all whom I lov'd thee, and who lov'd me;
> When I have put our seas 'twixt them and me,
> Put thou Thy sea betwixt my sins and Thee.
> As the tree's sap doth seek the root below
> In winter, in my winter now I go,
>   Where none but thee, th'Eternal root
>   Of true Love I may know.

God, as the eternal root of true love, is the source of all loving; to know Him is eternal life because He in that love unites us with all, and that wholeness is life indeed. This—the quest for life and light—motivates the poet to choose separation and darkness:

> Seal then this bill of my Divorce to All,
> On whom those fainter beams of love did fall;
> Marry those loves, which in youth scattered be
> On Fame, Wit, Hopes (false mistresses) to Thee.
> Churches are best for Prayer, that have least light:
> To see God only, I go out of sight:
>   And to 'scape stormy days, I choose
>   An Everlasting night.

Abstracting from these particular examples, we could say that distinction always implies unity: creation would simply not cohere if it were merely fragments. All that is manifests the oneness of God. Apparently paradoxical juxtapositions point us to His unity.

Astonishing Doctrine

This takes us to the second way in which Jesus leads us to the divine way of knowing and the knowing of the divine, leads us into the life of the Holy Trinity: through His teaching. It is so characterized by paradox that "the people was astonished at his teaching." Paradox is linked with eschewing what the contemporary French philosopher, Jean Borella, has called "epistemic closure." This is limiting how much (or how deeply) we know by using concepts that allow only a certain aspect (or certain aspects) of what we are considering to be taken into account. At one extreme there is closure, which considers only what can be measured, and no quality can be perceived; at the opposite extreme, where paradox opens up discourse, there is dis-closure, and God Himself is beheld. It is of course to this *dis*closure that the doctrine of Jesus tends. It is spiritual, not solid body, think-ing. It goes beyond what is merely rationally apprehended to reach the heart or intellect of Man.

The most obviously paradoxical teaching we have already touched upon; it is put in its most unqualified form in Saint Luke's Gospel: "Whosoever shall seek to save his life shall lose it; and whosoever shall lose his life shall preserve it." It conveys the literal truth of death being necessary for birth into eternal life, but it is not an exhortation not to bother with seat belts and so on. The spiritual meaning is that in seeking to preserve our egoic life invested in matter and oriented toward partial advantage, we lose the life found in God. By tran-scending this egoic life, withdrawing from the merely sensual and imitating the universal beneficence of God, we enter into His life. Subjectively, from the point of view of one living entirely in this world, this is a death; objectively, it is being "born of the Spirit." The spiritual journey is a quest to die before we die so that even while on earth our life may be "hid with Christ in God." Here, "Death is Birth"—a teaching that necessarily shocks the uninitiated.

This sense of paradox is present throughout the teaching of Jesus, sometimes in ways that our familiarity with the texts renders less than obvious. For example, in the parable of the Good Samaritan, the answer to the question "Which now of these three, thinkest thou, was neighbor unto him that fell among the thieves?" is obviously "the Samaritan," since he is the one who "had compassion" on the wounded traveler "and went to him and bound up his wounds." Yet "neighbor" means one who is near, and the Samaritans are by definition distant from the Jews (to whom this parable was first told), since they worship apart from Jerusalem, which Jews say "is the place where men ought to worship." The far (the Samaritan) is the near (the compassionate) in God, who is all compassion and love. The episode that immediately follows this parable in the Bible is the story of Martha and Mary, which we have already looked at. It too has the aspect of paradox: Martha who is doing what appears to be the good thing (feeding the Lord) is reprimanded, and Mary who is apparently neglecting the good (by not doing this) is commended. Again, the resolution of the paradox is in the higher, divine unity in which nothing is neglected.

Peter, likewise, is reprimanded for what seems entirely good: he wants to stop the Lord from suffering "many things of the elders and chief priests and scribes" and being killed. He is told very bluntly by Jesus, "Thou art an offence unto me." The seeming good is but an earthly one: the real good is the Friday on which, in the depths of the spirit where all men are one, Jesus breaks through everything that blocks access to the divine unity. The ultimate good is the divine presence. This means in practice openness to that presence, since "God is love" and always wants to give that good to us. From a perspective that limits itself to partial goods belonging to this world, that leads to paradox. Hence Saint Paul can write counterintuitively, "I take pleasure in infirmities, in reproaches, in necessities, in persecutions, in distresses for Christ's sake: for when I am weak, then am I strong." He has been told by God, "My strength is made perfect in weakness." This is because God can work best when we are not getting in His way. It is as though, to go back to the image of God as a cook preparing a marvelous creation, it does really help if we do not obtrude ourselves in the kitchen saying, "I know you like lightly fried onions—I'll chop some up for you now," when something else altogether is in the mind of the Creator—it would be better for us to be out of the way sipping sherry in the living room. Our nourishment is the goal; the best we can do is to let the cook cook.

Jesus Himself goes as far as to present moral weakness as strength: the apparently bad as good. He tells the tale of a steward, who was accused of wasting his master's goods and brought to account, who "called every one of his lord's debtors unto him" with a view to being received by them "into their houses." To this end, he reduced their debt, and, surprisingly, "the lord commended the unjust steward because he had done wisely." One edition of the Bible has an endnote pointing out that although the lord commended the prudence he did not condone the dishonesty, but this misses the point. It comes back to the divine unity. God in Christ identifies Himself with all humanity, especially those in need. He is the lord in question, so when with apparent dishonesty the steward is letting people off their debts, he is doing precisely what his master wants him to do. "Blessed are the merciful: for they shall obtain mercy" and be received into "everlasting habitations."

Giving God Permission

All these paradoxes point to God as the supreme good; they open minds and hearts to transcendent reality. As indicated above, openness to this reality is our ultimate good since only the presence of God can really make us happy. This is the heart of recovering a contemplative spirit. Jesus says, "Behold, I stand at the door, and knock: if any man hear my voice, and open the door, I will come in to him, and will sup with him, and he with me." In William Holman Hunt's celebrated painting of Jesus so standing, *The Light of the World*, this door is depicted as shut and having no handle on the outside. It can therefore only be opened from the inside. This represents the permission that Christ seeks from us to enter our lives with His light. God always graciously respects our freedom; He will not force His way in. The whole of the spiritual life consists in giving God permission. It is seeking not so much to fashion as to be fashioned. It is aiming not so much to change the world as to be changed by God. It is to want to say not so much "I have done great things" as "He that is mighty hath done to me great things." We simply have to give permission for them to be done to us, and we shall be blessed.

Jesus tells us how. Nine times in His seminal teaching on the mount He indicates who they are who are blessed. Each of these nine categories of people gives a particular permission to God. In a sense, they are all contained in the first, which is essentially giving God permission to be God. This permission is the beginning and the end of the entire spiritual journey. It is the beginning because "he that cometh to God must believe that he is." It is the end because it is only with the final surrender of all that we are to Him "that God may be all in all." If it seems odd that God should need permission to be God, we have only to recall that antecedent to the gift of Himself needs to be the gift of freedom to accept that gift. This starts with creation, a marvel of God giving ground: giving space for being to be and earth to be created. The miracle of the human person is the culmination of this marvel, in which He allows the person to be His image and ambassador in creation, accepting or not His kingship. An even greater marvel is His reaching out in Christ, who, when that kingship has been refused, waits patiently at the door. It is He who says to us, "Blessed are the poor in spirit: for theirs is the kingdom of heaven."

This is about giving God permission to be God, because to be poor in spirit is to know that we are not God and do not provide for ourselves. The life of the ego is a false simulacrum of Him. The one who is poor in spirit acknowledges this and yields up the illusion that egoism is true life. The Greek word for "poor" (πτωχος) is the same as the word for "beggar," which comes from the Greek word meaning "cringe" (πτωσσω). To be poor in spirit is to know that we receive everything from God. It is to go to God with empty hands to receive everything as a gift from Him. It is to know that we have no righteousness of our own. An outstanding exemplar of this openness to receiving God as God is Saint Francis of Assisi, who renounced his entire earthly inheritance before his father by stripping himself naked and saying, "Until now I have called you father here on earth, but now I can say without reservation, 'Our Father who art in heaven,' since I have placed all my treasure and all my hope in Him." This is allowing God to be God: all-providing, all-sustaining, all-merciful. The one who gives this permission is given "the kingdom of heaven," which is nothing less than God's kingly power. Giving up everything is being given everything. The receptivity is all.

Aspects of Receptivity

The next permission that we are taught to give is an aspect of this. It is giving God permission to provide. It is proposed in this promise: "Blessed are they that mourn: for they shall be comforted." This may seem more like giving God permission to take away from us and to be only about accepting and mourning our losses. Yet God, the all-generous, does not take anything away without wanting to give something better. More deeply understood, this promise is about allowing God to give us what He wants to give by accepting the emptiness in our lives as a space in which to receive it. He is "the God of all comfort" and wants to comfort us with nothing less than Himself. Every loss is an opportunity to allow this. Indeed, it is often at times of bereavement that people are especially comforted by His presence. The receptivity is all, and loss can increase it.

Another aspect of allowing God to be God is giving Him permission to be Lord. This is accepting that we are not ourselves Lord. Those that do this are promised the earth: "Blessed are the meek: for they shall inherit the earth." Chapter Three touched on how this promise works, pointing out how the Bible bears witness to the relation between Man's closeness to God and the fecundity of the earth. If we are humble enough to allow God to be Lord, He will bless us with the earth, for it and its fruit are His. God seeks also permission to satisfy us. We can choose to allow this by seeking to do what is right, since that is what fulfills who we are. Hence, "Blessed are those which do hunger and thirst after righteousness: for they shall be filled." In this hunger we are filled with nothing less than God. We need only not to be satisfied with ourselves, not to be bloated in our complacency. That cannot truly feed us: only God can. He is our true satisfaction.

To be truly receptive to God, we need to be willing to receive His mercy. It may seem unnecessary to say that since of course we want to receive mercy, yet sometimes this is an unrealistic wish for a divided mercy: mercy for the self but not for others. That cannot be, for mercy is one and undivided in God, and either His merciful presence is allowed in or it is not. Hence, "Blessed are the merciful: for they shall obtain mercy." Obtaining mercy is the same as giving permission to God the all-merciful to be present; that presence entails being merciful to others—it is not possible for it to be divided. "Freely ye have received, freely give" is not so much an exhortation as a metaphysical necessity.

The next promise given is all about receptivity: "Blessed are the pure in heart: for they shall see God." I have already considered it at length. It is about being willing to listen to God, having a heart for Him, open and willing to hear. It is about giving Him permission to speak. It is worth adding that it is also about giving Him permission to be present. It is the redeeming presence of Christ and the purifying presence of the fire of the Holy Spirit that make us whole of heart so that we can listen to God. We give permission for that, opening the door to Christ and saying, "Come, Holy Spirit!"

So far I have considered the promises attached to allowing God to be present as king and lord; as the One who is righteous and merciful; as the One who heals and makes whole. The next promise is attached to giving Him permission to be a Father: "Blessed are the peacemakers: for they shall be called the children of God." It is in knowing God as Father that we know others as brothers and sisters and all humanity as a single family. All these permissions for God to be present are made strong and definitive by giving Him permission to stay. We give that when we do not waver from commitment to what He wants when it causes trouble for us. The promise attached to this is the same as that attached to allowing Him to be present as God. This commitment and reward are expressed in the beatitude "Blessed are they which are persecuted for righteousness' sake: for theirs is the kingdom of heaven." The final blessedness is when the inner presence of God so replaces outward considerations that one's reputation can be trashed and He is still allowed to stay: "Blessed are ye, when men shall revile you, and persecute you, and shall say all manner of evil against you falsely, for my sake." To this is attached the promise, "Great is your reward in heaven."

We Are Invited

This teaching of Christ is also a portrait of Christ. The Crucified One is the showing forth of the blessedness of the beatitudes. He supremely allows God to be God: He is "the express image of his person." On the Cross He gives God the final permission, allowing Himself to be taken "out of this world unto the Father." His life and teaching are one. They invite us to be "buried with Him by baptism unto death: that like as Christ was raised up from the dead by the glory of the Father, even so we also should walk in newness of life." They invite us to die before we die so that we "shall not be hurt of the second death" after we die. They invite us to be one with Him as He is one with the Father, finding in Him healing and wholeness.

It is the Holy Spirit who gathers us into this unity. He is the Spirit of contemplation, the love with which the Son gazes upon the Father. We cannot actually see the Spirit, who is like the wind which "bloweth where it listeth," but we can see the effects of the Spirit as we can see the effects of the wind. The final chapter, therefore, will look at what characterizes a person who has recovered a contemplative spirit. It is my goal to be such a person, and I hope that by this point I have helped you to clear out of the way something of what might stop you from wanting it to be your goal, if indeed you are not already running there before me.

Chapter Nine:
The Spirit

Being Childlike

his book started with a quotation from the Bible. It is time to revisit it since it points to what a person with contemplative spirit has become: "Verily I say unto you, Except ye be converted and become as little children, ye shall not enter into the kingdom of heaven." Such a person has responded to the Savior's admonition, "Ye must be born again." She or he has, by the power of the Holy Spirit, become as a little child. The book started with poetry also, and this is the best way of describing this state. Thomas Traherne expressed in a poem called *An Infant Eye* how such a one sees the world:

> A simple Light from all Contagion free,
> A beam that's purely Spiritual, an Eye
> That's altogether Virgin, Things doth see
>   Ev'n like unto the Deity:
> That is, it shineth in an heavenly Sense,
> And round about (unmov'd) its Light dispence.

There is no contagion: no looking for any base advantage. The gaze is simple: it sees all as one, without complication. It is spiritual: it sees the deep spiritual reality of things. It is virgin: it has not been corrupted by a false way of looking. It looks the way God looks, from His point of view, bringing things to light without being disturbed by them. It sees from the very heart of all that is. Traherne comments elsewhere on the Scripture verse about becoming "as little children" that we are to become such "in the peace and purity of all our soul" so that "only those things appear, which did to Adam in Paradise, in the same light and in the same colors: God in His works, Glory in the light, Love in our parents, men, ourselves, and the face of Heaven: Every man naturally seeing those things, to the enjoyment of which he is naturally born."

Henry Vaughan, another English poet of the seventeenth century, writes about what this is like from his own recollections of childhood:

> Happy those early days, when I
> Shined in my angel-infancy!

He recalls an awareness of the eternal in nature:

> When on some gilded cloud, or flower,
> My gazing soul would dwell an hour,
> And in those weaker glories spy
> Some shadows of eternity.

Truly seen, the world is a manifestation of eternity. Its radiance is there for those with eyes to see. Vaughan explains that he

> felt through all this fleshly dress
> Bright shoots of everlastingness.

Traherne's most famous and most poetic prose is on the same theme, recalling his own childhood vision:

The corn was orient and immortal wheat, which never should be reaped, nor was ever sown. I thought it had stood from everlasting to everlasting. The dust and stones of the street were as precious as gold: the gates were at first the end of the world. The green trees when I saw them first through one of the gates transported and ravished me, their sweetness and unusual beauty made my heart to leap, and almost mad with ecstasy, they were such strange and wonderful things. The Men! O what venerable and reverend creatures did the aged seem! Immortal Cherubims! And young men glittering and sparkling Angels, and maids strange seraphic pieces of life and beauty! Boys and girls tumbling in the street, and playing, were moving jewels. I knew not that they were born or should die; But all things abided eternally as they were in their proper places. Eternity was manifest in the Light of Day, and something infinite behind everything appeared; which talked with my expectation and moved my desire.

This is living in the moment, in the eternal now. Everything is seen in its stillness by a soul not sold to the devices of change. Eternity is apprehended as it would have been in the innocence of our race.

Knowing knows no bounds: the heart is unconfined and reaches beyond what appears. There is an awareness of God through everything, corresponding to the soul's natural yearning for the divine.

Wonder

Above all, there is wonder. This is essential for thinking, for philosophy, and indeed for life. G.K. Chesterton wrote, "The world will never starve for want of wonders; but only for want of wonder." The way we see things determines who we are, how we undertake things, and indeed whether we undertake anything at all. Traherne wrote a poem entitled *Wonder* that recalls how this quality illuminated his childhood:

> How like an Angel came I down!
>   How Bright are all Things here!
> When first among His Works I did appear
>   O How their GLORY did me Crown?
>
> The World resembled His *Eternity*,
>   In which my Soul did Walk;
>   And every Thing that I did see,
>   Did with me talk.
>   The Skies in their Magnificence,
>   The Lively, Lovely Air;
> O how Divine, how Soft, how Sweet, how fair!
>   The Stars did entertain my Sense,
>   And all the Works of GOD so Bright and pure,
>   So Rich and Great did seem,
>   As if they ever must endure,
>   In my Esteem.
>
> A Native Health and Innocence
>   Within my Bones did grow,
> And while my GOD did all his Glories shew,
>   I felt a Vigour in my Sense
> That was all SPIRIT. I within did flow
>   With Seas of Life, like Wine;
> I nothing in the World did know,
>   But 'twas Divine.

The world reflects the eternal realm. Everything talks with the child: it all has meaning. Everything he sees is grasped in its spiritual essence. He in effect sees God. The poem continues beyond what I have cited in the spirit of the prose passage quoted above. The final stanza is of special interest for indicating the constituents of the Edenic state of childhood: it shows ownership and division to be absent from it. The word "proprieties" in it means "properties" in the sense of something belonging to one person rather than another. Here it is:

> Proprieties themselves were mine,
>   And Hedges Ornaments;
> Walls, Boxes, Coffers, and their rich Contents
>   Did not Divide my Joys, but all combine.
> Clothes, Ribbons, Jewels, Laces, I esteemed
>   My joys by others worn;
> For me they all to wear them seemed
>   When I was born.

Under one aspect, pursuing the spiritual goal of complete integration means giving up everything. Under another, and this is the one in view here, it means enjoying everything. And this latter—that of the child—is the more real: indeed, it endures for all eternity. It is having the hands open to receive everything from God, rather than closed with a miserly grasp on one little thing. The child (which is to say, the spiritually integrated person) as it were owns ownership itself ("Proprieties themselves were mine"). That means that he has entered into the complete oneness that contains every other oneness (including individuals having this or that). On the literal level, the child does not know that this is so-and-so's land he is walking on and that over there is someone else's: to him it is just land. On the spiritual level, the enlightened soul does not distinguish between "mine" (thought of as good) and "yours" (thought of as bad). To put it another way, this soul does not know good and evil for it is no longer affected by the eating "Of that forbidden tree, whose mortal taste / Brought death into the world, and all our woe": everything just is—there are no longer particular things on which a parody of God's blessing has been bestowed by the self. Divisions remain, but they are *within* the unity, enriching rather than limiting: hedges are ornaments; walls, boxes, and coffers combine rather than divide the joy taken in them.

To the unenlightened eye, this might seem unrighteous. A little child can be forgiven for not knowing that something belongs to another person, but for a grown person to act as though he doesn't is simply dishonest. Yet this misses what is wrong in thinking of anything as being in an absolute sense "mine." In reality, it all belongs to God. All that can really be "mine" is a duty to use it in a particular way at a particular moment. The worst of this attitude, though, is that it severely limits our joy. At the deeper level, prescinding from the concept of ownership of *other* people's property is not the intellectual prelude to thievery but the necessary precondition for unselfish conviviality. It enables one to delight in what is good for others, without casting upon it the blight of the thought, "That is not good because it is not *mine*." It is precisely the virtue that is the opposite of envy. It does not curse others' joy as not being its own or limit its joy to what the self (acting as though it were God) "blesses" as its own: it takes joy in *everything*. So the child in the poem esteems finery worn by others as though they wore it for him. It is the same for the spiritually integrated person as for the child. It is all his because it is God's and God is his because he is God's. There is scriptural justification for this: Saint Paul, writing to the Corinthians, says simply, "All things are yours." It is the mindset of heaven, where everyone's happiness belongs to everyone. It is paradisal living.

Community and Gratitude

I hope it is clear by now that someone who has recovered a contemplative spirit (become again as a little child) will be happy. How could she or he not be, with all the happiness on earth and in heaven at her or his disposal? Such a person feels no need to limit joy to what belongs to the self and therefore knows unlimited joy. This finding joy in others' blessings builds community; that community is the beginning of a new culture, one that receives everything and everyone as a gift. This is what every thing and every person truly is: a gift from God—there is no other fount or motive of existence. For every person, to be received as a gift is to be recognized and acknowledged in his or her true being. This recognition makes it easier to receive others as a gift, and so it goes on. The joy that surpasses the limits of the self spreads, and little by little a new way of knowing comes about—or rather the old way of knowing that we had when *we* were new to this world, and that our race had in its infancy. That is how our culture can be transformed. Ignoring the limits, boundaries, and division of the self and its "knowledge of good and evil," our culture can learn to refuse nothing good, so that the good there is to be seen is always recognized. People can rejoice together in this good.

There is a concomitant quality that makes for courteous and happy living: gratitude. If there is good all around, it is natural to be grateful. It can actually work the other way too, which is why habitual gratitude is a helpful spiritual practice. If one makes a point of saying thank you to God for all the good things of the day in one's evening prayer, one notices the good more. That leads to a less partial and more integrated heart: it is a way into the wholeness of God, a way of receiving the ultimate good. In fact, gratitude is so important spiritually that Meister Eckhart, the great Christian mystic and teacher, was able to say, "If a man had no more to do with God than to be thankful, that would suffice." If you are grateful, you have noticed God's goodness! You have (to quote Wordsworth) "a heart / That watches and receives." The receptivity is all.

Pleasure and Pain

It may be thought that this idea that life can be lived full of childlike wonder, happiness, and gratitude is a tad naive. The fact of the matter, it might be countered, is that people's perspectives are unavoidably altered by the promise of pleasure or the prospect of pain. Children live otherwise only because of their lack of experience. When we get older, we are not just going to be happy for other people, we are going to mesh or clash with them according to whether they give us pleasure or cause us pain. Yet Scripture presents an alternative. Saint Peter exhorts his readers to a different way of relating:

Seeing ye have purified your souls in obeying the truth through the Spirit unto unfeigned love of the brethren, see that ye love one another with a pure heart fervently: being born again, not of corruptible seed, but of incorruptible, by the word of God, which liveth and abideth for ever.

This is the love that comes with being born again with the pure heart of a child. It is a love, however, that does not grow old and weary. It is incorruptible, because it comes from the eternal Spirit of God. Another saying of Saint Peter can help us to understand how this love can transcend the promise of pleasure or the prospect of pain, or, to put it another way, how it can escape the passions of hope and fear. He writes, "One day is with the Lord as a thousand years, and a thousand years as one day." God's relation to time is not the same as ours. He has it all at once; we have it spread out, one bit after another. It is like a bicycle wheel. God, in eternity, is at the central point of the hub. He is so much at the center, that although the wheel is going round, He remains still. We, in time, are at the outside of the tire. We are so much on the outside that for us movement completes the circle that in God is all present in a single point and thus at once. Yet time does not have that fullness of reality that is there in that point where God is. There is total and absolute reality. The relative reality of time is contingent, dependent for what substance it has on God. It hovers between the really real of God and the unreality of nothingness. Time is spread out very thinly; in God there is no extension.

The same is true for the other, spatial, dimensions of creation. God is the absolute, the giver of being, the source of all possibility. To include them in our consideration, we can imagine instead of a wheel a sphere. God is perfectly still at the center of this sphere, for in Him there is no extension. Extension belongs to the created. Physical things are contingent—dependent for their reality on God—and changeable. They are spread out and move about. They are therefore weaker not only than God but than what is spiritual. Their mutual assaults are the action of the weak on the weak. The truly strong, the truly real, the spiritual, cannot be hurt in this way: nothing else can take its space because it is not extended and does not suffer from the limitation of space. It perdures; what belongs to space and time is weak and is therefore all going to end.

Shakespeare expressed this in a more poetical way. In *The Tempest*, Prospero has, by his magical art, put on a show, which ends with a suddenness that is disconcerting. He comments,

> Our revels now are ended. These our actors,
> As I foretold you, were all spirits, and
> Are melted into air, into thin air;
> And like the baseless fabric of this vision,
> The cloud-capped towers, the gorgeous palaces,
> The solemn temples, the great globe itself,
> Yea, all which it inherit, shall dissolve;
> And, like this insubstantial pageant faded,
> Leave not a rack behind. We are such stuff
> As dreams are made on, and our little life
> Is rounded with a sleep.

Life in space and time, even life in the most magnificent palaces, is such stuff as dreams are made on. It will all be dissolved.

In the light of this, and of what has just been said about time and space having only a relative reality compared to the absolute reality of God, pleasure and pain no longer have a necessarily directive force for those with hearts purified by the Spirit of God. Instead of valuing things that belong to time and space, such a heart values what belongs to eternity. It sees that pleasure cannot be put into a bank account. One experience of pleasure followed sometime later by another does not mean there are now two experiences of pleasure. The first one is forgotten. Although the circumstances can be remembered and similar pleasure can again be sought, the pleasure does not remain. A good meal had ten years ago no longer pleases. With regard to pleasure, one plus one does not equal two.

Similarly, such a heart can see that pain does not accumulate like a bad debt. One experience of pain followed sometime later by another does not mean there are now two experiences of pain. Health, of course, can decline, but pain disappears with time. With regard to pain, one plus one does not equal two. It follows from this that pleasure seeking and pain avoidance are not the highest values.

They need not compel, for they are limited to time, which has only an ambiguous reality. Only God is really real. He alone is the absolute point of reference for the Spirit-purified heart. The purity of heart that is sought in Him and given by Him lives unendingly, unlike pleasure and pain, and all the pageant of this world. The point is forcefully made by this poem of Herbert, which he called *Virtue*—another word for purity of heart:

> Sweet Day, so cool, so calm, so bright,
> The bridal of the earth and sky,
> The dew shall weep thy fall tonight;
> > For thou must die.
>
> Sweet Rose, whose hue angry and brave
> Bids the rash gazer wipe his eye,
> Thy root is ever in its grave,
> > And thou must die.
>
> Sweet Spring, full of sweet days and roses,
> A box where sweets compacted lie,
> My Music shows ye have your closes,
> > And all must die.
>
> Only a sweet and virtuous soul,
> Like season'd timber, never gives;
> But though the whole world turn to coal,
> > Then chiefly lives.

Gold

The final conflagration of the apocalypse can turn the world to charcoal, and "a sweet and virtuous soul" will still live. It has a greater reality than everything material. Symbolically, it is the "gold tried in the fire" offered to us by Christ. The fire of the final dissolution is nothing other than the presence of God meeting the impurity that is so fallen from Him that it no longer has being enough to keep it in existence. The purified soul has already met that fire. This is the Holy Spirit, which when the followers of Christ "were all with one accord in one place" appeared to them in the form of "cloven tongues like as of fire, and it sat upon each of them." This Spirit purifies the heart of each person who wants to be inwardly transformed so as to have a heart of gold where once there was a tarnished heart. It is the fire of which Jesus spoke, saying, "I am come to send fire on the earth." The Spirit spreads as fire does, though from person to person rather than from thing to thing. In *The Living Flame of Love*, Saint John of the Cross gives an image of the purified soul as a log so thoroughly ablaze that it is no longer possible to distinguish which is the log and which is the fire. This does not contradict the symbol of gold, since gold is traditionally associated with the sun, which is fire. It is the noblest of metals since it is not in its essence subject to decay or alteration; such is the soul purified by the fire of the Spirit. It, like gold, is the presence of that Spirit in the world. As the substance of gold cannot be altered by heat or by acid, so the purified soul shares in the immutability of God.

Like the innocent child in Traherne's poem *Wonder*, the purified soul senses that all is spirit. Indeed, three of the four traditional elements symbolize the Spirit. Air is the Spirit especially when experienced as wind, as when "suddenly there came a sound from heaven as of a rushing mighty wind, and it filled all the house." Water symbolizes the Spirit because it imitates the universal presence of God and cleanses the body as the Spirit cleanses the soul; it also revivifies the soul as water revivifies the body. Fire's symbolizing of the Spirit has just been explained; that leaves earth, which is the heaviest and least spiritual of the traditional elements. Yet even solid matter appears as a symbol of the Spirit when it is gold. And to the purified soul, everything has a golden aspect: it is all seen in terms of what is noblest about it. It is seen from the perspective of God, who "saw everything that He had made, and behold it was very good." It is seen as the manifestation of His providential purpose.

Seeing the Big Picture

It is seeing the "upper side" of what is woven on the loom, as in the weaver poem cited in Chapter Two. Even before the shuttles fall silent, that can in a certain sense be seen. Threads of Spirit and matter are interwoven in the rich fabric of our life on earth. The former are the golden threads; the silver threads are the reflection of the Spirit in the understanding of the mind. The inner eye of the purified heart will see these, and they will define the pattern. It is not that the vista in itself is different for such a heart: it is simply *seen* differently. As T. S. Eliot wrote, "The end of all our exploring will be to arrive where we started and know the place for the first time."

A poetic account of this kind of looking is given by Traherne:

> Pure Empty Powers that did nothing loathe,
>> Did like the fairest Glass,
>> Or Spotless polished Brass,
> Themselves soon in their Objects Image clothe.
>> Divine Impressions when they came,
> Did quickly enter and my Soul inflame.
>> 'Tis not the Object, but the Light
> That maketh Heaven; 'Tis a Purer Sight.
>>> Felicity
> Appears to none but them that purely see.

Loathing nothing (as in the first line) is not refusing to see any part of the picture: it is that whole and wholesome seeing referred to in Chapter Two. "Divine Impressions" are received by the person who sees the whole and sees the whole in each thing: one, that is, who contemplates God and sees Him in everything. What exactly is seen doesn't matter: what matters is the purity of sight. This is quite simply the way to happiness.

To recover it is to recover our essential being. Earlier in the poem, Traherne describes this being (as prior to its clothing in a body) thus:

> Then was my Soul only All to me,
>> A Living Endless Eye,
>> Just bounded with the Sky
> Whose Power, whose Act, whose Essence was to see.
>> I was an Inward *Sphere of Light*,
> Or an Interminable Orb of *Sight*,
>>> An Endless and a Living Day,
> A *vital Sun* that round about did *ray*
>>> All Life, All Sense,
> A naked Simple Pure Intelligence.

Seeing (or knowing) is of the essence. Traherne identifies this pure seeing with light, rhyming "light" with "sight." This is consonant with the active or creative aspect of seeing: it is a participation in the divine "let there be light." It echoes the words from Scripture quoted in Chapter One: "When thy eye is single, thy whole body also is full of light." It also fits with the traditional idea that purified souls radiate light, being what Jesus calls His followers—"the light of the world." This is represented in depictions of saints by halos, painted in gold to indicate spiritual purity. The endless and living day of the inward sphere of light corresponds to God's eternity, the vantage point of a naked, simple, pure intelligence. It sees all in the light of eternity.

That means that things are seen differently from how they would be seen by unpurified souls. Perhaps it is to such souls that Saint Paul addresses the reproach, "What hast thou that thou didst not receive?" The purified soul receives all as gift. Participating in the reciprocal love of the Holy Trinity, which is the Spirit, it can only receive what comes its way as an expression of love. It has therefore what the *Cloud* author calls "a kind of well-pleasedness." Meister Eckhart says that when you reach this stage, "what was previously an obstacle to you is now a great help." Difficult things that cause a soul not yet purified to stumble actually help one that is purified. It is as though the fire of the Spirit has so set it alight that a big damp log is to it but fuel to the fire, although it would have smothered a lesser conflagration, and a great gust of wind is as it were the action of a giant bellows, although it would have blown out a smaller blaze. Each passing problem roots its faith ever deeper in God, who never changes; each treachery roots its hope ever deeper in God, who is always faithful; each coldness from another compels its love to embrace God, whose love never grows cold.

Saint Thérèse of Lisieux, who was such a soul, said, "I always see the good side of things." For her, suffering was a spiritual opportunity inviting her to be closer to God, her greatest good. If God is all-loving, then it is necessarily the case that He intends good in everything: it is only a matter of having the inward eye to see it. That such positive vision is so very heroic need not discourage us from taking steps toward it. It is not a question of being either so pure of soul that everything makes us happy or so impure in our outlook that everything makes us miserable. Just seeing one good aspect in a difficult situation is a step in the right direction. Once we begin to look toward God, He will draw us toward Himself and the pure sight of the inward eye. Saintly exemplars remind us that God can work this miracle in people. As William Blake pointed out, the difference between a devil and an angel is only the way they see things. Our life is given to us that we might walk toward the angelic perspective.

Without Partiality

This perspective expects everything from God. Blake wrote, "It is not because angels are holier than Men or devils that makes them angels, but because they do not expect holiness from one another, but from God only." It is from God only that wisdom comes, for "the wisdom that is from above is first pure, then peaceable, gentle, and easy to be intreated, full of mercy and good fruits, without partiality, and without hypocrisy." Being pure of heart and soul involves having no affectation, putting up no barriers to others, and being "without partiality." That is to say, the only agenda is God's agenda. Saint Peter said, "God is no respecter of persons: But in every nation he that feareth Him, and worketh righteousness, is accepted with Him." The pure in heart share the universal acceptance of God. They are not partial.

This entails not simply being unselfish but, furthermore, not seeing with partiality. That is why it matters that we should not accept as an absolute the way of knowing that is prevalent in our culture. This is calculating. It measures so as to bend to a particular and partial purpose. Saint Thérèse of Lisieux boldly said that God was bad at arithmetic. She meant simply that He is not calculating: He gives us far more than we deserve. The abundance of the natural world witnesses to this fecundity of grace. Yet we live in a social milieu in which, even if everything is not reduced to its financial implications, it tends to be assessed according to measurement rather than quality. C. S. Lewis offered an interesting reflection on the spirit in which this approach was born. He argues in *The Abolition of Man* that magic and science were the fruit of the same seed: "One was sickly and died, the other was healthy and throve. But they were twins. They were born of the same impulse." In *English Literature in the Sixteenth Century*, he adds, "Bacon and the magicians have the closest possible affinity," and he observes in Bacon "a contempt for all knowledge that is not utilitarian" and a seeking of knowledge "for the sake of power." Magic is all about manipulation of nature for the sake of partial advantage; the Baconian empiriometric enterprise has a similar agenda—it appears, in Lewis's words, in an "unhealthy neighborhood" and "inauspicious hour." It cannot therefore be thought to share the pure light that is a participation in God's way of knowing. Of course, in bringing this to notice I am not arguing that either the pioneers or the present-day practitioners of this way of knowing are ungodly or evil: I am simply affirming that this way of knowing cannot be allowed an absolute suzerainty without cutting us off from God.

His pure wisdom is without partiality and also "peaceable, gentle." For the pure of heart, avoidance of violence is not powerlessness. Blake understood this. He dramatized in a poem a futile taking to arms to right injustice in which

> The hand of Vengeance found the Bed
> To which the Purple Tyrant fled;
> The iron hand crush'd the Tyrant's head,
> And became a Tyrant in his stead.

And he contrasts with this futility the true power of suffering and prayer:

> . . . vain the Sword & vain the Bow,
> They never can work War's overthrow.
> The hermit's Prayer & the Widow's tear
> Alone can free the World from fear.
> For a Tear is an Intellectual Thing,
> And a Sigh is the Sword of an angel King,
> And the bitter groan of the Martyr's woe
> Is an arrow from the Almighty's Bow.

The tear is "intellectual" in the sense of belonging to the heart or intellect of a person: to that center which is capable of unmediated contact with the light of God. God is almighty, so what He responds to—the suffering and prayer of His people—has real power, if what one has in mind is power to do good rather than to gain a partial and passing advantage.

God's Mother

Such is the power of the pure in heart. One person above all has it. Indeed, with the courage of my convictions, I have put this book under her protection. She is the epitome of everything I have been saying about the pure soul, except that with her there was no need for any process of purification: she has always had perfect purity. I will start with a fifteenth-century English poem about her—"makeless" in the second line means "peerless," and "ches" in the fourth means "chose." Here it is:

> I sing of a maiden
> That is makeless:
> King of alle kings
> To her son she ches.
>
> He came all so still
> There his mother was,
> As dew in Aprille
> That falleth on the grass.
>
> He came all so still
> To his mother's bower,
> As dew in Aprille
> That falleth on the flower.
>
> He came all so still
> There his mother lay,
> As dew in Aprille
> That falleth on the spray.
>
> Mother and maiden
> Was never none but she:
> Well may such a lady
> God's mother be.

The poem is explicit that there is not anyone like her, yet nonetheless she is the model of all who aspire to the perfect contemplation

266

of God, since it is only through having His Word, which she so lovingly received, dwelling in us that we can hope to enter into the knowing and loving of the Father in the power of the Spirit. So I will first go through the poem reflecting on what she can teach us and then look at what emerges (and other relevant considerations) in the light of Scripture.

The first point to note is that she chose to be the mother of the King of kings. It may seem that such a marvel is entirely God's doing. In a sense that is true, yet He chooses to do it only with the consent of the woman concerned. There is always that huge respect and courtesy on His part. As it was for Mary, so it is for us. If we want to know God through the Word that He has spoken, we have to consent to the presence of that Word. Knowing, as I hope I have shown, is something we choose to do. We actively pay attention to what we contemplate. Beholding is more than having eyes; hearing is more than having ears. Knowledge is cooperation. We give God permission to be beheld by us. We make His Word welcome.

His Word is the King of kings. He is sovereign over all powers. That means that in welcoming Him, we find ourselves at the heart of every act and present to every presence. We know from within. That is a different way of knowing creation, a way that knows the essential being of each thing; it is the only way to know God, who "is a Spirit."

The middle three stanzas of the poem are about God's work in the coming of the Word. It is "all so still . . . / As dew in Aprille." The thrice saying emphasizes what has already been alluded to: that God speaks in "a still small voice." It cannot be otherwise: God in Himself is the perfect repose of omnipotence—it is only the weak who feel the need to make a scene. It is in stillness and quietness that we know Him; it is in a receptivity that mirrors Mary's that we make Him welcome; it is as the earth open to the blue of the sky that we become the place where the dew falls. The three middle stanzas are nearly the same, imitating the almost imperceptible dew-like way in which God comes, but there are two variations: in the second line, indicating an increasing intimacy with Mary, and in the fourth, indicating an increasing fecundity. God comes where "his mother was . . . to his mother's bower . . . there his mother lay" and "as dew . . . that falleth on the grass . . . on the flower . . . on the spray." So it is with the life of grace: God becomes more intimately present very gently, and spiritual growth and fecundity come like the growth of a seed to one who "knoweth not how."

Knowing God involves both the activity of choice (indicated in the first stanza) and the passivity of waiting upon Him (indicated in the middle three stanzas). The final stanza puts these together by describing Mary as "mother and maiden." Outwardly, these are opposites, but in the God-bearer they are one. She is the fruitful mother by her own consent but also the virgin who allows nothing of this world to occlude her receptivity to the Most High.

The final stanza also picks up the second line of the first by emphasizing the uniqueness of God's mother. If we turn now to Scripture, we see that this is no barrier to our imitation of her perfect receptivity. That is made clear by this passage from Saint Mark's Gospel:

> There came then his brethren and his mother and they said unto him, Behold thy mother and thy brethren without seek for thee. And he answered them, saying, Who is my mother, or my brethren? And he looked round about on them which sat about him, and said, Behold my mother and my brethren! For whosoever shall do the will of God, the same is my brother, and my sister, and mother.

God's mother is each of those who "sat about him." That other Mary, Martha's sister, is therefore equally His mother because she "sat at Jesus' feet, and heard his word." She knows "one thing is needful"—being receptive to the Lord. To listen to the Lord, to pray "thy will be done," to live a life formed by this attention and prayer: this is to share in the unique privilege of Mary, the Mother of God.

She indeed shares her privilege with us. She is, to quote Words-worth again, "our tainted nature's solitary boast," and so through her the human race itself hears the words, "Thou hast found favour with God." The blessing of God upon her comes upon us if we join ourselves to her by imitation. Her own consent to God's plan models ours for us. It is an agreement to these words of the angel: "The Holy Ghost shall come upon thee, and the power of the Highest shall overshadow thee: therefore also that holy thing which shall be born of thee shall be called the Son of God." It is saying yes to the Holy Spirit, who declares that "Jesus is the Lord." It is a welcoming of "that holy thing" through whom we know the Father, the presence of His Word. It is a believing that the miracle of the transformation of the human heart and soul can be accomplished, "for with God nothing shall be impossible." Above all, it is saying, "Behold the handmaid of the Lord; be it unto me according to thy word." A handmaid is receptive to the least indication of the one she serves; those who contemplate say with the psalmist, "As the eyes of a maiden unto the hand of her mistress; so our eyes wait upon the LORD our God, until that he have mercy upon us." Our eyes too say, "Be it unto me according to thy word," because they know that they were fashioned by that Word, and it is only by being made anew through Him that our seeing can contemplate the glory of the Father. It is not simply a matter of doing what is right or avoiding what is wrong: it is in one's very being that this fashioning anew happens. It requires a receptivity as of wax to the seal; the harp to the harpist; the mirror to the light.

This is the beginning of the contemplative life. The manner of its continuance is announced in Mary's canticle of praise, which is literally—that is, liturgically—a daily part of contemplatives' lives:

> My soul doth magnify the Lord, And my spirit hath rejoiced in God my Saviour. For he hath regarded the low estate of his handmaiden: for, behold, from henceforth all generations shall call me blessed. For he that is mighty hath done to me great things; and holy is his name. And his mercy is on them that fear him from generation to generation. He hath shewed strength with his arm; and he hath scattered the proud in the imagination of their hearts. He hath put down the mighty from their seats, and exalted them of low degree. He hath filled the hungry with good things; and the rich he hath sent empty away. He hath holpen his servant Israel, in remembrance of his mercy; As he spake to our fathers, to Abraham, and to his seed for ever.

The contemplative magnifies the Lord: like John the Baptist she says, "He must increase, but I must decrease." Her joy is in God, not in what passes. She knows that in humbling herself she will be exalted.

She is blessed because she gives permission to God for what He wills. She prefers that the Almighty should do things to her rather than that she should exercise her own power. She totally respects Him. She knows that the proud heart can know nothing, the humble and receptive heart everything. She hungers for God, who she knows shows mercy as He ever has.

To be a contemplative is to allow oneself to be impressed by God: to give the things that speak of Him due weight. So Mary, when she had heard what was said by the shepherds about the angelic announcement of "tidings of great joy," "kept all these things, and pondered them in her heart." And when she did not understand what her Son said about the claims of His Father's business, she "kept all these sayings in her heart." The contemplative does the same with His words given to us through the Scriptures.

She is not exempt from suffering, like Mary, who was told by Simeon, "A sword shall pierce through thy own soul." She knows that the word God speaks in the events of our lives, as in the Scriptures, is "quick, and powerful, and sharper than any two-edged sword, piercing even to the dividing asunder of soul and spirit, and of the joints and marrow, and is a discerner of the thoughts and intents of the heart." Yet she has confidence and trust that the discernment is so that the path to true joy may be found and that "the dividing asunder" is so that her immortal spirit may be freed from what passes so as to be fit for the enjoyment of paradise. In her heart she stands with Mary "by the cross of Jesus" and with the Apostle John receives her as her mother. She knows her sorrow, but also her faith. She waits with her in the "upper room . . . with one accord in prayer and supplication," ready to receive the Holy Spirit.

Mary, the contemplative par excellence, stands for the whole Church as she prays by the power of the Spirit to the Father in the name of the Son. Pope Saint John Paul II, speaking to young people, identified her as "the best Teacher for achieving knowledge of the truth through contemplation." He highlighted the importance of learning from her for the culture of our time in these words:

> The drama of contemporary culture is the lack of interiority, the absence of contemplation. Without interiority culture has no con-

tent; it is like a body that has not yet found its soul. What can humanity do without interiority? Unfortunately, we know the answer very well. When the contemplative spirit is missing, life is not protected and all that is human is denigrated. Without interiority, modern man puts his own integrity at risk.

The lack of interiority comes from a materialist epistemology that is only willing to know what can be measured in space and time. It threatens the integrity of Man because it can see only in a fragmented way, and as is the knowing, so is the knower. Mary is, according to the saint, "the incomparable model of contemplation and wonderful example of fruitful, joyful and enriching interiority." She shows us the way to recovering a contemplative spirit.

As was said in the first chapter, her color is blue. This is because she is the pure one, the immaculately conceived; she is the Queen of Heaven; she is the one who looks on the earth from the place of light. I want to come back to that color now, since it is both her color and that of every contemplative. It is the color whose meaning I seek; it is the color of where I want to be; it is the color of my heavenly home. In the first chapter I considered it as light beckoning toward paradise; in this last I want to consider it as pigment, the trace on earth that points to heaven.

Ultramarine

I mentioned briefly its traditional source in Chapter Six when considering Yeats's poem *Lapis Lazuli*. This precious stone was used to make the blue pigment known as "ultramarine." It was not easy to find, hence the name of the pigment, which means "beyond the sea." The sea in question would have been the Mediterranean, considered (as its name implies) as being the middle of the earth. Traditional Christian maps, such as the *Mappa Mundi* preserved in Hereford Cathedral, show Jerusalem as their central point because it is spiritually central. However, lapis lazuli came from beyond there: farther to the east. Symbolically, it comes from a place that Jerusalem only represents: paradise, the home of our first parents. The *Mappa Mundi* marks this as its most eastern point with a picture of Adam and Eve being expelled from it. It is the place where the sun rises—the orient, the place of the origin of mankind. The east symbolizes also the resurrection of Christ, through whom paradise is restored. Blue is the color of paradise, and the stone used for its pigment traditionally comes from the direction of paradise, from its very approach. Lapis lazuli is the stone of paradise.

It is celebrated in a long poem about stones by a French bishop of the eleventh and twelfth centuries, Marbode de Rennes. It is, he writes,

> By nature with superior honours graced,
> As gem of gems above all others placed.

He claims for it the power to bring peace:

> Its soothing power contentions fierce controls,
> And in sweet concord binds discordant souls.

Its heavenly radiance requires a purity from one who uses it:

> But he who dares to wear this gem divine
> Like snow in perfect chastity must shine.

Coming from the earth, however, lapis lazuli itself needs to be purified for its true meaning to emerge, just as the heart needs to be purified before it can see God. It has an admixture of calcite and pyrite in it, producing white streaks and specks of gold amidst its blue—as it were, clouds and stars in the sky stopping it from being entirely blue. These need to be removed to produce pure ultramarine. The calcite is characterized by the element earth and the pyrite by the element fire. The removal of these leaves a pure ultramarine, which is characterized by the element water. This element is not identified with water completely literally: it is rather the fluid essence of creation. The result of the refining process therefore is a solid that represents the fluid, or, to give its symbolic meaning, it is an embodiment of the spiritual. Ultramarine has all the symbolic implications of water outlined in Chapters One and Three: it represents the universal presence of God; it is the liquid counterpart of light; it is the sign of eternity. And its color is the color of water: blue. The pigment, the water, and the color mean the same thing: the presence of the Spirit that gives life, the promise of paradise, the hope of heaven.

Concomitantly, they are associated with the qualities that make a soul receptive to this spiritual life and heavenly happiness. These are themselves aptly symbolized by water, which, to quote a distinguished commentator on the use of ultramarine, "is completely obedient." He goes on:

> And water obeys with grace because whenever it is transformed, its transformations are unfailingly beautiful. Unifying blankets of snow are countless filigree crystals, glistening dew drops are innumerable perfect spheres, and intangible mists magically arise, softly envelop and silently vanish. When liquid water scatters or gathers, its movements are always fluent, if not hypnotic. It follows smooth, elegant, economical curves to assume whatever shape circumstances ask of it. . . . Water's graceful obedience is the result of being completely in-tune with the realities around it. It has no selfish agenda. It does not calculate or negotiate but instantly, selflessly and unconditionally does whatever is required of it.

This of course is the state of a soul totally receptive to the promptings of the Spirit. It follows that contemplating water or its embodiment, ultramarine, or simply the color blue in their essence, tends to make a soul fit for heaven. It makes the one contemplating like what is contemplated in its manifestation (even to the extent of becoming identified with it) and thus capable of knowing that which is manifest through it: the heavenly realities. Such is the intention behind the fourteenth-century diptych (two paintings hinged together) altarpiece reproduced on the covers of this book: King Richard II of England (depicted on the left side) contemplates, with the help of the intercession of saints, the Virgin and angels clad in ultramarine blue and holding out to him the Savior Child offering golden and immutable purity (depicted on the right side). Mary is *stella maris*, the star of the sea, the one who perfectly embodies this essence of obedient water: "Be it unto me according to thy word." The ultramarine blue in her robe resonates with the soul and draws it to receptivity, a receptivity that is open to the heaven that it images.

Being difficult to find and difficult to refine, ultramarine was historically particularly expensive. In fact, it is recorded as having been literally worth its weight in gold: the color of heaven had, as it were, the value of the heart ready for heaven. Lapis lazuli was used medicinally as well as for making paint pigment. In particular, it was used for healing diseases of the eye. It was therefore used to put right how people see. The blue stone making whole the eye so that it can see the blue of heaven points to the Spirit making whole the eye of the heart so that it can look toward the heavenly homeland. The meaning of blue is related to the seeing as well as the seen. Ultimately, they are one, for God is only seen in God. The meaning of blue, the pigment of which is rare on earth but the heavenly light of which we see abundantly as we look toward the sky, is the divinely inspired longing for God in the human heart. What is seen in earth and sky speaks of what is in the heart. They are one, and they call us to the work of fulfilling our deepest desire: the Eden project of the heart; the quest for purity; the preparation for seeing God.

Sapphire

The old Greek word for sapphire (σάπφειρος) is said to have been used for lapis lazuli. In the Greek version of the book of the prophet Ezekiel, it is used to indicate the appearance of the throne of God: "Above the firmament . . . was the likeness of a throne, as the appearance of a sapphire stone: and upon the likeness of the throne was the likeness as the appearance of a man above upon it." From this throne and the One upon it radiates "the glory of the LORD," before which the prophet falls on his face.

The book of Exodus (in the Greek version) describes that upon which God stands as sapphire:

> Then went up Moses, and Aaron, Nadab, and Abihu, and seventy of the elders of Israel: And they saw the God of Israel: and there was under His feet as it were a paved work of a sapphire stone, and as it were the body of heaven in his clearness. And upon the nobles of the children of Israel He laid not His hand: also they saw God and did eat and drink.

Evagrius Ponticus, a fourth-century monk and theologian, alludes to this text when explaining an experience of one purified in heart praying:

When the mind—after having stripped off the old man—has been reclothed in one who comes from grace, then it will see its state, at the moment of prayer, similar to sapphire or to the color of the sky. This is what Scripture describes as the place of God—what was seen by the ancients on Mount Sinai.

In the knowing of the purified heart is the Known. The blue is in the seeing as well as in the seen. The meaning is the same: it is the place of God. This is both heaven and the heart that has been purified so as to be able to behold Him. The seeing becomes possible both because of the purification and because of God's gift of His light. Evagrius explains:

> If one wishes to see the state of the mind, let him deprive himself of all representations, and then he will see the mind appear similar to sapphire or the color of the sky. But to do that without being passionless is impossible, for one must have the assistance of God who breathes into him the kindred light.

This "kindred light" is the light of God experienced when the intellect or heart is in a state that is pure and prepared for it. This "state of the mind is an intellectual peak, comparable in color to the sky. Onto it, there comes, at the time of prayer, the light of the Holy Trinity."

This is seeing in the light of God, which colors the mind with the color of heaven. This is true knowing. This whole book has been about knowing, so I owe you before I finish it a conclusion about how we truly know.

The Final Word on Prayer

The answer is simple: true knowing comes from prayer. Evagrius writes, "Prayer is the state of mind that comes to be from the single-light of the Holy Trinity." Prayer is an entering into the light of God that shows us things as they truly are: utterly dependent on their Creator and speaking of Him. It is not necessary to master an encyclopedia to know truly: it is enough to pray. A single Hail Mary said from the heart is a more true knowing than the mastery of a shelf full of academic journals. It comes from the heart and goes to the heart: to the most pure heart of Mary and through her to the heart of God. We have cultivated too much knowledge of the periphery. It is time to return to the heart; to go back to that first innocence of our life and of our race; to begin again from the place where we touch our Maker. A prayer, any prayer, from the heart is so precious to Him that the wonder is that we could have ever imagined that anything else could be more important. He longs for a word from the heart more than any lover ever longed for a token of love. Giving it is for us too the perfection of love. It is ours to give. We can do it now.

So, at the end of all these words, I have one word for you: pray.

And if these words have helped in any way at all, or even if they haven't, then I ask your prayer for me also. I make Shakespeare's valediction my own:

> . . . my ending is despair
> Unless I be relieved by prayer,
> Which pierces so, that it assaults
> Mercy itself, and frees all faults.

Notes

Initial quotation: Martin Heidegger, *Poetry, Language, Thought*, translated by Albert Hofstadter (New York, 1975) p.223. The title of the lecture, "…Poetically Man Dwells…," is a citation from Hölderlin's poem *In Lovely Blueness*.

Introduction: Restoring the Wonder of a Child
"Verily I say…" Matthew 18.3.
Bible quotations are from the King James Version.

Some Poetry: "We need to recover…" *Evangelii Gaudium* (Rome, 2013) paragraph 264; "true love is…" ibid. paragraph 215; "There was a time…" *Ode on Intimations of Immortality from Recollections of Early Childhood* lines 1–9; "Except a man…" John 18.3.

The Doors of Perception: "If the doors…" *The Marriage of Heaven and Hell*; "willing suspension…" *Biographia Literaria*, Chapter 14.

Just a Monk: "Faith cometh by hearing" Romans 10.17.

Some More Poetry: "to thee / Science appears" Book Two, lines 216–26; "ye who are fed" Book Eight, lines 430–35.

The Atoms of Democritus: "For man has closed himself up…" *The Marriage of Heaven and Hell*; a poem—"Mock on, Mock on…"; Democritus was…—Sylvia Berryman, "Democritus," *The Stanford Encyclopedia of Philosophy* (Fall 2010 edition), Edward N. Zalta (ed.), URL = http://plato.stanford.edu/archives/fall2010/entries/democritus/; *Il Saggiatore* —Henri Bortoft, *Taking Appearance Seriously* (Edinburgh, 2012) p.39.

Newton's Particles of Light: "by convention" Sylvia Berryman, "Democritus," *The Stanford Encyclopedia of Philosophy* (Fall 2010 edition), Edward N. Zalta (ed.), URL = http://plato.stanford.edu/archives/fall20 10/entries/democritus/ paragraph 2—Atomist Doctrine.

Galileo, Violence, and Rape: "I cannot sufficiently admire…" Henri Bortoft, *Taking Appearance Seriously* (Edinburgh, 2012) p.37; Kant, "after a plan…" Henri Bortoft, *The Wholeness of Nature* (Edinburgh, 1996) p.17, quoting *Critique of Pure Reason*, translated by Norman

Kemp Smith (London, 1964) p.20; Bacon—ibid. p.243, quoting Caroline Merchant, *The Death of Nature* (London, 1982) p.168; "a fragile mythology…" Peter Kingsley, *Reality* (Point Reyes, CA, 2003) p.254.

Solid Body Thinking: Plotinus—Robert Bolton, *The Keys of Gnosis* (Hillsdale, NY, 2004) p.66, quoting *Enneads* 3,6,6; "Fear not them…" Matthew 10.28; "calculative thinking" Henri Bortoft, *The Wholeness of Nature* (Edinburgh, 1996) p.174; Its artistic expression…—Owen Barfield, *Saving the Appearances: A Study in Idolatry* (Middletown, CT, 1988) p.94; "ignorant armies…clash by night" Matthew Arnold, *Dover Beach*.

Getting Things Done: An intelligent book about Britain's prisons—Andrew Coyle, *The Prisons We Deserve*; *Paradise Lost*, end up eating not fruit but ashes—Book Ten, lines 564–66.

The Receptive Heart: Solomon asks…—1 Kings 3.5–14; "And this is life eternal…" John 17.3; "without him was not any thing made…" John 1.3; "There is some soul of goodness…" Shakespeare, *Henry V*, Act 4, Scene 1, lines 4–5; "In the sweat of thy face…" Genesis 3.29.

A Fresh Look: "garden eastward…" Genesis 2.8; "Nature is only squalid…" *Look to the Land* (Hillsdale, NY, 2003) p.114.

Reading Nature, Word, and God: Benedictine teacher—Louis of Blois, *The Rule of the Spiritual Life* (London, 1871) Chapter 28; a philosophermonk—Dom Illtyd Trethowan.

Tradition: an author of the last century—see *The Essential Writings of Frithjof Schuon* (Shaftesbury, 1991).

PART ONE: CONTEMPLATING NATURE

"For the invisible things of Him…" Romans 1.20.

Chapter One: Light and Color

God Is Light: "The light of the body…" Luke 11.34–36; "false secondary power" Wordsworth, *The Prelude* (version of 1805), Book Two, line 221; "God is light" 1 John 1.5; Plato saw the sun as a symbol…—C.H. Dodd, *The Interpretation of the Fourth Gospel* (Cambridge, 1953) p.139; the *Poimandres* says…—ibid. p.33; Philo of Alexandria—ibid. pp.55–56; Other traditions testify—J.C. Cooper, *An Illustrated Encyclopaedia of Traditional Symbols* (London, 1978) pp.96–97; "God is a Spirit" John 4.24; "God is light…" 1 John 1.5.

A Glory Passed Away: "The Rainbow comes and goes..." *Ode on Intimations of Immortality from Recollections of Early Childhood* lines 10–18; "O Rose..." Blake, *The Sick Rose*; The rose is a very rich symbol...— J.C. Cooper, *An Illustrated Encyclopaedia of Traditional Symbols* (London, 1978) pp.141–42.

Let There Be Light: "And God said..." Genesis 1.3; "In the beginning..." Genesis 1.1; the last book of the Bible declares...—Revelation 22.5; "on things above..." Colossians 3.2; "every good gift..." James 1.17; "The sun shall be no more thy light..." Isaiah 60.19; "there is no variableness..." James 1.17.

God in the Dark: According to Nicholas of Cusa...—*Nicholas of Cusa: Selected Spiritual Writings*, translated and introduced by H. Lawrence Bond (New York, Mahwah, NJ, 1979), introduction, p.46; "the earth was without form..." Genesis 1.2; "God divided the light..." Genesis 1.4; It is not essentially evil...—J.C. Cooper, *An Illustrated Encyclopaedia of Traditional Symbols* (London, 1978) p.50; "An horror of great darkness..." Genesis 15.12; "when the sun went down...A smoking furnace" Genesis 15.17; "The endurance of darkness..." *The Collected Works of St. John of the Cross*, translated by Kieran Kavanaugh, OCD, and Otilio Rodriguez, OCD (Washington, DC, 1979) p.685; "darkness was upon the face of the deep..." Genesis 1.2; "And God said, Let there be light..." Genesis 1.3; "In Him we live..." Acts 17.28.

The Sun and the Moon: "And God said, Let there be lights..." Genesis 1.14; "Let them be for lights..." Genesis 1.15; "trailing clouds of glory..." *Ode on Intimations of Immortality from Recollections of Early Childhood* lines 65–66; "God made two great lights..." Genesis 1.16; coats of skins—Genesis 3.21; Traditionally, the sun and the moon...—René Guénon, *Symbols of Sacred Science* (Hillsdale, NY, 2004) pp.410–12; Saint Thomas Aquinas's definitions...—ibid. pp.413–14, quoting *De Veritate* q.xv,a.1—*Ratio discursum quemdam designat, quo ex uno in aliud cognoscendum anima humana pervenit; intellectus vero simplicem et absolutam congnitionem (sine aliquo motu vel discursu, statim in prima et subita acceptione) designare videtur.*

The Mother of All Journeys: Saint Benedict...in his Rule...—Chapter 41; "in part..." 1 Corinthians 13.9; "face to face" Corinthians 13.12.

The Stars Also: "made the stars..." Genesis 1.16; "And they that be wise..." Daniel 12.3; "the soul that rises..." *Ode on Intimations of Immortality from Recollections of Early Childhood* line 60; She noticed stars...— *Thérèse de Lisieux: Oeuvres Complètes* (Paris, 1992) p.97.

Children of Light: "walk as…" Ephesians 5.8; "to walk in the light" 1 John 1.7; "put on the armour of light" Romans 13.12; "the light of the world" Matthew 5.14; "believe in the light…may be the children…" John 12.36; "good works…shine before men" Matthew 5.16; "the light of the LORD" Isaiah 2.5; "as children of light" Ephesians 5.8; "shine as lights…" Philippians 2.15; "as the stars…" Daniel 12.3.

The Dayspring from on High: "the one Morning Star…" the *Exultet* in the Easter Vigil liturgy; "the dayspring…" Luke 1.78; "the light shineth…" John 1.5; "The people which sat in darkness…" Matthew 4.16; "for a light…salvation unto…" Isaiah 49.6; "shall have the light…the light of the world" John 8.12; "the true Light…" John 1.9; "I am come a light…" John 12.46; "thou will light…" Psalm 18.28; "my light…" Psalm 27.1; "O send out…"Psalm 43.3; "O LORD my God…" Psalm 104.1–2; "his face did shine…" Matthew 17.2; "the darkness is past…" 1 John 2.8; "the darkness comprehended it not" John 1.5; "upon the face…" Genesis 1.2; "And it was about…" Luke 24.44–45; "In the end of the Sabbath…" Matthew 28.1–3; "Fear not ye…" Matthew 28.5–6; "Then opened he…" Luke 24.45; "the dayspring from on high…" Luke 1.78.

Color: "by the things that are made…" Romans 1.20; If you look at the sky—Henri Bortoft, *The Wholeness of Nature* (Edinburgh, 1996) pp. 43–44, citing Goethe's work.

The Meaning of Blue: J.C. Cooper, *An Illustrated Encyclopaedia of Traditional Symbols* (London, 1978) p. 40; Udo Becker, *The Continuum Encyclopedia of Symbols*, translated by Lance W. Garmer (London, 2005) p. 43; Richard Rohr and Andreas Ebert, *The Enneagram: A Christian Perspective*, translated by Peter Heinegg, p. 125; there is no explicit mention of this color—Gladstone, *Studies on Homer and the Homeric Age* (Oxford, 1858); "our tainted nature's…" in his poem *The Virgin*; "Unto the pure…" Titus 1.15; "in spirit and in truth" John 4.23.

The Red Horse: Udo Becker, *The Continuum Encyclopedia of Symbols*, translated by Lance W. Garmer (London, 2005) p. 43; J.C. Cooper, *An Illustrated Encyclopaedia of Traditional Symbols* (London, 1978) pp. 40–41; "And there went out another horse…" Revelation 6.4; "as blood" Revelation 6.12; "the seven angels…the vials of the wrath of God…" Revelation 16.1; "…upon the rivers…" Revelation 16.4; "shall the sun be darkened…" Matthew 24.29; "the elements shall melt…" 2 Peter 3.10; "darkness over the whole land…" Mark 15.33; "with a loud voice…" Mark 15.34; He is made sin…—2 Corinthians 5.21; "unto the end" John 13.1; the Scottish poet—Robert Burns, *A Red, Red Rose*.

Green Grows the Grass: "O the greenness…" *Hildegard of Bingen: Selected Writings*, translated by Mark Atherton (London, 2001) p.35; J.C. Cooper, *An Illustrated Encyclopaedia of Traditional Symbols* (London, 1978) p.40; Udo Becker, *The Continuum Encyclopedia of Symbols*, translated by Lance W. Garmer (London, 2005) entry for "green."

They Clothed Him with Purple: J.C. Cooper, *An Illustrated Encyclopaedia of Traditional Symbols* (London, 1978) p.40; Udo Becker, *The Continuum Encyclopedia of Symbols*, translated by Lance W. Garmer (London, 2005) p.319; "away into the hall…the whole band…" Mark 15.16–17; the ancient dye used…—Spike Bucklow, *The Alchemy of Paint: Art, Science and Secrets from the Middle Ages* (London, 2009) p.208.

How Colors Relate: two triangles—René Guénon, *Symbols of Sacred Science* (Hillsdale, NY, 2004) p.336; "put on Christ" Galatians 3.27; "all things were made" John 1.3; "God is light" 1 John 1.5.

The Rainbow: "This is the token…" Genesis 9.17; "The appearance of the bow…" Ezekiel 1.28; reigns on a rainbow—Udo Becker, *The Continuum Encyclopedia of Symbols*, translated by Lance W. Garmer (London, 2005) p.243; "droppeth as the gentle rain…" Shakespeare, *The Merchant of Venice*, Act 4, Scene 1, lines 185–86; Talmudic thought—Udo Becker, op. cit. p.243; assimilated to the serpent—René Guénon, *Symbols of Sacred Science* (Hillsdale, NY, 2004) p.375–76; symbol of Christ—John 3.14; of the devil—Genesis 3.1.

Unweaving the Rainbow: "destroyed all the poetry…" cited in Penelope Hughes-Hallet, *The Immortal Dinner: A Famous Evening of Genius and Laughter in Literary London, 1817* (Chicago, 2002) p.138; "Do not all charms fly…" *Lamia*, Part Two; "There is merely an inability…" Ludwig Wittgenstein, *Remarks on Colour*, edited by G.E.M. Anscombe, translated by Linda L. McAlister and Margarete Schättle (Oxford, 2007) section 2, paragraph 12; "peering eyes" Edgar Allen Poe, *Sonnet to Science*.

Chapter Two: Life and Wholeness

Life and Light: "With thee is the fountain…" Psalm 36.9; "In him was life…" John 1.4; "the resurrection…" John 11.25; "the light of the world…" John 8.12; "might have life…" John 10.10; "the true Light…" John 1.9; "green tree" Luke 23.31.

Beyond Time and Space: "I choose them all"—*Je choisis tout* in *Thérèse de Lisieux: Oeuvres Complètes* (Paris, 1992) p.84.

The Pattern He Has Planned: popular verses—*Just A Weaver* by Benjamin Malachi Franklin; "The sufferings of this present time" Romans 8.18; "Your sorrow…" John 16.20.

Adam, Eve, and Us: "the tree…" Genesis 2.9; "hid themselves…" Genesis 3.8; "Thy will…" Matthew 6.10; "have it more abundantly" John 10.10.

Looking at Darkness Within: the beam to the mote—Luke 6.41–42.

Loving Welcome: "knowledge of good and evil" Genesis 2.9; "Peace, peace…" Jeremiah 6.14; "Repent what's past…" *Hamlet*, Act 3, Scene 4, line 150; as Dante observed…—*E'n la sua volontade è nostra pace*, *The Divine Comedy: Paradiso*, Canto 3, line 85; "murmuring" *Rule of Saint Benedict*, Chapter 34; "not yea and nay" 2 Corinthians 1.19; an entire therapy—Rogerian Therapy, developed by Carl Rogers.

Wholeness of Spirit: "the second death" Revelation 20.6; in the Decalogue—Deuteronomy 5.20; "Come ye blessed" Matthew 25.34; "For I was an hungred…" Matthew 25.35–36.

Seeing the Whole: "the imagination of the whole…" *The Prelude* (version of 1805), Book Thirteen, line 65; "My main concern…" quoted in HRH the Prince of Wales, Tony Juniper, and Ian Skelly, *Harmony: A New Way of Looking at Our World* (London, 2010) p.180; "eidetic intuition" Robert Sokolowski, *Introduction to Phenomenology* (Cambridge, 2000) Chapter 12; "for the invisible things…" Romans 1.20; "little bit (two inches) of ivory" letter to J. Edward Austen, 16 December 1816.

The Music of Eternity: "with an eye made quiet…" *Tintern Abbey* lines 47–49; Heisenberg—HRH the Prince of Wales, Tony Juniper, and Ian Skelly, *Harmony: A New Way of Looking at Our World* (London, 2010) p.180; "eternal power…the things that are made" Romans 1.20.

All Is Everywhere: The Scholastics linked…—René Guénon, *Symbols of Sacred Science* (Hillsdale, NY, 2004) p.410, footnote 10; Aquinas taught…—*Summa Theologiae* 1a. 8, 3; "to see a World…" *Auguries of Innocence* line 1; "there are diversities of gifts…the same spirit" 1 Corinthians 12.4; "all the members…all the members rejoice" 1 Corinthians 12.26.

The Spiritual Life of a Potato: Henri Bortoft, *Taking Appearance Seriously* (Edinburgh, 2012) pp.73–74; "dark Satanic Mills" *And did those feet…* in the preface to *Milton: A Poem* line 8.

Creatures Great and Small: the Bible tells us—John 10.14.

Heaven: "nothing is secret" Luke 8.17.

Holiness: Christ thanked...—Matthew 11.25; To such belongs the kingdom—Mark 10.14; toil in the vineyard—Matthew 20.1–16.

Family and Community: "I am come..." John 10.10.

The Catholic Church: "There is one body..." Ephesians 4.4–6; "That they all..." John 17.21; "that they may be..." John 17.22–23.

God: "was not any thing..." John 1.3;

Life and Death: "See, I have set..." Deuteronomy 30.15.

Stillness: "Whoever saves a life..." Mishnah Sanhedrin 4:5; "Our Lord in the Garden..." *J'entre dans la Vie: Derniers Entretiens* (Paris, 1983) p. 58; "Peace I leave with you..." John 14.27; "All was sadness..." *Manuscrits Autobiographiques* (Lisieux, 1957) p. 15; "Be still..." Psalm 46.10; "nothing in particular" *Spiritual Letters* (London, 2003) p. v; "how to find stillness..." Peter Kingsley, *Reality* (Point Reyes, CA, 2003) p. 94; the Word through which...find eternal life—John 1.3, 17.3.

The Present Moment: the sacrament of the present moment—the title of a book by Jean-Pierre de Caussade, SJ; "Behold, now..." 2 Corinthians 6.2; "the seal's wide spindrift gaze..." Hart Crane, *Voyages* section 2; "Two lads..." Act 1, Scene 2, lines 63–65; "become as little children..." Matthew 18.3; "no thought for the morrow" Matthew 6.34; "All time belongs to Him..." Preparation of the Easter Candle.

Intensive Living: "Abide in me..." John 15.4; everything needed should be within—*Rule of Saint Benedict*, Chapter 66; as the first Christians did—Acts 2.44–45; the abbot is to look...—*Rule of Saint Benedict*, Chapter 55; cast out all sense...—*exue omnem proprietatem, Speculum Monachorum—Instructio Vitae Ascenticae*, part 8 in *Opera Quae Quidem Conscripsit Omnia...* (Cologne, 1672) p. 443; "our bourne of Time and Place" Tennyson, *Crossing the Bar* line 13.

Celestial Living: "hid with Christ..." Colossians 3.3; "God shall wipe away..." Revelation 21.4; "there are also celestial bodies" 1 Corinthians 15.40; "the doors being shut" John 20.26; "endureth unto everlasting life" John 6.27; "He that eateth my flesh..." John 6.56.

Difference and Hierarchy: "O, when degree is shak'd..." *Troilus and Cressida*, Act 1, Scene 2, lines 101–10; "Each thing meets..." ibid. lines 110–24; "might have life..." John 10.10; "the wolf catcheth them..." John 10.12.

Fragmentation in Our Time: "in tiny shreds..." Peter Kingsley, *Reality* (Point Reyes, CA, 2003) p. 122; "Seeing many things..." Isaiah 42.20;

"distracted from distraction..." *Four Quartets—Burnt Norton* part III; "no thought for..." Matthew 6.34.

Fragmented Thought: animals to be in effect machines—Letter to the Marquis of Newcastle, 16 November 1646; a common mind—André Gushurst-Moore, *The Common Mind* (Tacoma, 2013).

Entropic Collapse: Robert Bolton, *The Order of the Ages* (Hillsdale, NY, 2001) Chapters 9 and 10; "the shadow of death" Luke 1.79; "the earth was without form..." Genesis 1.2.

A Binary World: Plato thought that two...—J.C. Cooper, *An Illustrated Encyclopaedia of Traditional Symbols* (London, 1978) p.114; "the tree of the knowledge..." Genesis 2.17; no longer as one—René Guénon, *Symbolism of the Cross*, translated by Angus Macnab (London, 1975) pp.47–48; "the tree of life" Genesis 2.9.

Recovery: "all for You..." *The Collected Works of St. John of the Cross*, translated by Kieran Kavanaugh, OCD, and Otilio Rodriguez, OCD (Washington, DC, 1971) p.676; "all for me..." ibid.; "A condition of complete simplicity..." T.S. Eliot, *Four Quartets—Little Gidding* V; "selleth all" Matthew 13.44; "love the Lord thy God..." Matthew 22.37.

Chapter Three: Man and Cosmos

The Great Book of God: "And the vision of all..." Isaiah 29.11–12; "the great book of God" *The Rule of the Spiritual Life*, Chapter 28, in *Spiritual Works of Louis of Blois, Abbot of Liesse*, edited by John Edward Bowen (London, 1871); *Omnis mundi creatura...*—Alanus de Insulis; "exempt from public haunt..." *As You Like It*, Act 2, Scene 1, lines 15–17; He made, male and female...—Genesis 1.27; "To me the meanest flower..." *Ode on Intimations of Immortality from Recollections of Early Childhood* lines 204–5; her body was an envelope—in a letter to Mère Agnès de Jésus, *Thérèse de Lisieux: Oeuvres Complètes* (Paris, 1992) pp.593–94.

Water: J.C. Cooper, *An Illustrated Encyclopaedia of Traditional Symbols* (London, 1978) pp.188–89; a symbol of the Holy Spirit—Saint Cyril of Jerusalem, *Catechetical Instructions* 16 (*De Spiritu Sancto*); distinguished by His indistinction—*Meister Eckhart: Preacher and Teacher*, translated by Bernard McGinn (Mahwah, NJ, 1986) p.169; a symbol of His mercy—Shakespeare, *The Merchant of Venice*, Act 4, Scene 1, lines 184–86; "For in the wilderness..." Isaiah 35.6–7; "O that thou hadst hearkened..." Isaiah 48.18; a river pouring from the Temple—Ezekiel

47.1–5; "Every thing shall live..." Ezekiel 47.9; On its banks—Ezekiel 47.12; "a pure river of water..." Revelation 22.1; "Whosoever drinketh..." John 4.14; "He that believeth on me..." John 7.38; "This spake he..." John 7.39.

Trees: J.C. Cooper, *An Illustrated Encyclopaedia of Traditional Symbols* (London, 1978) pp.176–79; René Guénon, *Symbolism of the Cross*, translated by Angus Macnab (London, 1975) Chapter 9; "A man's reach should exceed his grasp..." *Andrea del Sarto* lines 97–98; implicit vertical pole—René Guénon, *Symbols of Sacred Science* (Hillsdale, NY, 2004); "its supporting central cedar pole..." *The Silken Tent*, lines 5-7; "And let it be..." 2 Samuel 5.24; "I AM THAT I AM" Exodus 3.14; "the tree of life..." Genesis 2.9; "fruit every month...for the healing..." Revelation 22.2; "the tree of the knowledge..." Genesis 2.17; an inverted tree—René Guénon, *Symbols of Sacred Science* (Hillsdale, NY, 2004) Chapter 51; "Look unto the rock..." Isaiah 51.1.

Birds: J.C. Cooper, *An Illustrated Encyclopaedia of Traditional Symbols* (London, 1978) pp.20–23; "the Holy Ghost descended..." Luke 3.22; "came in to him..." Genesis 8.11; Saint Benedict had a vision—Pope Saint Gregory, *The Dialogues*, Book Two, Chapter 34; the eagle...—J.C. Cooper, op. cit. p.58; "youth is renewed..." Psalm 103.5; "Behold the fowls..." Matthew 6.26; "seek those things..." Colossians 3.1; "set your affection..." Colossians 3.2.

Contemplating the Cosmos: "The heavens declare..." Psalm 19.1; "the invisible things..." Romans 1.20; "the innocent brightness..." *Ode on Intimations of Immortality from Recollections of Early Childhood* line 196; "was not any thing made..." John 1.3; "He that hath seen me..." John 14.9; "the invisible things...even his eternal power..." Romans 1.20; "moved upon the face..." Genesis 1.2; "Let there be light" Genesis 1.3; "We do not want merely..." "The Weight of Glory," a sermon in the Church of Saint Mary the Virgin, Oxford, on June 8, 1942.

The Centrality of Man: "The letter killeth..." 2 Corinthians 3.6; "It is thou, O king..." Daniel 4.22; "he was driven..." Daniel 4.33; "Whosoever will save..." Luke 9.24; "the spirit giveth life" 2 Corinthians 3.6; in perceiving the cosmos we find ourselves at the center *et seq.*—Jean Borella, *La Crise du Symbolisme Religieux* (Paris, 2008) pp.24–44.

All This Is Mine: "You never enjoy...Till you can sing..." *Centuries of Meditation* (London, 1960) the first century, section 29; "All things are yours...all are yours..." 1 Corinthians 3.21–23; "To come to possess..." *The Collected Works of St. John of the Cross*, translated by Kieran

Kavanaugh, OCD, and Otilio Rodriguez, OCD (Washington, DC, 1979) p.67; as Abbot John Chapman pointed out—*Spiritual Letters* (London, 2003) p.v; "Whoever knows how to die…"op. cit. p.681; "Whoever will lose his life…" Luke 9.24; "as little children…enter into…" Matthew 18.3; "The skies were mine…bounds nor…" op. cit. third century, section 3; "God said…" Genesis 1.26; the child like whom the gospel…—Mark 10.15; "When I consider…" Psalm 8.3–9.

My World, My Body: The human soul…contains the cosmos—Robert Bolton, *Self and Spirit* (Hillsdale, NY, 2005) p.37; "The fantasia of a fallen gentleman…" T.E. Hulme, *The Embankment*; "O if we but knew…" Gerard Manley Hopkins, *Binsey Poplars*; "Thanks to our bodies…" *Evangelii Gaudium* (Rome, 2013) paragraph 215.

Theurgy: "the winds and the sea" Matthew 8.27; "greater works" John 14.12; "The effectual fervent prayer…" James 5.16–18; "Cursed is the ground…" Genesis 3.17–19.

The Earth Mourneth: "The earth mourneth…" Isaiah 24.4–5; those rebelling—Jeremiah 5.23–24; "Your iniquities…" Jeremiah 5.25; "How long shall the land mourn…" Jeremiah 12.4; gives them their identity—Genesis 2.19.

Healing and Harmony: "We know that all things…" Romans 8.28.

Working but in Alliance: "the first / Poetic spirit…" *The Prelude* (version of 1805), Book Two, lines 275–76; "abated or suppress'd" ibid., Book Two, line 278; "after years" ibid., Book Two, line 276; the angels of little children—Matthew 18.10; "Even as an agent…" *The Prelude* (version of 1805), Book Two, lines 272–75; "His mind…" ibid., Book Two, lines 245–50; "spreads, / Tenacious of the forms…" ibid. lines 253–54; "What exists for thinking…" Peter Kingsley, *Reality* (Point Reyes, CA, 2003) p.190; "Self and world…" Henri Bortoft, *Taking Appearance Seriously* (Edinburgh, 2012) pp.201–2; Plotinus…observed…—HRH the Prince of Wales, Tony Juniper, and Ian Skelly, *Harmony: A New Way of Looking at Our World* (London, 2010) p.305; "God is a Spirit" John 4.24.

Man as Microcosm: Robert Bolton, *Self and Spirit* (Hillsdale, NY, 2005) Chapter 3; Robert Bolton, *The Order of the Ages* (Hillsdale, NY, 2001) pp.82–85; there are those who give themselves to prayer—Robert Bolton, *Keys of Gnosis* (Hillsdale, NY, 2004) p.85.

Offering It Up: Robert Bolton, *Keys of Gnosis* (Hillsdale, NY, 2004) Chapter 10; "Love ye your enemies…" Luke 6.35; "With the same measure…" Luke 6.38; "When thou makest a feast…" Luke 14.13–14.

In a Sense Everything: "The soul is in a sense…" *anima est quodammodo* *omnia*, Aristotle, *De Anima*, Book Three, Chapter 8—medieval Latin translation quoted in Henri Bortoft, *Taking Appearance Seriously* (Edinburgh, 2012) p.226; "The Soul, the Imagination..." *The Prelude* (version of 1805), Book Thirteen, line 65; "is the express / Resemblance..." ibid., Book Thirteen, lines 86–90; "in our life alone..." *Dejection: An Ode* line 48; "Ah! from the soul itself..." ibid. lines 53–58.

Heart of Man, Heart of the World: at the same angle—HRH the Prince of Wales, Tony Juniper, and Ian Skelly, *Harmony: A New Way of Looking at Our World* (London, 2010) p.128; the heart of Man is the heart of the world—René Guénon, *Symbols of Sacred Science* (Hillsdale, NY, 2004) p.406; a sacred cave—Pope Saint Gregory, *The Dialogues*, Book Two, Chapter 1; "closet...pray to thy Father" Matthew 6.6.

PART TWO: CONTEMPLATING THE WORD

"In the beginning was the Word..." John 1.1.

Chapter Four: Symbol and Language

Half a Sixpence and the Creed: Language is in a sense...—René Guénon, *Symbols of Sacred Science* (Hillsdale, NY, 2004) p.7; derived from the Greek—*Oxford English Dictionary*; an appeal to us to remember—Jean Borella, *Histoire et Théorie du Symbole* (Lausanne, 2004) p.81; "pleasant to the sight..." Genesis 2.9; as Philo of Alexandria observed...—C.H. Dodd, *The Interpretation of the Fourth Gospel* (Cambridge, 1953) p.141; According to Eriugena—Jean Borella, op. cit. p.53.

Beyond Being: ...in the same book of the Bible in fact, love—1 John 4.8; "Behold, when I come..." Exodus 3.13–14; "In him we live..." Acts 17.28; *Deo esse est dare esse*—cited in Vladimir Lossky, *Théologie Négative et Connaissance de Dieu Chez Maître Eckhart* (Paris, 1998) p.205; Being is *only* the symbol...—Jean Borella, *La Crise du Symbolisme Religieux* (Paris, 2008) p.294.

God Knows Best: "in part...through a glass..." 1 Corinthians 13.12; Being exists because...—Jean Borella, *Histoire et Théorie du Symbole* (Lausanne, 2004) p.235; "the covering..." Isaiah 25.7; "face to face" 1 Corinthians 13.12.

Depth of Being: he believes that forms...—Jean Borella, *Histoire et Théorie du Symbole* (Lausanne, 2004) p.104; To undertake this...—Jean Borella, *La Crise du Symbolisme Religieux* (Paris, 2008) p.55; "of making many books..." Ecclesiastes 12.12; comes from the Greek word—

The Meaning of Blue

Oxford English Dictionary; "always partakes..." J.C. Cooper, *An Illustrated Encyclopaedia of Traditional Symbols* (London, 1978) p.7; what we see is meaning—Henri Bortoft, *The Wholeness of Nature* (Edinburgh, 1996) p.131; incompleteness on its own level—Jean Borella, *Histoire et Théorie du Symbole* (Lausanne, 2004) p.87; "the glorious liberty..." Romans 8.21.

All about God: the beauty of a rose...—Jean Borella, *La Crise du Symbolisme Religieux* (Paris, 2008) p.13 note; "Everything that exists..." René Guénon, *Symbols of Sacred Science*, translated by Henry D. Fohr (Hillsdale, NY, 2004) p.10; "Indeed, there are traces..." Owen Barfield, *Poetic Diction: A Study in Meaning* (Middletown, CT, 1973) pp.79–80; Chapter Three of Saint John's Gospel—verses 5 and 8; "contemplation by which..." Bonaventure, *The Soul's Journey into God*, translated by Ewert Cousins (New York, 1978) p.69; "The whole of this perceptible universe..." *Revue des Sciences Philosophiques et Théologiques*, Volume 95, Number 2 (Paris, 2011) p.363 (*universus enim mundus iste sensilis quasi quidam liber est scriptus digito Dei, hoc est virtute divina creatus, et singulae creaturae quasi figurae quedam sunt, non humano placito inventae, sed divino arbitrio institutae ad manifestandam et quasi quodammodo significandam invisibilem Dei sapientiam*); "corporeal...and visible creature..." ibid. p.348 (*corporea...et visibilis creatura, iam ipse scriptus intus ac foris; ut per ea quae facta sunt intellecta, ea quae fecit Sapientia conspicuatur*).

Missing the Point: only to the extent...—Jean Borella, *Histoire et Théorie du Symbole* (Lausanne, 2004) p.157; "We look not..." 2 Corinthians 4.18; "For the invisible things of him..." Romans 1.20; "very good" Genesis 1.31.

Eyes to Look; Ears to Hear: "Seeing many things..." Isaiah 42.20; To read a symbol...—Jean Borella, *Histoire et Théorie du Symbole* (Lausanne, 2004) p.81; "If thou wouldest believe..." John 11.40; "Christ, who is the image..." 2 Corinthians 4.4; to have seen Him...—John 14.9; "the light of the knowledge..." 2 Corinthians 4.6; "Faith cometh by hearing" Romans 10.17; the faith that perceives...—Pope Francis, *Lumen Fidei* (Rome, 2013) section 29.

The Power of Words: "And God said, Let there be light..." Genesis 1.3; "And God said, Let the earth bring forth grass..." Genesis 1.11; "And God said, Let the earth bring forth the living creature..." Genesis 1.24; "For as the rain..." Isaiah 55.10–11; "And Isaac his father..." Genesis 27.32–35; "And out of the ground..." Genesis 2.19; implies something

288

unforeseen—Jean Borella, *La Crise du Symbolisme Religieux* (Paris, 2008) p.356; ancient traditions agree—René Guénon, *Symbols of Sacred Science*, translated by Henry D. Fohr (Hillsdale, NY, 2004) p.9.

A Confusion of Languages: "And the whole earth..." Genesis 11.1–4; People journey from the east... to make Himself known—Jean Borella, *La Crise du Symbolisme Religieux* (Paris, 2008) pp.358–61; "Go to, let us go down..." Genesis 11.7; subsequent chapter—Genesis 12.

The Name of the Lord: "Sing and rejoice..." Zechariah 2.20; "all nations" Isaiah 2.2; "They shall beat their swords..." Isaiah 2.4; "every man heard..." Acts 2.6–8; "whosoever shall call..." Acts 2.21; "ever learning..." 2 Timothy 3.7; "hath in these last days..." Hebrews 1.2–3.

The Word Was Made Flesh: "the way, the truth..." John 14.6; the Word made flesh—John 1.14; who is God—John 1.1; "all things..." John 1.3; "They are spirit..." John 6.63; "the words of eternal life" John 6.68; Heaven and earth...—Mark 13.32; made clean—John 15.3; healed—Luke 7.7; come to faith—John 4.41; "The imaged Word..." Hart Crane, *Voyages*, last stanza.

Words Give Us Meaning: metaphysical or supernatural essence—Jean Borella, *La Crise du Symbolisme Religieux* (Paris, 2008) p.356; Words disclose to us—Henri Bortoft, *The Wholeness of Nature* (Edinburgh, 1996) pp.310–11; the use of words in poetry—Henri Bortoft, *Taking Appearance Seriously* (Edinburgh, 2012) p.139; Helen Keller..."We walked down the path..." Henri Bortoft, *The Wholeness of Nature* (Edinburgh, 1996) p.312, quoting Helen Keller, *The Story of My Life* (London, 1959) p.23; "Language is the house of being"—"Letter on Humanism" in *Basic Writings*, translated by David Farell Krell (London, 2008) p.147.

Poetry, Puns, and Paradoxes: "Like as the waves..." Shakespeare, Sonnet 60; some editors—Stephen Booth, *Shakespeare's Sonnets: Edited with Analytic Commentary* (New Haven, CT, and London, 1977) p.239; After the eating of the fruit...—Genesis 3; no one is good...—Matthew 19.17; "All our righteousnesses..." Isaiah 64.6; paradox of Epimenides—Jean Borella, *La Crise du Symbolisme Religieux* (Paris, 2008) pp.297–309; "Words strain..." T. S. Eliot, *Four Quartets*—Burnt Norton V; "Words, after speech..." ibid.; "always now" ibid.

Numbers: J. C. Cooper, *An Illustrated Encyclopaedia of Traditional Symbols* (London, 1978) pp.113–18; Wolfgang Held, *The Quality of Numbers 1 to 31* (Edinburgh, 2012); the tree of the knowledge...—Genesis 2.17.

Architecture: "a machine for living in" *Vers Une Architecture* (1923); a monk-architect—Dom Paul Bellot; the consciousness of a city—Émile Mâle, *The Gothic Image* (London, 1961) p.398; represents the heavenly Jerusalem—ibid. p.397; a book—ibid. p.390.

Chapter Five: Scripture and Hermeneutics

O Book! Infinite Sweetness!: "God shall wipe away..." Revelation 21.4; "Whereas I was blind..." John 9.25.

Hermeneutist and Hermeneutics: "the Spirit of truth" John 14.17; "into all truth" John 16.13; "No man..." 1 Corinthians 12.3; "all things were made..." John 1.3; "the way..." John 14.6.

The Whole Thing: "the word of God is quick" Hebrews 4.12; "the Word was made flesh..." John 1.14; "Thou shalt love..." Matthew 22.37; "For all Truth..." *A Priest to the Temple*, Chapter 4, quoted in *The English Poems of George Herbert*, edited by C.A. Patrides (London, 1974) p.77.

Eyesalve: "tree of the knowledge..." Genesis 2.17; "he is a liar" John 8.44; Adam and Eve know—Genesis 3.7; "God created man..." Genesis 1.27; "they were both naked..." Genesis 2.25; "Because thou sayest..." Revelation 3.17–18; The white is a symbol—J.C. Cooper, *An Illustrated Encyclopaedia of Traditional Symbols* (London, 1978) p.41; a symbol of the sacred luminosity—ibid. p.74; "As long as..." John 9.5–7; "single" Luke 11.34; "the one thing" Luke 10.42.

More about Trees: "And out of the ground..." Genesis 2.9; "very many trees..." Ezekiel 47.7; "And he showed me..." Revelation 22.1.

Not a Closed System: "If any man..." Luke 14.26; "Honour thy father..." Deuteronomy 5.16; "Let every one of you..." Ephesians 5.33; "He that hateth..." 1 John 2.11; "Whoever he be..." Luke 14.33; "I live..." Galatians 2.20; losing one's life...—Luke 9.24; the love that God is—1 John 4.16; "When I am weak..." 2 Corinthians 12.10.

Scripture and Symbolism: "I am the true vine..." John 15.1; "have it more abundantly" John 10.10; "I am the vine..." John 15.5; carry the connotation...—C.H. Dodd, *The Interpretation of the Fourth Gospel* (Cambridge, 1953) pp.171–73; "He that hath an ear..." Revelation 2.17; "the inner man" Ephesians 3.16; Characteristically, a stone...—Robert Bolton, *Self and Spirit* (Hillsdale, NY, 2005) Chapter 1; symbolized by a stone—1 Peter 2.6; "is one LORD" Deuteronomy 6.4.

History as Symbol: "pearl of great price" Matthew 13.46; a modern political leader—Tony Blair.

Get Thee Out of Thy Country: "the LORD had said…" Genesis 12.1; "Fear not, Abram…" Genesis 15.1; "Look now toward heaven…" Genesis 15.5; "that turn many…" Daniel 12.3.

The Journey to the Promised Land: "a new king over Egypt" Exodus 1.8; "their lives bitter with hard bondage" Exodus 1.14; "was very meek…" Numbers 12.3; "unto a land…" Exodus 3.8; "And Moses stretched out…" Exodus 14.21–22; "Thus the LORD…" Exodus 14.30; "Harden not your heart…" Psalm 95.8; an ambivalent symbol—J.C. Cooper, *An Illustrated Encyclopaedia of Traditional Symbols* (London, 1978) p.50; "clean over Jordan"—Numbers 3.17; "Thus saith the LORD…" Joshua 24.2; "I have given you…" Joshua 24.13.

The Greatest Journey of Them All: "And it came to pass…" Luke 9.51; lovingly laments—Luke 19.41–42; "We go up to Jerusalem…" Luke 18.31–33; "How am I straitened…" Luke 12.50; "through the cities…" Luke 13.22; between the departure…—John 13.30–17.26; "a certain man…" Luke 9.57; "Foxes have holes…" Luke 9.58; "no continuing city" Hebrews 13.14; "the author and finisher…" Hebrews 12.2.

Prayer: the angelic salutation—Luke 1.28; "Blessed art thou…" Luke 1.42; announced by the angel—Luke 1.31; "the name which is above…" Philippians 2.9; its presentation to us of the Mother of God—John 19.27; to see whom…—John 14.9; "Our Father…" Matthew 6.9; "Thy kingdom come…" Matthew 6.10; "Lead us not…" Matthew 6.13; the appeal of the blind…—Matthew 9.27, Mark 10.48; "God be merciful…" Luke 18.13.

A Loving Letter: "Contemplative prayer…" *The Book of Her Life* chapter 8 in *The Collected Works of St. Teresa of Avila*, translated by Kieran Kavanaugh, OCD, and Otilio Rodriguez, OCD (Washington, DC, 1976) Volume 1, p.67; "He shall teach…" John 14.26; "What is Scripture…" Pope Saint Gregory the Great, *Letters* 4.31; "I live…" Galatians 2.20; the Son reveals—Matthew 11.27.

Spiritual Reading: "And I say unto you, Ask…" Luke 11.9–13; knowing Him as Lord—1 Corinthians 12.3; knowing the Father—Matthew 11.27.

Seven Wonderful Promises: "Opening the ears" Isaiah 42.20; They are the following: eating…—Revelation 2.7, 11, 17, 26–28, and 3.5, 12, 21; "He that hath an ear…" Revelation 2.7, 11, 17, 28, and 3.6, 13, 22.

Hearing: "Blessed are they…" Luke 11.28; "Listen…" *Rule of Saint Benedict*, Prologue; "Knowledge linked…" Pope Francis, *Lumen Fidei* (Rome, 2013) section 29; "The sheep hear his voice…" John 10.3–4; tells us to open…—*et apertis oculis nostris ad deificum lumen, attonitis auri-*

bus audiamus divina cotidie clamans quid nos admonet vox, *Rule of Saint Benedict*, Prologue, verse 9.

Chapter Six: Liturgy and Sacrament

The Beginning and the End: "And a voice…" Revelation 19.5–7.

Emphasizing Meaning: the teaching of Dom Guéranger…—preface to *L'Année Liturgique*; Saint Paul…—Galatians 4.19; "Except a man…" John 3.3; "Blessed be the God and Father…" Ephesians 1.3, 5–6.

A Great Ring: "I saw Eternity…" *The World*.

The Day, a Life, and Eternity: "Lord, now lettest thou thy servant…" Luke 2.29; the last words of Jesus…—Luke 23.46.

After the Pattern of Christ: "the tender mercy of our God…" Luke 1.78–79; "about the sixth hour" Luke 23.44; "He that is mighty…" Luke 1.49; Simeon's song—Luke 2.29–32; "No man hath seen God…" John 1.18; "will reveal him" Matthew 11.27; "Before Abraham was…" John 8.58; "All that could ever…" *Sermons & Treatises*, Volume 1, translated and edited by M.C. O'Walshe (Shaftesbury, 1987) Sermon 29, p. 220; through a glass…—1 Corinthians 13.12.

Soaring Above: "The soul in which God…" *Sermons & Treatises*, Volume 1, translated and edited by M.C. O'Walshe (Shaftesbury, 1987) Sermon 29, pp. 216–17.

The Value of Uselessness: "the voice of a great multitude…" Revelation 19.6; "O God, who cause…" collect for the Mass for the twenty-first Sunday in ordinary time; "Unwavering, unflagging…" *Lectures on Justification*, Chapter 13.

Daily Fare: "fared sumptuously…" Luke 16.19; "O come…" Psalm 95.1–7.

Poor and Needy: *La Tradition Médite le Psautier Chrétien* (Paris, 1974) pp. 466–69; "They that be whole…" Matthew 9.12; "wretched, and miserable…" Revelation 3.17; "Blessed be ye poor…" Luke 6.20; "For your sakes…" 2 Corinthians 8.9; "the Holy One of God" Mark 1.24; "God be merciful…" Luke 18.13; was justified…—Luke 18.14; "offered up prayers…" Hebrews 5.7; "A great multitude…" Revelation 7.9; "was not left in hell…" Acts 2.31; "consulted that they might…" Matthew 26.4; "the sign of the prophet Jonas" Matthew 12.39.

The Mother of Us All: "we spend our years…" Psalm 90.9; "is soon cut off" Psalm 90.10; "hid with Christ in God" Colossians 3.3; "Jerusalem which is above…" Galatians 4.26; "a better country…" Hebrews 11.16;

Psalm 137...—*La Tradition Médite le Psautier Chrétien* (Paris, 1974) pp.741–45; "a river went out of Eden..." Genesis 2.10; "the habitation of devils..." Revelation 18.2; "the LORD did there..." Genesis 11.9; symbol of weeping—J.C. Cooper, *An Illustrated Encyclopaedia of Traditional Symbols* (London, 1978) p.192; "our bourne of Time and Place" Alfred Lord Tennyson, *Crossing the Bar* line 13; "we delight in God..." *Exposition of the Psalms* 121–150, translated by Maria Boulding, OSB (New York, 2004) p.237; "for here we have..." Hebrews 13.14; "cast pearls before swine" Matthew 7.6; "through a glass darkly" 1 Corinthians 13.12.

Sacraments and Symbolism: "in these last days" Hebrews 1.2; make "a name" for himself—Genesis 11.4; "O! The one Life..." *The Aeolian Harp* lines 25–33; God is love—1 John 4.16.

Baptism: "the darkness and the light..." Psalm 139.12; "so many of us..." Romans 6.3; "as Christ was raised up..." Romans 6.4; "the Holy Ghost descended...from heaven..." Luke 3.22.

Oil: "it is to be noted that there are two sorts..." Gulielmus Durandus, *Rationale Divinorum Officiorum* (Antwerp, 1614) Book One, Chapter 8, p.38; "For my thoughts..." Isaiah 55.8; "My word...that goeth forth..." Isaiah 55.11; "The one to be baptised..." Gulielmus Durandus, ibid.; "no man can say..." 1 Corinthians 12.3; "chrism is named..." Gulielmus Durandus, op. cit., Book One, Chapter 8, p.39; "the invisible things of him..." Romans 1.20; "into all truth" John 16.13; "be ready always..." 1 Peter 3.15.

Healing: "Is any sick..." James 5.14–15; Gulielmus Durandus, *Rationale Divinorum Officiorum* (Antwerp, 1614) Book One, Chapter 8, p.38; as Julian of Norwich taught—"love was what He meant...Our Lord's meaning was love" *The Revelations of Divine Love*, translated by Elizabeth Spearing (London, 1998) section 86, p.179; "the tongue is a little member..." James 3.5; "Confess your sins..." James 5.16; "Be of good cheer..." Matthew 9.2; "Smooth open hearts..." *Confession*; recommends confession—*The Cloud of Unknowing*, Chapter 28.

The Ultimate Bonding: "Love is that liquor..." *The Agony*; Durandus points out...—Gulielmus Durandus, *Rationale Divinorum Officiorum* (Antwerp, 1614) Book Three, Chapter 7, p.71; "as sounding brass..." 1 Corinthians 13.1; the *Catechism of the Catholic Church*—see Section Two, Chapter 1, article 3; "White vestments are used...red vestments are to be used..." Gulielmus Durandus, op. cit., Book Three, Chapter 18, p.83; each particle...—Robert Bolton, *Self and Spirit* (Hillsdale, NY,

2005) p.15; "In midst of the Mass…" B text, Passus 19, lines 4–14; "The Word was made flesh…" John 1.14; "The Lord has always revealed…" *The Collected Works of St. John of the Cross*, translated by Kieran Kavanaugh, OCD, and Otilio Rodriguez, OCD (Washington, DC, 1979) p.666; "Let us make man…" Genesis 1.26; "Be it unto me…" Luke 1.38; "My Father giveth you…" John 6.32–33.

Sex as Symbol: "Husbands, love your wives…" Ephesians 5.25,28–32; "His invention…" *The Screwtape Letters* (London, 1942) p.49.

More about the Greatest Journey: threefold declaration of peace—John 20.19, 21, 26; three hours of darkness—Mark 15.33; dawn…messenger "whose countenance…" Matthew 28.1–3; "unto the end" John 13.1; "troubled in spirit" John 13.21; love that serves others—John 13.4–17; "This is my body…" 1 Corinthians 11.24; "answered nothing" Matthew 27.12; "never a word" Matthew 27.14; asks for forgiveness—Luke 23.34; One who finishes—John 19.20; "the day the LORD…" Psalm 118.24; "the light shineth…" John 1.5; "the darkness and the light…" Psalm 139.12; "I, if I be lifted up…" John 12.32; Jesus was to accomplish—Luke 9.31; "A new heart…" Ezekiel 36.26; "for if we have been planted…" Romans 6.5; "Peace be unto you" John 20.19.

PART THREE: CONTEMPLATING GOD
"And this is life eternal…" John 17.3.

Chapter Seven: The Father of Mercies

Beginning Again: "Some trust in chariots, and some in horses" Psalm 20.7; "But we will remember…" ibid.; "Ye have taken away…" Luke 11.52.

God in Ordinary Life: "we live and move…" Acts 17.28.

The Father: "save the Son…" Matthew 11.27; "He that hath seen me…" John 14.9; by the Holy Spirit—1 Corinthians 12.3; Saint Irenaeus teaches—*Against Heresies*, Book Four, Chapter 20, paragraph 1; the prodigal—Luke 15.11–32; "no man hath seen…the only begotten Son…" John 1.18; "God is love" 1 John 4.16; "Deep calleth unto deep" Psalm 42.7; "how to give…" Luke 11.13; He knows what our needs are—Matthew 6.32; "the Father of mercies…" 1 Corinthians 1.3.

Touching the Truth of God: "herein is love…" John 4.10; "Whom having not seen…" 1 Peter 1.8; "thou…canst not tell…" John 3.8.

One Thing Needful: "Now it came to pass…" Luke 10.38–42; the tree of the knowledge…—Genesis 2.17; "I have discovered…" *The Vision of God* in *Nicholas of Cusa: Selected Spiritual Writings*, translated by H. Lawrence Bond (Mahwah, NJ, 1997) pp. 251–52; "the wolf…" Isaiah 11.6; "Silence is not God…" *The Epistle of Discretion* in *The Cloud of Unknowing and Related Treatises*, edited by Phyllis Hodgson (Exeter, 1982) p. 115; hauntingly sung—by the Zeitgenössische Oper.

Purity of Heart: "Blessed are the pure in heart…" Matthew 5.8; all in all—1 Corinthians 15.28; "unto certain…" Luke 18.9; "stood and prayed thus…" Luke 18.11; "God be merciful…" Luke 18.13; "justified" Luke 18.14; "In Hell…" *The Last Judgement* in *Blake's Poems and Prophecies* (London, 1970) p. 369; "Judge not…" Matthew 7.1; "I give tithes…" Luke 18.12; the great divorce, as C. S. Lewis put it—in a book of that title; "the second death…the lake of fire" Revelation 20.15.

Joy and Woe: "Man was made…" *Auguries of Innocence* lines 56–58; "is but for a moment" 1 Corinthians 4.17; should not "murmur"—for example, in Chapters 34 and 40 of the *Rule of Saint Benedict*; their needs should be properly catered for—for example, in Chapters 31 and 48 of the *Rule of Saint Benedict*; "Be ye perfect…" Matthew 5.48.

God's Work: "He will be seen…" Chapter 34; "It is necessary that…" *The Cloud of Unknowing and Related Treatises*, edited by Phyllis Hodgson (Exeter, 1982) p. 88, lines 21–25; "We know not…" Romans 8.26; "a sharp dart" Chapter 6; "thick cloud" ibid.; "When thou…" op. cit., Chapter 7; "He that would become…" *Holy Wisdom; or, Directions for the Prayer of Contemplation*, Third Treatise, Fourth Section, Chapter 1, paragraph 10; "a pure, simple, and reposeful…" ibid. paragraph 5.

Forgetting: compares…to wheat growing—*Holy Wisdom; or, Directions for the Prayer of Contemplation*, Third Treatise, Fourth Section, Chapter 2, paragraph 18; "Father which is in heaven…" Matthew 5.48; "great value" *Rule of Saint Benedict*, Chapter 6; "Blessed are ye that hunger…" Luke 6.21; "Blessed be ye poor…" Luke 6.20; "thought for raiment" Matthew 6.28; "the lilies of the field" Matthew 6.28; "first the kingdom of heaven" Matthew 6.33; "shall be added" ibid.; "All our perfection…" *Holy Wisdom; or, Directions for the Prayer of Contemplation*, Third Treatise, Fourth Section, Chapter 6, paragraph 3; "Put a cloud of forgetting…" Chapter 5; "Who is it that calls…" Chapter 68; "though our outward man…" 2 Corinthians 4.16; "of God Himself…" *The Cloud of Unknowing*, Chapter 6; "Look that nothing remains…" *The Cloud of Unknowing and Related Treatises*, edited by Phyllis Hodgson (Exeter, 1982) p. 75, lines 18–21; "the brightest time" ibid. p. 82, line 19; "As soon as…" ibid. p.85, lines 13–16; "then is that thing…" Chapter 9; "offering up…naked blind feeling…Look ever…" ibid. p.86, lines 24–31.

Unknowing: "blind beholding" *The Book of Privy Counselling* in *The Cloud of Unknowing and Related Treatises*, edited by Phyllis Hodgson (Exeter, 1982) p.86, lines 13–14; "If thou wilt stand…" *Cloud*, Chapter 12; "The best knowing…" ibid., Chapter 70; "The soul loses all remembrance…" *Holy Wisdom; or, Directions for the Prayer of Contemplation*, Third Treatise, Fourth Section, Chapter 2, paragraph 25.

Being a Stinking Lump: "strive to work…" *Cloud*, Chapter 14; "Feel sin as a lump…" ibid., Chapter 40; "a lump…" ibid., Chapter 66; "All other sorrows…" ibid., Chapter 44; "the great desolation" *Holy Wisdom; or, Directions for the Prayer of Contemplation*, Third Treatise, Fourth Section, Chapter 5; "to feel her natural infirmity" ibid. paragraph 3; "she now sees…" ibid. paragraph 6; "She practises tranquillity…" ibid. paragraph 8.

Being Made One with God: "to be made one…" *Cloud*, Chapter 67; "I say that…" *The Cloud of Unknowing and Related Treatises*, edited by Phyllis Hodgson (Exeter, 1982) p.87, lines 27–30; "there is neither time nor place" *Holy Wisdom; or, Directions for the Prayer of Contemplation*, Third Treatise, Fourth Section, Chapter 1, paragraph 15; "this happy state…" ibid. paragraph 17; "a state of love…" ibid., Chapter 6, paragraph 3; "the union of nothing with nothing…" ibid., Chapter 6, paragraph 8; "whatever naturally pertains…" *De Aeternitate Mundi* (*prius enim naturaliter inest unicuique quod convenit sibi in se, quam quod ex alio habetur. Esse autem non habet creatura nisi ab alio; sibi autem relicta in se considerata nihil est: unde prius naturaliter est sibi nihilum quam esse*); "insubstantial pageant" Shakespeare, *The Tempest*, Act 4, Scene 1, line 153; "It is a great thing…" *The Spiritual Mirror*, Chapter 11, paragraph 1 in *Spiritual Works of Louis of Blois, Abbot of Liesse*, edited by John Edward Bowen (London, 1871) pp.185–86; "being delivered…" Romans 8.21; "such stuff…" Shakespeare, *The Tempest*, Act 4, Scene 1, lines 156–57; "the powers…" *Meister Eckhart: Sermons & Treatises*, Volume 1 (Shaftesbury, 1989) p. 7.

The Connection with Earlier Chapters: C.S. Lewis makes the point—*The Discarded Image* (Cambridge, 1964) pp.213–14; "A man's reach…" Robert Browning, *Andrea del Sarto* line 98; "although they do not…" *The Spiritual Mirror*, Chapter 11, paragraph 2 in *Spiritual Works of Louis of Blois, Abbot of Liesse*, edited by John Edward Bowen (London, 1871) pp.188–89.

Chapter Eight: Christ the Word Incarnate

Recapitulation: "gather together in one..." Ephesians 1.10; "Alpha and Omega..." Revelation 22.13; "hath seen the Father" John 14.9; "the way, the truth, and the life" John 14.6; "This is life eternal..." John 17.6; "To teach Doubt..." *The Everlasting Gospel* lines 45–46; "Whoso shall offend..." Matthew 18.6; "Thy faith hath..." Mark 10.52, Luke 17.19, and Matthew 9.22; "This Life's five Windows..." *The Everlasting Gospel* lines 96–100; a marginal annotation—*Blake's Poems and Prophecies*, edited with an introduction by Max Plowman (London, 1970) p.351; "the Lord from heaven" 1 Corinthians 15.47; "the greater light...the lesser light...the stars" Genesis 1.16; "the light of the world" John 8.12; "If with exultant tread..." Francis Thompson, *Ode to the Setting Sun*; "There lives the dearest freshness..." Gerard Manley Hopkins, *God's Grandeur* line 10; "the resurrection, and the life" John 11.25; "golden section" Scott Olsen, *The Golden Section: Nature's Greatest Secret* (Glastonbury, 2006); "gather together in one" John 11.52; "I am come..." John 10.10; especially the hungry...—Matthew 25.44–45; loves them as its true self—Mark 12.33; "made by him" John 1.3; every rock— 1 Corinthians 10.4; His sacrifice in every bull—Louis Charbonneau-Lassay, *The Bestiary of Christ*, translated and abridged by D.M. Dooling (New York, 1992) p.20; "Whom say ye...Thou art..." Mark 8.28; He is the One...—John 1.1–3.

The Word of God: "the only true God..." John 17.3; a Greek lexicon—Liddell and Scott, *A Greek-English Lexicon* (Oxford, 1968) pp.1057–59; "GOD, who at sundry times..." Hebrews 1.1–2; "as one having authority" Matthew 7.29; "a still small voice" 1 Kings 19.12; not in wind... 1 Kings 19.11–12; "If ye continue..." John 8.31–32; Isaiah prophesied— Isaiah 42.7; "If the Son..." John 8.36; "The Father spoke one Word..." *Maxims and Counsels* #21 in *The Collected Works of St. John of the Cross*, translated by Kieran Kavanaugh, OCD, and Otilio Rodriguez, OCD (Washington, DC, 1979) p.675; "troubled about many things" Luke 10.41.

A Most Excellent Book: "a most excellent book" *The Spiritual Mirror*, Chapter 10, paragraph 7 in *Spiritual Works of Louis of Blois, Abbot of Liesse*, edited by John Edward Bowen (London, 1871) pp.179–80; *The Sacrament of the Altar*, slightly adapted from *Medieval English Lyrics*, edited by R.T. Davies (London, 1968) p.196.

More about Prayer: "when he had sent..." Matthew 14.23; "itself maketh intercession" Romans 8.26; "filled with madness..." Luke 6.11–12; "If any man be…" 2 Corinthians 5.17; "the LORD God formed man…" Genesis 2.7; "though our outward man…" 2 Corinthians 4.16; "hath made him…" 2 Corinthians 5.21; "being in an agony…" Luke 22.44; "My God…" Matthew 27.46; a cloud overshadowed Him—Mark 9.7; "our griefs…our sorrows" Isaiah 53.4; "By his knowledge…" Isaiah 53.11; "enjoyed all the delights…" *J'entre dans la Vie: Derniers Entretiens* (Paris, 1983) p. 58.

Being Made Conformable: "know him, and the power…" Philippians 3.4; "If any man will come after me…" Luke 9.23; "Thou losest here…" *King Lear*, Act 1, Scene 1, line 252; "Seek ye first…" Matthew 6.34; "without him…" John 1.3; "one pearl of great price" Matthew 13.46.

Twin Sisters: "the other side of coincidence of contraries" *The Vision of God* in *Nicholas of Cusa: Selected Spiritual Writings*, translated by H. Lawrence Bond (Mahwah, NJ, 1997) p. 252; "And many false prophets shall rise…" Matthew 24.11–12; "take upon 's…" *King Lear*, Act 5, Scene 3, lines 16–17.

More about Paradox: "unto Jesus…" Hebrews 12.2; "the other side of coincidence of contraries" *The Vision of God* in *Nicholas of Cusa: Selected Spiritual Writings*, translated by H. Lawrence Bond (Mahwah, NJ, 1997) p. 252; "suffereth long" 1 Corinthians 13.4; "for the joy…" Hebrews 12.2.

More Twins: "Alpha and Omega…" Revelation 22.13; "even the wind…" Mark 4.41; "the Lamb that was slain…" Revelation 5.12; "that liveth for ever…" Revelation 5.14; "the coincidence of contraries" *The Vision of God* in *Nicholas of Cusa: Selected Spiritual Writings*, translated by H. Lawrence Bond (Mahwah, NJ, 1997) p. 252; "I tell you the truth…" John 16.7.

Astonishing Doctrine: "the people was astonished…" Mark 11.18; "epistemic closure" in *Histoire et Théorie du Symbole* (Lausanne, 2004) p. 97ff. and in *La Crise du Symbolisme Religieux* (Paris, 2008) p. 243ff.; "Whosoever shall seek…" Luke 17.33; "born of the Spirit" John 3.6; "hid with Christ…" Colossians 3.3; "Which now of these three…" Luke 10.34; "had compassion…and went to him…" Luke 10.33–34; "is the place where…" John 4.20; "many things of the elders…" Matthew 16.21; "Thou art an offence…" Matthew 16.23; "God is love" 1 John 4.16; "I take pleasure in infirmities…" 2 Corinthians 12.10; the tale of a steward—Luke 16.1–9; "called every one…" Luke 16.5; "into their houses" Luke 16.4; "the lord commended…" Luke 16.8; One edition of the Bible—the Catholic Revised Standard Version; God in Christ identifies

Himself...—Matthew 25.31–46; "Blessed are the merciful..." Matthew 5.7; "everlasting habitations" Luke 16.9.

Giving God Permission: "Behold, I stand at the door..." Revelation 3.20; "He that is mighty..." Luke 1.49; "he that cometh to God..." Hebrews 11.6; "that God may be..." 1 Corinthians 15.28; "Blessed are the poor in spirit..." Matthew 5.3; "Until now..." Bonaventure, *The Soul's Journey into God, The Tree of Life, The Life of Saint Francis*, translated by Ewert Cousins (London, 1978) p.194.

Aspects of Receptivity: "Blessed are they that mourn..." Matthew 5.4; "the God of all comfort" 2 Corinthians 1.3; "Blessed are the meek..." Matthew 5.5; "Blessed are those which do hunger..." Matthew 5.6; "Blessed are the merciful..." Matthew 5.7; "Freely ye have received..." Matthew 10.8; "Blessed are the pure..." Matthew 5.8; "Blessed are the peacemakers..." Matthew 5.9; "Blessed are they which are persecuted..." Matthew 5.10; "Blessed are ye, when men shall revile you..." Matthew 5.11; "Great is your reward..." Matthew 5.12.

We Are Invited: "the express image..." Hebrews 1.3; "out of this world..." John 13.1; "buried with him..." Romans 6.4; "shall not be hurt..." Revelation 2.11; "bloweth where it listeth" John 3.8.

Chapter Nine: The Spirit

Being Childlike: "Verily I say..." Matthew 18.3; "Ye must be born again" John 3.7; "A simple Light..." *Traherne's Poems of Felicity*, edited from the manuscript by H.I. Bell (Oxford, 1910) p.10; "in the peace and purity...all things appear..." *Centuries of Meditation* (London, 1960) the third century, section 5; "Happy those early days..." *et seq.—The Retreat*; "The corn was orient..." ibid. the third century, section 3.

Wonder: "The world will never..." *Tremendous Trifles*; "How like an Angel came I down!" *The Poetical Works of Thomas Traherne*, edited by Gladys I. Wade (London, 1932) p.5; "Of that forbidden tree..." John Milton, *Paradise Lost*, Book 1, lines 2–3; "All things are yours" 1 Corinthians 3.23.

Community and Gratitude: "If a man had no more..." *Sermons & Treatises*, Volume 1, translated and edited by M.C. O'Walshe (Shaftesbury, 1989) Sermon 27, p.209; "a heart / That watches..." *The Tables Turned*.

Pleasure and Pain: "Seeing ye have purified..." 1 Peter 1.22–23; "One day is with the Lord..." 2 Peter 3.8; "Our revels now are ended..." *The Tempest*, Act 4, Scene 1, lines 148–58.

Gold: "gold tried in the fire" Revelation 3.18; "were all with one accord…" Acts 2.1; "cloven tongues…" Acts 2.3; "I am come to send fire…" Luke 12.49; "suddenly there came…" Acts 2.2; "saw everything…" Genesis 1.31.

Seeing the Big Picture: "The end of all our exploring…" *The Wasteland*; "Pure Empty Powers" stanza 6 of *The Preparative* in *The Poetical Works of Thomas Traherne*, edited by Gladys I. Wade (London, 1932) p.13; "Then was my Soul…" stanza 2 of *The Preparative* in *The Poetical Works of Thomas Traherne*, edited by Gladys I. Wade (London, 1932) p.12; "let there be light" Genesis 1.3; "When thy eye is single…" Luke 11.34; "the light of the world" Matthew 5.14; "What hast thou…" 1 Corinthians 4.7; "a kind of well-pleasedness" Chapter 49; "what was previously…" *Meister Eckhart: Selected Writings*, translated by Oliver Davies (London, 1994) Sermon 25, p.228; It is as though…never grows cold—Luke Bell, *Paradise on Earth* (Rattlesden, 1993); "I always see the good side of things" *Thérèse de Lisieux: Oeuvres Complètes* (Paris, 1992) p.1004.

Without Partiality: "It is not because…" *The Last Judgement* in *Blake's Poems and Prophecies* (London, 1970) p.369; "the wisdom that is from above…" James 3.17; "God is no respecter of persons…" Acts 10.34–35; He argues in *The Abolition of Man*…—Michael Ward, *Planet Narnia: The Seven Heavens in the Imagination of C.S. Lewis* (Oxford, 2008) p.107; In *English Literature*…—ibid.; observes in Bacon…—op. cit. p.144; "unhealthy…inauspicious…" op. cit. p.107; "The hand of Vengeance…" *The Grey Monk* in *Blake's Poems and Prophecies* (London, 1970) p.333; "…vain the Sword…" op. cit. pp.332–33.

God's Mother: "I sing of a maiden…" slightly adapted from *Medieval English Lyrics*, edited by R.T. Davies (London, 1968) p.155; "is a Spirit" John 4.24; "a still small voice" 1 Kings 19.12; "knoweth not how" Mark 4.27; "There came then…" Mark 3.31–35; "sat at Jesus' feet…" Luke 10.39; "one thing is needful" Luke 10.42; "our tainted nature's…" in his poem *The Virgin*; "The Holy Ghost shall come…" Luke 2.35; "Jesus is the Lord" 1 Corinthians 12.3; "for with God…" Luke 2.37; "Behold the handmaid…" Luke 2.38; "As the eyes of a maiden…" Psalm 123.2; "He must increase…" John 3.30; "tidings of great joy" Luke 2.10; "kept all these things…" Luke 2.19; "kept all these sayings…" Luke 2.51; "A sword shall pierce…" Luke 2.35; "quick, and powerful…" Hebrews 4.12; "by the cross of Jesus" John 19.25; with the Apostle John…—John 19.26; "upper room" Acts 1.13; "with one accord…" Acts 1.14; "the best Teacher…The drama of contemporary culture…the incomparable model of contemplation…" Madrid, 3 May 2003.

Ultramarine: Spike Bucklow, *The Alchemy of Paint: Art, Science and Secrets from the Middle Ages* (London, 2009) Chapter 2; "By nature with…Its soothing power…But he who dares…" Marbode de Rennes, *De Lapidibus*, translated by J.M. Riddle, *Sudhoffs Archiv*, Beiheft 20 (Wiesbaden, 1977) pp. 42–43, cited in Spike Bucklow, *The Riddle of the Image: The Secret Science of Medieval Art* (London, 2014) Chapter 2; a distinguished commentator—Spike Bucklow in Chapter 4 of *The Riddle of the Image: The Secret Science of Medieval Art* (London, 2014); the fourteenth-century diptych…—op. cit., Chapter 4; Mary is *stella maris*…—op. cit., Chapter 5; "Be it unto me…" Luke 1.38.

Sapphire: "Above the firmament…" Ezekiel 1.26; "the glory of the LORD" Ezekiel 1.28; "Then went up Moses…" Exodus 24.9–11; "When the mind…" William Harmless, SJ, and Raymond R. Fitzgerald, SJ, *The Sapphire Light of the Mind: The Skemmata of Evagrius Ponticus* in *Theological Studies* Volume 62 (2001) p. 518; "If one wishes to…" op. cit. p. 521; "state of the mind…" ibid.

The Final Word on Prayer: "Prayer is the state of mind…" William Harmless, SJ, and Raymond R. Fitzgerald, SJ, *The Sapphire Light of the Mind: The Skemmata of Evagrius Ponticus* in *Theological Studies* Volume 62 (2001) p. 526; "my ending is despair…" *The Tempest*, epilogue, lines 15–18.

FORWARD BY
THE AUTHOR

This might surprise you but like many anti-speed camera campaigners, I've never been a fan of speed cameras. But the difference I suspect, is that I've always had an appreciation that they are and always have been an effective, valuable and yes a clumsy method of reducing road traffic casualties on our roads.

I realised very early on that speed cameras had very little to do with speed and more to do with our basic levels of awareness. I was able to put this into print in 2008 in my first book, 'The Real Drivers Guide to Beating the Speed Camera'. However, whilst it provided an easy and effective solution to beating fixed speed cameras, I was never completely satisfied that I hadn't nailed down mobile speed cameras too. An understanding of how mobile camera vans work would have rounded the book off nicely but despite being proud of my first book I always regretted the inability to include mobile cameras and so despite publishing it, I never marketed it.

In 2019, I had the most incredible stroke of luck. I was faced with being made redundant and had three months to find a role to get redeployed into. I unsuccessfully went for job after job and quite literally was left feeling like the last player to be picked for the football team. To be fair if it was a football team, then I would completely accept and expect to be picked last.

Then, right at the 11th hour, a job became available within the

Safer Roads Department for a Road Safety Technician.

It truly felt like a gift from God.

I was invited out for a day to see what the job was like and if I was interested in doing it which I obviously was. But even on that very first day, the answer as to how mobile cameras worked presented itself to me in glorious technicolour. Again, nothing to do with speed but due to the deterioration of another of our motoring cognitive functions that affect most, if not all motorists. And more encouragingly, it genuinely is a truly simple fix.

So now I have the complete set, the final piece of the puzzle, the element that was missing from my first book, and it has only taken 12 years since its publication to find it.

My first book is available on Lulu.com in paperback and as a 'free download' which it will always remain. I think that my first book is an excellent accompaniment to Beating Speed Cameras – FAST! As it delves into much of what I speak, in far greater detail, if that's your thing.

This has allowed me to keep this book much shorter and to the point, whilst covering all of the speed camera bases.

ABOUT THE BOOK

The author is both an ex Department for Transport Approved Driving Instructor, Road Safety Technician and Safety Camera Van Operator who has brought his unique blend of knowledge and skill into print, to both help motorists fight back against all speed cameras, whilst improving their safety on the road.

We all want to make the roads safer and we all want to be free from persecution. Well, for the first time ever, we can have both. The Secret to achieving this is understanding why all road users, motorists and bikers alike get caught in the first place. Once understood, this gives drivers and bikers the very real fighting chance to never get a speeding ticket again.

Developing this understanding was the hard part, the easy part is yours, putting it into action.

Discover not only where the motoring community got it wrong, but also where the road safety got it wrong too.

Beating Speed Cameras – FAST! Reveals these secrets that have remained hidden and unaddressed for the last 3 decades.

For the first time, bringing this understanding into the light of the public domain, to give all motorists, a very real and genuine chance to fight back.

BEATING THE SPEED CAMERA –

FAST!

Forward by the author

About The Author

PART 1

Understanding Why We Get
Caught by Speed Cameras

CONTENTS

PART 2

*Using our understanding to
beat the speed camera*

CONTENTS

ABOUT THE AUTHOR

Thomas Heavey was a fully qualified Approved Driving Instructor until the mid-1990s.

He has a deep passion for road safety and motoring and believes that these two interests don't have to clash. After the birth of his first child he became very active in the online Speed Camera debates which were rife at the time, but took particular interest in the views and opinions of both road safety campaigners and anti-speed camera activists.

After a successful 5 year career as an ADI where he helped in excess of 250 people to pass their driving test, he left to start a long career spanning 25 years with two UK Police Forces. The majority of his time spent was spent working on the front desk and a brief 2 year spell in the Control Room. In 2019, when faced with redundancy and right at the 11th hour, his dream job as a Road Safety Technician became available, of which a significant part of this role was being trained to operate the Safety Camera Vans.

In 2008 Thomas wrote his first book entitled 'The Real Drivers Guide to Beating the Speed Camera', although this book offered the motorist protection from fixed 'Speed Cameras', the answers to why motorist get caught by Mobile Camera Vans, has always proved elusive and unclear, until he became a camera operator and could finally witness, first hand, the reasons why millions of motorist fall foul of camera vans each year.

Tom's careers as an Approved Driving Instructor and his work with Mobile Safety Camera vans has placed him in a unique position, where he has been able to combine these two knowledge bases, and create the most definitive and unique self-learning guide to protect all road users from the perils and pitfalls of being caught by not only safety camera vans, but all safety cameras.

The author is very pleased that finally he is able to give all motorists a fighting chance to finally beat fixed and mobile safety cameras and not through the pressures of contesting them in court, but by exploiting the bikers and drivers natural talent to completely avoid getting a ticket in the first place.

"Getting caught by a Speed Camera is very much like running into a glass door, you didn't see it because you never anticipated that it was there".
Thomas Heavey

"I don't think we'll ever be able to take the speed out of the motorist, but by enhancing a motorists' awareness, anticipation, concentration, knowledge, observation and sense of responsibility, we can certainly remove some of the dangers out of speed".
Thomas Heavey

"Current road safety centres very much on speed reduction, I'd like it to concentrate on less punitive measures and more education".
Thomas Heavey

"Never, ever speed around a blind bend, its highly dangerous, gives you little chance of being able to stop

within the distance you can see to be clear and there just might be a camera van waiting on the other side of it".
Thomas Heavey

PART 1

*Understanding why we get
caught by speed Cameras*

CHAPTER 1

Introduction - Do Safety Camera
Vans Reduce Casualties?

Do speed cameras save lives? There are numerous studies that have been undertaken over the last three decades that really prove beyond any doubt that fixed and mobile speed cameras are an effective method for reducing casualties on our roads. Unfortunately for motorists it looks like speed enforcement is not going anywhere soon.

Road safety organisations, campaigners and activists have made great strides in road casualty reduction over the last few decades, but those gains appear to be stalling. For example, UK road deaths in 2017-2018 were 1793, the following year 2018-19 they had only fallen by 9 to 1784 and the latest figures for 2019 – 20 were 1748 a fall of just 36, better but not significantly. So I suspect that those in charge of improving road safety are actively looking for new methods of casualty reduction to keep the downward trend going. And we may not like the solutions they come up with.

(Independent studies by Newcastle University discovered that casualties on North Yorkshires roads dropped by 20% as a direct result of introducing Safety Camera Vans).

In the mid 2000's I recognised the advancement of motoring technology and envisioned that the rise of fully automated or driverless vehicles could be upon us within 20 years or so. I foresaw the innovations such as power steering, assisted braking systems and GPS and others not yet thought of, would all starting to come together, eventually replacing all of our skills as motorists in an unholy marriage of technology. 12 years later and were almost there. The end of road for drivers and bikers alike is in sight. I often thought how sad it would be, that this is the legacy that todays' motorist, my generation, will leave for the next. This, I fear is where current road safety initiatives are leading us.

I believe that we are at a point in time now where we have to change the road safety narrative.

The old GATSO cameras are dying a death, some police forces in the UK have stopped operating them altogether and have effectively switched them all off. Why? Well despite popular belief that they are a cash generator, they have become, for several police forces, unaffordable and uneconomical to run and for many that do still run them, they have very few that are operationally viable. This I suspect is due to safety camera revenue going to central government as opposed back into the road safety schemes running them. But that's another story.

Whilst GATSO's may be petering out, new types of camera are being developed, fixed digital state of the art cameras that never need a film to be changed and the much maligned mobile camera vans are likely here to stay, for the foreseeable future at least.

Yes, there is also research to the contrary, the '85th percentile' for example which you can read about and much more, in my first book 'The Real Driver Guide to Beating the Speed Camera'. I suppose the reason that both sides are still clashing is because of one simple reason, in one way they both have a point, safety

cameras do save lives and yes, they do it by punitively perse-
cuting and punishing motorists. There are alternatives, talks,
open days, re-education, re-training but they are considered expensive and less effective. So road safety will always naturally
revert to speed reduction as a casualty reduction tool.

The speed awareness courses on offer, are an educational way
to give the motorist/biker the chance to avoid getting penalty
points and the negative financial implications that can come
with them.

So, the argument against speed cameras and safety camera vans
will never end and has proved so far, to be a fruitless with anti-
camera activists forever on the losing side. Especially as speed
reduction also seems to be the main casualty reduction tool in
the road safety industries arsenal. So maybe now is the right
time for a new approach, time to change the narrative.

CHAPTER 2

Contesting Speeding Tickets
– Is it worth it?

Fighting speeding fines through the courts is also becoming more expensive, difficult and with an ever diminishing chance of success. Why? Because the days of the 'loophole finder' are virtually at an end. In the early days, cases could be over-turned by creating doubts over the accuracy and operation of the equipment. Most if not all of these loopholes have now been closed. The camera enforcement equipment is annually serviced and calibrated, the calibration is checked regularly at a fixed distance by the operators, to ensure accuracy of distance measurements and also the alignment of the camera and laser is performed when every new site is visited. Roughly 2-3 sites per day per safety camera van. All of the Road Safety Techni-cians' are highly trained in the operation of the equipment and accredited by approved sources. So there is very little left in the way of loopholes, to prove the invalidity of a ticket. And the cost of trying can run into £1000s even tens of £1000's, the risk of failure has never been higher.

A headline from 10/09/2019 on the BBC stated 'Man spends £30,000 fighting £100 Speeding Ticket'. He failed.

Less than 1% of motorists who get a speeding ticket today con-test them, which is probably a wise decision.

There are however five acceptable defences you can use to appeal for a speeding fine.

1. You weren't speeding.

2. It wasn't you driving when the speeding offence happened.

3. There wasn't proper notice of the speed limit.

4. The speeding vehicle caught on camera has been misidentified.

5. Your car was stolen.

CHAPTER 3

Fighting back

The opportunity to successfully fight a speeding ticket on technicalities through the courts, has all but gone. Many who have tried, have found it ended as a very expensive failure. But there still remains one legitimate, unbeatable and very powerful means of fighting back against all speed cameras. And that is you.

The most powerful, reliable and effective road safety and speed camera detection device ever created is the human brain.

The reason why I believe that the best way to beat speed cameras by using the brain, over other all other methods, is that the weaknesses that motorists have, that speed cameras joyfully exploit, are the same weaknesses that get us into road traffic collisions, where people get seriously injured and killed. So by targeting and repairing these weaknesses it's possible, that not only will speed camera activations be reduced, but road safety will at the same time, be improved. Nobody could seriously argue that this is a bad thing. Who knows, in the future we may even be able to lay the founding argument for an increase to the speed limit.

So by quickly, simply and easily improving a few basic skills, common to both bikers and drivers around their thought processes, you'll improve your safety, keep yourself free from prosecution and all whilst maximising our enjoyment and freedom of the roads.

The two major benefits of using this method to protect yourself from speed cameras, is first that the method prevents you from getting a speeding ticket in the first place, so there is no contesting in court and secondly, that safety camera devices are not 100% reliable. For a device to know the location of a live camera van site, the device has to be told first, if it hasn't been told, it doesn't know.

With my history as a Department for Transport Approved Driving Instructor (DfTADI) and today as a Road Safety Technician/Safety Camera Operative, I have gained a combination of skills and knowledge that have afforded me both a unique perspective and the opportunity, to witness, study and understand in real time, why motorists and bikers get caught out by Safety Camera Vans. This has been achieved by literally witnessing their actions at the time of the committing the offence.

But more importantly, what they need to do to stop getting caught.

I think that it's only fair, that motorists and bikers alike get this chance, the opportunity to fight back.

CHAPTER 4

*How do mobile speed cameras
actually work?*

The narrative that mobile cameras only work for very limited amounts of time in a particular spot isn't true, in effect they work in three distinct ways, by lowering average speed, self-regulating traffic speed and memory. Let me explain.

Simply put, speed cameras work by lowering the average speed, thus when a collision does occur, its risk of serious injury or death is also lowered. Therefore reducing casualties.

I often use this as a way of reasoning speed reduction as a casualty reduction tool. Take a 30mph speed limit, now force drivers to drive at 20mph, now 10mph, and now 0mph. It's obvious that the casualty rates will drop from whatever they were, all the way down to zero.

But this isn't a good thing for motorists, far from it, because it provides an all too easy, yet unimaginative option that favours those that make the rules. Resulting in most road safety interventions being designed around speed reduction and then ultimately, enforcement. Needless to say, that enforcement will always be around for as long as there are people presenting a risk. So the best approach, is to take yourself out of that equation.

Besides the immediate effect of slowing vehicles within specific low to high risk areas where camera vans are present, camera vans also effect average speeds in surprising ways. I spoke recently with a motorist who had managed to get 9 points on his licence within two years. He told me that it was amazing how for the next 2 years, he suddenly developed the skills to safely control his speed and stick to the speed limits. This particular motorist and there are many others, then effectively became a speed reduction tool in the road safety arsenal, because his lower average speed, created a speed reduction effect on all those following behind, effectively self-regulating the traffic. I dare say that he may have unwittingly prevented many others from getting tickets. *(Many a time I have seen motorists about to overtake a slower moving vehicle, only to abort when they realised the reason they were driving to the speed limit was because of a camera van).*

Memory is also a useful speed reduction tool because many drivers and bikers remember where they have previously seen camera vans and slow their speed down within these higher risk areas, before the camera van becomes a threat. This happens irrespective of whether there is a speed camera van present or not and an effect that lasts long before and after, the camera van has gone. So again it's 'mission accomplished'.

It's well documented and irrefutable to any train of reasonable thought, that collisions involving lower speed, increase survivability and reduce injury. So again, the argument against speed reduction and speed camera vans was always remain, a non-starter.

So speed cameras and camera vans work by reducing the average speed on roads that present a higher risk. They work initially due to their presence and secondly because motorists remember where they are. Memory also creates a form of self-regulation for traffic because even when the van is not present, vehicles slow down for them. So even when a camera van is not present, its memory still remains.

CHAPTER 5

The Three E's – Education,
Enforcement and Engineering

To be fair, other methods of casualty reduction are always being explored, in the fields of education, engineering and enforcement (The three E's of road safety) but all too often, education is the poor relation and heavy reliance placed on engineering and enforcement.

I feel low reliance on education is due to the heavy dependence on statistical data as opposed to a willingness to gaining an understanding of the cognitive functions and decisions made by motorists and their relation to road traffic collisions. I think that collision forms don't and can't give a clear and unbiased account of a road traffic collision because they are based on what we see or have witnessed, but there is no account of what a motorist was doing or thinking at the time. This has led to flawed conclusions that weigh heavy and undue blame on a motorists' use of speed.

I think in one way, our fixation with excessive speed, yes whilst dangerous in itself, ignores many more and equally dangerous problems on our roads, for example the levels of anticipation, awareness, concentration, knowledge, observation and responsibility. These are all black holes in the national road safety strategy and yet, may account for the majority of those killed and seriously injured on our roads. It's possible that our lack of focus within these areas may be the cause of our faltering casualty reduction efforts. It's not just 'speed' that kills. There are many who get killed and seriously injured below the speed limit, through lacking in these basic qualities and yet, never or rarely get recorded as such.

This lack of focus on a more nuanced approach to education is excused and maintained by the belief, that any education would have to focus on virtually complete retraining, which for over 30 million motorists is considered to be 'prohibitively expensive'.

However to improve safety and reduce persecution, comprehensive re-training isn't necessary, I believe it is possible to produce impressive casualty reduction numbers by focussing on the six key areas of a motorists awareness, anticipation, concentration, knowledge, observation and responsibility.

We can very quickly and effectively lower the risk of collision involvement, whilst at the same time reduce, even eliminate the threat of all fixed and mobile speed cameras.

Reducing casualties is ultimately the goal, speed reduction is currently the method which I believe can be changed into a win-win scenario for both motorists, bikers and casualties to finally, get the authorities off the motorists back.

CHAPTER 6

Empowerment.

I think one of the added benefits of improving your knowledge and skills, is that it does give you a sense of empowerment. You get the feeling that you know a little bit more than others do about motoring and that's a great feeling. If someone complains to you that they got ripped off with a speeding ticket, you'll know that it wasn't the speed that got them, but more likely, it was a weakness somewhere else in their driving. Almost definitely somewhere in the areas of, **awareness** (didn't see the signs, didn't know what the speed limit was so kept speeding until I did), **anticipation** (never expected the van to be around the corner), **concentration** (I was on the phone, or daydreaming, chatting etc.), **knowledge** (not remembering camera van or fixed camera locations, not noticing new signs have gone up on a new site), **observation** (not seeing the signs that exist, not seeing a 9 foot van or 7 foot camera and even driving straight passed it without seeing it), **responsibility** (driving and riding at speed though the areas where people live, creating safety fears and complaints leading to the creation of new sites that may just catch you out one day, they may have even been the source of the complaint, that got the camera put there, that eventually caught them).

If you ever get the chance to speak to someone who has been caught speeding, dig down a little bit and you'll soon discover that it wasn't just excessive speed that caught them out, but rather what they were doing in addition to the excessive speed.

I would advise anyone to take their advanced driving test if they can and you'll see and experience exactly what I mean.

CHAPTER 7

12 Speed Camera Myths Busted

1. Camera van must be visible

No, there is nothing in law that states that a camera van has to be visible. If they wanted to they could literally be camouflaged. However, out of fairness to the motorist, camera vans are usually highly conspicuous.

2. Do all speeding fines based on the 10% + 2mph rule?

The 10% + 2 mph threshold is only a guideline that is variable between forces before they prosecute. Some do just go by 10% meaning that you can get prosecuted in a 30mph limit by just doing 34mph.

Some forces also give a little extra 10% plus 3mph, here you wouldn't get prosecuted until you were doing 37+mph giving the motorist a greater chance of avoiding a ticket.

This could be deemed to be a little unfair and not standard across the board and some would be prosecuted at 34mph whilst another motorist won't be prosecuted until they reach 37mph. Unfair?

3. Cameras are just a money making scam.

According to North Yorkshire Police, in 2017 safety cameras cost slightly more to run than the income they generated. So on a local level, they're not. Many forces are finding that the fixed camera sites are becoming increasingly unaffordable to run, resulting in the turning off of many fixed cameras and downsizing the fleet of mobile camera vans.

4. Police Officers should be out fighting crime, not persecuting motorists.

The Mobile Camera vans are operated by highly trained and qualified police staff leaving the maximum number of police officers to fight crime.

5. Speed Cameras only catch motorists travelling in one direction?

Mobile camera vans can catch people speeding in both directions. This is also true of Gatso cameras, they certainly have the capability to catch motorists in both directions but there are none that I'm aware of that do so, because of the risk of the flash affecting the motorists visibility.

6. Can I get caught twice in the same day?

Technically, you can get caught twice within minutes. Usually because the two times you have been caught may class as two separate journeys. However getting caught in some force areas twice within 20 minutes will only be classed as one offence. Again unfair?

7. Will signalling to other motorists of the presence of a speed camera van get me in trouble?

Technically yes, this is an offence but one that many operators will ignore because they're effectively doing the camera van operators job for them, to slow traffic down.

8. Is it illegal to obstruct a vans view of the road?

Yes, obstructing the vans view of the road whilst being operationally deployed for a policing purpose, is an offence. Don't try it because it's really annoying and could land you in court and may cause the camera van to revisit the site sooner than should was planned.

9. Camera vans only target speeding motorists?

This isn't true, Camera van operators also target people using mobile phones and not wearing their seatbelts.

Additionally some camera vans are equipped with ANPR which is used for tracking criminal activity and has also proven useful in tracking the movements of missing persons.

10. How long do camera vans stay on the same site?

Camera vans usually stay on site for around 1 hour and 30 minutes. This is usually because that's about the limit of recording time they have on their memory cards.

Once finished at a site, they'll file everything away, move to a new site and set everything up again with fresh memory cards.

11. If I go on a speed awareness course, do I have to disclose this to my insurance company?

The simple answer is yes, you should disclose to your insurance company that you have been on a speed awareness course. If you haven't and you get involved in a collision, it could easily invalidate your insurance claim.

12. Are camera vans obliged to put out temporary 'speed camera' warning signs if there are no permanent speed camera signs?

No, they are not obliged to put out temporary signs. This could be due to the weather or traffic conditions where it would not be safe. But also because signs have been damaged or stolen (surprisingly on occasion by people who don't want speeding motorists to be warned that they're driving towards a camera van).

CHAPTER 8

Facts and Stats

The first speeding ticket was issued on January 28th 1896 in Paddock Wood, Kent. A constable spotted a driver named Walter Arnold speeding down the street. Since the constable didn't have a motorised vehicle, he chased him down on his bike. Arnold was doing 4 times the blistering speed of 8mph. Yes, the speed limit then was 2mph. The limit was raised later that year to 14mph.

(Source – needs either BBC, Money Week, Ohio History, USA Today)

The following data is from the report 'Do Speed Cameras Save Lives' by Cheng Keat Taug" Sept 2017.

London School of Economics:

1. Around 50 million people are hurt in road traffic collisions globally every year.

2. Around 1.2 million of these don't survive their injuries

3. According to the Department for Transport, speeding either excessive or inappropriate accounts for more than 60% of fatal collisions in the UK in 2015.

According to iNews "Over three quarters (78%) some 31 million adults admit to speeding, with over two million drivers (five per cent) speeding on every journey they make. While a further 4.7 million (12 per cent) say they speed on most journeys".

New research from Direct Line Insurance also discovered that "Half of all drivers in the UK, some 20 million people, believe it is acceptable to break the UK speed limit.

CHAPTER 9

Some Eye Watering Headlines

'Colossally stupid' motorcycle rider caught doing 180mph....
by his own helmet camera – Sunday Times Driving 3 Dec 2019

Police search for 176mph biker BBC News 24 Sep 2007
(He was eventually jailed for 28 days)

12 months prison for 139mph speeding biker MCN 20 July 2009
(He did this over the brow of a hill)

CAUGHT BY COPS AT 137MPH – ON HIS ARSE. Visor Down 20
Apr 2008
This Dutch biker clocked a new record in the Netherlands after
being snapped passing a speed camera on his arse, with his bike
a few feet in front of him.
(Ouch)

Biker caught speeding at 122mph with 14 year old son on back
of motorcycle – Telegraph – The Telegraph 2 Feb 2009

CHAPTER 10

Abusers and Accusers

One thing that is abundantly clear is that camera vans are Marmite. There mainly two types of people who approach the van to speak with the operators, the abusers and supporters. With the latter being by far the rarest.

Most abusers approach the van with nonsensical points to make, here are a few:

1. Are you with the road safety team? Then why are you parked on the brow of a hill?

When I asked him where the brow of the hill was, he couldn't find it.

2. "You're causing an obstruction!"

What am I obstructing?

"You're parked on double yellow lines!"

Yes, I'm fully aware of that, that's not causing an obstruction, that's parking on double yellow lines, which we're authorised to do for a policing purpose.

"But you're causing an obstruction!"

Is that all you've come to do, give me a bit of grief?

"Yes"

3. This one usually gets his phone out so he can 'big it up' on social media.

Pointing his camera phone through the window says things like:

"Why you hiding here?"

"You're a thief!"

"You're a parasite"

"How much do you get paid for doing this?"

This one will usually be ignored and the window closed on them. Camera operators have no desire to be somebodies social media post of the day.

And you can intersperse a great many expletives within all of that too.

All pretty unpleasant stuff really, when all they're trying to do is their job.

I think that the abuse that camera operators receive, has been created by the lack of understanding, at both the road safety community and motorist levels, of speed cameras and therefore their inability to explain just how they work. This lack of understanding feeds directly into the levels of abuse the camera operators get, because up until now, they've never fully understood the reason behind why they were caught.

We've never recognised before that it wasn't their just their speed that was at fault and I don't think the road safety community recognised that either. We've never really spared any thought or given any consideration to the motorists' sense of awareness, anticipation, concentration, knowledge, observation or responsibility in relation to road traffic casualties in an effort to find a better, more acceptable solution for motorists, for our road safety problems.

This lack of understanding has led most motorists, to always believe that the rest of their driving was fine and they were being prosecuted, for something they felt in control of, their speed. Had we understood from the beginning that it wasn't just speed that earned the motorist a speeding ticket, then the relationship between camera vans and motorists would have possibly been better. As it stands, motorists are being prosecuted for speeding without being fully informed as to why, for as long as these errors remain unchecked, then riders and bikers will just continue to fall foul of them.

It is in this respect, that I believe speed cameras have always been very much mismarked, because had they been called 'concentration cameras' or 'awareness cameras', then the motorist would have known exactly what it was they were being prosecuted for and would have been in a better position to correct it and prevent repeat offences.

One discussion that illustrates this lack of a genuine understanding was with a solicitor, he accused the operator of hiding around a bend, catching motorists as they emerged. What he failed to recognise and give acknowledgement to, was the fact that these drivers being caught speeding, were driving around a blind bend at an excessive speed.

Arguably, the issue wasn't just the motorists' speed, but in addition, their lack of anticipation. There was no anticipation of any hazard being there, a child, a cyclist, a pedestrian and in this case failing to anticipate the presence of the camera van.

Yes bikers, you can be a bunch of bastards too, regularly giving the operators a variety of hand signs.

And what's the hand on the hip thing about when you're riding past?

Rarely, but it's nice all the same, you get a thumbs up from a driver or a nod from a biker and when a camera operator gets them, they're very much appreciated.

So try to give the Road Safety Techs a break. They're doing an important job keeping our roads as safe as they can for us, our families and our friends.

Give them a break.

CHAPTER 11

*The Worst of Advice, The
Best of Advice –*

*Understanding How We Became
Vulnerable to Speed Cameras*

For many drivers and bikers, the journey to getting their first speeding ticket started the day they passed their driving test. The driving test itself is a construction or collection of driving techniques all brought together with the singular purpose of keeping you and other road users safe. It's as simple as that. From the basic use of the hand and foot controls, all the way through to more advanced manoeuvring and road craft techniques, all have their origins in road safety.

As you progressed with your driving, as skills became second nature, the instructor added more and more safety features/ techniques to your driving until the day arrived, that you could carry out all of these skills independently.

The day of the driving test was always nerve wracking, not just for the novice taking their test, but also for their instructors too. Who having spent half the lesson prior to the test, trying to dispel myths of quotas and examiner ogres, then had to wait for your return, nervously wringing their hands back in the test centre waiting room and hoping that their words of encouragement worked. All the time wondering, if the journey home was going to one of celebration, or one of dissemination.

Once the test is passed, you earned the next stage in your right of passage through life, the glorious freedom of the road. This is the point in time where things started to go wrong and where the start of your journey towards your first speeding ticket began. It's a common process, one that will be familiar to virtually every driver or biker as they started to change the things they had been taught.

I only ever fully understood the extent of the changes I had made to my driving when I started training as a Driving Instructor. My first advanced lesson was brutal beyond words with every error I was making, every technique I had diverged from, being highlighted by the second.

For me, the day I'd passed my driving test, I remember wanting to create my own driving style after receiving the worst piece of driving advice I'd ever received and now consider to be the worst piece of driving advice ever given:

'Now go out there and really learn how to drive'.

What on earth did it mean? I don't think anyone ever truly did and I've never met a single motorist who was able to explain it.

How were young and new motorists supposed to interpret it? Was it that they should look towards the more experienced drivers and riders around them, for clues and incorporate elements of their driving into their own? After all, they've already gone out there and learned how to really drive.

Some, thankfully a minority create their own non approved techniques.

Most if not all of us, started to remove some of those safeguards the instructor put into place while teaching us to drive. Our road positioning became less important, speed increased, attitude (yes that changed for some), braking becomes later and harder, acceleration became harsher, manoeuvring accuracy out the window.

But most importantly, our cognitive group of skills also suffered as a result of using our mirror less, our concentration and observations reduced, resulting in our awareness of the things around us and therefore the ability to anticipate becoming weaker. This combination of weakened driver and rider qualities and harder driving technique, resulted in our collision risk increasing and for the purposes of this book, our vulnerability to fixed and mobile safety cameras too.

Imagine the effect that changing their driving style had on the new and inexperienced driver or biker. With limited experience and trying out new and unauthorised driving techniques would have sent their collective collision rate soaring. Maybe, we are wrong to blame a young motorists collision rates on inexperience, maybe, it was the changes the more experienced motorists advised them to make.

The positives about now knowing why we're vulnerable to speed cameras of any type, is that we're already half way to fixing it.

I think advising new and young drivers and bikers to 'now go out there and really learn how to drive', trashes everything their instructor taught them, by effectively telling them that it was wrong, that they'd only been taught to pass a test. Nothing could be further from the truth, they were trained to be safe and competent. The last thing they need is to be told from day one that driving is somehow different to the way they were taught.

I can't emphasise enough how tragically bad those ten words are as motoring advice.

Don't give it.

The best motoring advice you can give to any new fledgling motorist is:

'Remember what you have been taught and never change a thing, just add experience to what you have learned'. Keep yourself up to date with changes and read and update your Highway Code, it's not just for the test'.

You can always add, "And don't drive like me, I'd never pass the test again".

This advice is clear and concise, its telling the new motorist that to remain a really safe and competent driver, all they have to do is remember and drive by the skills they were taught.

By passing the test, they have proved they have achieved good, competent and safe basics, now all they need to add to that is the experience to enhance and improve those skills, not remove them.

PART 2

Using Our Understanding to Beat the Speed Camera

CHAPTER 12

Psychomotor and Cognitive Skills

The relationship between your cognitive and psychomotor skills are essential to becoming a truly safe and prosecution free driver or rider.

Your cognitive skills basically translate into the understanding of your surroundings, what you see and what you hear. Great cognition comes from, first and foremost, heightened levels of concentration and observation, not the tunnel vision extreme single point concentration that becomes narrower the faster you drive or ride. But a very well rounded assessment of your surroundings to the front, rear and sides of your vehicle that only comes from effective observation, allowing you to continually assess and reassess those surroundings, as you progress on your journey.

This essential level of concentration and observation then naturally leads to the enhanced levels of awareness that you need to spot and anticipate hazards, for instance the potential for other vehicles to emerge from junctions that may not have seen you, children, and yes, safety camera vans.

Your psychomotor skills are the actions that your hands and feet take in response to the information that has come from your cognitive skills. Which is why, if your cognitive skills are badly informed, your psychomotor reactions will be flawed. You brain will be effectively sending the wrong instructions to your hands and feet, heightening your own personal risk, which may manifest itself as nothing at all but could present itself as a collision or a road traffic offence or in a thousand other ways.

This is also why I think that the way our casualty statistics are recorded is inherently flawed. Largely focussing on the psychomotor aspects of motoring, whilst leaving the cognitive contribution to RTC's largely unexplored, resulting in a road safety approach that largely concentrates on speed reduction as a casualty reduction approach as opposed to considering a motorists cognitive function.

These black holes in road casualty data are important to fill and understand. Because it is these missing elements, that are likely to be the most common reasons for road traffic casualties but also the same elements that render us vulnerable to mobile speed cameras.

So with this approach to beating speed cameras, the additional result will be to reduce road traffic casualties at the same time. Meaning a win/win situation for road safety organisations and motorists alike. Fewer casualties does not have to mean the persecution of motorists. On the contrary, fewer road traffic casualties could even lay for foundations for increases in some speed limits.

CHAPTER 13

*The Six Qualities of a Great Motorist/
Biker and How Enhancing These Will
Stop You Getting Caught by Speed
Cameras.*

These six qualities are fundamental to beating safety/speed cameras and unsurprisingly, they are all focussed on the cognitive functions of the driver or rider. They are also the key to reducing your collision risk, protecting your licence from penalty points and your wallet from fines.

It works by placing them into the correct order and for the purpose of this exercise, I'll split them into three groups because they go hand in hand:

1. Observation and concentration.
2. Awareness and Anticipation
3. Knowledge and Responsibility

To beat any and all speed cameras, it is essential to have great levels of observation which only come from a great level of concentration. The effect that this has, is that it will naturally raise your levels of awareness and anticipation giving you the ability to react appropriately. Effectively repairing the disconnection between your cognitive and psychomotor skills that virtually all of us, have allowed to deteriorate over time.

Then finally, knowledge and responsibility. All of these qualities when applied to road users are fundamental to road safety, you're not only lowering your risk to speed cameras but also your collision risk.

These are the same qualities that give you and all other road users, the best protection from both prosecution and injury. In other words, they lower your risk of being caught by a speed camera van whilst improving the safety of all of us at the same time. This is why I believe that this method of protecting yourself against prosecution, is by far the best and only truly legitimate way of beating speed cameras, because it comes from you, your skills, your experience and judgement as motorists and bikers.

CHAPTER 14

Observation

Observation: The action or process of closely observing or monitoring something or someone.

Observation is obviously a highly important quality of a motorist. That goes without saying. But, the question with observation is are we doing it correctly? Are we doing it right?

As soon as we've passed our driving test, our observational skills are one of the first to deteriorate. We tend to use our mirrors a lot less, therefore reducing our awareness of the things going on around us. We drive/ride faster which in itself narrows our fields of vision. The result of this is that hazards get missed and sometimes they're important things like speed camera signs, cyclists, pedestrians, children, cars emerging from junctions. The most common form of collision is a rear end shunt at roundabouts, caused because a motorist failed to look forward before moving off only to realise that the car in front hadn't left yet. That's an observational error but could also be put down to a lack of awareness, anticipation even knowledge.

Concentration and observation are the bedrock to everything that follows. You need your eyes to feed your brain all of the information it needs to make you aware of everything that is going on around you, to spot hazards as they emerge and anticipate the potential of hazards you cannot yet see which ultimately give your hands and feet instructions on what to do next.

So if your observations aren't collecting enough information about your surroundings, your brain may sent the wrong instructions to your hands and feet.

In other words, if shit goes in, then shit comes out.

So observations and I mean great, effective observations are the gateway to great, safe and prosecution free motoring.

How to improve your observation

To make sure you've got everything covered, you have to organise your observations into 'zones of vision'. And there are many around you. There are three zones of vision to the front of you, the immediate, intermediate and the distant, respectively informing you what is happening now, what is coming next and what is coming after. These observations are rolling and keep you prepared well in advance of hazards such as the potential for vehicles to emerge into your path, children at the side of the road who may run into it, parked vehicles, fixed and mobile speed cameras or any number of other hazards that may be present.

The same observations apply also to the sides, rear and blind spots of your vehicle, which will keep you informed of hazards present or approaching from the sides and behind.

But without a decent level of concentration, your observations may miss necessary and important hazards leaving you, the motorist or biker, vulnerable.

CHAPTER 15

Concentration

Concentration: The action or power of focussing all ones attention.

Concentration or the lack of it, was the motorists' greatest weakness when it came to fixed speed cameras or the dreaded and much maligned 'Gatso'. These were the subject of my first book 'The Real Drivers Guide to Beating the Speed Camera' published in 2008. Where I pondered the question, how could a motorist, whilst driving through a well signed area allow themselves to drive passed a bright yellow, 9ft tall Gatso camera at speed, which was inevitably going to cost them £60 and 3 penalty points on their licence? How could some motorists even manage to achieve this feat multiple times?

It was at this point that I understood that fixed speed cameras had very little to do with speed and everything to do with concentration. Speed cameras had been marketed badly, they should have been called 'Con-cams' or 'Concentration Cameras' because that's exactly the weaknesses that they were exploiting and continue to exploit today. What they exposed, was a motorist not only driving at speed, but even more unforgivably, whilst doing it with low levels of awareness, concentration and observation.

I can't help but think that if we as motorists knew and understood this from day one, would it have changed our attitudes and behaviour towards them. Might we have instead thought to ourselves, "right I know what happened there, I wasn't concentrating hard enough'. At least then we would have had the chance to modify our driving and riding behaviour, to focus and concentrate on our observation that bit harder and make sure there was no repeat of the same mistake.

It's a similar story for Safety Camera vans, but they take it a step further and additionally exploit weaknesses in anticipation and awareness which up until now, has remained unknown. The lack of effective observation has led many drivers and bikers to miss the speed camera warning signs which has resulted in millions driving and riding around blind bends, at speed.

Was a camera van hiding around a blind bend, or did the road user fail to anticipate he presence of a camera van and decide to drive over the speed limit on a blind bend?

Why were the safety camera signs ignored? Were they even seen in the first place?

So reduced levels of concentration inevitably leads to reduced levels of awareness and anticipation which are the enemies of the speed camera van and they will catch you out for them.

Maybe Safety Camera Vans should be named 'Anticipation Cameras'. At least then, the motorist will have had this fault in their driving instantly revealed to them. That the problem wasn't just necessarily their use of speed, but a weakness with their anticipation also.

When operating a speed camera van, it's quite fascinating to see the inattention of road users in 'real time'. There are many different levels of inattention too. The vast majority, hit the brakes the second they have seen the camera van but others take longer to react. This is where we can gauge the reduced levels of awareness and concentration. On any given stretch of road, a motorist with decent observational skills will spot the camera van at the exact same time as the camera van spots them and it's just a case of who is faster on the draw? The laser or the brake? They'll be watching their letter box for the next two weeks wondering if they're going to get a 'Notice of Intended Prosecution' but living with a chance that they won't.

The problem with this motorist was that they failed to antici-pate the presence of the camera van. So we know their antici-pation levels are low which stems from low levels of concen-tration and observation. Which kind of blows apart the age old excuse of 'I only suffered a momentary lapse of concentration, your honour'.

But then there are others, and many of them who get much, much closer to the camera van before spotting it. They're con-sidered to have much reduced levels of concentration and will suddenly realise that they have been speeding in view of the camera van for quite some time. It would be comical if it weren't so tragic to see them hit their brakes, so long after they have been hit with the laser. This motorist was speeding with very low levels of awareness and observation and if faced with an emergency situation probably wouldn't have known about it until it was over.

They may have only been doing 37mph in a 30mph limit, they'll claim persecution and they'll probably get sympathy. Would you want them driving anywhere near you or your fam-ily?

And finally, there are the drivers and bikers who fail to see the camera van completely. Some who speed into view and con-tinue to speed on the approach and then past the van, completely oblivious to its presence. For them, the day they receive their NIP will come as a shock, a bolt out of the blue, because they never even knew the van was there. For these drivers and bikers, there is no speed that is safe for them to drive or ride at. What they need is taking off the road.

There is another group of surprise speeders, they come into view at ow below the speed limit, then as they approach it inexplicably accelerate above the camera van threshold.

All of the others, the ones who speed and didn't get caught we'll never know about their standard. Some undoubtedly will possess elevated driver and rider qualities, others may have dreadful qualities but just choose not to speed. An area worthy of a future visit.

Low levels of driver quality also explains the other common accusation thrown at camera vans from motorists', that they didn't expect the camera van to be there or they were hiding around the corner. Is it more likely that despite the signage, their low levels of observation and concentration wouldn't allow them to anticipate the presence of the van?

Remember, forces have few camera vans and potentially several hundred camera sites, so it's often weeks or months after seeing a camera van before they will reappear on site. So the best way to protect yourself, is to always expect a camera van to be around the next bend.

Also be aware that not all camera van sites are signed and additionally, camera vans are not obliged to put out temporary signs to warn motorists of their presence.

So the rule of thumb is. Never drive or ride around a blind bend at speed. The rule of always driving within the distance you can see to be clear was never so important when it comes to dealing with speed camera vans.

CHAPTER 16

Awareness and Anticipation

*Awareness: Knowledge or perception of a situation or fact.
Anticipation: The action of anticipating something,
expectation or prediction.*

Anticipation is probably the most important skill when it comes to dealing with speed cameras but along with awareness develops as a natural consequence of the quality of your combined observation and concentration. The better these qualities are, the better your anticipation will be and grow to be. And the opposite is also true.

So reduced levels of 'concentration and observation' inevitably result in reduced levels of 'awareness and anticipation' which safety camera vans will ravenously feed from and punish for poor levels. But a good standard of concentration and observation will send your standard of awareness and anticipation soaring, improve both your safety and protection from prosecution.

Whilst operating a speed camera van, it's quite fascinating to see the inattention of road users caused primarily by sub-standard observations and concentration, in 'real time'. There are many different levels of inattention too.

Great awareness only comes from a great levels concentration and observation. Without these, your level of awareness is going to be negatively affected and therefore, so is your vulnerability as a road user to prosecution and road traffic incident. It is vitally important that your levels of awareness is fully and constantly informed. Because a lack of concentration creates a disconnection between the psychomotor and cognitive functions or more simply put, what our brains are telling our hands and feet to do.

CHAPTER 17

Knowledge

*Knowledge: Facts, information and skills acquired
through experience or education, the theoretical
or practical understanding of a subject.*

Knowledge is a great thing to have, a joy to use but a pain to get because it only comes from learning. For motorists it comes from the Highway Code and the driving manuals which are essential reading for all motorists. There are always new signs, road markings and techniques being advised, so keep yourself up to date with changes in knowledge.

CHAPTER 18

Responsibility

Responsibility: The state or fact of having a duty to deal with something or of having control over someone.

Respect

Respect: Having due regard for the feelings, wishes or rights of others.

The first step you should take to reduce your risk of collision and prosecution is to take some responsibility for your own driving/riding. As discussed, we know that pretty much all of the loopholes that were once used to squash speeding tickets have now been closed and as new ones emerge, they'll be closed too. The best protection from getting caught now, is down to you and pretty much you alone.

Most counties and states have mobile camera sites numbering in their hundreds and new ones can be set up very quickly. There doesn't have to be a history of collisions, complaints of speeding are enough to create a new site. These complaints are genuine concerns from other motorists as well as residents. Many often disturbed by vehicles screaming through their estates and outside their homes, where their children go to school, play and they also have to live and work. So they complain, the authorities go out and assess the sites, confirm there is a speeding problem and within days, there is a new speed camera site. A road some have been used to driving or riding down, with little consideration for those that have to live there, who have been shown little or no respect for their right to peace and quiet in a safe environment. Then they will show the driving licences of the road users denying them this right, the same respect being shown to them, none.

The greatest problem for motorists with a new speed camera site, is that it's new. Motorists and bikers will usually find this out the hard way.

I know of one such road where three camera technicians caught over 550 offenders in three, one and a half hour sessions. The road is well signed, the vans were highly conspicuous. It's a 40mph speed limit leading into a residential area. Two of the motorists within that time were clocked at 88mph, one was in the wet.

Besides the elevated risk these motorists presented, they also showed a lack of respect for the residents. In part, this lack of respect from motorists and bikers themselves was one of the main reasons they received penalty points. Their driving led to complaints, those complaints led to the creation of a new camera site and the new camera site caused many hundreds of motorists to fall foul of the weaknesses in their driving.

The solution is simple, have a little more respect for locals and new camera sites won't be created.

Summary

A local radio host once asked the question 'shouldn't motorists be considered responsible enough to set their own speed limits?' Or something very similar.

I think that this book has shown that were nowhere near ready for that kind of a leap just yet. The barrier is that our motorists' cognitive skills aren't ready for it.

The early days of the Covid-19 pandemic has also shown us what happens when we leave motorists to their own judgement, when speed enforcement was removed from the roads, motorists countrywide, went crazy. Complaints of speeding and the roads being treated like a racetracks went through the roof, I think what prevented many collisions from happening was that traffic volume decreased by 73% all the way down to 1955 levels.

So should motorists be allowed to judge for themselves what a safe speed is? The answer I'm afraid is clearly no.

This book could also be seen as a double edged sword, yes it gives the motorist the tools they need to protect themselves from speed cameras, but it also gives the road safety community a new impetus on the importance of speed reduction. If a motorist now gets a speeding ticket, it can no longer be considered the persecution of an innocent motorist as the faults committed, that led to the speeding ticket, have now been identified.

We've also learned that whilst two motorists may get speeding tickets on the same stretch of road driving at the same speed, the levels of risk they present can be wildly different.

We've learned that mobile and fixed speed cameras do prevent death and serious injury on our roads. By their very existence they are taking the speed out of road users with low awareness, whilst they are travelling through higher risk areas.

We've also questioned the possibility that the road safety community fixation with speeding, whilst ignoring education, may be the very reason why the falls in toad traffic casualty have all but stalled.

Importantly, we've learned that getting caught speeding, has very little to do with speed and everything to do with the deterioration of our motoring cognitive function such as awareness, anticipation, concentration, knowledge, observation and our sense of responsibility. And that to beat speed cameras in all of their forms, the motorist merely has observe a little better, understand what they see a little better and then send the right signals to the parts of their bodies in charge of the controls.

But more importantly, we've established that if we can learn to beat the speed the speed camera, then we also learn the skills that help to reduce casualties on our roads. Ultimately reducing the need for them and effectively passing them out completely.
That's changing the narrative.

Thomas Heavey ©2020

THE 'REAL DRIVERS' GUIDE TO BEATING THE SPEED CAMERA

FORWARD

Over the last few years, I have found myself embroiled in the speed camera debate. A thoroughly enjoyable debate, that has always been highly emotive, lively and quite often aggressive. One thing for sure though that became clearly evident, was the stubbornness from both sides, to yield an inch. I have always been in a position where I have found, that both sides have a point, as well as a part to play, but neither side, had got it quite right either. But when you try to tell either of them this, the expression 'banging your head against a brick wall' was never so appropriate and as a consequence, I had no alternative but to withdraw.

My own beliefs became increasingly isolated within the debate, as I altered from being an absolute supporter of the camera, to realising that yes, they also had their flaws. I do firmly believe speed cameras prevent deaths and injury, but also that there are better methods and practises that are largely overlooked. Ways that enhance the driving experience and prevent the motorist from constant and relentless punishment. So there lay the problem, how do you give everyone what they want, fewer road traffic casualties, whist at the same time, fewer speed cameras? Today, I'm going to give you the answer.

Sick of reading about the dreadful and ultimately avoidable daily waste of life on our roads, I began writing with that sole intention in mind. After a few months, the result was a document that I couldn't seek the support or either side, as it finds deep flaw in both their arguments and as such, opposes their beliefs. So I decided to turn it into a book.

Aside from the debate though and infinitely more important, the book reveals the game that speed cameras play, how they save lives and catch so many speeding motorists in the process (2.1 million in 2006). Armed with this information and using all of my experience and knowledge from my time as an Approved Driving Instructor, I have been able to bring together, six traditional driving techniques formulated to provide the ultimate defence against them and created:

'The Real Drivers Guide to Beating the Speed Camera'

It has been designed to put the 'real' back into the 'real motorist' as it uses driving skills, not technology, to beat the speed camera.

The lessons learned will allow the motorist, to level the playing field against the speed camera and put into use the most powerful defence against them ever created, the human mind.

Utilising 'real' driving skills, goes so much further than the simple speed camera detector or reliance on risky and potentially freedom wrecking court defences, because as well as providing the motorist with the ultimate protection against the speed camera, the motorist is also armed with the power to prevent the need for more. Protection, that is not limited to just protecting driving licences but extended to reduce casualties on every inch of our roads.

Ultimately, the aim of the book is to make the roads safer and speed camera free and all without ruining the motoring experience.

At last, the motorist has a new option in protection from the dreaded speed camera, but for the first time, the protection is preventative and comes before the nippy (notice of intended prosecution) is ever issued.

Thomas Heavey

CONTENTS

Part 1

Part 2

Part 3

Introduction

If, like so many others, you have a real desire to see the end of the speed camera, then the first and most important step you must take, is to completely understand, just how motorists get caught out in the first place.

You MUST acknowledge and accept the possibility they really do save lives. Once you discover how they save lives, but in the process detect ever increasing numbers of motorists (2 million + in 2006 in the UK alone) can you start to take the measures that will prevent you, from becoming another speed camera victim.

In the utopian world, if every motorist were to learn a few simple techniques to modify their driver behaviour and standard, then it is possible that the speed camera would become valueless and ineffective as a road safety measure, eventually breaking the dependence we have on them. However, as this is unlikely to ever happen, then the best action you can take is to protect YOURSELF against their ever expanding numbers and ever increasing efficiency. You will also learn that by protecting yourself from the speed camera, you will also be protecting yourself from hurting others around you. After all, the best possible protection against the speed camera is YOU.

It is important to say, that this book is not about speed, I am not going to lecture you that the best way to avoid the speed camera, is not to speed in the first place, even though it is. I am leaving 'use of speed' as it has always been, a choice, left to the individual motorist and I'll make no apology for that. For this book, I am going to concentrate on something infinitely more important, education.

The point of this book is primarily intended to improve road safety, regardless of whether you speed or not and protect your licence in the right way, by helping you, to make the right choices.

Collisions will happen irrespective of whether you are travelling at 28mph or 38mph, it is the outcome of that collision that is determined by speed. So the primary aim is not to reduce the severity of a collision by reducing speed, but one of completely avoiding the collision by improving the driver's skills.

One of the resulting effects of improving skills is that you will enhance your experience as a motorist, by developing a far greater awareness of your environment. This improved awareness will benefit you in four ways.

1. Your chance of being involved in a collision will be greatly reduced.
2. Your chance of getting caught by a speed camera will also be greatly reduced:
3. By creating fewer casualties on the road, you will also reduce the need for further speed cameras and finally:
4. Your confidence and therefore enjoyment from motoring will be enhanced.

Effectively, you will be attacking speed cameras on two levels, first by protecting yourself against them, you are making them less cost effective and then by reducing your collision risk, you are not contributing to the need for more.

Speed and speeding is an issue that is always going to remain with us and being realistic, no-one, is ever going to be able to put an end to it.

Personally, I have always been a supporter of speed cameras, because I have always had to be (the reasons for which will become clear later) but when the government recently relaxed the placement criteria for speed cameras and announced plans to digitise several thousand of them, I was filled with a kind of dread, that foresees' a nation infested with little grey and yellow boxes.

Our local authorities are now free to place speed cameras at locations deemed to be potentially hazardous, without having to meet the old camera placement criteria. This change in policy, in one respect can only be a good thing, as we no longer have to wait for 3 or 4 human beings to be killed or seriously injured, before something is done about it. The flip side is the blighting of our landscape as well as the loss of freedom and livelihood caused by this potentially rapid increase in the reliance and spread of speed camera technology.

Strangely, this is something that I both support, because of their valuable contribution to road safety and oppose, because of their unsightliness and their potential to punish motorists instead of addressing their driving issues. There is a better way to improve road safety whilst also returning to the motorist, the freedom and enjoyment that they so desire.

Even though I support speed cameras, I also find that, along with many current and future road safety initiatives, they are ruining the very fabric of what constitutes motoring by the gradual erosion of the ability of the motorist, to make decisions. It is true that they are a very blunt and simple tool, but they are undeniably very effective in addressing the hugely complex issue of road safety.

Having said this though, I have also discovered that 'speed cameras' harbour one huge flaw, a flaw that exposes the weaknesses of current road safety policy. Yes, they prevent many from being killed and injured, but over time, a few simple motorist modifications could easily result in preventing thousands more.

Besides the death and injury that speed cameras prevent, it is also true that they make vast amounts of money in the process. 2.1 million times £60 a throw adds up a very lucrative industry, gleaning around £126 million pounds per year out of the motorist (a figure that is surely set to increase). Not something that the authorities are ever likely let go of, so easily as bowing to the complaints, of a few disgruntled motorists.

Much of the opposition demands their immediate removal, but offers nothing to prevent the increase in casualty rates and carnage that would certainly follow.

The government are in possession of overwhelming and independent evidence, that prove beyond their own doubt, that speed cameras are an effective and necessary life saving road safety measure. So, no amount of complaining is ever going to sway the Governments determination to reduce casualties on our roads, by whatever means necessary and available, however blunt.

As it appears extremely unlikely, that speed cameras will be removed from our roads in the near future, so I have brought together the tools that I have been using for years, to make the speed camera obsolete for you. By simply readdressing a few traditional driving methods, not only will you have re-developed the skills to spot any fixed speed cameras, but at the same time, you will reduce your chances of being caught out by mobile cameras and increase your protection from the involvement of a serious and life altering collision.

As 'real motorists', we need to take the responsibility for road safety back into our own hands or the government, bless them, will continue to develop and employ more casualty reduction measures, that are designed to beat the motorist into submission, rather than focus on motoring development. After all, driver education costs money, speed cameras don't.

The first part of the book is going to examine just how speed interacts with our driving. Then we are going to explore the argument surrounding the speed camera debate and discover why the debate is making no ground. We shall see that it is the statisticians, who are compromising a meaningful debate, which in turn, is hindering real progress in road safety. Undoubtedly, some great minds have contributed to the speed camera debate, but are they really the right minds?

I have always questioned the validity of statistical and scientific reasoning behind road safety, as their conclusions seem increasingly, to have been based on data which is pitifully inadequate. Casualty stats are generally based on what we see or are told, not necessarily on what really actually occurred. We see a vehicle travelling at speed and the assumption is that speed caused the collision, what we didn't see was the motorist thinking about the next holiday, the argument he just had with his wife, him fiddling with his radio or talking on his hands free mobile phone. Additionally, he or she is unlikely to ever admit that he or she was not concentrating on the job of driving, and as a consequence, in many cases, the blame is wrongly heaped onto a little excessive speed instead of addressing the real issues and hence, 'speed kills' when the real culprit was diminished concentration, inattention, poor observation or any of the many other common driver errors.

Over the last few years we have seen the blame speed is apportioned with for casualty rates, fluctuate wildly. Excessive speed was once blamed as a contributory factor in 35% of all serious collisions, then lack of concentration was apportioned some blame and that figure dropped to 12%. A 'Transport Research Lab' report was then misinterpreted and speed was then blamed for 7% of collisions. This was soon again amended and at the last count, the blame speed now gets is 15%, all of this has occurred within the last few years. Talk about our safety experts chasing their own tails!

This is precisely why I have a real distrust of road safety statistical analysis. It is little wonder that dealing effectively with road safety is such an over complicated, expensive and difficult task that offers little, in terms of serious casualty reduction, when statisticians have not even started to explore the contribution of the thousands of combinations of other errors made whilst driving, errors that still remain unchecked and yet, have an effect, on the level of blame that speeding is apportioned with. For example many deaths occur on the road due to weak mirror work, poor observation, lack of concentration etc?

After, we have explored how speed cameras work (for which you have to look much deeper than just the overall annual road casualty numbers to understand) we can start to look at ending their reign of terror on our driving licences.

As it stands, the future of motoring looks bleak, speed cameras are at the forefront of automated road safety and their growth in numbers is a direction that I personally, no longer relish taking. Very recent advancements in speed camera technology have created the indestructible speed camera. It has 4 cameras that can cover four lanes of traffic with video back up and can take photos of traffic travelling in either direction. Additionally, this new breed of camera can be installed in pairs, with the other taking a photo from the front to enable easy identification of the driver. The defensive loopholes against them are certainly in the process of being closed.

It has also been said, that we already have the technology to develop fully automated vehicles with no need for a driver. This technology could be widely available within 20 or so years. Other initiatives include speed limiters for cars and motorbikes and even monitoring of a vehicles speed by satellite. Is this the legacy that we really want to leave for future motoring generations?

This may surprise you, but you already own the best and most accurate speed camera detector and casualty reduction tool on the face of the planet, the brain, and by the end of this book, you're going to switch it on.

PART 1

1

AN UNDERSTANDING OF SPEED

We all believe that we are good and responsible drivers, who can handle a bit of speed, but do we really understand at which point speed becomes excessive? There appears to be so many of us with this belief, who have got this judgement completely wrong and for some, driving at any speed is excessive. Knowing when 'use of speed' truly becomes excessive is all down to awareness. To achieve good awareness, our observations and concentration also have to be good. Good observations come from knowing where we should look and understanding what we see, not where we think we should.

This is one of the primary reasons why we have speed limits. They are set purely due to the number of hazards present on any particular road, the greater the number, or potential number of hazards, the lower the speed limit. To some extent, speed limits have removed some of the need for us to think. They have been set at an estimated maximum 'safe' speed and any variations in our use of speed, is expected to be contained within that maximum speed limit.

Obviously motorways have very few hazards and so, have a higher speed limit.

Poor use of speed is usually described in one of three ways, excessive, inappropriate or too slow for the conditions, which is normally described as failing to make good progress. Driving too slow for the conditions can also have a negative effect on some motorists who feel they are being held up. A result of this is that it makes many motorists, feel that they have to overtake.

If done badly, overtaking is probably the single most dangerous manoeuvre we can perform.

2

Excessive Speed

Excessive speed is basically exceeding the posted speed limit for any particular road. The speed limit already incorporates a certain level of risk to all road users, but this level is deemed to be acceptable. Exceeding it is therefore deemed unacceptable, as going over any speed limit increases the risk we present to ourselves and other road users.

Speed possesses an irrefutable ever present risk that increases as we accelerate. The faster a vehicle is travelling the higher collision risk increases, until it reaches the point of certainty. Speed also has an inseparable relationship with our driving standard. If our driving standard is weak, then the point of certainty arrives much sooner. In effect it is possible that some motorists can drive far safer at say 40mph, than some others can at 20mph purely due to differences in driving standard (but don't get your hopes up just yet).

A fine example of how an improved standard lowers speed collision risk can be found with the police forces in the UK. There are many police chases on our roads every year. The police officers heightened motoring skills, render them less vulnerable to a collision, than those they are chasing and invariably it is the offender who, in most cases, comes off worst. This does not mean that the police officer has made speeding safe, but rather, has just reduced their collision risk, just that little bit, to give them the edge. A police officer driving at high speed, irrespective of training has a collision risk that still exceeds normally acceptable boundaries and as such, on occasion, it is the police officer who suffers.

Increased speeds interact with our awareness as we are gradually giving ourselves less and less time to react to hazards. The speed limit on any particular road takes into account the number and frequency of hazards. When we start to exceed these set speed limits, we then begin to encounter hazards at a far faster rate which is where we can experience a certain amount of 'sensory overload'. In other words, there is far too much going on, for us to concentrate on effectively. But instead of our heads imploding, we then employ a degree of compensation to deal with this sensory overload, by selecting what we feel we need to observe, from what we should be observing and as a result, hazards start to get missed. Over the years, this selective observation becomes increasingly natural and irrespective of what speed we are driving at, hazards get missed, including speed cameras. What I have described here is a part of the natural erosion of our driving standard.

(Hazard – A hazard on the road is anything that could cause us to have to change our speed or direction. Hazards can be comprised of anything from a pedestrian to a parked car).

Speed limits are in place simply to give us as much time to as possible to observe as much as possible, but even within the speed limit, hazards still get missed.

Now in the real world, we know that people will not stop speeding, but by improving our observational powers, it is possible to manipulate collision risk, so as the motorist can maintain the same average speed if they choose to, whilst at the same time, reducing their collision risk and vulnerability to speed cameras. This is not casualty reduction by speed enforcement but rather casualty avoidance by driver improvement.

However, there are several levels of excessive speed that range from being slightly over the limit, to being grossly in excess of it. Excessive speed to the extreme, not only renders observational skills virtually useless but the motorists who use extreme speed, if we can call them motorists, are not only driving well beyond the limits of their own capabilities, but also up to and possibly beyond the limits of their vehicles capabilities. This renders them a huge and unacceptable, road safety liability.

Hence, when I talk about excessive speed, it is only aimed at those who use it with a good degree of responsibility. For the idiots on the road, there is not much that can be done to improve their little dance with the devil.

Driving over any limit can exceed the brains capacity to recognise the hazards that we need to observe. But if we are completely honest with ourselves, most of us do not observe well enough in the first place. This is the primary reason that many fail to see and react to hazards at any given speed, not just because of how our speed is used.

To a certain extent, this is supported by the fact that most fatal collisions occur whilst vehicles are travelling within the posted speed limit. It would appear therefore, that even the legal limits are set too high for many motorists. Poor standards of observation have increased the potential for collisions to occur, irrespective of what speed a vehicle is travelling at. This is precisely why an increase in the speed limit or the removal of speed cameras now, is completely inconceivable.

For the motorist who possesses good awareness skills, their collision risk is far lower, even when driving at the same or even higher speeds than average. It's not necessarily speed alone that makes speed dangerous but the thought process that is used behind it.

3

Inappropriate Speed

Inappropriate speed relates to poor use of speed within the speed limit. For example, driving passed a school at 30mph at 3:30 in the afternoon when the kids are coming out could easily be described as reckless. But also driving passed a line of cars on a narrow road, where your view of the pavement is obstructed, at 30mph, could also be just as reckless.

Use of inappropriate speed points to either recklessness or unacceptably low hazard perception skills. As experienced motorists, you must use your experience and judgment to decide on the appropriate speed for the road you are travelling on. Don't base your judgement of appropriate speed just on what you can see, but also what you can't.

As most collisions appear to have occurred within the speed limit, so it appears that inappropriate speed, is probably more of an issue than excessive speed.

There are three main types of inappropriate speed, there is that which we all know of driving at a speed too fast for the road, traffic and weather conditions, and there is that which is driving to fast for our own skill. If our concentration is distracted from the job of driving because of a phone call for instance, or you're upset or angry you are not concentrating on the road, irrespective of what speed you are travelling at (this is possibly why motorists using mobile phones have been calculated to increase their collision risk 4 fold).

However, the third I believe is far more common, driving to fast to take account of our naturally diminished awareness.

This is quite possibly the major cause of collisions that occur within the speed limit.

Speed cameras have no effect on incidents caused by inappropriate use of speed, as these collisions occur within the speed limit. But this argument, from another perspective, still emphasises the importance of speed cameras, as we don't really want these oblivious motorists, who crash within the speed limit, driving any faster, in any given location. And in all honesty, those who have already been caught out by the 'speed camera' have placed themselves amongst this group.

Correct use of speed has always been related to road, traffic and weather conditions. On a clear road, in good conditions we should be able to keep up to the posted speed limits; this is called 'making good progress' by not driving too slow.

Everything we come across on the road that does or could cause us to change speed or direction is, as said earlier, classed as a hazard, whether it consists of parked cars, junctions, pedestrians, road works traffic lights and so on. On the approach to these hazards, a reduction in speed from the posted speed limit may very well be appropriate.

Certainly driving down a residential road, with cars parked on both sides and only enough room for one vehicle to get through, would be entirely inappropriate for a vehicle to negate at 30mph and yet so many motorists do.

This is where the motorist is expected to use their awareness and hazard perception skills. Yet many can't and so the local authority response is to create more speed reduction tools such as 20 mph signs, within these more than obvious areas (*Recently calls have been made for all residential roads to be restricted to 20mph, then this new limit to be enforced with thousands upon thousands of speed cameras*).

This lack of hazard perception is certainly not confined to side streets and is present pretty much everywhere else in the motorists daily driving.

So, inappropriate speed is not allowing your mind to deal effectively with any particular set of hazards within the speed limit. This is caused in two ways, either through driving too fast for a particular set of hazards or lack of concentration which leads to reduced awareness.

If our hazard perception skills were excellent, then there would be no need for speed limits, as the motorist would be capable of selecting a safe and appropriate speed for the road, weather and traffic conditions.

4

Is there an acceptable level of road traffic casualty?

It has been said that only 5% of all road traffic collisions, are genuine accidents. This figure is probably still true today, because even though the number of road traffic casualties has reduced, traffic volume has gone up. What this is saying, is that even if everyone were to drive to a perfect standard, then simply because of the inherent risk of having vehicles on the road, a minimum of 160 people would still get killed each year.

This then suggests that there must be a minimum acceptable level of death on the road in order for the roads to exist and therefore even driving within the speed limit, is never absolutely safe. To completely eliminate death from our roads, we would have to remove all vehicles and we know that this will never happen.

In 2005, three thousand two hundred and one people were killed on British roads, so the acceptable level of death must therefore be more than 160 but less than 3201.

By setting our speed limits as they are, a certain level of injury and death is inherent. It must be accepted that some collisions will naturally occur and that some people will sadly get killed as a result of them. But separating the genuine accidents, from the avoidable collisions is no easy task.

Having speed limits set as they are, combined with current driver standard dictates that we should expect a minimum of 3200 deaths to occur. Understanding the relation between death and speed, we know that increasing the speed limit now, as requested by some groups, can only result in an increased number of deaths, because collisions will increase at greater speeds unless something is done to address the average driving standard.

5

Speed Limits

Your powers of observation and awareness should be developed enough to know constantly what speed limit you are driving in. If you find yourself unsure of the speed limit in an urban area, keep to an appropriate speed within 30mph. Check into residential roads for any other speed limit signs. If the road you are on is a 30mph limit, then the residential road will post no change of speed limit. In addition, if the road you are on is a road with a 30mph speed limit, there won't be any repeater signs to inform you. (Be aware that some roads now make use of 20mph speed limits and these do not display repeater signs either). Generally, when you are within an area restricted to a 30mph speed limit, there are no repeater signs and you are only informed of the speed limit, when you enter the area. So if you feel you have missed the speed limit sign, keep to 30mph until you know different.

The National Speed Limit is represented by the following sign.

This is the only sign to which two speed limits apply, depending what type of road you are travelling on. On motorways we all know that the speed limit is 70mph for cars and bikes unless otherwise stated. (Refer to the 'Highway Code' for speed limits that refer to specific types of vehicle).

The speed limit on dual carriageways is also 70mph when the national Speed Limit applies. I thought that I'd mention it here because all too often, I have seen motorists sticking to 60mph whilst on dual carriageways. On single carriageways the national speed limit is however, 60mph.

It is possible therefore to drive from a 60mph limit into a 70mph limit without any new speed limit signs informing you of the change. Incidentally, this little snippet occasionally pops up in pub quizzes.

We all possess many bad points about our driving in amongst the many positive points. It is this combination of driving styles that gives our motoring nation its character. But it is also this combination that predetermines the number of people who are killed and seriously injured every year. Safe driving is determined by our thought processes, which help us to make those vital decisions whilst driving. Because many of us have low awareness then it renders some motorists vulnerable to getting this thought process wrong, then we get the measures to redress the balance which usually results in curbing speed.

We know that 2.1 million motorists were caught by speed cameras in 2006 in the UK alone, Later on we will find out just how they were caught and believe me, it has little to do with speeding.

It has recently been reported in the press, that there are now in the region of 10 million motorists with points on their driving licenses, 4 million of those for speeding and we also have nearly 1 million motorists with 9 points who are now on the verge of losing theirs. It appears therefore, that **at least** as many as 1 in 3 British motorists are failing to observe the road as well as they should be.

This is precisely why speed limits and speed cameras to enforce them are currently so vitally important. With at least 1 in 3 motorists, driving under par, all that the motorist is waiting for is someone else to make a mistake, within the same space and time for a collision to occur. The speed camera will reduce the severity of that collision by ensuring that the impact speed had been reduced, assuming of course, that the camera had been seen in the first place.

Each and every one of our 32 million motorists has developed their own particular blend of driving style, so to address each one individually, is an absolute impossibility. The intelligence gathered regarding the causation of road traffic collisions identifies speed as a major cause, with the most common driver error now being attributed to lack of concentration. However, of the two, speeding, whether excessive or inappropriate, is infinitely more simplistic to control with innovation and appears to be the preferred option.

Speed is without doubt a major contributor to the number of people seriously hurt or killed on our roads, but it is not the only factor and in many cases it is not the causation factor. Any other error, either single or combined we possess, can and all too often ultimately results in a collision. The severity of that collision will be determined by the speed the vehicle was travelling at.

In most cases, it is my belief that excessive speed, in all but the most extreme cases, is secondary to the fault that caused the collision in the first place. Take away the primary reason for the collision and what could have been a tragedy turns into a non-event.

Many road safety organisations have an over zealous, single minded pre-occupation with speed reduction as an answer to all our woes. It seems to be the answer to all road safety problems. In one way they are absolutely right, reduce the speed limits everywhere to 10mph and there will be very few fatalities and serious injuries. The more speed can be hammered down, the safer the roads will inevitably become. But this type of casualty reduction is far too narrow-minded and unimaginative, because speed reduction as a road safety measure, only reduces the impact speed of a vehicle when involved in a collision. Whilst this has the effect of reducing the severity of a collision by possibly changing a fatal collision into a serious injury collision (good thing), an injury collision into a damage only collision (good thing) and so on, it fails to prevent the collision in the first place (bad thing). This is currently how road safety is working, but would it not be far better to remove the primary cause of a collision to prevent it from occurring in the first place?

I agree with many of the anti-speed camera organisations who call for a return to education as a means to improve road safety, but do not share their requests for the complete removal of the speed camera; we are not ready for that yet. I also find that road safety policies are being dictated by ideologies that are far too simplistic and amateur, that attempt to reduce casualties by targeting a very limited number of true collision causation factors.

Establishing accurate road casualty causation statistics is an extremely difficult task, as many witnesses only see what occurred from an external view point and will be oblivious, to what errors were being made inside the vehicle, at the time of the occurrence. And if the driver who was at fault survived, he or she is hardly likely to admit that they were driving particularly badly at the time and occasionally they are instructed, not to admit liability. This is incredibly bad and shameful advice to give to anyone, as it can prevent us from getting to the true root cause of many fatal and serious collisions.

We know all of the types of error that motorists make, as we see them everyday whilst driving and sitting beside others in their cars. Most of us will also know, that we don't signal or use our mirrors as often as we should (both of these incidentally, given the right circumstances are potentially fatal errors), but are we aware of the many other errors we ourselves possess, many of which combined with a little excess speed are a potentially fatal mix?

6

Common Driver Errors

When we were learning to drive, we were taught to a certain standard. A common myth is that the Driving Instructor just taught us to pass a driving test. In most cases, including my own, this is just not true. The Approved Driving Instructor (ADI) taught you to drive that way for a reason.

They would have started off with an explanation of the controls and then progressed on to moving off and stopping and so on. What most learner drivers didn't realise, was that as they progressed through their course of lessons, the instructor was also putting in place, all of the motoring safety guards that you need to survive today's roads. The learner was being moulded into a motorist. With moving off from the side of the road, you were taught correct observation, including your blind spot and combined with the correct use of accelerator, brake, clutch and signals. When steering, you were taught to push and pull the steering wheel instead of crossing your hands. All of these methods and techniques were designed with safety in mind, to reduce your risk of getting involved in a collision. Some lessons were more important than others, but all having a value in keeping casualties to a minimum when performed properly.

Once we passed our driving test, the story is the same for virtually everyone when we began the process of removing these safety guards. We began crossing our hands, not using our indicators as often as we should and so it started. Some of the safety guards we removed are virtually insignificant in terms of road safety but others, such as keeping a safe distance or maintaining high standards of awareness, were incredibly important to maintain. Through our motoring development, we went on to remove more and more safeguards as our individual experience and driving styles progressed.

Below is a list of common errors, how many of them can you honestly say that you have just as good a standard of today, as when you passed your test? Or would you even know now, if you were doing it correctly? Don't just read the list but really think about each one and how it relates to your own driving.

Mirror work
Road positioning
Use of speed (includes excessive and inappropriate speed) Anticipation
Attitude
Concentration
Awareness
Sense of Responsibility
Indication
Emergency Stop
Knowledge
Overtaking
Bad / inconsiderate parking
Crossing hands on steering wheel
Harsh acceleration
Harsh braking
Leaving foot over clutch in between gear changes
Never or rarely practiced an emergency stop
Reversing manoeuvres (have you ever reversed from a side road into main road?)
Observations including blind spots (Do you know your zones of vision?)
Failure to recognise or see road signs
Hazard recognition skills

This list is merely a brief example and should not be taken as comprehensive. Most of the experienced motorists I have observed possess weakness in most, if not all of these areas and more besides. These errors combined with our normal use of excessive and inappropriate speed is what's creating the numbers of road casualties that we currently see. Maybe we should not be judging ourselves by how much experience we have, but on how good our technique is.

But incredibly, this is not entirely bad news, because by addressing the most important of these weaknesses we can reduce road casualties whilst leaving our 'use of speed' alone. As opposed to the anti-speed theorists who are largely addressing speed, whilst leaving the other, more important areas alone.

WARNING
(You may find this next bit a little upsetting)

The motorist is impossible to categorise by the severity and combination of mistakes they make, there are just too many groupings. Many of our motorists, even with years of experience will find that, contrary to their own belief, the motoring experience they have accumulated on the road over the years, counts for very little. A novice who has recently passed the driving test will be of a far superior technical driving standard on average than someone with say, 20 years experience who has allowed their driving standard to slip. The only thing that the novice lacks is the only thing the average driver has; experience.

However, after passing the driving test, the newly qualified driver then begins their own quest to develop their own particular blend of driving style. Whilst these changes are happening their standard and safety is in freefall and their risk of becoming a casualty goes through the roof. It is because of these voluntary changes that nearly all drivers make to their driving, that causes so many young motorists to get killed and injured every year and not because of the standard of driver education. When they are developing this new driving style, they are doing it whilst relatively inexperienced. So understandably this all too often includes young motorists who while stripping away the safeguards, they are also introducing unsafe levels of in-appropriate and excessive speed which is a highly volatile mix.

Therefore, the real advice the experienced motorist should be giving to our fledgling motorists, is that once they have passed the most basic of driving tests, then they should maintain the minimum standards that they were taught and add experience to them. If the novice achieves this, they would be well on their way to driving at an advanced standard and you would have given them, the best chance of surviving today's roads. But if they have to make changes, then do it gradually and slowly, to allow the time, to incorporate the new driving style and to fully understand the changes that they are going through.

(Interestingly enough, when I took advanced driving lessons, it took more time for the instructor to repair the damage that I had done to my driving, than it took to learn to drive in the first place).

The errors we commit ultimately lead to the collisions we're involved in. The inappropriate and/or excessive use of speed only serves to enhance the severity of any collision. So as standards are today, proper use of speed is incredibly important to master and adhere to.

The correct use of speed is based on a judgment; part of that judgment has been done for us in the form of speed limits (giving rise to the acceptable numbers killed on the roads, if there is such a thing), the remainder so far, has been left up to the motorist. The speed limits all over the country have been set for decades, in the main, they are accepted as accurate. However, on occasion they need to be amended or corrected to reflect the changing conditions, hence, now we see the slow introduction of 20mph speed limits, which I don't think anyone has ever complained about. There will also be examples where the speed limit could be increased.

7

Road Safety Features

There is an idea that the reductions in road casualties we have seen over the years, have been brought about by the good driving ability of the common motorist. An idea that now no longer seems to be entirely accurate. Over the years this government has invested billions into our complex road networks, to make them safer. Many safety devices have been created to reduce the number of deaths on the roads, which for many years have brought our fatality rates down and are keeping them down. It is for these reasons and improvements in vehicle design and road engineering that fatalities are reducing, sadly not because of our average driving standard. Driver standards have remained virtually unchanged for many years.

Such road safety initiatives include:

Traffic lights
Roundabouts
Pedestrian crossings
Railway crossings
Dual carriageways and motorways
Road Humps
Yellow Lines
Speed Limits
Chicanes
Tarmac Composition
And yes, Speed Cameras

All of these and many more besides, have been created to improve safety and reduce casualties, in areas where the perception of hazard risk is present, such as junctions, outside schools, high density pedestrian areas, country roads etc. Some have been placed in these areas to force the driver to slow and they work, because they reduce the speed of those with poor hazard recognition skills, that for many motorists are under developed or forgotten. In effect enforcing a thought process, rather than relying on the motorist to think for him or herself. This is quite insulting but unfortunately, true.

8

The Impact of Road Safety/Speed Camera's on Our Driving.

Speed cameras; contrary to popular belief do so much more than affect speed. We now know that when driving, we all make multiple mistakes, some we are aware of and others are not so obvious. But they are there all the time.

A collision can occur because of any combination of these errors and then the severity of the collision is generally determined by the speed, at which we are travelling.

A speed camera will slow us down if we notice that it is there, but it will not make us naturally drive any better. So in the event of a collision occurring because of our other errors it will tend to be less severe. Because of this reduced speed, the motorist has also been given more time to react. This has without doubt prevented many collisions from occurring, reduced the severity of many others and saved many unappreciative motorists, from the pain of knowing that they have killed someone. There are just as many families who have loved ones sitting next to them now, who would not have otherwise been there.

The reality though is that none of us drive through a Speed Camera intentionally and yet, they catch out thousands, every week. This really is damning confirmation that as well as excessive speed there must be other issues with our driving. For example, motorists who get caught out by speed cameras must have poorer concentration and awareness levels, than those who manage to slow down for them. So this also clearly shows

that there exists a divide in driver skill, attention and awareness. It gives a clear indication that the motorists who set off a
speed camera, possesses one of the most lethal errors within a
driver's makeup, inattention. And to top it all, they are willing
to do drive like this at speed, rendering them infinitely more
vulnerable to collision and the gatso. So for those who slow
down enough to drive through the camera, at a speed which
is not going to set it off, the outcome of any collision now
involved in for whatever reason; is going to be significantly reduced. Safety Cameras, like many other road safety initiatives
compensate for the motorists naturally weakened driver technique, in particular those whose error base includes excessive
speed. And within the limited area of camera placement, the
roads have been made significantly safer.

Speed cameras are present on less than 1% of our road net-
work, leaving the motorist to carry on driving to their normal
standard elsewhere. The safety camera can only produce a positive result within its placed area and a few hundred yards beyond. The desired behavioural change to the average motorist
passes, once they are clear of these areas. Without having made
any permanent change to the driver's behaviour, their collective bad driving habits result in death and injury elsewhere,
maintaining the numbers of road casualties and promoting new
speed camera sites. Looked at from another view, the numbers
of people killed within safety camera sites is reducing, but overall casualty reduction appears to have flat-lined, so the numbers
of those killed away from camera sites, must have increased.
This would indicate a worsening of driver behaviour that is
being balanced by road safety initiatives. With fatalities also
occurring away from speed camera sites, this can only mean one
thing........more cameras.

PART 2

9

Driving Methods, Defensive and Altruistic

To begin this section, I would like to talk about what a 'real' driver should be. If we all drove to the perfect standard then, we would achieve very small road casualty numbers indeed.

It is thought, that the acquisition of a comprehensive motoring knowledge encourages favourable attitudes towards driving and I have to admit, that in my experience this is true. Ideally, motoring should be based on altruistic motives or in other words, with a regard for the safety of everyone else, but for this depth of knowledge and understanding to be taught to novice drivers, would be prohibitively expensive, for it to become common place within driver education (although this is now being considered).

Instead, driver education came up with a compromise whereby novice drivers are taught 'defensive' driving techniques as opposed to altruistic, in which they were and still are taught, to develop a style of driving designed to preserve their own safety.

Altruism: An unselfish concern for others

Altruistic driving cannot be taught in the classroom or learned from a book, it can only be learned through many years of good quality motoring experience.

For most of us, including myself, immediately after being released from the constraints of our driving instructors and mentors, we began to develop our own, very personal relationship with the motor car, a journey it seems that many of us were lucky to survive. Probably the first two things we re-taught ourselves were to cross our hands on the steering wheel and to start driving a little faster, just like all those other people that we admired and considered to be good quality motorists. Then came the slow degradation of so many of our other driving skills, that saw more serious flaws or bad habits creeping in, such as driving too close to the car in front, not using our mirrors or observational skills as often as we should and so on. Later some of us have taken this to mean that we should begin practising handbrake turns, wheel spins, and power slides and most of us are wrongly under the impression, that we are better drivers for it.

(I used to practice wheel spins in a car park under a bowling alley in Coventry, because it echoed and made it sound better but I wasn't very good at them. Well...what do you expect from a 1977 Talbot Alpine 1.3 in champagne?......I loved that car).

This is not the experience that we were ever intended to develop though, and as much as we believe we have improved since passing the driving test, many of us would probably fail the driving test if we were expected to take it again.

This theory was recently tested by 'What Car' magazine when they retested 20 experienced drivers and discovered that 75% of them failed on some serious errors that could easily result in fatal consequences. However, you also have to consider that most, if not all of these drivers would have raised their game for the occasion and is probably not a reflection on their normal daily standard.

10

So What Happened to Our Driving?

This first chart (fig1) is going to try to explain our journey from novice to experienced driver.

It also explains why so many young drivers have such a high collision risk over experienced drivers. And it also explains why many experienced motorists would not pass the driving test, if required to do so again. This brings into question the age old beliefs that the more experience you have, the better driver you must be.

fig1

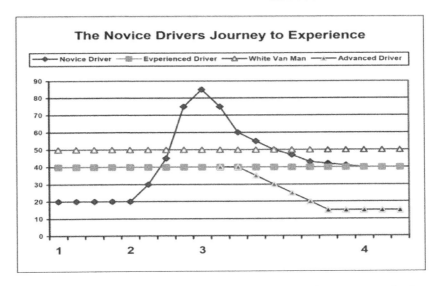

The Novice Drivers Journey to Experience

Great driving is not based on experience but on technique. Truly great drivers can only be created by adding experience to solid motoring foundations.

Adding experience to a poor technique does not develop a good driver. Many motorists have years of experience, but sadly it seems is wasted experience. To illustrate this point 'White Van Man' has more miles under his belt than most and yet he has developed a far higher collision risk than our average driver to become one of the 'high risk' groups of drivers on the road. So could it be possible, that contrary to popular belief, the more experience we get, the worse drivers we become?

Novice Driver

At point 1 the novice driver has just taken up driving lessons, their collision risk would be high as they have yet to develop driving skills and experience. However, the novice collision risk here is contained in a controlled environment by the Driving Instructor (ADI) that keeps collision risk to a minimum.

Novices driving without the constraints of an ADI have a higher collision risk.

Between point 1 & 2 the ADI is working very closely with the novice to turn them into a real motorist, everything from basic vehicle control, steering, manoeuvres, junctions, traffic lights, roundabouts, effective observations etc. you get the picture. But the instructor is also trying to promote good attitudes, awareness, knowledge, confidence and responsibility into their driving to produce a well-informed, safe and competent driver, who has in place, all of the safe guards to prepare them for today's roads. This motorist is then tested on their knowledge and ability and if successful, given the green light. This young and inexperienced motorist has a collision risk that is probably going to be at the lowest point that it ever will be throughout their motoring lifetime. Lower than that of most experienced motorists. So what happened that gave them such high fatality rates?

From point 2 though is where, in many cases it all goes tragically wrong. Free of the constraints of the ADI, the young and vulnerable motorist starts to make changes. Changes to their driving styles that inevitably result in the newly qualified driver (NQD), removing many of the motoring safe guards, the instructor had put into place. Observations and therefore awareness becomes weaker followed by a degradation in mirror and observational work, speed gets faster and so on.

What results from this re-education, is a collision risk of the newly qualified driver that rises rapidly and results in greater numbers of young drivers, being involved in serious collisions, which are out of proportion with the rest of the motoring community. Young motorists do have a higher collision risk than the average motorist, but they didn't start out that way.

From point 3 onwards, as experience kicks in, the collision risk of the NQD slowly starts to reduce, eventually settling around the same level as today's experienced drivers. Many newly qualified drivers sadly never make it this far.

As the novelty of the car begins to fade, it is increasingly used as a means to get from A to B rather than for recreational reasons. Collision risk begins to reduce and eventually settles around the average driver standard.

This is a journey that many of us should recognise.

(Also at point 3, I have shown what happens to the collision risk of the average driver who made the decision to become an advanced driver, which is incidentally the same route I took).

Had the novice only been told to keep the skills they had learned just after passing the test and then added experience to them, then our NQD's could have been, the safest group of motorists on the road.

The answer to reducing the casualty rates in young drivers is not making the driving test harder, or expecting the novice to have a minimum of 100 hours driving time with their instructor, this may have some minimal casualty reduction benefit, but not as much as desired as all that is likely to occur, is a delaying of the skills degradation process. But by preventing the degradation of skills that all too often happens just after passing the driving test, would yield the greatest possible casualty reduction in novice drivers.

One way in which this could possibly be achieved, without hitting the young motorist too hard, is to adopt a process similar to that which ADI's have to undergo, a 'test of continued ability' after 12 months whereby the novice has to re-take the driving test under the same stringent criteria. This is one possible way to inspire the novice driver to keep up his standard if he wishes to keep his licence.

It also has to be said that many novice drivers do follow the ideal path, retain their skills and add experience to it. These are quite probably amongst the safest and best drivers on the road and yet, as they are grouped with the worst, they are unjustly punished by the insurance industry.

Just to illustrate this point, some years ago, I had a group of friends who were probationary police officers. Before they were allowed to drive the liveried police vehicles, they were required to undergo a test of basic driving competence. One of the lads approached me, knowing I had been an ADI and asked if I would take him out for an assessment, which I did. I tested him on all aspects of his driving ability and made the appropriate corrections which took a further three or four hours, after which he got through the tests.

Needless to say, I was approached by several more Police Officers who were in need of the same treatment. (I have to say at this point that at no time were any of these officers charged for these services). Anyway, one of the officers was a young female who was not very confident, as her driving had been the brunt of some jokes by her colleagues. One of her colleagues told me beforehand that she would probably be hard work. However, on taking her for her assessment, I found that she was not overly confident in her ability. At the end of the assessment though, I could find very little wrong with her driving ability that could not be put right within minutes. She had not long passed her driving test and yet her ability was far superior to that of her more experienced colleagues.

She went on to pass the assessment with ease.

Experienced Driver

Throughout all of this, the experienced driver is trundling along as he/she always has done. His driving style has developed quite a few errors by this point in time, which is reflected in their elevated collision risk. Errors such as speeding, weaker observational powers and so on have all made their contributions but a slower overall average speed has reduced the average motorist's collision risk leaving him feeling that after all these years and all this experience, that he must be a good driver.

White Van Man

Even though white van man has gained way more experience than most motorists on the road, he also possesses a disproportionately higher collision risk than the average motorist, why?

Well, 'Van Man' has developed in the exact same way as the average motorist. 'Van Man' spends so much time on the road that he has developed a far more aggressive driving style. This is probably due to the pressures placed on him to meet targeted deliveries etc. In addition, he has also developed a far more lazy driving style than many other motorists with fewer observations included. Van mans speed may also be a little higher than average, this has all combined to create his higher than average collision rate.

It just goes to show that our perception of what a real driver should be is impaired, most of us have no idea of what a motorist should be and much of the advice we give to young motorists, is dreadfully flawed. We should be pointing our critically blame laden fingers back at ourselves for a change and try to understand where we ourselves are getting it wrong.

All of us at one point in time had driving perfection in the palms of our hands, only to let it go to eventually see our standard settle within the realms of motoring mediocrity.

What it really meant, when we were told to go out and learn how to drive, was that we were expected to retain all of the skills and techniques we learned as novices and then, add experience to them. Over the years, as our experience grew, we were supposed to become more altruistic with our attitudes but sadly, it appears that its meaning has been somewhat lost down the years.

It is interesting and worthy of note to explore what happened through this transition, to our risk of being involved in a collision.

Every element of driving a vehicle defensively has been developed into a driving technique. For example, the reason why we push and pull a steering wheel as opposed to crossing hands, is so as we retain complete control of the steering, all of the time. When we cross our hands, at one point both hands will be on the same side of the steering wheel and then if we need to steer further, then one or both hands have to be repositioned. Now this repositioning may only take half a second longer, than if we were pushing and pulling the wheel as suggested, but if this error were to occur at 40 mph, you could have travelled an additional 30 feet before being able to steer again whilst correcting this mistake, over the motorist who was pushing and pulling. These sorts of distances can make huge differences in determining the motorist's ability to avoid a collision. However, you will probably never find any statistics on collisions that have occurred due to this error. This is one scenario that I will now use to explain how speed cameras compensate for poor driving habits.

A motorist drives in a 30mph limit at 40mph and is not in total control of the vehicles steering.

Another vehicle pulls out in front of him 30 feet away; it takes him ½ a second to reposition his hands on the steering wheel to allow further steering, by which time he has travelled 30 feet. Too late, and the collision occurs just as he has regained control of the steering wheel.

The same vehicle at 40 mph in a 30 limit but with total control of the steering, when the same vehicle pulls out in front of him 30 feet away. He is now able to steer immediately giving himself a chance to avoid the collision.

Now with a speed camera present

The same vehicle at 30mph, not in control of the steering would travel a distance of approximately 22.5 feet before regaining control of the steering wheel, but would have a much lower impact speed and still has almost 8 feet left in which to steer.

The same vehicle driving at 30mph, in full control of the steering has 30 feet to steer and stands the greatest chance of completely avoiding the collision.

Effectively the speed camera, by forcing us to reduce our speed is in the same way, allowing a degree of compensation for all of the other errors that we make.   There are thousands of examples such as this one and driving instructors, will be able to give a potentially fatal scenario for virtually any driving error. So it is by no means unreasonable to conclude that many serious collisions are not caused because of speed alone, but because there are many other factors that contribute towards collision causation. If all that we see is the speed of a vehicle, then speed gets all of the blame. It follows therefore that by improving certain aspects of driving, other than that of speeding we can realistically reduce the chance of getting involved in a serious collision. Obviously keeping to the speed limits or below, currently gives us the greatest chance of reducing collisions, but expecting 28 million motorists to stop speeding is in reality, impossible. So the best practical way to reduce collisions is to address driver standard. This is where the philosophy behind this book can be summed up in one simple statement.

'You can't take the speed out of the motorist, but you can take some of the risk out of speed'.

I am a firm believer that anyone expecting our nation of motorists, not to use a bit of excessive speed is living in dreamland. But what the statisticians say is occasionally right, speeding is dangerous and has been linked to many deaths and serious injuries. However, I also believe that mildly excessive speed will not actually increase the risk you present on the road exponentially (yes, I did get that out of the dictionary) provided that the other errors you make are reduced. This can be achieved relatively simply and quickly by instead of hammering down a little excessive speed that may influence a half percentage improvement in road safety, improve the basic standard of the motorist instead and influence a 5% improvement in their driving. This would allow most motorists to avoid speed camera activations whilst at the same time, helping to reduce road casualties. Or in other words, you can't take the speed out of the motorist, but you can remove some of the danger out of speed.

I have heard it said many times by motorists that they were penalised for speeding when they were driving on a perfectly safe road. The reality is that even a car that is parked on the road has an element of risk attached to it, as it becomes a hazard. There are no perfectly safe roads.

Simply due to the presence of a vehicle on the road, risk exists. When you get into that vehicle, risk is then slightly raised and continues to climb as you pick up speed. Eventually, speed reaches a point whereby either, the limitations of the vehicle or the ability of the motorist get exceeded and total loss of control is inevitable. Because of the degradation of our driving skills, we all too often see these limitations being exceeded at speeds well within the posted speed limits. It is your basic driving standard that determines how sharply that 'speed risk' rises.

As you progress through the book it will become abundantly clear, that most collisions are caused because the motorist failed to see the potential of a hazard or failed to see the hazard itself. Then when the collision occurs, the severity of that collision is then determined by the speed at which the vehicle was travelling at. However, if the hazard was spotted because of good hazard perception skills, then the collision is far more easily avoided and what could have been a fatal road traffic collision now becomes a non incident, with no change to the motorists' use of speed.

> *Did you know that the average cost that a fatal road traffic collision incurs, is now heading towards £1.5million and a serious injury collision around £400,000.*

Use of speed though has to be reasonable, irrespective of whether it is excessive or inappropriate, go beyond the boundaries of reason and you enter the realms of information overload, where there, you start prioritising hazards instead of dealing with them all.

11

Speed Cameras Are Not On The
10 Most Dangerous Roads.

This is one of the more ridiculous arguments against speed cameras. Speed cameras are not on the most dangerous roads and they never will be.

This is simply because the 10 most dangerous roads in the UK are constantly changing or fluid. Place speed cameras on the current 10 most dangerous roads and the collision rate will fall as expected, dropping them out as one of the 10 most dangerous roads. Then, a whole new set of 'Ten Most Dangerous Roads' will emerge. This argument, if continued, will only encourage the continued growth of speed cameras on our roads, until all roads have been exhausted.

This is one way in which the anti-speed camera lobby are themselves contributing to the growth of speed cameras.

12

The 85th Percentile

The 85th percentile is an argument that pro speeders use, to try to justify a notion that raising speed limits will actually make our roads safer.

The 85th Percentile is a method that American engineers use to determine the 'safe speed' of mainly open roads. It is done by taking the speed of all motorists on that road, removing the speed of the top 15% and then taking an average of the remainder (there are several interpretations that I have come across that differ as to how this theory is calculated).

However, they freely admit that this theory appears to fall apart when applied to urban roads. There are several major reasons why we cannot apply this theory to British roads. In the main these surround the facts that American roads had far lower speed limits anyway, they are also straighter, they have virtually double the numbers killed and seriously injured (KSI) than in the UK and the most striking error within this theory, is that the 85th percentile is based on an 'assumption'. An assumption that most motorists (85%) are responsible and capable enough of determining just exactly what a 'safe speed' for any given road should be.

So are most motorists capable of selecting a safe speed?

It has been stated that only around 1 in 5 speed cameras are actually active (have you ever been flashed and never been nipped?). If this is the case, then we can now calculate that if they were all active, then 5 times as many motorists would be caught out by speed cameras, than the current 2.1 million. This is the part of road safety that I find particularly frightening, as it means we have at least 10,500,000 (32%) of British motorists who are at times literally driving around at speed and unaware of their surroundings. This tells us that at least $1/3^{rd}$ of British motorists, are incapable of selecting a safe speed for their surroundings, simply because they are unaware of what their surroundings are. Add to this, that there are now around 40% of motorists with penalty points on their licences then it must undermine somewhat the theory that most motorists are safe and responsible drivers.

It appears that the most appropriate UK formula should currently be 66th percentile or less.

13

Has Road Safety Flat Lined Since Speed Cameras Were Introduced?

This next chart (fig2) clearly illustrates how road death statistics have been behaving since 1950. As you can see, over time, effecting these reductions has been somewhat of a bumpy ride. Since the mid 90's to the present day, the numbers killed have steadily began to reach a plateau, this has erroneously been blamed on speed cameras. Fig2

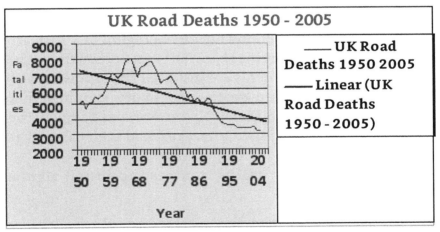

However, we can see that the line of trend clearly indicates that the numbers killed on our roads should still be in the region of 3900 deaths per year. But something clearly happened in the early 90's that changed all of that and forced the numbers killed on the roads to drop sharply below the expected line of trend.

The statistics I have used here are all of the actual numbers from 1950 to the present day with the trend line representing all years. Later I will show you how by being selective of the years you choose, can statistically alter the perception of how road safety is behaving.

It is noticeable that over the last few years, the decline in the numbers killed has decayed somewhat. Today we seem to have reached a casualty 'plateau' in the numbers who are being killed and seriously injured each year. The truth is that reaching this plateau was always inevitable.

We have been heading for it, for the last 5 decades. In fact, on closer inspection, there is an uncharacteristic drop in KSI around the early 1990's of around 8%, which is just about the time when speed cameras made their first appearance on our roads. This is how our roads react to road safety initiatives, it pushes the numbers down and when the treatment levels off, so do the reductions.

It takes on average 60 cameras to prevent one death on the road, so 6000 of them currently prevent in the region of 100 deaths every year. Effectively forcing the fatality rate down from 3300 to 3200, if no further cameras are installed the following year, the numbers of prevented deaths and injury should remain steady at around 3200. This is not a failure of speed cameras but an indication that 6000 cameras have reached their casualty reduction limit.

To prevent another 100 deaths, you need to install another 6000 speed cameras.

We can see more clearly here, that reaching a road casualty plateau was inevitable. When we look at annual road casualty numbers as a whole it is obvious that over time, the rate at which road casualties numbers have been falling, has been decaying. What this means is that at some point in time, road casualty numbers must eventually level off or reach a plateau. Fig3

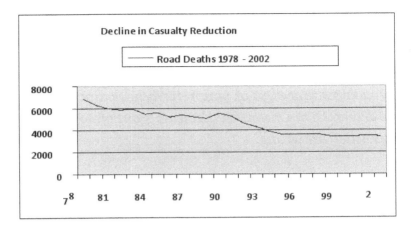

After all, the numbers can only go so low.

Once we have reached the bottom of the curve, as we appear to have today, the numbers become quite vulnerable to fluctuation, they can go back up as easily as they came down. However the fluctuations will tend to be small and any rises are no indication of failure. Once you have squeezed 95% of the achievable road casualty reduction out of the motorist, it then becomes increasingly difficult, to squeeze out any more. For the managers amongst you, how do you increase the efficiency of anything that is already 95% efficient? This dispels the statistical conspiracy theory that 'Speed cameras have claimed over 5000 lives since their creation'. Had it not been for speed cameras, then this flat line would quite possibly have occurred, when road casualty numbers were in the region of 3900 instead of 3200.

This particular theory gained some considerable notoriety and had many people fooled. It worked by carefully selecting a grouping of 4 or 5 years when we experienced a steeper than usual decline in road traffic casualties. A line of false trend was then created, which gave the appearance that road casualties were falling faster before speed cameras were introduced, than after. This imaginary difference has become known as the fatality gap. This gap was then measured to calculate that if speed cameras had not been created, then over 5000 fewer deaths would have occurred on our roads. This is just one example of how statistics can be manipulated to prove, just about anything you like.

> *(Did you know that 80% of motorists' believe that they are above average drivers? This means that at least 3 out of 5 motorists, who hold this belief, are wrong.*

14

Have Speed Cameras Claimed 5000 Lives Since They Were Introduced?

Or
Have We Been Hoodwinked?

The following charts depict how statistics can be manipulated to show just about anything we want them to. Below we will see how the claim that speed cameras, have caused the deaths of over 5000 people since they were installed, was created. It has been achieved by carefully selecting years, when we experienced unusually high falls in casualty rates. The selected years I have used are the years 1990 to 1993. However selecting the 1988 to 1989 trend when casualty numbers were going up, would then have shown that road deaths should currently be in the region of eight or nine thousand.

So here is the statistical recipe that duped some into believing that speed cameras are claiming lives.

Firstly (fig4) take the actual numbers of road traffic casualties and put them into a chart. Just for good measure, add a trend line to show what the actual trend looks like.

Fig4

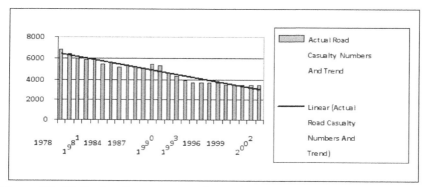

Next (fig5) find a few years when there was an unusually steep decline in road traffic collisions and then, only using these few years, add another trend line and hey presto, it looks as though road casualties should have been falling far faster than they have been.

Fig5

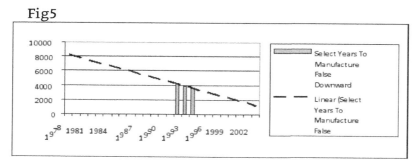

However, select three different years when trend was going up (fig6) and OOPS!!! Now we can interpret that speed cameras have prevented the deaths of over 20000 people since their inception, but that would be dishonest!!!

Fig6

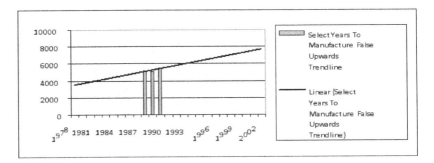

Next, (fig7) superimpose both the real trend line and the manufactured trend line onto the chart and then the imaginary **fatality gap** is manufactured. The difference between the two is then calculated to be in the region of 5000 to date and climbing and then the blame is heaped on the humble speed camera, like shovelling penalty points on your wife's driving licence.

Fig7

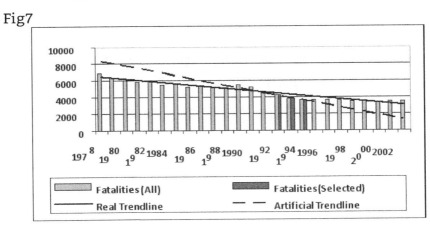

This is precisely, in my view, why statistics have no place in road safety except, for the most basic of functions, because they can make just about anything look exactly how they want it to, the truth is that this fatality gap never existed, it was manufactured to lend weight to an argument.

Ever heard the expression 'Science can prove that an elephant can dangle from a tree with its tail tied to a daisy'? Me neither but it's apparently provable, but we all know the reality.

Just to turn this argument on its head a little further, I have taken a look at pedestrian fatality rates since 1980. As you can see, there was a downward trend in the numbers being killed, from 1941 deaths in 1980 down to around 1000 killed today.

However, I have split the chart into two, showing the trend we were following before speed cameras and then the new trend in casualty rates after speed cameras were introduced. As you can see the trend line changed. Instead of 1000 pedestrians being killed each year there are now 671 representing a decrease of 329.

So there is a fatality gap, but it does not represent the number of lives that speed cameras have claimed, but the number of lives that they have saved (fig8).

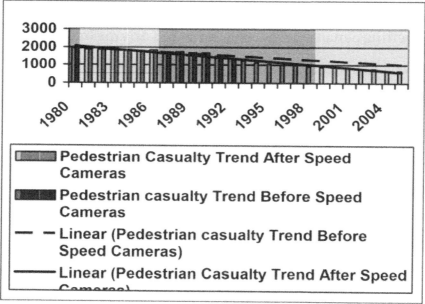

The final point to note here is that speed cameras are present on less than one half of one percent of British roads. It is not surprising that they do very little to reduce the levels of death and injury among motorcyclists and other road users and casualty rates within these groups appear to have stalled. But as you can see, the reductions in child and pedestrian deaths are self evident.

15

Speed and Concentration

One of the more recent theories in the debate is that of the relationship between speed and concentration, in that the faster you travel, the more you concentrate. As if to suggest that increased speeds, promote better concentration, resulting in safer drivers. It sounds perfectly reasonable, doesn't it?.....sadly it is not. This argument has already stumbled at the first hurdle but I just want to make sure that it stays there.

I have to agree that some motorists do increase their levels of concentration when their speed increases. But is this increased concentration effective and directed at what we should be concentrating on? By now, you probably already know the answer.

It has to be said that a good driver possesses certain qualities, one of which is concentration. A good driver will also keep his levels of concentration elevated, from the moment he enters his/her vehicle and retains this level of concentration, throughout their driving. However, there appear to be some motorists who admit to having low levels of concentration whilst driving at low speeds and even some, who have claimed that they are vulnerable to falling asleep at the wheel, because of the boredom created by having to drive at low speed.

What happens with any motorist is that the faster they get, the more intense concentration becomes. But instead of this intense level of concentration encompassing all zones of vision, it increasingly becomes tunnelled and only directed to the road ahead. Faster still and concentration is limited to the path of the vehicle and not, what is at the side of the road. Yes, this is a far more intense level of concentration, but at the same time, virtually valueless.

This intensity is due to the desire for self-preservation, rather than defensive or altruistic motives.

The collision risk with this motorist is climbing rapidly because speeding has a detrimental effect on your concentration, which in turn lowers awareness and therefore increases collision risk. Low levels of concentration when you start driving, even at low speed, make a driver a high potential risk on the road. Even as speed starts to climb, and concentration levels rise, a driver is concentrating on far less, than he should be and retains a high collision risk throughout his journey. Concentration is not just to do with how hard or intensely we are concentrating, but more precisely with what we are concentrating on.

16

How do Speed Cameras Work?

Quite simply, speed cameras work by forcing the motorist to reduce speed, but what also happens is that the levels of the motorist's awareness and concentration are, for a short time, elevated. The forced reduction in speed allows for a reduced impact speed if a collision does occur, but most importantly the reduced speed allows for a far greater reaction time that prevents many collisions from occurring in the first place. As the cameras are mainly situated in highly pedestrian areas, then it really is no coincidence, that the greatest reductions in those killed and seriously injured, are with pedestrians and children.

However, the national combined statistics that we tend to look at don't reflect this and you really do have to look beyond these numbers to discover that. Irrespective of the fact that the numbers of road casualties appear to have reached a plateau, they really are saving lives beneath the surface. After all, with all of these speed cameras (approx 6000) we would have expected to see the numbers of road casualty fall, which has many motorists believing that speed cameras don't work. Then, when we see that they are raking in £126mllion per year, it is easy to understand why some only see them as a stealth tax. They only make this money by the exploitation of weaknesses in driver ability or more realistically, speed cameras have created a tax on bad driving.

The manner in which the speed camera operates is far from simplistic, they work in much the same way as a burglar alarm does, a burglar alarm won't prevent a burglary from happening but it merely moves the burglary onto a different location. So to prevent further burglaries elsewhere, you need to put up more burglar alarms. You can't stop a burglar from burgling, much in the same way as you can't stop someone who is vulnerable of being involved in a collision from having one, but you can reduce their chances within specific areas.

Speed cameras also have the similar effect of altering the type and location of a collision, so when collisions do occur elsewhere, so the need for the speed camera increases. If all motorists improved their concentration and awareness, the numbers of collisions in new locations would decrease which in turn, would slow and even prevent speed camera growth.

The movement of casualty location is something, which I call 'Casualty Transgression'. For example: the speed camera prevents a child or pedestrian from being killed in one area by the unobservant motorist but it does nothing to prevent them from killing somewhere else. The spread of speed cameras is currently locked into this cycle. It is down to the motorist to break it (not the speed camera, the cycle).   Now when we consider that speed cameras, in the main, have been placed in highly pedestrian areas, then this is where we should be looking, to see if speed cameras have really given us something, in return for all of the fines we have paid and the points that have been etched into our driving licences.

Even though we know that road casualties have currently reached a plateau, the reductions in children and pedestrians who have been killed or seriously injured just keeps on falling. Pedestrian deaths really are, at a 40 year low (fig9).

Fig9

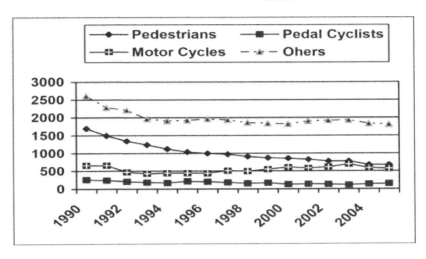

One of the main problems with speed cameras is that they are present on less than 1% of our roads. They have been placed in the main, in highly pedestrian areas and as such the casualty rates for pedestrians has fallen which is welcome news. But because their spread is currently so limited, there are not enough of them yet to influence much of a change with motor cycle users and all other road users. Pedal cyclist death has been fluctuating, because whilst they are slightly safer whilst within the vicinity of a speed camera, their vulnerability increases again when outside of them. You may well also note that between 1994 and 2003, the numbers of motor cyclists killed was steadily increasing whilst the numbers of other road users remained fairly static. Motorcyclists incidentally are increasingly coming under the road safety spotlight. Recent suggestions have called for limited engine size, acceleration rates and top speed. Not something to make the biking community very happy.
Yet another example of how those involved in road safety, can be blinkered to the real issues and end up spoiling the enjoyment and freedom of the British motorist.

So we can conclude that speed cameras have not failed to halt the numbers killed or seriously injured on our roads, instead this casualty reduction plateau has been reached by the increases in some areas and reductions in others. We can translate this to mean that speed cameras are currently targeting specific groups of road user and currently the biggest winners are among our most vulnerable, a trend that has been on-going since 1993. As you can see, the decline in child and pedestrian deaths is completely out of sync with the national trend.

Here are a few more statistics courtesy of the Department for Transport:

- 3,201 people were killed on Britain's roads in 2005, 1 per cent less than in 2004. The number of people seriously injured fell to 28,954, 7 per cent lower than in 2004. Total casualties in 2005 were 271,017, 3 percent fewer than in 2004;
- 141 children were killed on the roads in 2005, 25 less than in 2004, a fall of 15 per cent. The total number of children killed or seriously injured fell by 11 per cent to 3,472;
- Total pedestrian casualties fell by 5 per cent between 2004 and 2005, and the number of killed or seriously injured pedestrians was down 5 per cent. 12 per cent of all road accident casualties and 21 per cent of those who died in road accidents were pedestrians;

And one or two of my own

- Motor cyclist deaths in 1992 stood at 469 in 2005 they were 569, an increase of 18%. Motor cycle deaths showed reductions in only 6 out of 13 years, displaying a fluctuating trend.
- Other vehicle user death in 1992 stood at 2209 in 2005 they were 1813, a reduction of 18%. Other vehicle deaths showed reductions in 8 out of 13 years.
- Pedal cycle deaths in 1992 stood at 204 in 2005 they were 148 a reduction of 28%. Pedal cyclist deaths showed reductions in 8 out of 13 years. There numbers killed over 2004 and 2005 remained steady as 671 cyclists died whilst using our roads in each of these years.
- Pedestrian deaths in 1992 stood at 1347 in 2005 there were 671, a reduction of 50%. Pedestrian deaths showed a

reduction in 12 out of 13 years.

17

The Growth of the Speed Camera

Speed camera numbers are set to grow massively because we are currently trapped in this 'catch 22' type of situation. A major part of the problem is that current road safety initiatives are looking towards treating the roads with speed cameras, chicanes, speed humps and so on instead of treating those who use the roads. This is a hugely slow, expensive and laborious process that involves reducing the numbers of casualties on certain stretches of road.

I also believe that these speed reduction initiatives are partially to blame for increased levels of congestion.
Then WE get charged for it….hey ho.

If we were to treat the motorist instead, there would surely be far greater casualty reductions made. Instead of reducing casualties on certain stretches of road, the educated motorist takes their reduced collision risk with them on all roads.

The only way to stop the speed camera, is to treat the motorist, and that is what I intend to do within the final chapters of this book. Because by treating the motorist, cameras will stop flashing and the numbers of killed and seriously injured will begin to fall as a natural consequence of driver ability, not because of enforced road safety initiatives. And as a result, we the motorist, will not create the need for any more of these much maligned devices (will we, eh!!) The reason why the new '10 Most Dangerous Roads' are constantly changing, is also the same reason why speed camera numbers are still growing, despite of the fact that national statistics appear to have reached a plateau. This is down to a theory that I call 'Collision Transgression'.

18

Collision Transgression

'Collision Transgression', in its simplest form means that a motorist who poses a risk on the roads, is unlikely to change his or her behaviour until that change is either enforced upon them or they are involved in some tragic circumstance. Speed cameras are only likely to alter driving habits, whilst the motorist is in the vicinity of one.

Once free of them their driving behaviour returns to its normal elevated risk. The motorist then collectively continues to drive in this manner until someone has been injured or killed. The pain created by this event is usually enough, to influence a behavioural change. Which is why I believe driver education, after a tragic collision is almost valueless, as the driver is unlikely to revert to the same standard as prior to the collision. The collision has itself affected that particular individual driving style. The same goes for speed awareness courses after having been caught by one. The experience in most cases is enough to influence a more observant behavioural change.

In areas where speed cameras have been erected, the casualty reductions are proven, the average driver has been forced to slow down achieving the desired behavioural change and what would have been a casualty, has now been prevented. But this has only prevented the collision occurring within this area.

Evidence of this is reflected in how the types of casualty have altered. We have seen a marked reduction in child and pedestrian casualties. This reduction caused by the increase in speed cameras, located within the areas that pedestrians and children frequent. If speed cameras were ineffective then surely reductions within these areas would not have been realised. This goes a long way to support the theory that intelligent speed camera placement really works.

New sites for speed cameras are constantly emerging, why?

Because safety cameras, currently change the type and location where collisions occur. The previously high-risk areas have been addressed or treated and so, the problem moves onto another area, creating the need for ever more cameras in new locations.

This is also why the overall number of fatalities has remained fairly steady over the last few years, as the old camera placement rules, kept the number of speed cameras they were allowed to erect down. Without these rules, more cameras would have been erected and more lives saved. These rules have now been relaxed and the continued and rapid growth of the speed camera is set to continue.

Currently, to significantly reduce road casualty numbers there must be a massive increase in the number of speed cameras, or a change in driver behaviour.

I can only currently visualise a worsening of driver behaviour which is why the rest of us need to protect ourselves.

19

Are The Motorists That Speed Cameras Catch 'Innocent'?

The first point to realise, is that speed cameras have very little to do with speeding, obviously speeding plays its part, but the reasons why over two million motorists get caught out each year is entirely more dangerous.

In 2005 the 'Direct Line Insurance Company' reported the results of a survey claiming that 94% of the motorists they spoke to admitted to speeding.

(The research was carried out by you Gov from March 18th-21 March 2005. A total of 2,059 UK adults aged 18 and above were questioned).

This means that over 30 million British motorists now potentially admit to speeding. However, last year only 2.1 million of these motorists were caught. So why is it that only 6.5% of all our speeding motorists get caught? The answer lies in recognising that there is more than one group of speeding motorist. There are those who speed and are observant enough to spot the speed camera but the one fault common to all motorists, who get caught by speed cameras is not speed, but lack of awareness. The difference is with how observant they were whilst driving at speed, not the speed itself. So speed cameras have suffered an identity crisis, had they been called concentration cams (someone would have christened them 'Concams' no doubt) from the outset, motorists would have probably put their hands up and accepted the punishment. They had been caught driving without good awareness and also at a speed that, had they hit a pedestrian, they would have almost certainly been killed.

However, I mentioned earlier that speed cameras harboured a deep flaw as they only detect those not concentrating who are driving over the speed limit. There are many thousands more who are driving to the same oblivious standard under the speed limit. It is no surprise that the majority of fatal collisions occur whilst motorists drive within the speed limit. This is why education as opposed to speed enforcement is vastly more important than any speed reduction measure. This is also why the government are considering proposals to lower the speed limit and enforce the changes with more speed cameras.

The vast majority of Speed Cameras are now very well sign posted, road marked and have additionally been painted yellow. In other words they should be highly visible to all motorists. And yet, every year, around 2 million motorists fail to see all of the accompanying signage and markings and still drive passed a speed camera, apparently oblivious to its existence, until it's too late that is. The speed camera is effectively catching a motorist when he or she is at their most dangerous, a motorist who is not only driving at speed, but is also not concentrating on the road, which is a highly volatile mix. Incidentally, this is happening at least 4 times every minute, on one half of one percent of British roads alone. It begs the question of what really is the true extent of low awareness on 100% of our roads.

We all suffer from many lapses in concentration every time we drive. These same lapses are now blamed as the root cause of many deaths on the road each year and now appear to be the number 1 cause of fatal and serious injury collisions. This subject just happens to be the focal point of this entire book, to raise awareness and concentration levels that will not only result in creating your own defence against the speed camera, but unlike any other speed camera detection method, will reduce your chances of being involved in a potentially fatal collision on 100% of our roads.

Here I'm going to give you three examples of speeding motorists and their reactions when approaching a speed camera.

The Observant Motorist

This motorist spots the speed camera from afar and is well prepared, to deal with it safely and in good time. Even though he may have been utilising a little excessive speed on the approach, he recognised early that the speed camera was there and so was able to reduce speed smoothly and safely, causing no inconvenience to the other road users around him. Additionally he was under full control of his speed and did not need to keep an overly obsessive eye on his speedometer. Therefore, allowing good, effective observation. This motorist could have stopped before reaching the speed camera.

The Partially Observant Motorist

You just know that this motorist had his head in the clouds and speeding at the same time.

Only partially aware of his/her surroundings, they didn't see the signs, didn't see the road markings and didn't see the speed camera until it was almost too late, when the only course of action left, was to perform a partial emergency stop, that would just get his or her speed reduced from 39mph to 30mph. This was not an involuntary reaction but a deliberate attempt to save £60 and 3 points. This particular manoeuvre is only dangerous if there is another speeding motorist, equally as dippy following too closely behind. It is good defensive driving to keep your distance from this unpredictable motorist.

The 'Unobservant Motorist'

This motorist was completely oblivious on the approach of

either the speed limit or the presence of the speed camera. They may have been concentrating enough to perform the basic control functions, but were oblivious to their surroundings. Their low awareness and hazard perception skills caused the speed camera, like most other hazards on the road to become, well invisible until they sailed passed and were woken up by two short flashes that were caught in the corner of their eye.

This motorist was still doing 39 at the point of reaching the speed camera.

Now take these three examples and swap the speed camera for a child stepping into the road.

20

The Speed Camera Debate

Sadly, it seems that the speed camera debate is set to rage on, the governments pre-occupation with addressing speed will continue and the anti speed camera lobby, arguing that most motorists are generally safe and responsible drivers. The stubbornness of both sides to concede an inch, continually trying to prove that speed cameras do and don't work, has created a barrier to a really meaningful discussion. It seems as though the best way forward, is to detach from it.

The government are partially right that speed does have a detrimental effect on road safety, but this does not apply to all motorists. The speed camera protesters are also only partially right as there are motorists out there who can use a little excessive speed with a degree of responsibility, whilst at the same time having collision risks that are far lower, than some who drive well within the speed limits. But nowhere near the number they would like to believe exist. This stubbornness and unwillingness to reason from both sides, is only contributing to speed camera numbers increasing.

In my opinion, neither side of the debate have enough understanding of true collision causation factors, to take the discussion forward.

Yes, there are too many dangerously unobservant motorists on the roads, to justify the removal of speed cameras and yes there are motorists who do speed and possess the skills to deal with speed safely. These same skills are the ones that also allow them to avoid getting caught by speed cameras in the first place.

So there you have it, a third point of view but this time from an ex-driving Instructor and not a statistician. A view based on the most basic motoring principals of reducing collision risk by using, good old common sense and very real driving skills. The faults that cause us to drive through the speed camera are the same ones that cause so much pain and suffering. Reduce our chances of speeding through a speed camera and we will also reduce our risk of seriously injuring or killing someone.

As we have seen, speeding does have a negative effect on road safety, the more you speed the worse that effect is. There is no such thing as a 'safe road' as your risk begins the instant you get into your car and that risk increases as you accelerate. The risk we currently possess is not just based on our use of speed, but on many other factors also. By addressing these other factors, it is possible to reduce collision risk without altering the real motoring experience.

PART 3

21

How to Beat the Speed Camera

The final and most important chapter of this book is going to tell you how to 'Beat the Speed Camera'. This is going to be a personal journey for you that will:

1. Protect your driving licence from receiving points from a speed camera.
2. Improve your confidence, awareness and hazard recognition skills that will not only help you to spot speed cameras, but dramatically reduce your chance of being involved in a collision.
3. Will enhance the enjoyment of the driving experience.

I realised long ago, that one of the main problems with road safety, is that most motorists enjoy the sensations or buzz they get from speed. As this is something that we enjoy, then it is surely going to be incredibly difficult to give up. I also realised that the best case scenario in the interests of road safety, would be for all motorists to become advanced drivers, but such a task, would be impossible to achieve.... After asking myself, how can you improve road safety without destroying the enjoyment and freedom of the motorist? I had a 'Baldrick' moment and came up with a cunning plan.

I realised that no-one can take speed out of the motorist, but by using real motoring skills and driving techniques, it is entirely possible to remove some of the danger out of speed. It seemed to be the perfect solution. So I looked at the driver errors we make, that contribute to the most serious road traffic collisions. I discovered that if we were to even partially repair these other errors, then collisions would be avoided, even at speed because we are removing the causation factors out of the collision equation. What has resulted is a method of improving the basic driving standard, of our experienced motorists. Whilst taking nothing away from the motoring experience and results in improving road safety without enforcement.

For instance, I will not be dealing with steering, most of you cross your hands whilst steering, but as an error, it contributes very little in terms of being a threat to road safety. Most of us can cross our hands on the steering wheel and remain in good, almost complete control of the steering (just looks bad because it's not text book). So my purpose here is not to make an advanced driver out of you, but to raise your game a little. I intend to take away none of your enjoyment, but make you safer. Hopefully, if enough take up the challenge, we could influence some real reductions in the numbers killed and seriously injured on our roads.

What follows is a list of six self-help driving exercises or challenges. These in no way will ever turn you into an advanced driver, but they will serve to protect your driving licence from speed cameras and reduce your risk of being involved in a collision. They are ultimately designed to improve your awareness and concentration on the road, which is how you are going to spot the speed camera and ultimately improve your own personal road safety. I have included the emergency stop as an exercise, as it is probably the most important lesson you can refresh yourselves on. Over my own motoring years, I have seen plenty of dreadful examples by experienced motorists.

The exercises are designed to build a defence against speed cameras in two ways, by protecting you against them and then by preventing you from contributing to the need for any more.

I want you to take on, one exercise per week, the reason for this is because I want you to read and reread the exercise, for you to become really familiar and comfortable with its content. Then practise it, until it is fully incorporated in your driving, before moving on to the next exercise.

The first lesson is 'Mirror Signal Manoeuvre', back to basics a bit I'm afraid, but you may find that there is quite a bit, that you had forgotten. Please remember that this is all integral to the finished product, you.

22

Exercise 1 Week 1 Mirror –
Signal – Manoeuvre

This is the first exercise on the road to beating the speed camera and as such, I am going to take you back to basics. Beating the speed camera is all about developing your awareness on the road and this is where it all starts. To beat the speed camera you need to possess well developed and effective observation skills which mean to the sides and rear of the vehicle as well as to the front.

We all know the old saying of Mirror - Signal – Manoeuvre. But there is far more to it than many of us really remember.

The mirror signal manoeuvre or MSM routine is, in reality only the start of the routine and actually looks more like this, MSMPSL. But let's start at the beginning. Can you remember what PSL stands for?

Mirror

It is vitally important that we use our mirrors before any changes of speed or direction and I emphasise the word BEFORE.

1. Moving away/Accelerating – One of the main reasons for this is to ensure that you are not in the process of being overtaken, so you are ensuring that it is safe to pull away and accelerate. Should someone be in the process of passing you, then you know to hold back for a few seconds. Once safe you can pull away but don't forget to check your 'blind spot', or 'kill zone' as some bikers refer to it.

2.	Decelerating and/or stopping – Use you mirrors before slowing down and/or stopping, just to ensure that any vehicle behind you is not travelling too close. This will allow you to brake at an appropriate pace. In any event, braking should always be smooth and comfortable and never harsh, except for in an emergency.

3.	Turning left or right – These are areas where you will make greater use of your door mirrors or wing mirrors for those of us who still have them. Use your interior mirror first to check behind, before you start to slow down and then as you are slowing check your left door mirror before turning left and right mirror if turning right (sorry, but I'm not trying to teach you to suck eggs here).. This will obviously allow you to see anything that may be coming up on the side of you. The last thing you want is a cyclist hanging off your roof rack. That would be the last thing he wants for that matter.

4.	Bends – even on the approach to left and right hand bends, check your mirrors so as you are aware of what anyone behind you is doing, because once you have started to go around the bend, you will probably lose sight of them. Especially important if the vehicle behind is travelling at a rate of knots and after the bend you encounter a queue of stationary traffic.

5.	On the straight – on good straight roads, the general rule is that you should be using your interior mirror in the region of every three or four seconds. This is the sort of time frame that I usually use when using my interior mirror because if there are any changes in the traffic conditions behind me, then I become aware of them at the earliest possible moment. I therefore have more time to make any crucial decisions that may arise. Also whilst on straight roads, don't forget to periodically check your door mirrors. You may know that there is nothing there but it is never-the-less an excellent habit to get into. Better to use them when you don't need to, then not use them when you do.

Using your mirrors should not just be an action, but a real effort to understand what is going on behind you. You need to look out for anything that could be interpreted as a hazard such as a cyclist, a vehicle approaching too fast and be prepared to act on that information. The possibilities are endless and it is the proper use of your experience that will determine the course of action that you take. This may include abandoning the intended manoeuvre completely, in the interests of not only your safety, but that of everyone (Altruism).

Signal

You may have heard people saying, that they use their indicators at every turn or corner and I tend not to place much faith in this type of driver. Continually using your indicators is, to a certain extent wrong and during a driving test would be picked up and marked as an error. The reason for this is that you only need use your indicators, if the signal would be appropriate and to know if it is appropriate, you must have been using and interpreting what you saw in your mirrors and ahead. You only need give a signal to inform other road users of your intentions, if there's no other road users around that would benefit from you giving a signal, then, you don't need to give one. Someone giving a signal when there is no need is a strong indication that they are not fully aware, of what is occurring around them. Similarly, those who don't give signals when they should are at risk of misleading those road users around them.

To use your indicators correctly, use your mirrors first and understand what you see, then decide if a signal is appropriate or not. But remember that if signals need to be given, then they should be given in plenty of time to warn others of your intentions, before you start to execute them.

Manoeuvre

This is the interesting one as the 'manoeuvre' part of the routine is further split into its own component parts and these are known as PSL or 'Position – Speed – Look'.

So the whole Mirror Signal Manoeuvre process looks like this:

Mirror – Signal – Position – Speed – Look

This is what every novice should be telling him or herself every time they turn a corner and what every experienced driver, should be doing naturally.

Position

After you have used your mirror and given your signal if you needed one, the next thing to check is your position in the road. If you are turning left then you should maintain your general road position. This under normal circumstances should be just left of centre, if turning right you should move the vehicle out close to the centre lane markings, if it is safe to do so. As we said earlier, use your mirror before making this change of direction.

Speed

Next you need to adjust your speed to make the turn safely and comfortably. This speed will be determined by the road, traffic and weather conditions, how sharp the turning is and how far you can see into the road itself.

Look

Finally, before turning you must take a look ahead to ensure that it is safe to cross the path of any oncoming traffic but also to look into the road into which you are turning.

There is a golden rule to remember here and that is you, as the motorist, must give way to pedestrians who are crossing the road into which you are turning. This is another crucial reason to maintain a steady speed at junctions.

Practice this every time you drive because this is going to serve as the base for the rest of the book. It is basic stuff, but it is hugely important, not just to get right, but for it to become second nature. As an experienced motorist you should not find this too difficult. The reason I want this so ingrained is because later we will be dealing with the most dangerous manoeuvre we as motorists can make, overtaking, where the MSM routine takes on a rather interesting twist.

So to recap, for this week try to get into your heads, not the routine of mirror signal manoeuvre but that of:

Mirror – Signal – Position
– Speed – Look

23

EXERCISE 2 Week 2 Overtaking

I have included overtaking within these pages because over-all, it is one of the most, if not **the** most dangerous manoeuvre that we can possibly make. Generally conducted at high speeds, any collisions that ensue because of poor overtaking methods are highly likely, to result in tragedy. If executed badly it will almost certainly result in two vehicles travelling towards each other at speeds of 60mph plus, thus giving an impact speed of around 120mph. Needless to say, that there is not much that could survive such destructive forces.

However, having said this, the overtaking manoeuvre, is very easy to get right and its execution is based on that most basic and important of driving rules.

MIRROR – SIGNAL – MANOEUVRE

We are going to cover this exercise whilst the basic Mirror – Signal – Manoeuvre routine is fresh in your minds. However, the interesting thing when applying the MSM routine to overtaking is that you use it in a reverse order and now it looks something like this.

POSITION – SPEED – LOOK – MIRROR – SIGNAL

The first thing you need to decide is whether or not you need to overtake at all. If the vehicle in front is driving to the speed limit or you might be turning off soon, then the right answer is obviously, no.

Once you have made the decision to overtake, then you must

ensure that the road you are travelling on is suitable for over-taking. Just take a minute now and try to think of all the places that you shouldn't overtake. There are many of them, but try to think of at least 6.

Some examples are found at the end of this section.

Once the decision has been made to overtake and the road and traffic conditions are suitable, then the first thing you need to do is get yourself in position;

POSITION – You need to position your vehicle close enough behind the vehicle in front, so as you can pull out and pass it in the shortest possible time as soon as you get the opportunity. Also position the vehicle slightly out towards the centre of the road to give yourself the best possible view of the road ahead.

SPEED – Your speed should be matched to the vehicle in front and you should also be in the right gear, one which leaves you with enough power in reserve, to accelerate passed the intended vehicle, quickly and safely.

LOOK – Your position in the road will allow you to get the best view of the road ahead, if it does not, do not overtake. Remember, if there is any doubt what-soever, **DON'T OVERTAKE**.

Once you have decided that it is safe to go, you may like to flash your headlights to warn the vehicle in front, that you intend to overtake them. But be careful as flashing headlights is often misinterpreted. He/she might think you are telling them to get out of the way. Flashing of headlights is only intended to warn other road users of your presence.

If you are in the process of being overtaken, **DO NOT ACCELLERATE,** as some numb nuts do. This is an extremely irresponsible thing to do and to some extent, goes back to using your mirrors properly. Also bear in mind, that it may be necessary or prudent for you to take your foot off the accelerator and/or apply the brake, if someone is overtaking you badly.

MIRROR – Final look in the mirror just to ensure that you are not in the process of being overtaken yourself, if you are, be prepared to abandon your overtaking. If it is safe to both the front and rear then:

SIGNAL – By now you should have already ascertained that it is safe and necessary to indicate your intentions, so give your signal to inform the other road users both in front and behind of your intended manoeuvre. Then **GO**, accelerate quickly and move back into the left in good time.

There you go, now you know how to overtake in perfect fashion. But remember, how safe you are when you are overtaking is based on following that most basic of routines, the MSM routine, only this time reversed.

Position – Speed – Look – Mirror – Signal

Places where you should not overtake:

1. On the approach to a bend
2. On the approach to a humpback bridge
3. On the approach to crossroads
4. Where there is a no overtaking sign
5. Where to overtake would mean you crossing a solid white line on your side of the road down the centre of the carriageway.
6. On the approach to a pedestrian crossing
7. Anywhere where you cannot be absolutely sure that it is safe.

Please refer to the Highway Code.

Remember, don't pull in too quickly if you can avoid doing so, you must never cause any other driver to have to change their speed or direction.

24

Hazard Awareness/Recognition Skills

Excessive and inappropriate speed affects every area of driving. The faster you go, the straighter the driving line needs to be, and so road positioning can suffer. But more importantly, when any of us are driving, there are certain observations that we must make to ensure that it is safe for us to proceed, these observations must be conducted all around the vehicle. To organise these observations you need to split them into their respective areas, otherwise known as, zones of vision.   There are three zones of vision to the front, two to the near side, two to the off-side and one to the rear. These areas must be consulted regularly whilst driving to keep you well informed of your surroundings. Then, you will be better equipped to anticipate any situation and prepared to deal with it in good time. This then potentially gives you the ability to ultimately change a fatal collision into a non-incident or remove the threat of the speed camera.

Earlier we spoke about the relationship between speed and concentration. The suggestion that increased speed actually increases concentration and therefore allowing motorists to travel faster improves road safety.

What actually occurs is that the balance of observation is dangerously affected. The concentration on the furthest frontal zone of vision is increased but narrowed dramatically whilst all other zones of vision become increasingly neglected. It follows that the risk then posed within these areas, to other vehicles and especially pedestrians, has increased dramatically. This is where we then get the excuses of, "I didn't see him" or "He came out of nowhere". When in reality, they were not seen because the zone of vision the victim occupied, was not considered important or just overlooked.

Increased speed reduces observation and as a consequence increases risk dramatically.

This is where Road Safety Cameras play such an important role; they are placed within proven high-risk areas. The motorists who comply with speed limits have no problem with them, having no need even to acknowledge their existence. Those that don't comply with speed limits are forced to comply or run the risk to their licence and pocket with little consideration given to the potential victims of their driving habits. But we know that just merely keeping to the speed limit is not enough. Collisions are caused in the main because of a lack of awareness that leads to hazards getting missed. The majority of poor motoring awareness must occur whilst within the speed limit. Speed cameras therefore cannot have a positive effect on poor standards of driving whilst within the speed limit. In effect, the camera is limited to the number of deaths and serious injury it can prevent because it only has a very limited area of effectiveness i.e. above the speed limit. It follows then, that to increase the life saving potential of the camera, you must lower existing speed limits and enforce them. This is an idea that is currently under consideration.

As far as speed cameras go, this is by far the most important lesson to learn. As we have discussed previously, speed cameras have very little to do with speeding but have everything to do with our levels of concentration, awareness and hazard recognition.

So what is a hazard? A hazard can be absolutely anything that is present on the road from a bend, pedestrian, parked car or just about anything that causes us or could cause us to alter our speed or direction. What we have to realise as motorists is the potential dangers these hazards can produce. For example, a parked car can hide the presence of a child or around the next bend could be an unexpected queue of traffic or a mother or father for that matter, pushing a pram.

Your hazard awareness is the skill that determines the actions you take when faced with these problems behind the wheel. Strong hazard perception skills will help you to anticipate the possibility of an incident and prepare you to deal with it, before it arises, rather than as it or after it arises.

It is the lack of these same skills that cause so many of us drive through speed camera's each year. Low observation leads to low awareness of just about everything, including speed cameras. Raise your level of observation and hazard recognition and not only will you become a far better motorist, but you'll also make the road safer for you. It will also be developing the very skills you need, to stop you from ever driving through a speed camera too quickly again.

In the first lesson, Mirror – Signal – Manoeuvre, we discussed how to use our mirrors effectively, from this we should now be far more aware than before of just what is occurring behind us. Now we are going to learn how to read the road ahead just as effectively. First we need to talk about 'zones of vision'. There are three zones of vision to the front of the vehicle, the immediate, intermediate and distant. All three zones should be scanned constantly when motoring.

Distant

The distant zone of vision relates to the furthest possible view you have of the road ahead. It is used to give you the earliest possible indication of any possible hazards that you may be approaching and as such, gives you the longest possible time to prepare. This is also where you should first be capturing the location of a speed camera and as such will avoid any late and harsh braking, had you failed to spot it until it was within your immediate zone of vision. The distant zone of vision will include all possible hazards from pedestrians to traffic lights. If you spot pedestrians for example, are they young are old? If so, are they messing around or acting sensibly, confused or drunk? All these questions will prepare you as you approach them. Will you need to adjust your speed or direction? If so, will your actions interfere with anyone else on the road and so on? The greatest benefit here is that you have set the alarm bells ringing, at the earliest possible moment.

Further examples could include:

1. A line of parked cars – What are they concealing?
2.   A bus – is it going to be pulling into the bus stop, what type of people are getting off? If the answer is school kids or the elderly then alarm bells should start to ring, even the weather plays its part; if it's raining they may be walking with their head to the ground. Chances are that nothing will happen, but one day, it just might.
3.   Traffic lights – will they still be on green or red when you get there or will they change?
4.   A bend in the road ahead, how sharp is it, how far around it can you see, is there anything on the other side out of view and if there is, can you stop in time?

Intermediate

The intermediate zone of vision will now consist of everything you saw in the distant zone but now, it's that little bit closer and it will have also altered a little.

Now your awareness of what you saw earlier is becoming clearer and you will be building a clearer picture, of just what is going on up ahead. If you had spotted a speed camera in your distant zone of vision, then your speed will now have been adjusted, to the speed limit of the road you are travelling on. The sound of the engine and steadiness of your right foot, should be telling you that your speed is constant and as such, only periodic checks of the speedometer are now required, to ensure you maintain a steady speed. At the same time your checks of your zones of vision continue to ensure that the safety of those around you remains intact.

Immediate

You should now be well prepared and well aware of most things that are occurring within your immediate zone of vision. However, you must still be ready for the sudden and unexpected, as these will tend to occur within your immediate zone of vision.

With all of these zones of vision, how we observe what is contained in them, is the very cornerstone to all of the decisions that we make whilst driving, but this has to be effective observation. For your observations to be effective, they also have to be correct and ensure that you are looking in the right place at the right time. It is ineffectual observation that causes us to miss potential hazards on the road.

Concentration and observation come at a price, at first you will possibly find that once again, after years of motoring, that driving is making you tired. The levels of concentration needed to survive today's road is huge. But don't worry if you are getting tired, as this is quite a natural reaction to your new found powers of observation. After a short while, you will find that maintaining this higher level of concentration becomes second nature. Never again will you arrive at your destination not remembering the journey that you just made on auto pilot.

Distractions

There are many obvious distractions that can reduce your concentration and therefore awareness from the job of driving and come from a myriad of sources. These can include conversation, Radio/CD's, Mobile phones and screaming children. It is also important to realise that if you drive while you are upset, distressed or angry, your mind will not be fully on the job. This increases your risk of missing a speed camera or more importantly it increases your collision risk. So you must always be prepared to drop out of any conversation with a passenger or on the mobile, better still, turn the mobile off when you drive. Even if you normally use a hands-free kit, a conversation on a mobile takes much of the concentration and mental ability away from the job of driving.

If the kids are playing up, pull over and deal with it whilst parked up, just make sure you do it safely.

The result of good effective observation is readiness. Later we will readdress the emergency stop as it was one of the first and most important manoeuvres we were taught. But having good quality observation may very well result in the motorist never having to perform one. Good quality observations are absolutely fundamental to road safety and once attained, speed cameras no longer present themselves as a problem. Pedestrians are amongst our most vulnerable group of road users, especially the under 15's and the over 60's. This is because young adults are still developing their senses of awareness and danger recognition, and some of our more senior citizens are beginning to lose theirs which makes them unpredictable.

A little expression that has remained with me for a long time now is the one that follows. It sums up quite a lot really.

Think of them, think for them

25

Exercise 4 Week 4 Braking Distances

It is also worth saying at this point that the braking distances published in the Highway Code, are still as pertinent today as they have ever been. They relate to the minimum safe stopping distances, which some vehicles today are still only just maintaining. If you can stop well within these distances, then great.

There is another point to stopping distances that is largely overlooked. And that is of the section pertaining to thinking distance. Your ABS may well stop your vehicle within 45 feet at 30 mph but that 45 feet only starts from when you have started to brake. The weakened hazard perception skills of our average motorists will certainly delay the application of a brake pedal, over the motorist who recognises a hazard early enough to stop. No amount of ABS will stop a car if the danger has not been seen. Effectively it is the unaware driver, who is artificially extending braking distances and rendering them as valid today as the Morris Minor they were tested on.

I find this is an interesting subject, because many motorists believe that braking distances, as per the Highway Code, are largely irrelevant. Many are also under the impression that the improved braking performance of modern vehicles, should allow them to be able to drive at ever increasing speed. This idea though possesses, an element of risk compensation because as vehicles themselves become safer, motorists are inspired to take more risks which in turn helps to keep casualty levels elevated. But irrespective of how a vehicles braking performance has been improved, the most important element of braking has remained virtually unchanged throughout motoring history, thinking distance.

Braking distances are only a measure of a vehicles minimum allowable standard of braking performance. For instance, a vehicle travelling at 70 mph should be able to come to a complete stop within 315feet or 96metres. It only takes a vehicle three seconds to cover this distance at this speed.

If your vehicle can stop within half this distance, it does not translate that you should be allowed to drive your vehicle at 140mph. Because the faster a vehicle is travelling, the less the motorist is able to observe and therefore react to and as such, the higher your collision risk soars. At 140mph on a public road in uncontrolled conditions, it would go through the roof.

Your braking distance is reliant on three highly important factors:

1. Your reaction time

You reaction time is purely dependent, upon how effectively you are observing. How effectively you observe is dependent upon the speed you are travelling at. For example, the average reaction time of a motorist, irrespective of the speed at which he or she is travelling at, is in the region of two thirds of one second. A very good reaction time would be in the region of ½ a second. This human reaction time, by definition, is the time it takes to realise that there is a problem and then getting your foot off the accelerator and onto the brake and is commonly known as the thinking distance. It does not sound much until you fully realise, the distance that you are travelling at, per second, any given speed. To calculate how many feet you are travelling at, in one second just multiply your speed by 1.5. So at 30 mph, you are travelling at roughly 45 feet per second, at 60 mph you are travelling at roughly 90 feet per second and so on.

Whilst in a 30 mph speed limit and travelling at 30 mph, an alert driver will come to a stop within 75 feet, at 60 miles per hour; you would have only just started braking. ABS is not going to be much help here.

2.   The braking performance of your vehicle is also dependent upon the condition of your brakes and tyres. If either of these possesses weaknesses then your braking distance will be lengthened.

3.   How you use your brakes is also an incredibly important factor. For example, if your brakes lock due to over braking then your tyres will lose some traction with the road, and cause the vehicle to travel further than it should. This is why I have included the Emergency Stop as an exercise, because managing to achieve the best possible braking effect that your vehicle has to offer, will reduce the impact speed, damage and level of injury of any collision that you may be involved in *(Incidentally, reducing the severity of a collision will in turn also reduce the need for speed camera placement).*

Your overall stopping distance is made up of two parts, thinking distance and braking distance, which only when added together, gives the overall stopping distance. As you can see, the faster a vehicle is travelling at, the further it will travel before even beginning to reduce its speed. Let us say you were travelling at 50 mph in a 30 limit and a vehicle pulls out in front of you that is 75 feet away. At 30mph you would expect to be able to stop your vehicle well within that distance. Travelling at 50mph in the same circumstances and you would still be travelling at around 35mph when you hit it.

Travelling at 70 mph and you will have achieved virtually no speed reduction what so ever.

Another important factor to notice is that the braking distance at 60 mph is not twice that of 30 mph, but is in fact 4 times the distance. So if you are travelling at high speed, your chances of reducing that speed on impact is seriously impaired.

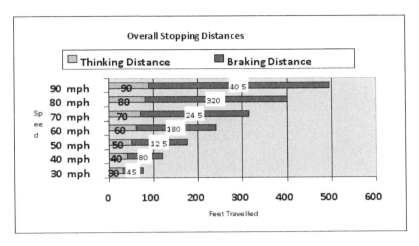

Oh and for the benefit of a good friend of mine, the overall stopping distance at 140mph is 1120 feet, just shy, of a quarter of a mile.

26

Exercise 5 Week Emergency Stop

Even though this is probably one of the most important lessons you will ever learn, I have saved it until now because I wanted you, to have been given the time to develop your awareness to a good standard. After all, I don't want you go out practising the emergency stop, with some idiot 2 feet off your bumper, sort of defeats the object really.

First, you need to find a safe place to practise it, preferably a quiet side road with not much traffic, (on a Sunday afternoon maybe when the rugby's on the TV).

During this exercise, the thinking distance will have been removed from the overall stopping distance (Refer to lesson 5 – Braking distances) and we will just be concentrating on ensuring that you fully understand how to achieve the best possible braking power from your vehicle.

The rate at which all vehicles come to a stop from 30mph will differ depending on the vehicles inherent braking performance, but all should be able to come to a complete stop well within the recommended braking distance, which at 30mph is 45 feet.

There are three points to master with this particular manoeuvre.

1.   That you come off the accelerator and onto the brake pedal as quickly and accurately as possible. *(I have seen a chap once, come around a bend far to fast whilst I was crossing the road, he panicked and went for his brake, missed and re-connected with the accelerator pedal. Needless to say I had*

to make a quick dash for the pavement. He then continued to plough into two cars waiting at traffic lights).

2.   That you apply the maximum braking power to the brakes without them locking up. You have to apply pressure to the brake, up to the point just before the wheels lock. If you achieve this you will have squeezed the best possible performance out of your brakes.

3.   You must leave your clutch pedal well alone until just before you come to a complete stop, only then depress it. The reason for this is because you will also be employing the natural engine braking capability of the vehicle. Imagine driving down a level road and just simply taking your foot off the accelerator pedal, what happens, the car naturally begins to slow down. This natural braking ability, combined with the foot brake will cause the vehicle to stop more quickly. It may only be a few feet quicker, but it could make all the difference between stopping short and making contact. And if contact does occur, it will be at a slightly more reduced speed.

Now because this is a mock emergency stop, you MUST ensure that it is safe to practice this manoeuvre. So before you hit the brake pedal, make sure that there is nothing around you that your vehicle could interfere with.

So the routine here will be:

1.   **MIRROR – Ensure it is safe to perform the emergency stop. Also ensure that the road is clear to the front as you don't want to startle anyone else.**

2.   **BRAKE – Brake to achieve the maximum braking pressure without locking the wheels.**

This may take three or four attempts, before you really start getting comfortable with it.

3.   **MIRROR – Check whilst braking for anything travelling too close behind that could cause further injury or damage. (Of course within this situation there will be no-one behind as you will have already checked – WON'T**

YOU!!!!)
4. CLUTCH – Depress the clutch just before stopping to ensure that you make full use of the engines natural braking ability.

In a real emergency situation the most important thing is to hit your brake first and then check your mirror. The reason for this is because all too often, someone is travelling too close behind (Refer to lesson 6 – The Two Second Rule) and you can then prepare yourself for the possible secondary impact. This will help to reduce the injury to yourself and passengers and also minimise the distance that you will inevitably be pushed forwards. So in a real emergency situation your actions would now look like this:

1. BRAKE – Start braking immediately and under full control
2.   MIRROR – Check your mirror so as to prepare you for any secondary impact or prepare for any evasive manoeuvre necessary.
3.   CLUTCH – Press the clutch down only just before the vehicle comes to a complete stop.
4.   MIRROR – Just before stopping, for any final preparations you may need to make.

Skidding

With the emergency stop, always comes the risk of your wheels locking, as we discussed earlier, this causes the wheels to lose traction with the road and as such the vehicle will travel further. Another consequence of your wheels locking up is the possibility for the back end of the vehicle to slide either to the left or the right. If this does happen, then we need to control it and this is done with two actions.
Firstly you steer into the skid, if the back end is sliding to the left you steer to the left, if the back end is sliding to the right, steer to the right. And secondly relax, but don't completely release the pressure on the brake pedal, to get the wheels moving again. Then re-apply a little pressure if you need to bring brak-

ing, back up to its maximum performance.

Finally, you should practice this manoeuvre fairly regularly and especially when you drive a new or different vehicle. The more you practice, the less you will find that you will panic when confronted with a real emergency situation. Having said this, the more your awareness and concentration has improved the less vulnerable you become and as a result, far less likely that you will get yourself into an emergency situation.

Not one that is of your making anyway...

27

Exercise 6 Week 6

The 2 Second Rule

Only a fool breaks the two second rule.

We've all of heard it, but not many of us practice it and yet, it is never-the-less one of the most important rules we can stick to when driving. Most rear-enders today could be avoided if this simple rule were used more prolifically.

The basis of this rule is that you should allow a two second time gap, between your vehicle and the vehicle in front. This should give adequate time for you to pull up safely, if the car in front should need to perform an emergency stop. That is provided that you have been alert and observant. (It is also possible that by now, you may be able to spot the hazards in front of the vehicle in front of you even before he does).

It is said that the two second rule works best at speeds over 20 mph, at speeds under 20 mph then you should allow 1 yard for every mile per hour of your speed, however....I find that the two second rule works pretty well at all speeds.

To check if you are at the correct distance behind the vehicle in front, you need to pick out a marker at the side of the road, such as a road sign, lamp post or a motorway bridge etc. Then either count two seconds or simply say (in your head if your mates are in the car).'Only a fool breaks the two second rule' as this takes roughly two seconds to say at normal speech speed.

'Only a Fool Breaks the Two Second Rule'

From this you can actually work out roughly how far you are from the vehicle in front.

At 30 mph you are travelling at roughly 45 feet per second, so a two second time gap places you 90 feet away from the vehicle in front. Now what is your overall stopping distance at 30 mph? Remember? No! Ok, the answer is 75 feet. You are placed well within the distance you can see to be clear.

Next time you are driving, time the distances between other vehicles on the road, you will find that many are within half a second. At 30 mph that is roughly 22.5 feet away from the vehicle in front. At this gap, if the vehicle in front came to a sudden stop, say against an artic, you wouldn't have even started braking when you joined the collision. And besides all of the potential injuries to you and your family, if you were the last one in, whose insurance would have to foot the bill?

Keeping to the 'two second rule' would have seen you stop within 75 feet, 15 feet short of the problems ahead and the cost, inconvenience, not to mention the injury, is someone else's problem.

Two further points to remember with this rule is that in wet weather conditions, you must at least double the distance between you and the car in front (4 seconds) and in icy weather, this distance should be at least ten times greater.

For this week, practice keeping your distance, it will become second nature very quickly. There will be times when you leave such a gap that others will not think twice about filling. When this does happen, just drop back slightly to regain the 2 second time gap. The journey time you may lose in practicing this, will be negligible.

28

Avoiding Parking Tickets

Parking tickets can just as easily be avoided, as a speeding ticket. You only have to think…

I have to say, that I have read so many stories of people complaining, that they got a parking ticket because there were not enough spaces or they didn't know they couldn't park there or blah, blah, blah. I have to say that in all of my 24 years of driving I have never had a problem finding places to legally park my car,

Most of the time, I have managed to locate a place in a designated car park, on other occasions I have used the rules of the road to my advantage, but you can't use them if you don't know them.

Some years ago, I went for a day out to a local festival in a local park called the Brampton. The car park was full and the surrounding roads were also packed. There was however a stretch of completely empty road, very near to the festival that was contained within a 30mph limit. There were no 'No Parking' signs or yellow lines and neither was it a clearway and yet, not a single car was parked there. Most motorists were put off because it is an odd looking piece of road that slightly resembles a dual carriageway, but it's not.

I chose the prime parking space and left my car there for the rest of the afternoon. Later when I returned, the whole stretch of road was covered with parked cars. For some reason the word 'Sheep' sprung to mind.   On another occasion I went to the theatre, however, this time I had already parked in a car park.

But whilst I was in the queue for the performance, I noticed that there were double yellow lines right outside of the theatre door. These were accompanied by a sign saying that there was no parking here between 7am and 7pm and yet, there was not a soul parked there. Next time, I know exactly where I will be parking.

So, a little knowledge does seem to go a very long way. It is quite easy to find a parking space, if you only know where to look. This is another area where the Highway Code, bless it, is an extremely useful document indeed.

On the other hand, a snippet in the local press had a story of 30 or 40 cars that had all received parking tickets while attending a Stoke City football match. It seems that all it takes is one vehicle to park badly and then 39 more followed. Strangely the word 'Sheep' reared its woolly little head again. So hopefully, over this last piece in his book, I'm going to show you how to avoid getting your own ticket and turn you from a sheep, into a shepherd.

Before I do that though, I want to discuss parking a little, just to emphasise how dangerous a parked car can be.

I was unfortunate enough some time ago, to end up in a conversation with a male who had killed a young child. Initially, even though I couldn't vent it, I was quite angry towards this young man. He had told me what had happened and also that the reason he failed to see the child was because of 3 or 4 parked cars that had obscured his view. Had this lad treated the parked vehicle as he should have, it is more than possible that the child would still be alive today. But having said this, I also discovered that these parked cars, were parked illegally and had they not been there, then things could have been so much different. The view would not have been obscured, he could have seen that the child's mother did not have full control over the child (hazard recognition again!!!) and he may well have had enough information, to modify his driving enough to have dealt with the situation, who knows?

So when you park, think carefully about it because your vehicle could well be creating a hazard that someone else has to deal with, if they deal with it badly and many do, then tragic things can happen. You may never get punished for it, but rest assured, poor parking has almost certainly contributed to the deaths of many innocent people.

Ok so let's lighten up a little.

So where shouldn't you park? The Highway Code pretty much covers all bases, but we'll go through some of the basics now:
1. On a bend
2. On the approach to the brow of a hill.
3. Within 10 metres (32 feet) feet of a junction.
4. Directly opposite a junction.
5. On a clearway/urban clearway
6. On yellow lines when restrictions are in place.
7. Where there is a solid white line down the left hand side of the carriageway.
8. Where there is a no parking sign.
9. Where there is a solid white line down the centre of the carriageway and parking would cause passing vehicles to cross that line.

The basic rule is that you can park anywhere, where it is safe and legal without causing an obstruction. Follow these few simple rules and you won't have to go through the stress of trying to contest a parking ticket as you won't get one in the first place.

AND FINALLY.....

So there it is folks, how to use the best qualities of a motorist, to beat speed cameras and avoid parking tickets. And all without ever having to go through the stress and trauma, of going to court and taking the risk of ending up with a worse punishment, than if you had paid up in the first place.

We have learned that speed cameras only work because they exploit weaknesses in driver ability, weaknesses that began to develop soon after passing the driving test, weaknesses that ultimately cost lives and livelihood.

You can disguise these weaknesses with technology, or you can try to defend these weaknesses in court. But both are a poor substitute for 'real driver' skills.

For now, we can still enjoy the motoring experience. However road safety technology is constantly improving and if as motorists, we do not change our qualities and attitudes, to take the responsibility for road safety back, then, I shudder to think of the motoring legacy we will leave for future generations.

Do we really want to be remembered, as the generation that destroyed the motoring experience?

Good luck to you all and safe driving.